Please return/renew this item by the
last date shown to avoid a charge.
Books may also be renewed by phone
and Internet. May not be renewed if
required by another reader.

www.libraries.barnet.gov.uk

BARNET
LONDON BOROUGH

Lizzie Williams

A green and friendly country straddling the equator in the Great Lakes region of East Africa, it is the outstanding natural beauty and special animals that attract travellers to Uganda. Although game viewing doesn't equal that of neighbouring Kenya and Tanzania in terms of numbers and variety of species, some parks do have savannah animals, as well as enjoyable boat cruises to see hippo, crocodile, buffalo and waterbirds. But what Uganda has in abundance is an exceptionally rich population of primates living in the beautiful tangled forests. And with more than half of all Africa's bird species, it's also one of the world's top birdwatching destinations.

Bwindi's 'impenetrable' forests and the slopes of the Virunga volcanoes at Mgahinga are home to the fragile population of mountain gorillas. An hour's audience with these magnificent creatures is truly one of the most exciting and memorable wildlife encounters on earth. Chimpanzees can be tracked in several forests too or can be seen in Ngamba Island Chimpanzee Sanctuary, and the striking golden monkey has recently been habituated in its natural habitat for people to visit.

With much of the country dominated by lakes and rivers, you can raft or kayak the whitewater rapids on the River Nile, paddle a traditional dugout canoe across picturesque Lake Bunyonyi, or fish for the mighty Nile perch around the Ssese Islands. And in Uganda's misty mountains there are challenging glacier climbs in the Rwenzoris or volcano climbs in the Virungas or Mount Elgon.

The urban areas too have distractions. Kampala, a fast-growing characterful city spread over numerous hills, is as famous for its pumping nightlife as it is for its chaotic traffic, while many of the regional towns are surrounded by brilliantly green terraced hillsides and are home to exceptionally friendly people, colourful markets and thousands of *boda-bodas*.

Kidepo
Valley
National
Park
*Lorungole
(2750m)*

Kidepo Valley National Park

○Kotido

Moroto ○ *Moroto
(3084m)*

*Napak
(2537m)*

*Kadani
(3060m)* ▲

Lake
Opeta

Mount Elgon
National Park
◆

bale ○ ▲ *Wagagai
(Mount Elgon)
(4321m)*

KENYA

Malaba
○

sia
○

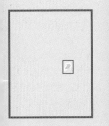

N

40 km

40 miles

Don't miss...

See colour maps at end of book

v

Itineraries for Uganda

Uganda is a compact country and the main draws are tracking the mountain gorillas and other primates, birdwatching and game drives in the national parks, and the exciting activities on the River Nile at Jinja. An itinerary of a week or 10 days around the circuit of good, fast roads will enable visitors to enjoy all these attractions. With more time you can add in another park or two, as well as community-driven activities such as cultural walks, cycling or mountain climbing; and you'll have time to relax at a nice hotel or resort. Travel is relatively easy; distances between the major sites aren't too great, public transport is frequent, and for those who prefer an organized tour, the countless Ugandan tour operators can arrange anything from an airport transfer or gorilla permit to a multi-day camping safari or fly-in lodge holiday. If you are going to see the gorillas, the allocation of your permit will determine how, when and what route you take to the southwest corner of Uganda, where they live, and other itineraries can easily be changed around.

ITINERARY ONE: 7-10 days
Gorillas and game parks

After arrival at Entebbe International Airport, there may be time for a stroll around the well laid out Botanical Gardens or the Uganda Wildlife Education Centre, and a half-day visit to the chimpanzee sanctuary on Ngamba Island in Lake Victoria. Kampala, the capital, deserves a day or two; it is a handsome and friendly city that has a range of comfortable hotels, exciting nightlife, fine public gardens and colourful markets. En route to or from the southwest, there are several options. You could spend a night or two in Lake Mburo National Park, where a boat ride is a good way of seeing a number of interesting species, or head for Queen Elizabeth National Park, which has most of the plains game people expect to see on safari, as well as a few surprises, such as the unique tree-climbing lions. A must-do here is the cruise on the Kazinga Channel, and you

Whitewater rafting, Bujagali Falls

Ngamba Island Chimpanzee Sanctuary

can track chimpanzees at Kyambura Gorge. Alternatively, head to Kibale National Park a little further north, which has the world's greatest concentration of primates. Once at Bwindi Impenetrable or Mgahinga Gorilla National Park (depending on gorilla permits), the full-day excursion can be a tough scramble through the dense rainforests, but coming face to face with these gentle giants makes it more than worthwhile. The impossibly pretty Lake Bunyonyi is a deservedly popular spot on the way to and from the gorillas, and the lovely lakeshore resorts are ideal for a day or two's relaxation.

TRAVEL TIP

Gorilla permits cannot be refunded or rescheduled; make sure you are at your accommodation near the trailhead the night before and at the gate promptly on time in the morning.

ITINERARY TWO: 10-21 days
Lakes, rivers and mountains

With more time, there are plenty of additional places and activities to add into an itinerary of Uganda. Just a couple of hours' drive to the east of Kampala, Jinja and nearby Bujagali are the centre of one of Uganda's biggest tourist attractions: the River Nile. You can see the source of the mighty river as it spills out of Lake Victoria and then ride the whitewater rapids by raft, jet-boat or kayak. Sunset and birdwatching cruises are a more sedate way to enjoy Bujagali Lake, and you can explore the local area on horseback, mountain bike or

Black-headed weaver, Lake Mburo National Park

Murchison Falls

Lake Bunyonyi

TRAVEL TIP

The numerous activities at Jinja and Bujagali based on and around the River Nile can be booked as 'combos' offering substantial discounts.

quad bike. How long you stay here simply depends on how much you want to do. The snow-capped Rwenzori Mountains, the highest range in Africa, straddle the border with the Democratic Republic of Congo (DRC), and there is exceptional hiking on the lower slopes and some challenging peaks to 5109 m for serious trekkers. Giant lobelia, heathers and other montane flora thrive and are quite unlike anything else you'll see in the country. There are alternative volcano climbs in Mgahinga Gorilla National Park, where you can also track golden monkeys and visit the Batwa pygmies, or you could climb Mount Elgon, a heavily forested an-

cient volcano straddling the Kenyan border. Located in the northwest, Murchison Falls National Park makes a rewarding three-day safari and has a wide diversity of vegetation and wildlife habitats, and the launch trip to the base of the falls gives excellent views of hippos, giant Nile crocodiles and mammals drinking at the water's edge. This trip can be combined with Kidepo Valley National Park, one of Uganda's secret destinations in the extreme northwest, that is only just opening up to visitors; it is a magical and virtually untouched wilderness of vast plains and stony mountains.

TRAVEL TIP

Consider flying into Entebbe in Uganda and out of Kigali in Rwanda (or vice versa), as Kigali is close to many of the attractions in southwest Uganda. But allow for extra visa and transfer costs.

Rwenzori Mountains National Park

Ziwa Rhino and Wildlife Ranch

x

Contents

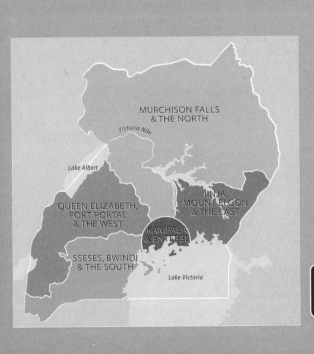

MURCHISON FALLS
& THE NORTH

Victoria Nile

Lake Albert

QUEEN ELIZABETH,
FORT PORTAL
& THE WEST

JINJA,
MOUNT ELGON
& THE EAST

KAMPALA
& ENTEBBE

SSESES, BWINDI
& THE SOUTH

Lake Victoria

Contents

Footprint features

Essentials

Planning your trip

When to go to Uganda

Straddling the equator, Uganda has a warm climate all year round with minor temperature fluctuations depending on the elevation and topography. More significant is the rainfall pattern when planning a trip. The heavy rainy season is March to May, and there are lighter rains in November and December. Generally there is some sunshine each day, even in the rainy seasons. From a practical point of view, it is probably best to try to avoid March-May, as the murram roads can become bogged (with trucks having to be dug out) and so journey times are extended. Gorilla tracking can become difficult as the forest trails are very steep and it is hard to keep your footing on the slippery slopes. During heavy downpours climbing, trekking and camping on the Rwenzori Mountains and Mount Elgon all increase in difficulty.

Many hotels have different high and low season rates, with the latter being significantly cheaper; it is always worth bartering. High season is generally June-September and December-March, and low season is October-November and April-May. Fares rise on public transport at peak holiday times like Christmas and Easter. As Uganda is on the equator, the times of sunrise and sunset hardly change throughout the year – sunrise is generally 0700-0800 and sunset 1800-1900.

What to do in Uganda

Birdwatching

For its size Uganda has Africa's greatest birdlife variety with over 1000 species recorded, including the rare shoebill stork, and some claim that you will be able to spot over 300 species in a day. Birders can join specialist tours visiting multiple sites, and, if well prepared, it is possible to see 450-500 species in 2-3 weeks. The prime birding sites are found in the western rainforests, including Bwindi Impenetrable National Park, Semliki National Park, Kibale National Park and the Rwenzori Mountains. Even Entebbe's Botanical Gardens has several easily identifiable species, and a fair number of species can be ticked off from a veranda of a hotel in Kampala. Birding Uganda, www.birding-uganda.com, is a good place to start for more information.

Boat rides, canoeing and whitewater rafting

Whether it's a casual 30-min paddle or a fully fledged expedition, a boat or canoe trip on one of Uganda's rivers or lakes is great fun. For wildlife enthusiasts, it's an excellent way of getting a close look at birds and game without frightening them away, and Lake Mburo and Queen Elizabeth National Park offer game-watching boat trips. Lake Bunyonyi in the far southwest near Kabale, and the Ssese Islands on Lake Victoria offer peaceful canoeing trips between their many islands. The River Nile at Bujagali near Jinja offers thrilling rafting or kayak rides through the cataracts and Grade V rapids.

Climbing and trekking

The snow-capped Rwenzoris offer some exceptional trips to both casual trekkers and experienced climbers. These lofty peaks are some of the most challenging ascents in East Africa, and the endless views, giant

Packing for Uganda

Before you leave home, send yourself an email to a web-based account with details of passport, driving licence, credit cards and travel insurance numbers. Be sure that someone at home also has access to this information.

A backpack or travelpack (a hybrid backpack/suitcase) rather than a rigid suitcase covers most eventualities and survives the rigours of a variety of modes of travel. Trekkers will need a smaller and sturdier pack that can withstand wet weather. A lock for your luggage is strongly advised – there are cases of pilfering by airport baggage handlers the world over.

A good rule of thumb when packing is to take half the clothes you think you'll need and double the money. Laundry services are generally cheap and speedy in Uganda and you shouldn't need to bring too many clothes. Bear in mind, though, that you may well travel through a variety of climates; it can be very cool at the top of the slopes at Bwindi but very hot and humid at Entebbe. Light cotton clothing is best, with a fleece for evenings and a raincoat for wet weather. On safari expect to get dirty, particularly during the dry season when dust can be a problem, or gorilla tracking, which can be very muddy. Try to have a clean set of clothes to change into at night, when it is also necessary to wear long sleeves and trousers to help ward off mosquitoes.

During the day you will need a hat, sunglasses and high-factor suncream. Footwear should be airy; sandals or canvas trainers are ideal. Trekkers will need comfortable walking boots that have been worn in, especially if you are climbing the Rwenzoris or Mount Elgon. Those going on camping safaris will need a sleeping bag, towel and torch, and budget travellers may want to bring a sleeping sheet. Finally, take a notebook and pen as it is good fun to write down the number of bird and animal species you have spotted.

vegetation and shimmering glaciers make the efforts all the more worthwhile. Mount Elgon, a heavily forested ancient volcano straddling the Kenyan border, also offers climbing excursions. There are guided walks in most of the national parks, which are ideal for birdwatching and perhaps spotting the smaller mammals, and some of the lodges or community-run camps offer nature and village walks.

Fishing

The giant Nile perch, the world's largest game freshwater fish that can weigh over 100 kg, is found in both Lake Victoria and the Murchison Nile. The main method of sport fishing is trolling with lures, and specialist tour operators and some of the lodges can organize trips with equipment and fishing guides. More casually, there are numerous places where a traditional canoe can be hired to fish for small tilapia or catfish; often while watching Nile crocodiles and hippos on the riverbanks and lakeshores.

Gorilla, chimpanzee and golden monkey tracking.

Of the estimated 880 mountain gorillas remaining, about half are located in Uganda either at Bwindi Impenetrable or Mgahinga Gorilla national parks. A number of gorilla groups are habituated and very accustomed to close contact with humans, and it is a great privilege to meet them in their spectacular forested and mountainous home. Golden monkeys are also extremely rare and a quite beautiful primate and can been tracked at Mgahinga, while chimpanzees can be seen in their forest habitat at Kibale and Kyambura Gorge.

Gorilla permits

It is necessary to have a permit to see the mountain gorillas in Uganda at Bwindi Impenetrable National Park (page 150) or Mgahinga Gorilla National Park (page 160); there is not much point in visiting both parks as the gorilla tracking experience is largely the same and equally rewarding. The choice of park largely comes down to a question of permit availability and they must be booked in advance. It is not advisable to turn up at the parks hoping that someone will drop out or not turn up, as this rarely happens. Always secure your gorilla permit before booking flights and accommodation. For what to expect when you go gorilla tracking, see box, page 155, and for more information about mountain gorillas see box, page 157.

The first and most expensive option of getting a permit is to go on an organized tour with a tour operator (arranged in Uganda or before you arrive), which will include the permit, transport and accommodation. The second and cheaper option is to do it yourself, but be prepared to spend some time planning well in advance. Before you decide, it is worth knowing about the way gorilla permits are allocated, as they are very strictly administered by the Uganda Wildlife Authority (UWA) (www.ugandawildlife.org).

Of Uganda's gorilla families that have been habituated (accustomed to the presence of humans), the majority are in Bwindi where nine groups can currently be visited. Eight permits are issued per day for each group, which means there are 72 permits available per day. There is one habituated group in Mgahinga, where eight permits are available per day. The cost of a gorilla permit at both is currently US$600 for most of the year. However there are low season rates (periods typically characterized by heavy rains) of US$350, which are valid 1 April-31 May and 1-30 November. Permits include the daily park entry fee and the services of guides and trackers. As changes to price are sometimes made, check with the UWA, the tour operators or the backpackers in Kampala (pages 55,

Going on safari

One of the main reasons for going to Uganda is to see the wonderful wildlife in splendid African landscapes, and in particular, Uganda is synonymous with gorilla tracking. There are 10 national parks and numerous wildlife reserves and sanctuaries. Most are administered by the Uganda Wildlife Authority (UWA), while others fall under the jurisdiction of the National Forestry Authority (NFA) or are in the private sector. Some are world famous like Bwindi Impenetrable National Park or Queen Elizabeth National Park, and have excellent facilities and receive many visitors, while others rarely see tourists and have few amenities.

The best time of day to spot animals on a vehicle safari is early in the morning and late in the afternoon, as many animals sleep through the intense midday heat. Animals can most easily be seen during the dry season when the lack of surface water forces them to congregate around rivers and waterholes. However, the rainy seasons, from October to November and March to May, are when the animals are in the best condition after feeding on the new shoots, and there are chances of seeing breeding displays and young animals. The disadvantage of the wet season is that the thicker vegetation and the wider

56 and 64) and Bujagali (page 97), who are also a reliable, up-to-date source of information.

To book your gorilla permit independently, you first have to contact UWA's reservation office by email inquiring about availability of the dates you intend to track the gorillas. Note that you need to consider at least a full day of travel from Kampala to Bwindi or Mgahinga and need to stay overnight near the park headquarters, as gorilla tracking starts promptly at 0800. If the exact dates you want are unavailable, the UWA will let you know the nearest dates. You can then book and they will hold the permits for up to seven days until they have received confirmation of your payment by electronic bank transfer. Make sure you get the official Uganda Wildlife Authority receipt/permit by email.

For Bwindi you can book many months in advance but for Mgahinga, the rules are slightly different. This is because the one habituated family there, Nyakagezi, are a nomadic lot and frequently move around within the mountains, sometimes crossing over the borders into Rwanda and the DRC. As such, gorilla permits at Mgahinga are ONLY available 14 days in advance. This makes it the better option for getting last-minute permits, but of course there are only eight permits per day at Mgahinga compared to 72 at Bwindi.

An easier option for booking a permit independently (especially from overseas) is to contact a Ugandan tour operator who, for a fee, will book a permit on your behalf. (Some tour operators are listed under Kampala, see page 64, or you can visit the Association of Uganda Tour Operators website, www.auto.or.ug.) The advantages are that you will have a better choice of dates, are most likely to get your gorilla permit confirmation faster, and a tour operator will probably accept credit cards. Expect to pay a fee of US$30-50 per permit. Finally, if you find you like the tour operator you're dealing with, they may well be able to persuade you to book a gorilla tour with them.

availability of water mean that the wildlife is more spread out and more difficult to spot; also, driving conditions are far harder as none of the park roads are paved. Mountain gorillas and chimpanzees can be seen at any time of year, but again in the rainy seasons, it can be slippery and hard going underfoot. Nevertheless, prices for accommodation and gorilla permits can be lower during the rainy seasons.

It is important to remember that, despite the expert knowledge of the guides, they cannot guarantee that you will see any animals (even primate tracking is never 100% guaranteed). When they do spot one of the rarer animals – a leopard perhaps – sharing their pleasure is almost as enjoyable as seeing the animal.

Organizing a safari

Most people visit the parks and reserves on an organized safari, which includes transport, accommodation, meals and park entry fees. Tour operators offer basically the same safari but at different prices, which is reflective of what accommodation is booked. For example, you could choose a three-day safari from Kampala to the Queen Elizabeth and Bwindi national parks and the options would be to camp (the companies provide the equipment) or stay in a lodge or tented camp safari, which would make it considerably more expensive. Everyone is likely to have the same sort of game-viewing

National park fees

Fees are valid 1 January 2014 to 31 December 2015. Entry is per 24 hours. Under 5s are free. The fees below are for international visitors. Foreign residents in Uganda and East African citizens have a cheaper fee structure. For more information contact Uganda Wildlife Authority (UWA), Kampala, T0414-355000, www.ugandawildlife.org.

Category A covers Murchison Falls, Lake Mburo, Queen Elizabeth, Kibale, Bwindi Impenetrable and Mgahinga Gorilla national parks.
Adult US$40
Children (5-15) US$20

Category B covers all other UWA protected areas.
Adult US$35
Children (5-15) US$15

Vehicle entry fees

The fees below are for foreign-registered vehicles. Ugandan- and East African-registered vehicles have a cheaper fee structure. Vehicle entry fees only apply to those parks and wildlife reserves which have drivable tracks (eg Murchison Falls and Queen Elizabeth). No vehicle fees apply to parks where there is only walking (eg Bwindi).

Motorcycles	US$30
Saloon cars	US$50
Minibuses	US$100
4WD vehicles	US$150

Guided walk
All protected areas
Adult US$30
Children (5-15) US$15

Guided game drives
Only for Murchison Falls, Queen Elizabeth, Kidepo, Lake Mburo national parks (minimum charge for vehicle and guide US$100).
Adult US$30
Children (5-15) US$15
Guide in your own vehicle US$20 per car.

Gorilla tracking
Bwindi Impenetrable National Park*
US$600 includes park entry fee.
No under 15s.
Mgahinga Gorilla National Park*
US$600 includes park entry fee.
No under 15s.
* Low-season gorilla permits, US$350. These must be pre-booked and are valid 1 April-31 May and 1-30 November.

Primate walk
Kibale National Park   US$150
includes park entry fee. No under 12s.

Chimpanzee tracking
Kyambura Gorge   US$50
excludes park entry fee. No under 12s.

Golden monkey tracking
Mgahinga Gorilla National Park
US$50 excludes park entry fee.
No under 12s.

experiences, but the level of comfort will depends on where you stay and how much you spend.

You can pre-book a safari from your home country, or though one of the many tour operators in Uganda. The **Association of Uganda Tour Operators (AUTO)** ① *www. auto.or.ug*, is a good place to start; some of these are listed under Tour operators in Kampala, page 64. Costs vary enormously depending on duration, season, where you stay and how many are in a group. At the very top end of the scale, and staying in the most exclusive accommodation expect to pay in excess of US$500 per person per day; for mid-range lodges, around US$200-400 per person per day; and for camping safaris using basic campsites or *bandas* and the services of a safari cook, about US$100-200 per person per day.

There is always the option of organizing your own safari. Unlike Kenya and Tanzania where there are long distances to the park gates, the most popular parks in Uganda, like Bwindi, Mgahinga, Queen Elizabeth, Kibale and Lake Mburo, can be reached by public transport or by hire car from Kampala. Many of Uganda's forested parks have no vehicle access in any case and can only be explored on foot. If you have arrived at one of the savannah parks by public transport (Queen Elizabeth and Lake Mburo, for example), the UWA park HQ can arrange guided game drives for a moderate charge in the park vehicles. Or a UWA guide can accompany you on game drives in your own or hired vehicle (see box, page 8, for UWA fees). Getting to the parks yourself, and organizing all arrangements including accommodation and gorilla permits (see box, page 6), considerably reduces the cost of a safari.

Getting to Uganda

Air

Uganda's only international airport, **Entebbe International Airport** ① *T0414-353000, flight information, T0414-320926, www.entebbe-airport.com,* on the shores of Lake Victoria, 40 km south of Kampala and 3 km from Entebbe, is efficient and modern. For getting to and from the airport, see page 38. An alternative and often more economical way to get to Uganda is to buy a cheap flight to Nairobi and then to travel overland or take a local connecting flight to Entebbe. It is essential to have a yellow fever certificate to enter Uganda.

From Europe
Direct flights from Europe are from London with **British Airways** (www.britishairways.com), Amsterdam with **Air France** (www.airfrance.com) and **KLM** (www.klm.com), who code share, and Brussels with **Brussels Airlines** (www.brusselsairlines.com). Indirect routes from Europe are with **Lufthansa** (www.lufthansa.com) from Frankfurt, which touch down in Addis Ababa, and **Turkish Airlines** (www.turkishairlines.com) from Istanbul which touch down in Nairobi. Flight time from London is eight to nine hours, and there is no jet lag coming from Europe as there is only a minimal time difference.

From North America
There are no direct flights from North America to Uganda. It is usual to fly via London, Amsterdam or Dubai if travelling from the USA. Alternatively, **Delta** (www.delta.com) and **South African Airways** (www.flysaa.com) have flights from New York to Johannesburg on a code-share agreement, from where there are direct flights to Entebbe, with **South African Airways**.

From Australia, New Zealand and Asia
There are no direct flights from Australia, New Zealand or Asia to Uganda, but a number of indirect routes via Kenya, the Middle East or South Africa. **Emirates**

(www.emirates.com) fly from Australia and New Zealand to Dubai, from where there are direct flights to Entebbe. Between them **Qantas** and **South African Airways**, on a code-share agreement, fly between Perth and Sydney and Johannesburg. **Singapore Airlines** (www.singaporeair.com) code share with **Qantas** (www.qantas.com.au) from Australia and New Zealand to Johannesburg via Singapore, and they also code share with **Ethiopian Airlines**, so there are flights from Singapore to Addis Ababa. Other options from Australasia are to Kenya via Asia. **Kenya Airways** have flights from Bangkok, Hong Kong, Guangzhou, Dubai and Muscat and Nairobi. From Johannesburg there are direct flights to Entebbe with **South African Airways**, from Addis Ababa with **Ethiopian Airlines**, and from Nairobi with **Air Uganda** (www.air-uganda.com) or **Kenya Airways**.

From Africa

Air Uganda fly to and from Entebbe and Bujumbura in Burundi, Dar es Salaam and Kilimanjaro in Tanzania, Juba in South Sudan, Kigali in Rwanda, Mogadishu in Somalia, and Nairobi and Mombasa in Kenya. Direct flights to/from Entebbe with other regional carriers include Addis Ababa with **Ethiopian Airlines** (www.ethiopianairlines.com), Cairo with **Egypt Air** (www.egyptair.com), Nairobi with **Kenya Airways** (www.kenya-airways.com), Kigali with **Rwandair** (www.rwandair.com) and Johannesburg with **South African Airways**.

There are no lake ferry services between Uganda and its neigbouring countries around Lake Victoria. However, there is an overnight service in Tanzania that links Mwanza on the southeastern shore with Bukoba on the lake's northwestern corner. The ferry takes cars, and buses also link Bukoba with Masaka (for travel to the southwest of Uganda) and Kampala. For details of the ferry and the border crossing between Tanzania and Uganda, see page 124.

Road → *See also Transport in Uganda, page 13.*

Bus

Long-distance buses connect Kampala with all the capitals of Uganda's neighboring countries. It's always a good idea to avoid travelling on buses overnight, as road traffic accidents are more common. There has been a ban on buses travelling overnight in Tanzania for some years now and Kenya implemented the same in early 2014. This shouldn't have any adverse effect on travelling, though, given that Nairobi (and Kigali in Rwanda) can be reached comfortably during daylight hours. It is only journeys to and from Tanzania that now require an overnight in Kenya and swapping buses in Nairobi – a little more time consuming, perhaps, but it does save what used to be a 35-hour bus journey from Dar es Salaam to Kampala.

Kenya There are regular departures and several long-distance bus companies ply the Nairobi–Kampala route (12-15 hours). The buses also stop at Kenyan's western towns of Nakuru (nine hours) and Eldoret (6½ hours). Currently **Easy Coach** (www.easycoach.co.ke) and **Queens Coach** (www.queenscoach.com) are recommended as they have the newest and most comfortable vehicles, and both usefully have modern terminuses at the Oasis Nakumatt Shopping Mall on Yusuf Lule Road in Kampala (see Transport, Kampala page 66). In Nairobi long-distance buses depart from the River Road area to the east of the city centre.

Border crossings

Uganda–Kenya
Busia, see page 106.
Malaba, see page 106.

Uganda–Tanzania
Mutukula, see page 124.

Uganda–Rwanda
Katuna, see page 141.
Kisoro–Cyanika, see page 163.

Uganda–South Sudan and Uganda–DRC
At the time of going to press, the FCO and US State Department had issued travel warnings against travel to the areas of DRC bordering Uganda and South Sudan, so use of these border crossings is currently not recommended.

Tanzania To get to and from Arusha (for Tanzania's northern circuit game parks and reserves), Moshi (to climb Mount Kilimanjaro) and Dar es Salaam (for Zanzibar), you'll have to change buses in Nairobi and stay overnight. **Note**: if you are travelling between Tanzania and Uganda via Kenya, you do require a visa for Kenya. However, you only need a transit visa, valid for seven days, which costs US$20 and is available at the border. The seven days may be long enough if you want to do additional things in Kenya on the way. From the western side of Lake Victoria in Tanzania, there are buses between Bukoba and Kampala via the border at Mutukulu (five to six hours). These also stop in Masaka, so in fact, if coming from this direction from Tanzania and going to the southwest of Uganda, there is no need to go to Kampala at all. (See Border crossing, page 124, and Transport Kampala, page 66).

Rwanda There are long-distance buses between Kigali and Kampala (8-9 hours, see Transport Kampala, page 66), which use the Katuna border post 105 km north of Kigali and 21 km south of Kabale (see Border crossing, page 141). You can also do the journey between Kigali and Kabale by *matatu*, swapping vehicles at the border. The other crossing is from Ruhengeri in Rwanda (although it's been renamed Musanze, this town is still widely known as Ruhengeri), near the Volcanoes National Park (Parc National des Volcans), where the mountain gorillas are visited in Rwanda. The route, 65 km in total, is via the Cyanika border 15 km south of Kisoro (see Border crossing, page 163). It can be done by *matatu*, swapping vehicles at the border, or alternatively private transfers can be arranged locally. It is very feasible to go over the border in either direction for gorilla tracking in Rwanda or Uganda, and many tour operators do so, depending on availability of gorilla permits. There is also the option of flying into one country and flying out of the other. However, consider the visa costs first (see box, page 33). **Note**: Rwanda is one hour ahead of Uganda and they drive on the right-hand side of the road.

Democratic Republic of the Congo (DRC) At the time of going to press, the FCO and US State Department advise against all travel to eastern and northeastern DRC due to insecurity and lawlessness. Should conditions improve the most likely option would be between Kisoro and Rutshuru across the Bunagana border, 12 km west of Kisoro, as this provides access to the DRC's Virunga National Park (Parc National des Virunga), where there are also habituated mountain gorillas. However, because of rebel activity in eastern DRC, unfortunately the park and the border are currently closed, and have been since 2012. The other crossings between Uganda and DRC include the Ishasha border, also to

Rutshuru, which is on the southwestern side of Queen Elizabeth National Park, and the Mpondwe border, just over 60 km southwest of Kasese, to Beni via Kasindi. While these borders are open and used by haulage trucks carrying goods into the DRC, again there is consistent rebel activity beyond the borders and travel is ill-advised.

South Sudan At the time of going to press, the FCO and US State Department advise against all travel to South Sudan due to renewed clashes between factions since the country gained independence from the north in 2011. The Nimule border is 120 km north of Gulu and 190 km southeast of Juba but this region is currently the site of refugee camps for the displaced people of South Sudan and travel is ill-advised except for specialist aid workers and NGOs.

Car

If in a private car, you must have a registration document, a letter of authorization from the registered owner if the vehicle is not owned by the driver, and a driving licence printed in English with a photograph. If in a foreign-registered vehicle, you'll need a *Carnet de Passage* issued by a body in your own country or in the country of origin of the vehicle (in the UK, the RAC or AA issue these). If crossing the border into Uganda in a car registered in a neighbouring country, you'll be issued with a temporary import permit (TIP). For all vehicles, you will be required to take out a road fee permit for a one-off fee of US$20 for 30 days, and third-party insurance for Uganda from one of the insurance companies who have kiosks at the border posts. All vehicle fees are paid in US dollars (cash).

Note: all formalities at the border can be done yourself. There have been a number of scams, especially at Malaba and Busia, the borders with Kenya, where would-be 'clearing agents' offer to process the vehicle and claim that some sort of bond needs to be paid to the Uganda/Kenya revenue authorities to import a vehicle. Ignore them, and anyone else offering assistance, and ensure you only pay road fees within the border buildings, and go into an insurance company's kiosk to pay for third-party insurance. Also make sure you keep all receipts in case you need to show them to police once in Uganda.

Overland trucks

Overland truck safaris are a popular and hassle-free way of exploring East Africa, and most itineraries visit many of Uganda's places of interest by road in a compact group. It's a great adventure, traversing the country and making friends whilst camping under equatorial skies. The standard route most trucks take through Uganda is from Nairobi on a two-week circuit. This goes via some of the Kenya national parks, a stop for whitewater rafting and the other adventures at Bujagali, Kampala, Lake Bunyonyi, tracking the gorillas, and returning to Kenya. Some companies also include Queen Elizabeth National Park and chimpanzee tracking at Kibale National Park. From Nairobi the standard route (in either direction) then heads south into Tanzania to Arusha for the Ngorongoro Crater and Serengeti, before heading south to Dar es Salaam, for Zanzibar. If you have more time, you can complete the full circuit that goes from Tanzania through Malawi and Zambia to Livingstone to see the Victoria Falls, and then another three weeks from there to Cape Town in South Africa via Botswana and Namibia. There are several overland companies with departures almost weekly from Nairobi, Livingstone and Cape Town. If you're flying into Kampala, there is also the option of joining one of these circuits there.

Overland truck safari operators
Acacia Africa, www.acacia-africa.com
Africa Travel Co, www.africatravelco.com
African Trails, www.africantrails.co.uk
Dragoman, www.dragoman.com

Exodus, www.exodus.co.uk
G Adventures, www.gadventures.com
Oasis Overland, www.oasisoverland.co.uk
Tucan Travel, www.tucantravel.com

Transport in Uganda

Air

Given that Uganda is a fairly small country and driving distances aren't huge on roads that are improving all the time, there has never been much of a necessity for flights connecting the major tourist destinations. However, there are 13 airstrips dotted around the country and **Aerolink** offers a comprehensive scheduled service from Entebbe International Airport for those short of time. A minimum number of four people are required for flights to operate so you may not always get your first choice of departure times and dates. They may also touch down at other places en route – for example the flight going to Bwindi (the Kihihi or Kisoro airstrips) may also stop at Kasese for those going to Queen Elizabeth National Park. There is also the option of chartering the whole plane and designing your own itinerary. They use Cessnas, typically seating up to nine passengers. You can book with them directly or a tour operator can build flights into a package tour.

From Entebbe, **Aerolink** (www.aerolinkuganda.com) fly daily to Bwindi Impenetrable National Park (Kihihi and Kisoro airstrips); Queen Elizabeth National Park (Kasese and Mweya airstrips); Murchison Falls National Park (Bugungu, Pakuba and Chobe airstrips); Semuliki Wildlife Reserve (Semliki airstrip); and Kidepo Valley National Park (Apoka airstrip). No flight is more than about 1¼ hours.

Costs of flights vary depending on availability and numbers but for a one-way flight expect to pay in the region of: Entebbe–Murchison Falls, US$240; Entebbe–Bwindi/ Queen Elizabeth, US$260; and Entebbe–Kidepo, US$405.

Charter flights to the above airstrips can also be organized with **Eagle Air** (www.eagleair-ug.com) from Entebbe, and with **Air Uganda** (www.flyuganda.com) based at Kampala Aeroclub at Kajjansi Airfield between Kampala and Entebbe.

Lake

See page 130 for details of how to get from Entebbe and Masaka to the Ssese Islands, by ferry or small local canoes.

Road

Boda-boda
The use of *boda-boda* bicycle taxis started in the 1960s and 1970s and they are now a ubiquitous form of African transport. The name in East Africa originated in the Uganda-Kenya border town of Busia where people without the paperwork needed to cross the 500-m no-man's land without using motor vehicles. The bicycle owners would shout out

boda-boda (border-to-border) to potential customers. These days bicycle *boda-bodas* have largely been replaced by mopeds or more powerful motorbikes, depending on the terrain. They are extremely useful in Uganda, but bear in mind they have a very poor safety record and accidents are common. You can flag down *boda-bodas* on the street, or else they may approach you; alternatively, you can get one from a 'stage'; usually a spot under a nice shady tree where the drivers hang out to chat and wait for custom. Agree the price with the driver before boarding the bike. If you are not sure, ask a local what you should pay. If the driver seems drunk or very young, find another one. If you want a *boda-boda* to slow down say '*mpola mpola*' ('slowly slowly'). Don't ride during a storm or downpour, as wet roads and sudden gusts of wind are a major cause of accidents.

Bus and matatu (minibus)

There is an efficient network of privately run buses and *matatus* across the country. A *matatu* is a minibus, usually a Nissan or Toyota, with a three-tonne capacity, hence the name – *tatu* means 'three' in Kiswahili. Fairly new regulations in Uganda mean that all public service vehicles have to be speed governed at 80 kph, standing is not permitted and everyone must wear a seat belt (police issue on-the-spot fines to passengers who haven't got seat belts on).

Larger buses provide a considerably more comfortable ride than *matatus*, have more space for luggage and are generally safer, better maintained and driven a little less recklessly. Buses can be any colour, while *matatus* have to be uniformly white with a blue stripe. The larger buses cover the long-distance routes and you will be able to reserve a seat at kiosks run by the bus companies at the bus stations, known variously as bus parks, stands or 'stages'. *Matatus* do some long-distances, but mostly go from town to town and leave when full from taxi parks (usually close to the bus parks). If you have problems finding the right vehicle, just ask around and someone will direct you. In towns *matatus* can be flagged down on the street for short journeys in the direction you are going. On all public transport and at the bus and taxi parks, keep an eye on your belongings and keep any valuables out of sight.

By far the most reliable bus service is the **Post Bus** ① *T0414-255511, ww.ugapost.co.ug*, which is well driven, runs to a fixed timetable and has some luggage space. Post Buses stop at all the post offices en route, and the time it takes to load and unload mail doesn't add much to the journey time. They run Monday-Saturday and all services leave at 0800 from the Kampala main post office on Kampala–Jinja road, near its junction with Speke Road. Get there by at least 0700 to buy a ticket as you can't pre-book. The routes are: Kampala–Gulu; Kampala–Kabale via Masaka and Mbarara; Kampala–Kasese via Fort Portal; Kampala–Hoima via Masindi; and Kampala–Lira via Mbale and Soroti. Naturally the routes run in reverse and most depart from the post offices at the end of their routes at 0700-0800. You need to enquire at the local post offices en route to ask when they expect them to arrive and depart. For an idea of fares, see Kampala Transport, page 66.

Car

Driving is on the left side of the road. Speed limits are 60 kph in built up areas and 100 kph on open roads. Police use speed guns and breaking the speed limit can result in an on-the-spot fine. All vehicle occupants must wear a seat belt at all times and a driving licence must be available for inspection. The key roads are in good condition, and many of the major routes have been rebuilt in the last few years to a very high quality. A normal saloon car is adequate in Kampala and along the major tarred roads between the large towns.

However, a 4WD, or at the very least a vehicle with high clearance, is preferable if you are going off the tarred roads or into the parks. The minor roads are constructed from murram (laterite), which is generally well maintained although there are some notorious stretches where travel is very slow, bumpy and pretty uncomfortable. In the dry season dust on these roads is a big problem, while in the wet, trucks often get bogged down and, as the roads are usually single track, this can cause big delays. Roads in the parks are rough gravel or dirt tracks and, during the rainy season, many are passable only with 4WD vehicles.

Driving in Uganda is not without its hazards. Things to be aware of include other road users' reckless driving, often without lights, with oversized, poorly secured loads; speeding *matatus* that may also brake suddenly to pick up passengers; large potholes; broken-down vehicles blocking the road; high speed bumps; children and livestock meandering across the roads; and wobbling bicycles transporting several stands of bananas. It is customary across East Africa to put piles of leaves on the road a few metres apart as a warning of a broken-down vehicle ahead, so slow down if you see this.

Fuel is available along the main highways and in towns, but if you're going way off the beaten track, consider taking a couple of jerry cans of extra fuel. Also ensure the vehicle has a jack and possibly take a shovel to dig it out of mud or sand. In remote areas petrol stations will not accept credit cards or have an ATM, so carry enough cash.

Car hire Most people visit the parks and reserves on an organized safari, but if you're confident about driving in Uganda, there is also the option to hire a car. (Most companies can also organize drivers for additional expense). Renting a car has certain advantages over public transport, particularly if you intend visiting any of the more remote regions of the country, or there are at least four of you to share the costs.

You generally need to be over 23, have a full driving licence (it does not have to be an international licence, your home country one will do – with English translation if necessary) and a credit card. Always take out the collision damage waiver premium as even the smallest accident can be very expensive. Costs vary between the different car hire companies and are from around US$70-80 per day for a normal saloon car; US$100-120 for a minibus; and US$140-170 for a 4WD. Deals can be made for more than seven days' car hire. It is important to shop around and ask the companies what is and what is not included in the rates and what the provisions are in the event of a breakdown. Things to consider include whether you take out a limited or unlimited mileage package depending on how far you think you will drive. Finally, 18% VAT is added to all costs. For car hire companies in Kampala, see page 67.

Hitchhiking
In the Western sense hitchhiking (standing beside the road and requesting a free ride) is not an option. However, truck drivers and many private motorists will often carry you if you pay, and if you are stuck where there is no public transport you should not hesitate to approach likely vehicles on this basis.

Taxis
Taxis are generally referred to as 'special hire'. It's always advisable to agree the fare before departure (*bei gani?* – how much?). Prices are generally fair as drivers simply won't take you if you offer a fare that's too low. Be aware that taxi drivers never seem to have change, so try and accumulate some small notes for taxi rides. If you find a taxi driver you like, get their mobile number.

Maps

The Michelin *Map of Africa: Central and South* (www.michelintravel.com) covers Uganda in detail. The better maps are Macmillan's 1:350,000 *Uganda Traveller's Map*, and Nelles 1:700,000 *Uganda Map*. These are available in the UK from **Stanfords** ① *12-14 Long Acre, Covent Garden, London WC2E 9LP, T0207-836 1321, and 29 Corn St, Bristol, BS1 1HT, T0117-929 9966, www.stanfords.co.uk*. Locally, **Uganda Maps** ① *www.uganda-maps.com*, produce attractive hand-drawn tourist maps of Kampala, Jinja and the Nile, southwestern Uganda and parks, including Queen Elizabeth and Lake Mburo. Try the bookshops in Kampala (page 63) and some of the upmarket lodges; **Uganda Wildlife Authority** offices also sell them.

Where to stay in Uganda

Hotels in the towns and cities usually keep the same rates year-round, but safari lodges have seasonal rates depending on weather and periods of popularity of overseas (especially European) visitors. Low season in East Africa is generally around the long rainy season from the beginning of April to the end of June, while there is a shorter low season around the rains in November. Room rates can drop considerably and it may be possible to negotiate rates, especially if you plan to stay a few days. For more expensive hotels (and national park entrance fees), a system operates whereby foreign or non-resident visitors are charged a higher rate than resident regional and local visitors. Most non-resident rates are published in US dollars – but these can be paid in Uganda shillings as well as foreign currency. This really makes no difference but check the rates and make a fuss if the exchange rate is not fair. Credit cards are widely accepted at the larger establishments, but may attract a surcharge of around 5%. VAT at 18% is added to all service charges, though this is usually included in the bill.

Hotels

With the exception of a couple of places in Kampala, such as the **Sheraton**, there are few international hotel chains in Uganda, which means much of the accommodation is locally owned, individual and characterful. Quality of local town and city hotels varies widely; some are newly built with good amenities, while others tend to be bland with poor service and dated decor; there are also a number of charming hotels that have been around since the colonial days.

Hotels at the top end charge US$200-300 for a double room and for this you should expect good en suite facilities, air conditioning or fans (although this depends on the local climate), mosquito nets, DSTV (satellite TV), Wi-Fi or hotel internet access and breakfast. Mid-range hotels cost around US$100-150 and offer the same but won't be as luxurious or reliable or have as many extra facilities like a swimming pool. Rooms in the US$40-100 range are often the best value with comfortable accommodation in self-contained rooms, hot water, fans, possibly DSTV, breakfast and perhaps a decent restaurant. At the budget end there's a fairly wide choice of cheap hotels for US$10-40. A room often comprises a simple bed, basic bathroom which is sometimes shared, mosquito net and fan, but may have an irregular water or electricity supply; it is always a good idea to look at a room first, to make sure it's clean and everything works. It is also imperative to ensure that your luggage will be locked away securely for protection

Price codes

Where to stay

$$$$ over US$300 $$$ US$150-300

$$ US$75-150 $ under US$75

Unless otherwise stated, prices refer to the cost of a double room including tax.

Restaurants

$$$ over US$30 $$ US$15-30 $ under US$15

Prices refer to the cost of a main course with either a soft drink, a glass of wine or a beer.

against petty theft. There may be a restaurant serving local Ugandan food or basics like chicken or fish and chips, and breakfast could be included but may not be substantial, with perhaps a cup of tea/coffee, bread and fruit. At the very bottom of the scale are bare cell-like rooms in concrete compounds often attached to a bar and referred to locally as 'board and lodgings'; these cost as little as US$6-8 but should nevertheless be avoided.

Hostels

Uganda remains a popular destination for backpackers and many gravitate in particular to the excellent backpackers' hostels in Kampala, Lake Bunyonyi, Jinja and Bujagali. These are well organized and offer several types of accommodation in dorm rooms with bunk beds, private rooms with shared bathrooms or more expensive en suite doubles, and campsites with 'lazy camping' (see below). Expect to pay around US$20-40 for a double, US$8-12 for a dorm and US$5-8 for camping. They vary from converted old colonial houses to purpose-built resorts with rustic thatched buildings. Facilities include hot showers, a restaurant and bar, internet of some kind (Wi-Fi or an internet café), perhaps a laundry service, DSTV, pool tables or a book exchange. They are generally a great source of local information and can organize a number of activities depending on their location; canoeing on Lake Bunyonyi or whitewater rafting at Jinja and Bujagali, for example. Additionally if you haven't yet booked a gorilla or other safari, the backpackers are the best places to arrange budget tours.

Uganda also has a number of hostels or guesthouses run by church groups and accommodation for rooms, dorms and camping is about the same price as the backpackers. Many are in attractive locations with a homely, friendly atmosphere and have spotlessly clean rooms with en suite or shared bathrooms, a communal lounge and terrace area, and generous and wholesome set meals in the restaurant, though no alcohol is served.

Campsites and bandas

There are campsites all over Uganda, including in the national parks (see below). Some also offer cheap rooms in chalets or *bandas*, which are simple cabins or huts, often with a thatched roof, and sometimes made of more permanent materials like stone or concrete. Standards vary from nothing more than a basic 'long-drop' toilet to good facilities with clean ablution blocks, hot water (often heated by a donkey boiler over a fire), a fireplace where you can cook, a tap for water and possibly a restaurant and bar. Camping rates are as little as US$3 per person and rise to US$12 per person for somewhere with exceptional facilities or in a particularly scenic spot, while a bed costs around US$10-20 per person.

Community-run camps and are often located near the national park gates but outside the park boundaries (hence park fees don't apply). At these, and with a bit of notice, filling local meals and beers and sodas can be provided. Inexpensive and interesting activities such as forest walks or village visits can be organized, and the local (often self-taught) guides are a mine of information on the flora and fauna and cultural aspects of the area. Profits go back into local initiatives like a clinic or a school, or for preserving a wetland or forest, so they are well worth supporting.

Many country lodges also have campsites; these can be found at Bujagali, the crater lakes around Kibale National Park and Lake Bunyonyi. In some there is the option of 'lazy camping', which means they provide a simple dome tent with mattresses and bedding. This is one of the cheapest options of accommodation, but is not to be confused with more expensive safari tented camps (see below). At campsites attached to lodges, there is also the option of eating in the restaurant, and some offer B&B rates to campers. Most campsites are guarded but despite this you should ensure that valuables are not left unattended. Camping should always have minimal impact on the environment. All rubbish and waste matter should be buried, burnt or taken away with you. Do not leave food scraps or containers where they may attract and harm animals, and be careful about leaving items outside your tent. Many campsites have troupes of baboons nearby that can be a nuisance and a hyena can chew through something as solid as a saucepan. Wild or 'free' camping is rarely done in Uganda.

Safari options

All safari companies offer basically the same safari but at different prices, which is reflective of what accommodation is booked. See also page 6.

Safari lodges and tented camps These vary and may be either typical hotels with rooms and facilities in one building, or individual cottages or permanent tents with a central lounge, dining and bar area. The tents will have a thatched roof to keep it cool inside, proper beds, a veranda and a small bathroom at the back. At night you may hear animals surprisingly close by. Standards at lodges and tented camps vary from the rustic to the modern, from the simply appointed to the last word in luxury. Nearly all are in superb locations with excellent views, or overlook waterholes or salt licks that attract game, and many have swimming pools. Efforts are usually made to design them to blend into their environment, with an emphasis on natural local building materials as well as traditional art and decoration. Rates vary widely from US$200-500 per couple depending on what's included, but most are full board, although extras like wine and liqueurs can be very expensive.

National park accommodation Park accommodation provided by the **Uganda Wildlife Authority (UWA)** is generally basic but good value. Many camps are conveniently located near the park HQ at the gate, while others are further into the parks and a 4WD may be necessary. All are most attractively sited, perhaps in the elbow of a river course or overlooking a lake, and they always have plenty of shade. Birds are plentiful and several hours can be whiled away birdwatching. There are campsites as well as *bandas*, some with an attached shower and toilet, otherwise there is a communal ablution block shared with campers (again, hot water may be heated by a donkey boiler). Bed linen, mosquito nets, drinking water and firewood are provided, but you will need to bring your own food and utensils. Kerosene lamps are usually provided, but you may want to bring torches and candles. Rooms cost US$20-30 and camping is US$8 per person, although remember if staying overnight within the park boundaries, park entry fees apply (see box, page 8). This is not as prohibitively expensive as it might sound, given that you are probably visiting the parks in any case and park entry fees are for 24-hours. Many UWA camps are used by the budget tour operators and safaris include park fees, tents and equipment, as well as food and a cook.

Food and drink in Uganda

Food

Traditional Ugandan food reflects the many different lifestyles of the various groups in the country, as well as historical international influences dating back to the 15th century, when the Portuguese introduced maize, cassava and (a little-known fact) bananas and pineapples to East Africa. Later culinary influences include British and Indian, which were introduced during the colonial times.

Local food is generally based around the main proteins of beef, pork, goat and chicken, and there's plentiful fish, mostly delicious tilapia found in all Uganda's lakes. These are usually accompanied with *posho* (known as *ugali* in other parts of East Africa), which is maize ground and boiled to form a stiff dough, and *matoke*, which is boiled and mashed plantains (you will see these green bananas all over Uganda). Indian additions to the menu include chapatti and *pilau* rice and you can't go wrong by adding tasty Ugandan groundnut sauce. Street snacks include samosas and hard-boiled eggs, cobs of roasted corn or maize, and *muchomo*, grilled meat on sticks. The best of these are pork 'sticks' – a few pieces of seasoned roast pork on a skewer – which are usually sold at informal little hole-in-the-wall restaurants called 'pork joints'. For something sweet try *mandazi*, a kind of sweet doughnut, or ready prepared peeled and sliced fruit such as oranges, pineapples, bananas, mangoes and papayas. These items are very cheap and are indispensable when travelling. Finally, no visit to Uganda is complete without trying the famous 'Rolex' – a chapatti wrapped around an omelet, with onions, cabbage and tomatoes. The name in fact, has nothing to do with the Swiss watch company, but is a collaboration of 'roll' and 'eggs'.

Most food is purchased in open-air markets. In Kampala and the larger towns these are held daily and, as well as fresh fruit and vegetables, they sell eggs, bread and meat. In the smaller villages, a market will be held on one day of the week when the farmers come to sell their wares. Markets are very colourful places to visit and, given how fertile Uganda is, the variety of fruits and vegetables available is vast. Other locally produced food items are sold in shops, often run by Indian traders, whilst imported products are sold in the few upmarket supermarkets, such as Nakumatt.

Eating out Kampala has excellent restaurants and there is a wide variety of international cuisine on offer, although any imported ingredients on the menu come at a price. Small town hotels and restaurants tend to serve either traditional Ugandan fare or a limited variety of bland food; omelet or chicken and chips, and perhaps a meat stew but not much else. Indian food is extremely good in Uganda and cheap, and an important option for vegetarians travelling in the country. Restaurant prices are generally low: it is quite possible to get a plate of hot food in a basic restaurant for US$5; even the most expensive places often charge no more than US$30 per person with drinks. Some larger hotels offer breakfast and dinner buffets. The standard of these varies enormously. The most important thing is to make sure the food has been freshly prepared and avoid dishes that have been sitting around for a long time on a buffet table. Near the national parks, most hotels and lodges will prepare a packed lunch if you are going out gorilla tracking or on a game drive.

Drink

Sodas (soft drinks such as Coke, Fanta and the like) are available everywhere, and sold either in cans or cheaper refundable 300 ml bottles. Bottled water is fairly expensive, but is available in all but the smallest villages. Tap water is reputedly safe in many parts of the country, but is only really recommended if you have a fairly hardy traveller's stomach. Popular throughout the country is *chai* (tea), which is served milky and sweet with the ingredients boiled together, but is surprisingly refreshing. Coffee, although grown in Uganda, is often instant powder and pretty insipid, although the more upmarket places serve the freshly ground real thing, and coffee shop chains are becoming popular in Kampala.

Ugandan beer is sold in 500 ml bottles and is quite acceptable and good value compared with the imported alternatives. There are two main breweries; **Uganda Breweries** (based in Port Bell) produces Bell lager and Guinness (under license), while **Nile Breweries** (based in Jinja), produces Nile Special, Nile Gold and Club lagers. Imported wines, spirits and beers are very expensive, although they're widely available and there's a reasonable choice, including wines from South Africa. Local spirits are sold in both bottles and sachets of one tot and include some rough vodkas and whiskies. Far more palatable but equally potent is Uganda's famous *waragi*, a type of gin made from sugar cane. Going under various names, you may be offered banana wine in the rural and mountain areas; this home-brew of fermented bananas and sorghum produces a highly intoxicating and foul-tasting alcohol – administer with care.

Festivals in Uganda

January
Nile River Festival, www.nileriverfestival. wordpress.com. Organized by **Kayak the Nile** at Bujagali, this is a weekend of whitewater racing for professional kayakers, plus displays when a ramp is erected in Bujagali Lake for spectators to watch their skills. It's also a good excuse for a party and events take place at **Nile River Explorers** and **Hairy Lemon** (see pages 100 and 94 for details).

September
Bayimba International Festival of the Arts, www.bayimba.org. Popular 3-day festival at the National Theatre (page 43) focusing on music, dance, theatre and visual arts from Uganda and other East African countries. It's a platform for emerging performers and the tickets of just a US$1 aim to promote the arts to all.

October
Kampala City Festival, www.kcca.go.ug. Formerly the **Kampala Carnival**, this street parade is organized by the council, **Kampala Capital City Authority** (KCCA), and follows a 2-km route down Nile Av. There are floats from the sponsors such as **Nile Breweries** and local hip-hop bands and cultural groups perform along the way.

How big is your footprint?

The point of a holiday is, of course, to have a good time, but if it's relatively guilt-free as well, that's even better. Perfect ecotourism would ensure a good living for local inhabitants, while not detracting from their traditional lifestyles, encroaching on their customs or spoiling their environment. Perfect ecotourism probably doesn't exist, but everyone can play their part.

The tourism industry in Uganda is very important for the country's economy and creates thousands of jobs. Many national parks and game reserves, valuable archaeological sites and museums are funded by visitor entry fees, which in turn promote their protection. Additionally, some of the tour operators and lodges fund conservation and community projects. By earning from tourism, the poorer people who rely on the land for their livelihoods are more likely to protect their environments for the benefit of tourism and these projects are well worth supporting.

Here are a few points worth bearing in mind:

- Think about where your money goes and be fair and realistic about how cheaply you travel. Try to put money into local people's hands; drink local beer or fruit juice rather than imported brands and stay in locally owned accommodation wherever possible.
- Haggle with humour and appropriately. Remember that you want a fair price, not the lowest one.
- Think about what happens to your rubbish. Take biodegradable products and a water bottle filter. Be sensitive to limited resources like water, fuel and electricity.
- Help preserve local wildlife and habitats by respecting rules and regulations, such as sticking to footpaths and not buying products made from endangered plants or animals.
- Don't treat people as part of the landscape; they may not want their picture taken. Ask first and respect their wishes.
- Learn the local language and be mindful of local customs and norms. It can enhance your travel experience and you'll earn respect and be more readily welcomed by local people.
- And finally, use your guidebook as a starting point, not the only source of information. Talk to local people, then discover your own adventure.

November

MTN Kampala Marathon, www.athletics uganda.co.ug, www.mtn.co.ug. Like Kenya and Ethiopia, Uganda is well known for producing some world-class athletes – attributed to training at high altitude – and it was Ugandan Stephen Kiprotich that spectacularly won the marathon in the 2012 London Olympics. The Kampala Marathon attracts some 20,000 runners and anyone can participate.

Nile Gold Jazz Safari, www.thejazzsafari. com. Again sponsored by **Nile Breweries** among others and held at the **Kampala Serena Hotel** (page 54), with afternoon and evening performances from quality musicians from across East Africa as well as food and dancing. Has also been hosted in Kigali and Nairobi.

Shopping in Uganda

Although the selection is nowhere near as good as that of Kenya and Tanzania, Uganda produces some interesting crafts and curios, including wood carvings, woven bark cloth mats and pots, decorated gourds, musical instruments, leather and sisal baskets and textiles. You may also see items from neighbouring countries, including soapstone carvings and *kikois* (colourful woven sarongs) from Kenya, or wood carvings from the DRC (interesting because the masks and figures are very distinctive and these days are rarely found). Kampala has some excellent quality curio shops (page 63), and some of the tourist lodges have shops too. On safari routes to and from the parks there are roadside stalls where vehicles can conveniently pull in. Prices in shops are largely fixed, though in the depths of the quiet low season, can be negotiable, while at stalls and markets prices are always negotiable. See page 23 for tips on bargaining.

Essentials A-Z

Accident and emergency

Police and ambulance: T999. **Fire**: T112.

Bargaining

Whilst most prices in shops are set, the exception are curio shops where a little good-natured bargaining is possible, especially if it's quiet or you are buying a number of things. Bargaining is very much expected in the street markets whether you are buying a tomato or a carved wooden statue. Generally traders will attempt to overcharge tourists who are unaware of local prices. Start lower than you would expect to pay, be polite and good humoured, and if the final price doesn't suit, walk away. You may be called back for more negotiation, or the trader may let you go, in which case your price was too low. Ask about the prices of taxis, excursions, souvenirs and so on at your hotel.

Children

Uganda is a good destination for family holidays but bear in mind some of the more popular activities are not permitted for children below a certain age: no under 15s for gorilla tracking; no under 12s for chimpanzee or golden monkey tracking; and adventure activities such as bungee jumping, whitewater rafting and mountain climbing also have age restrictions. However, Uganda is all about nature and smaller children will enjoy forest walks, seeing the animals on safari, boat and canoe rides, and it's the perfect place to introduce children to birdwatching. There are some activities specifically for children. For example, the **Uganda Wildlife Authority** (UWA) organizes nature walks and activities at Kibale National Park (page 215) for

under 12s and, at Bujagali (page 88), **Adrift** has family floats on the River Nile and **All Terrain Adventures** has quad bikes for kids and a mini-golf course. Children love camping, so even if you don't have your own camping equipment or can't afford an upmarket tented camp, there is the option of 'lazy camping' (see page 18) in places like Bunyonyi Lake. Many accommodation options can organize babysitting while parents go on the more adventurous activities. Enquire about this when making a reservation. With a bit of pre-planning, Uganda can be fun for the whole family.

Children get significant discounts for accommodation and, while adjoining rooms aren't common, putting extra beds into rooms is. In the national parks, entrance fees are half price for children under 15, and under 5s are free (see box, page 8). Seeing animals on safari is very exciting, especially when you catch your first glimpse of an elephant or lion. However, small children may get bored driving around a hot game park all day if there is no animal activity. Keep them interested by providing them with their own animal and bird checklists and perhaps their own binoculars and cameras. If you travel in a group, think about the long hours inside the vehicle sharing little room with other people. Noisy and bickering children can annoy your travel mates and scare the animals away. Most tour operators use minibuses for safaris so consider taking one for yourself or share it with another family.

Items such as disposable nappies, formula milk powders and puréed foods are only available in major towns and are expensive, so you may want to ring enough with you. It is important to remember that children have an increased risk of gastroenteritis, malaria and sunburn and are more likely to develop complications, so care must be taken to minimize risks. See Health, below.

Customs and duty free

The following items can be imported duty free: 400 cigarettes or 500 g of tobacco; 1 litre wines and spirits; 0.5 litre toilet water or 0.25 litre perfume. Narcotics, pornography and firearms are prohibited. Once in Uganda, be careful about accepting any wildlife-derived object from villagers and guides. Any souvenir made from an endangered species is prohibited. If you were to buy such items, you should always consider the environmental and social impact of your purchase. Attempts to smuggle controlled products out of Uganda can result in confiscation, fines and imprisonment under the **Convention on Trade in Endangered Species (CITES)**, www.cites.org.

Disabled travellers

There are few specific facilities for disabled people in Uganda. Wheelchairs are not accommodated on public transport, so the options are to self-drive or go on a tour. Most tour operators should be able to make special arrangements for disabled travellers. Contact the **Association of Uganda Tour Operators (AUTO)**, www.auto.or.ug, and ask if they can make a recommendation. Ugandan's themselves will do their very best to help, and being disabled should not deter you from visiting Uganda. Some of Kampala's larger more modern hotels have rooms with disabled facilities, and at least one of the lodges near the most popular national parks should have wheelchair access.

The excursion to see the gorillas is not completely out of bounds for wheelchair uses. Despite the arduous nature of gorilla tracking, porters have been known to carry wheelchairs. Contact the **Uganda Wildlife Authority (UWA)**, www.ugandawildlife.org, or **AUTO** (see above) for a specialist operator.

Electricity

220-240 volts AC at 50 Hz. Mostly square 3-pin British-type sockets, but older round 3-pin large or small sockets are still found in older hotels; a multi-socket adaptor that includes a 2-pin round socket for razors, phones, etc is advisable.

Embassies and consulates

For a list of Ugandan embassies abroad, see http://embassy.goabroad.com/embassies-of/Uganda.

Gay and lesbian travellers

Homosexuality is illegal in Uganda and, by law, could be punishable by a life sentence. Exercise extreme discretion. However, discreet behavior is generally tolerated by ordinary people, especially by those in the tourism industry. Gay clubs and bars are conspicuous in their absence.

Health

Before you go
See your GP or travel clinic at least 6 weeks before your departure for general advice on travel risks, malaria and recommended vaccinations. Make sure you have comprehensive medical insurance including full medical repatriation, with additional cover for extreme sports if appropriate. Get a dental check, know your own blood group and if you suffer from a long-term condition such as diabetes or epilepsy make sure someone knows or that you have a Medic Alert bracelet/necklace with this information on it.

Vaccinations
First of all confirm that your primary courses and boosters are up to date (diphtheria, typhoid, polio and tetanus). Vaccinations commonly recommended for travel in Uganda are yellow fever, hepatitis A and B,

meningitis and rabies, especially if staying for long periods in remote areas. Travellers will need to produce a yellow fever vaccination certificate on arrival in Uganda, and on arrival in other countries if travelling from Uganda.

Health risks
Altitude sickness

Uganda has 2 areas of high altitude: the Rwenzori Mountains, where the peaks reach 5109 m, and Mount Elgon, at 4321 m. Altitude sickness can strike above 3000 m, and is a response to the lack of oxygen in the air. The best way of preventing it is to ascend relatively slowly and to acclimatize to the rarefied air by spending some time walking at medium altitude. No specific factors, such as age, sex or physical condition contribute to the condition – some people get it and some people don't. Symptoms include headache, lassitude, dizziness, loss of appetite, nausea and vomiting. If the symptoms are mild, the treatment is rest, painkillers (preferably not aspirin-based) for the headaches and anti-sickness pills for vomiting. Should the symptoms be severe it is best to descend to a lower altitude immediately – the symptoms disappear very quickly with a drop of even a few hundred metres.

Bilharzia

Also known as schistosomiasis, bilharzia is a disease carried by parasitic snails living in fresh water. It occurs in most of the freshwater lakes of Uganda, including Lake Victoria, especially around the Ssese Islands, and can be contracted from a single swim or wade. Symptoms, which can appear within a few weeks, or even many months afterwards, include fever, diarrhoea, abdominal pain and spleen or liver enlargement. A single drug cures this disease, so get yourself checked out as soon as possible if you have any of these symptoms, or if you have spent prolonged time in infected water. Alternatively, avoid

swimming in any freshwater lakes (difficult given that most of Uganda's lakes are so inviting). Many places advertise themselves as 'bilharzia-free'. Bear in mind, though, that there is no way of testing this is true. Broad advice is that the parasite is not present in fast-moving water, so avoid stagnant water or still reedy shores, and don't wade or swim too close to villages where people who may be infected use the water to bathe or wash clothes. Chlorinated swimming pools are fine.

Bites and stings

Ticks usually attach themselves to the lower parts of the body – often after you've been walking in areas of long damp grass or where cattle have grazed – then swell up as they suck blood. You should use a pair of tweezers to remove a tick, gently rocking it out and being careful not to leave the head embedded in your skin as this can cause a nasty infection. Do not use petrol, Vaseline, lighted cigarettes. If travelling with children, check them over for ticks.

In areas of wet soil or sand the **jigger flea** can burrow its way into people's feet causing a painful itchy swelling which finally bursts in a rather disgusting fashion. Avoid these by wearing shoes. If they do become established, ask someone experienced to winkle them out with a sterile needle.

Putsi flies, also known as tumbo or mango flies in Uganda, lay their eggs under the skin of sheep and cattle, but also in damp fabric, including washing. The egg is transferred to the skin and a maggot grows and pops up as a boil. The best way to remove them is to cover the boil with oil, Vaseline or nail varnish to stop the maggot breathing, then to squeeze it out gently the next day. Avoid them in the first place by hanging clothes out to dry in direct sunlight until crisp; never lay them on damp grass. They can also be eradicated from clothing by ironing.

Tsetse fly is present in most game areas in Uganda, and can transmit sleeping sickness (African trypanosomiasis). Although this disease is extremely rare in humans, tsetse flies do administer a wicked bite.

Bites from **scorpions** are very painful but rarely dangerous to adults. Seek medical advice if a young child is bitten. Do not immerse the bite in cold water as this increases the pain. If camping, shake out boots and shoes, and check backpacks before putting them on.

Bites and stings can fester quite quickly in Uganda's moist climate. They can be relieved by cool baths, antihistamine tablets, or mild corticosteroid creams. Treat infected bites with an antiseptic or antibiotic cream or, even better, powder (these are available locally). If the redness around the infection spreads or you develop a fever, a course of antibiotics may be required. Fungal infections can also develop in moist climates so wear clean cotton socks and underwear.

Most snake species are non-venomous and even venomous snakes often inflict a 'dry bite' where no venom is injected. But if you are unlucky (or careless) enough to be bitten by a venomous snake, try to identify the culprit, without putting yourself in further danger. Do not apply a tourniquet, suck or cut open the bite wound; victims should be taken to a hospital or a doctor without delay.

Cholera

Cholera is spread through consumption of contaminated water and food in areas with very poor sanitation and lack of clean drinking water. The main symptoms are profuse watery diarrhoea and vomiting, which may lead to severe dehydration. However, most travellers are at extremely low risk of infection and the disease rarely shows symptoms in healthy well-nourished people. The cholera vaccine, Dukoral, is only recommended for certain high-risk individuals such as health professionals or volunteers.

Diarrhoea

Diarrhoea can refer either to loose stools or an increased frequency of bowel movement, both of which can be a nuisance, but symptoms should be relatively short lived. Adults can use an antidiarrhoeal medication to control the symptoms but only for up to 24 hrs. In addition, keep well hydrated by drinking plenty of fluids and eat bland foods. Oral rehydration sachets taken after each loose stool are a useful way to keep well hydrated. These should always be used when treating children and the elderly. If there are no signs of improvement the diarrhoea is likely to be viral and not bacterial and antibiotics may be required. Also seek medical help if there is blood in the stools and/or fever.

The standard advice to prevent problems is to be careful with water and ice for drinking. If you have any doubts then boil the water or filter and treat it. Food can also transmit disease. Be wary of salads (what were they washed in, who handled them), re-heated foods or food that has been left out in the sun having been cooked earlier in the day. There is a simple adage that says wash it, peel it, boil it or forget it. Also be wary of unpasteurized dairy products as these can transmit a range of diseases.

Hepatitis

Hepatitis means inflammation of the liver. Viral causes of the disease can be acquired anywhere in the world. The most obvious symptom is a yellowing of your skin or the whites of your eyes. However, prior to this all that you may notice is itching and tiredness. Pre-travel hepatitis A vaccine is the best bet. Hepatitis B is spread through blood and unprotected sexual intercourse: both of these can be avoided.

HIV/AIDS

Africa has the highest rates of HIV and AIDS in the world. Efforts to stem the rate of infection have had limited success, as many of the factors that need addressing such as social change, poverty and gender inequalities are long-term processes. Visitors should be aware of the dangers of infection from unprotected sex and always use a condom. If you have to have medical treatment, ensure any equipment used is taken from a sealed pack or is freshly sterilized. If you have to have a blood transfusion, ask for screened blood.

Malaria

Malaria is present in almost all of Uganda and prophylactics should be taken. Take expert advice before you leave home, and make sure you finish the recommended course of anti-malarials. It can start as something just resembling an attack of flu. You may feel tired, lethargic, headachy, feverish; or, more seriously, develop fits, followed by coma and then death. Have a low index of suspicion because it is very easy to write off vague symptoms, which may actually be malaria. If you have a temperature, go to a doctor as soon as you can and ask for a malaria test. On your return home if you suffer any of these symptoms, get tested as soon as possible.

To prevent mosquito bites wear clothes that cover arms and legs and use effective insect repellents. Repellents containing 30-50% DEET (Di-ethyltoluamide) are recommended; lemon eucalyptus (Mosiguard) is a reasonable alternative. Rooms with a/c or fans also help ward off mosquitoes at night.

Rabies

Avoid dogs and monkeys that are behaving strangely. If you are bitten by a domestic or wild animal, do not leave things to chance: scrub the wound with soap and water and/or disinfectant, try to determine the animal's ownership, and seek medical assistance at once. The course of treatment depends on whether you have already been satisfactorily vaccinated against rabies.

Sun

Protect yourself adequately against the sun. In Uganda do not be fooled into thinking that the sun is not harmful if it's foggy; the UV rays will still penetrate the mist. Apply a high-factor sunscreen (greater than SPF15) and also make sure it screens against UVB. Prevent heat exhaustion and heatstroke by drinking enough fluids throughout the day (your urine will be pale if you are drinking enough). Symptoms of heat exhaustion and heatstroke include dizziness, tiredness and headache. Use rehydration salts mixed with water to replenish fluids and salts and find somewhere cool and shady to recover. If you suspect heatstroke rather than heat exhaustion, you need to cool the body down quickly (cold showers are particularly effective).

If you get sick

There are private hospitals in Kampala, which have 24-hr emergency departments and pharmacies, and provide a high standard of healthcare. For cases of extreme emergency or surgery, visitors with adequate health insurance may be transferred to a private hospital in Nairobi, Kenya, which has the best medical facilities in East Africa. In other areas of Uganda, facilities range from government hospitals to rural clinics, but these can be poorly equipped and understaffed. It is essential to have travel insurance as hospital bills need to be paid at the time of admittance, so keep all paperwork to make a claim.

Useful websites

www.btha.org British Travel Health Association.
www.cdc.gov US government site with excellent advice on travel health and details of disease outbreaks.
www.fco.gov.uk British Foreign and Commonwealth Office travel site with useful information on each country, people, climate and a list of UK embassies/consulates.

www.fitfortravel.nhs.uk A-Z of
vaccine/health advice for each country.
www.travelhealth.co.uk Independent
travel health site with advice on vaccination,
travel insurance and health risks.
www.who.int World Health Organization,
updates of disease outbreaks.

Holidays

Uganda recognizes both Christian and
Muslim holidays in addition to fixed public
holidays. Government offices, post offices,
banks and forex bureaux will be closed but
many shops are open.
1 Jan New Year's Day
26 Jan Liberation Day
8 Mar Women's Day
Mar/Apr Good Friday
Mar/Apr Easter Monday
1 May Labour Day
3 Jun Uganda Martyrs' Day
9 Jun National Heroes Day
9 Oct Independence Day
25 Dec Christmas Day
26 Dec Boxing Day

Insurance

Before departure, it is vital to take out
comprehensive travel insurance. There are
a wide variety of policies to choose from,
so shop around. At the very least, the policy
should cover medical expenses, including
repatriation to your home country in the
event of a medical emergency. If you are
going to be active in Uganda, ensure
the policy covers trekking or whitewater
rafting, for example. There is no substitute
for suitable precautions against petty
crime, but if you do have something stolen
whilst in Uganda, report the incident to the
nearest police station and make sure you
get a police report and case number. You
will need these to make any claim from
your insurance company.

Internet

Internet cafés are widely available in
Kampala and all the main towns. Entebbe
International Airport has a Wi-Fi hotspot,
as do many restaurants and coffee shops
in Kampala. Places in other towns are
catching on, and increasingly many hotels
offer Wi-Fi for a fee. However, most safari
lodges in the more remote places won't
have internet, and if they do it is likely to
be via an expensive satellite connection.
There is the option of buying a USB/dongle
connection and loading it with airtime once
in Uganda; this can be organized at any of
the mobile phone shops/stalls (which are
everywhere) – try MTN or Orange.

Language

The official language is English, and it is
widely spoken. However, on a day-to-day
basis most Ugandans speak Luganda,
which is the most popular of more than
30 local languages. Kiswahili, the common
language across East Africa, is also spoken,
but not as widely as in Kenya and Tanzania.

Media

Newspapers
The main newspaper is *New Vision* (www.
newvision.co.ug), published in English.
Although it is government owned it has
considerable editorial freedom and no
advertising. It also has good events listings.
Its rival, *The Monitor* (www.monitor.co.ug),
is independent. Both papers have some
coverage of international news and sport.
The East African (www.theeastafrican.co.ke),
a weekly newspaper published in Kenya
but sold throughout the region, provides
the most objective reporting on East
African issues and has in-depth coverage
of international news. International
newspapers from the US, UK and Europe
are regularly available in Kampala (although
a day or so late). Most newspapers and

magazines are available from the many street stalls.

Radio

Radio broadcasts are mainly in English, but some are in Kiswahili and Luganda. The **BBC World Service** (www.bbc.co.uk/worldservice) is broadcast to Uganda, and can be received on a short waveband radio; check the website for frequencies. **Radio Uganda's Red Channel** (98 FM) is a government-owned English-speaking station with good coverage. **CBS FM** (88.8 and 89.2 FM) and **Radio Simba** (97.3 FM) are popular, commercial Kampala-based Lugandan stations and are the best bet for international music.

Television

There is a TV service run by the government that broadcasts for about 6 hrs every evening, mostly in English. South African DSTV (Digital Satellite Television) is widely available, with over 100 channels of film, music, sport and light entertainment. A number of hotels and bars have widescreen TV for watching big sporting events.

Money

Currency ➔ *US$1 = USh 2515, £1 = USh 4267, €1 = USh3510 (May 2014).*
The currency is the Ugandan shilling (written either USh or using /= after the amount, ie 500/=). Notes are 1000, 2000, 5000, 10,000, 20,000 and 50,000 USh; coins are 2, 5, 10, 20, 50, 100 and 500 USh. When changing money you will normally be given high denomination notes. These can be difficult to change so make sure that you have an adequate supply of smaller bills and coins for public transport and the like.

Changing money

As the USh is not a hard currency, it cannot be brought into or taken out of the country. However, there are no restrictions on the amount of foreign currency that can be brought into Uganda. US dollars, UK pounds and euros can be exchanged in banks or in the foreign exchange bureaux that are widespread. The bureaux tend to offer better rates than the banks and stay open longer hours, but commission rates can be steep. If you are bringing US dollars cash, try to bring newer notes; because of the prevalence of forgery, many banks and bureaux de change do not accept dollar bills that are more than five years old. Any with the slightest mark or tear will be rejected, even if they pass the 'electronic counterfeit detectors' that are in use everywhere. Sometimes lower denomination bills attract a lower exchange rate than higher denominations.

Credit and debit cards

Barclays, **Standard Chartered** and **Stanbic** banks with ATMs are found in all but the smallest towns, but remember your bank at home will charge a small fee for withdrawing from an ATM abroad with a debit and credit card. Credit cards are accepted by the large hotels, airlines, main car hire firms, tour operators and travel agents, but an additional levy of 3-5% will be charged. **Visa** is the most widely accepted card, followed by **MasterCard**, **AMEX** and **Diners** far less so.

Currency cards

If you don't want to carry lots of cash, prepaid currency cards allow you to preload money from your bank account, fixed at the day's exchange rate. They look like a credit or debit card and are issued by specialist money changing companies, such as **Travelex** and **Caxton FX**, as well as the **Post Office**. You can top up and check your balance by phone, online and sometimes by text.

Opening hours

Banks Mon-Fri 0800-1700 and Sat 0800-1300. Forex bureaux are open longer hours 7 days a week. **Post offices** Mon-Fri

0830-1700. Main branches also open Sat 0900-1200. **Shops** Generally Mon-Sat 0800-1800. Larger branches of the supermarkets stay open until late in the evening and are open on Sun morning. In Muslim areas, shops may close early on Fri.

Post

Posta Uganda, www.ugapost.co.ug, has post office branches across the country, even in the smallest of towns, and it also runs the reliable **Post Bus** service (see page 14). Sending post out of the country is cheap and efficient, and letters to Europe and the US should take no more than a few days. If you are sending home souvenirs, surface mail is the cheapest method but will take at least 6 weeks. Parcels must be wrapped in brown paper with string. There is no point doing this before getting to the post office as you will be asked to undo it to be checked for export duty. It's probably best to use registered mail for more valuable items so that you can track their progress. The post office has its own domestic and international courier service, **EMS**, and the main international companies are also represented in Uganda; check the websites for the nearest branch: **DHL**, www.dhl.co.ug, **Fedex**, www.fedex.com.

Safety

Overall, Uganda is very safe, with far less petty crime than is found in Kenya. Every bank, shop, store, restaurant, hotel and even the hospital has armed guards, which may alarm you at first, but you quickly get used to it. The most common crimes are pickpocketing, purse-snatching and thefts from vehicles, and many robberies happen in crowded places like markets and bus stations. The general common-sense rules apply to prevent petty theft: don't exhibit anything valuable and keep wallets and purses out of sight; always keep car doors locked and windows wound up; lock room doors at night; do not accept any food or drink from strangers as it may be drugged and used to facilitate a robbery; avoid deserted areas and always take taxis at night.

It's not only crime that may affect your safety; you must also take safety precautions when visiting game parks and reserves. If camping, it is not advisable to leave your tent or *banda* during the night. Wild animals wander around the camps freely at night, especially organized campsites where local animals have got so used to humans that they've lost much of their inherent fear. Exercise care during the day too; remember that wild animals can be dangerous.

Telephone → *Country code: +256.*

You can make international calls from public coin or card phones in boxes on the street or at post offices, which sell phone cards and are found in even the smallest towns. Most hotels and lodges offer international telephone services, though they will usually charge double the normal rate. In larger towns, private shops also offer international services, usually with additional internet. Calls between Uganda and Kenya and Tanzania are charged at long-distance local rates rather than international. If you have a mobile phone with roaming, you can make use of Uganda's cellular networks, which cover all larger towns and the main roads but not all the parks and reserves or the north of Uganda away from the towns. Sim and top-up cards for pay-as-you-go mobile providers – try **MTN** or **Orange** – are available almost everywhere, even in the smallest of settlements. Mobile phones are now such a part of everyday life in Uganda that many establishments have abandoned the local landline services and use the mobile network instead. You will see from listings such as hotels and restaurants in this book, mobile numbers are sometimes offered instead of landline numbers: they start T07.

Time

GMT + 3 hrs. There is a 1 hr time difference going west to Rwanda and the DRC, which are GMT + 2 hrs.

Tipping

It is customary to tip around 10% for good service; this is not obligatory or expected but greatly appreciated by hotel and restaurant staff, most of whom receive very low pay. Taxi drivers don't need tipping since the price of a fare is usually negotiated first.

How much to tip the guide/driver (on a camping trip the cook too) on safari is tricky. Remember that wages are low and there can be long lay-offs during the low season. However, excessive tipping can cause problems for future clients being asked to give more than they should. It is best to enquire from the company at the time of booking what the going rate is. As a very rough guide you should allow US$5-15 per person per day. Always try to come to an agreement with other members of the group and put the tip into a common kitty. For gorilla tracking you'll have a guide and 3-6 trackers and a recommended tip for the 1-day excursion is about US$20. This can be placed in the appropriate tip box for your gorilla group (found at UWA park HQ where the tracking begins and returns to) for distribution amongst the staff. Tips are usually given in Uganda shillings or US dollars.

Tour operators

See also Overland trucks, page 12, for companies offering overland trips.

UK and Ireland
Abercrombie & Kent, T0845-070 0600, www.abercrombiekent.co.uk.

Acacia Africa, T020-7706 4700, www.acacia-africa.com.
Africa Travel Centre, T0845-450 1520, www.africatravel.co.uk.
Africa Travel Resource, T01306-880 770, www.africatravelresource.com.
Expert Africa, T020-8232 9777, www.expertafrica.com.
Explore, T0870-333 4001, www.explore.co.uk.
Global Village, T0844-844 2541, www.globalvillage-travel.com.
Odyssey World, T0845-370 7733, www.odyssey-world.co.uk.
Okavango Tours and Safaris, T020-8347 4030, www.okavango.com.
Rainbow Tours, T020-7226 1004, www.rainbowtours.co.uk.
Safari Consultants Ltd, T01787-888590, www.safari-consultants.co.uk.
Somak, T020-8423 3000, www.somak.co.uk.
Steppes Africa, T01285-880980, www.steppestravel.co.uk.
Tribes Travel, T01473-890499, www.tribes.co.uk.
Volcanoes Safaris, T0870-870 8480, www.volcanoessafaris.com.
Wildlife Worldwide, T0845-130 6982, www.wildlifeworldwide.com.

Australia
The Africa Safari Co., T+61 1 800-659279, www.africasafarico.com.au.
African Wildlife Safaris, T+61 (0)3-9249 3777, www.africanwildlifesafaris.com.au.
Classic Safari Company, T+61 1 300-130218, www.classicsafaricompany.com.au.
Peregrine Travel, T+61 (0)3-8601 4444, www.peregrine.net.au.

North America
Adventure Centre, T1 800-228 8747, T+1 51-0654 1879, www.adventure-centre.com.
Africa Adventure Company, T+1 954-491 8877, www.africa-adventure.com.
Bushtracks, T+1 707-433 4492, www.bushtracks.com.

South Africa
Go2Africa, T+27-(0)21-4814900, www.go2africa.com.
Pulse Africa, T+27 (0)11-325 2290, www.pulseafrica.com.
Wild Frontiers, T+27 (0)72-927 7529, www.wildfrontiers.com.

Tourist information

Association of Uganda Tour Operators
(**AUTO**), 14 York Terrace, Kololo, T0414-542599, www.auto.or.ug, Mon-Fri 0900-1700. Useful for pre-planning.
Uganda Tourism, 42 Windsor Cres, Kololo, T0414-342196, www.visituganda.com. Mon-Fri 0800-1700, Sat 0945-1300. The staff here are very helpful. There is also a desk at Entebbe International Airport (page 38) and at the Garden City Shopping Mall on Yusuf Lule Rd (page 63).
Uganda Wildlife Authority (**UWA**), main office, 7 Kira Rd, between the British High Commission and the Uganda Museum, Kamwokya, T0414-355000, www.uganda wildlife.org. Mon-Fri 0800-1300 and 1400-1700, Sat 0900-1300. The UWA controls all Uganda's national parks and game reserves. Arrange to pay for and collect permits to see the gorillas in Bwindi and Mgahinga here and book *banda* accommodation in the national parks and game reserves.

The **backpackers hostels** in **Kampala, Jinja** and **Bujagali** are excellent sources of reliable up-to-date information about Uganda. See Where to stay in the relevant chapters. A useful publication for sale at the bookshops in Kampala is *The Eye Magazine* (www. theeye.co.ug), which is also online, and lists attractions, shops, restaurants and services.

Useful websites
www.fco.gov.uk UK's Foreign Office site, for the 'official' advice on latest political situations.
www.guide2uganda.com General tourism plus listings for expats like property and services, and daily forex rates.
www.monitor.co.ug Online version of the national daily *The Monitor* newspaper.
www.myuganda.co.ug Tourism info and a portal for advertisements for lodges and tour operators.
www.newvision.co.ug Online version of the *New Vision* newspaper.
www.traveluganda.co.ug Uganda Travel Planner with detailed travel and accommodation listings for all budgets.

General tourism
www.buganda.com In-depth history of the Buganda Kingdom.

Visas and immigration

Your passport must be valid for a full year after your planned arrival date in Uganda, and you must produce a yellow fever vaccination on arrival. Note: Visa regulations change frequently, so it's advisable to check with your nearest Uganda embassy or with a Ugandan tour operator before you travel. Almost all visitors require a visa, with the exception of some African countries. A a single-entry visa valid for 3 months costs US$50, and a multi-entry visa valid for 12 months costs US$100. Visas are issued at Entebbe International Airport and all land borders, or may be obtained from Ugandan embassies and consulates overseas. However, getting one on arrival is far easier and very straightforward; you'll need US$ cash to pay. Be aware that you may not automatically get a 3-month visa; the Ugandan immigration officer will issue one to match the date of departure that you have written on the arrivals/visa form. Double check it's enough time because over-stayers are fined heavily. Multi-entry visas are not available on arrival but only through embassies.

Before the visa expires you can apply for an extension of up to 6 months at the **Ugandan Ministry of Internal Affairs Immigration Office**, 75 Jinja Rd, Kampala, T0414-595 945, www.immigration.go.ug,

Borderless borders

Uganda, Kenya and Tanzania have an agreement that means you can move freely between the three countries on single-entry visas for each, without the need for re-entry permits as long as your 90-day visas remain valid. However, Rwanda is NOT part of this agreement, so if visiting Rwanda to track gorillas, say, be aware that you will be required to purchase another US$50 visa on re-entry to Uganda, and again new visas on re-entry into Kenya and Tanzania.

A new **East Africa Tourist Visa (EAV)** was introduced in the first half of 2014. An EAV is a 90-day, US$100 multiple-entry visa that allows travel to and between Uganda, Rwanda and Kenya, but NOT to Tanzania. The EAV holder is also allowed to move out of Uganda/Rwanda/Kenya (say to Tanzania, but you will need a separate visa for Tanzania) and return to Uganda/Rwanda/Kenya as long as the EAV is still valid. The holder of an EAV must enter the region in the country that issued the visa, and this visa cannot be extended. While regular visas are issued at the airports and borders, at the time of press the diplomatic missions of the three countries were only issuing EAVs but by the time you read this, they are also likely to be issued at the airports and borders.

So what does this mean to travellers to East Africa? It means that by scrutinizing your proposed itinerary carefully before you even think about booking flights, and working out the cheapest and easiest visa options, you can save a considerable sum on visa costs and in some instances avoid paying twice to go into the same country.

The following questions will help you work out your best option:

- Are you only going to Uganda? A single-entry visa is sufficient.
- Are you going to Uganda and Tanzania? Two single-entry visas are sufficient and both allow you to return to each.
- Are you going to Uganda and Rwanda? Two single-entry visas are sufficient if you are arriving into one and departing from the other, but an EAV is cheaper if you are returning from one to the other as it will allow you to return to each.
- Are you going to Uganda and Kenya? Single-entry visas for each are the same price as an EAV, and both allow you to return to each so it makes no difference.
- Are you going to Uganda, Kenya and Rwanda? An EAV is cheaper than three single-entry visas, and will allow you to return to each.
- Are you going to Uganda, Kenya and Tanzania? The three single-entry visas to Uganda/Kenya/Tanzania cost the same as an EAV plus a separate visa for Tanzania; both three separate visas and an EAV allow you to return to each so it makes no difference.
- Are you going to Uganda, Kenya, Tanzania and Rwanda? An EAV and a separate visa for Tanzania works out cheaper than visas for all four countries and will allow you to return to each.

The EAV scheme has been initiated by the tourism authorities of Uganda/Rwanda/Kenya: namely Uganda Tourism (www.visituganda.com), the Rwanda Development Board (www.rdb.rw), and the Kenya Tourist Board (www.magicalkenya.com); so contact them, or embassies, for up-to-date requirements. Alternatively, visit www.visiteastafrica.org, a website specifically set up by these tourist authorities to help explain the East Africa Tourist Visa.

open Mon-Fri 0800-1630. There are regional immigration offices in the larger towns; check the website for addresses. See also box, page 33.

Weights and measures

Metric. In markets items are often sold by the piece or pile (a carefully displayed pile of tomatoes or potatoes, for example).

Women travellers

Normal caution is required. In particular, dress modestly, be wary of unsolicited male company, move around in a group where possible, avoid sunbathing alone and take taxis at night.

Working and volunteering

There are no opportunities for travellers to obtain casual paid employment in Uganda. Most foreign workers are employed through embassies, development or volunteer agencies or through foreign companies. For the most part these people will have been recruited in their countries of origin. However, a number of NGOs and voluntary organizations can arrange placements for volunteers in Uganda for periods ranging from a few weeks to 6 months. Visit www.volunteerafrica. org, www.volunteeruganda.org or www. volunteerhq.org. In Bujagali, **Soft Power** is an organization that can arrange just 1-2 days of volunteering while you're there; it's an excellent way to enhance your holiday. See page 99 for more details or visit www.softpowereducation.com.

Contents

Kamapla & Entebbe

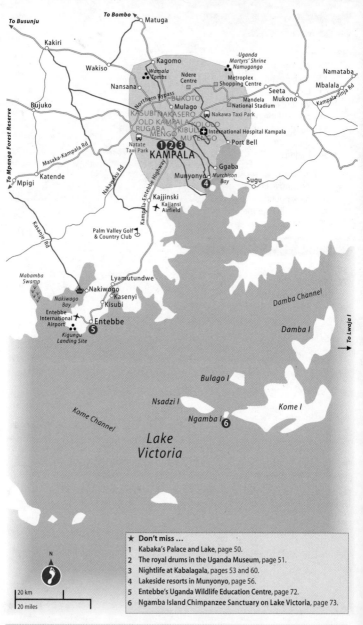

To Busunju

To Bombo

Matuga

Kakiri

Kagomo

Wamala Tombs

Uganda Martyrs' Shrine Namugongo

Wakiso

Nansana

Ndere Centre

Metroplex Shopping Centre

Namataba

Mbalala

Seeta

Mukono

Kampala-Jinja Rd

Bujuko

Northern Bypass

BUKOTO

Mulago

Mandela National Stadium

KASUBI NAKASERO

OLD KAMPALA

RUGABA MENGO

KIBULI KOLOLO MUTUNGO

Nakawa Taxi Park

International Hospital Kampala

Port Bell

Masaka-Kampala Rd

To Mpanga Forest Reserve

Mpigi

Katende

Natate Taxi Park

1 2 3

KAMPALA

Ggaba

Munyonyo

4

Murchison Bay

Sugu

Nakayuku Rd

Kampala-Entebbe Highway

Kajjinski

Kaijansi Airfield

Palm Valley Golf & Country Club

Kasanje Rd

Lyamutundwe

Kasenyi

Mabamba Swamp

Nakiwogo

Kisubi

Nakiwago Bay

Entebbe International Airport

Entebbe

5

Damba Channel

Damba I

To Lwaja I

Kigungu Landing Site

Bulago I

Nsadzi I

Kome I

Kome Channel

Ngamba I

6

Lake Victoria

N

20 km

20 miles

★ **Don't miss …**
1 Kabaka's Palace and Lake, page 50.
2 The royal drums in the Uganda Museum, page 51.
3 Nightlife at Kabalagala, pages 53 and 60.
4 Lakeside resorts in Munyonyo, page 56.
5 Entebbe's Uganda Wildlife Education Centre, page 72.
6 Ngamba Island Chimpanzee Sanctuary on Lake Victoria, page 73.

Situated just a few kilometres inland from Lake Victoria, Kampala was historically the capital of the Buganda Kingdom and was famously built on seven hills. Today's capital of Uganda now sprawls haphazardly over more than 20 hills and is still expanding rapidly. Viewed from a distance the skyline features glassy skyscrapers interspersed with thick green vegetation, dusty red roads and the clustered roofs of shanty towns, and the cathedrals, churches and mosques of the three religions, Catholic, Protestant and Muslim, which are perched on separate hills keeping a wary eye on each other.

In the crowded city centre you'll find legions of battered minibus and motorbike taxis, and clamouring markets thronged with roadside vendors, just like in any other African city. But Kampala has also witnessed rapid modern development since the early 1990s, and is now a sophisticated African city with a great deal of civic pride. It is partly still a work in progress: cosmopolitan restaurants are increasingly cropping up, and expected to open in the next few years are the towering Hilton and Intercontinental hotels, more expansive shopping malls and a new sleek expressway connecting Kampala with Entebbe.

Kampala is a friendly city and you can wander around and not worry about being hassled, which is a very pleasant change from other East African capital cities. It is small enough to explore without taking a city tour and, given that security has improved dramatically in the last few years, even the city's famously lively nightlife can be enjoyed safely.

Entebbe is situated on the shores of Lake Victoria, just 37 km from Kampala, and until 1962 was the administrative capital of the country. While it's the location of Uganda's international airport, it retains a peaceful atmosphere compared to Kampala, and is a rather pretty town, built on lots of small hills that slope down to the shores, with almost constant views of the lake.

Kampala

Kampala's city centre is located about 7 km to the north of Port Bell on the shores of Lake Victoria. Dominated by Nakasero Hill, it is largely made up of government buildings and is neatly bisected by the Kampala–Jinja road. Uphill, all is calm with pleasant colonial-style buildings and pretty streets lined with jacaranda trees and flamboyants. Most of the buildings, if not government offices or embassies, have been turned into apartments. Downhill all is frenetic: the streets are more congested with traffic and pedestrians and the huge street markets surround the chaotic *matatu* parks and Nakivubo Stadium. Some of the most important landmarks, like the two cathedrals (Anglican and Catholic), the Kibuli Mosque, the huge grass-thatched tombs of the Baganda kings, and the University of Makerere, are dotted around the city centre and can be seen on top of the hills. The city has always been known for its greenery and surprising number of trees, many of them inhabited by marabou storks. Although in recent times many of the valleys have been built over, the impression is still an extremely pleasant one: a mixture of blue sky, green open spaces, the red corrugated roofs of the old parts and the gleaming glass of the newer buildings.
▶▶ For listings, see pages 54-68.

Arriving in Kampala → *Altitude: 1230 m. Phone code: 0414/0312. Population 1.7 million. Colour map 2, B5.*

Getting there

Air **Entebbe International Airport** ① *T0414-353000, flight information, T0414-320926, www. entebbe-airport.com*, is on the shores of Lake Victoria 40 km south of Kampala and 3 km from Entebbe's town centre. Visas are available on arrival, and visitors will be asked to produce a yellow fever vaccination certificate. Facilities include bars and restaurants, curio and gift shops, post office, left luggage desk, ATMs and 24-hour bureaux de change (although exchange rates tend to be slightly lower than the forex bureaux in Kampala). There's Wi-Fi throughout the airport, and phonecards for the public payphones can be purchased at the post office, duty free shops or bureaux de change. There's a **tourist information desk** ① *T0414-321444, www.visituganda.com, daily 0800-1900*, in the arrivals hall.

All taxis serving the airport are run by the registered and reliable **Airport Taxi** ① *T0414-321292, www.airporttaxiug.com*, which are white with a yellow band across the side. A taxi from the airport to Kampala should cost roughly US$30-35, depending on the destination. Arrange a taxi and confirm rates at the **Airport Taxi** desk in the Arrivals hall. They can also be pre-booked to pick up from hotels for the return journey to the airport. A cheaper option is to take a taxi to Entebbe (roughly US$4-6), and from there frequent *matatus* (minibuses) go to Kampala, US$2. However, this is not a good option if you have a lot of luggage as they get crowded, and it's most certainly not a good idea to be at *matatu* parks after dark because of the danger of robbery.

The bigger hotels can arrange an airport shuttle bus service. Book this along with hotel reservations. They cost about US$50 for one or two people and US$70 for three to five people. Drivers meet passengers in the Arrivals hall. A shuttle can also be pre-booked through the **Airport Transfer Company Uganda** ① *T0713-805580, www.airporttransfers. co.ug*, or **Uganda Airport Transfers** ① *T0414-347 460, www.airporttransfersuganda.com*. Most of the hotels in Entebbe offer a free airport pick-up, and those that don't charge around US$10. The car hire companies (page 67) can arrange to meet clients at the airport, and **Hertz** and **Europcar** have desks in the Arrivals hall.

You will need Ugandan shillings to pay for a taxi and can change money or use an ATM inside the airport. Journey time is roughly one hour but longer in peak commuter traffic times. Peak hours are generally 0700-0900 from Entebbe to Kampala, and 1630 to as late as 2000 in the opposite direction Monday-Friday, when it could easily take two hours each way, so ensure you allow for plenty of time.

Road If arriving by bus from Nairobi, and other over the border destinations (see Getting to Uganda, page 9), you are likely to arrive at one of the bus company offices scattered around the city centre. Many of these are along or around the Kampala–Jinja road and the parallel De Winton Road, near the big junction with Yusuf Lule Road. **Easy Coach** and **Queens Coach**, have terminuses a little further to the north at the Oasis Nakumatt Shopping Mall, on Yusuf Lule Road.

For arrivals from other parts of Uganda, the main long-distance bus station is between the Old and New taxi parks near the Nakivubo Stadium. The **Post Bus** arrives and departs outside the main post office on Kampala–Jinja road, near its junction with Speke Road.

Matatus also cover the longer distances but, given that they stop off on the way, take much longer than buses. They arrive and depart at the Old and New taxi parks, but those from the closer places like Jinja and Entebbe also stop and pick up at various places on the main roads in and out of the city. Other *matatu* parks include Nakawa Taxi Park on the Kampala–Jinja road near the junction with New Port Bell Road, for Jinja and other destinations to the east; and Natete Taxi Park on the Masaka Road, about 1 km east of the junction with the Northern Bypass, for Masaka, Fort Portal and other destinations to the west. From all these places you will need to take either a special hire taxi or a *boda-boda* to hotels. ⏵ *See also Transport, page 66.*

Getting around
Unless you are staying outside the city centre you probably will not need to use public transport much as the city centre is compact and most places are within easy walking distance. However, a number of hotels and restaurants, and some sights such as the Uganda Museum, cathedrals, palace and Kasubi Tombs, are away from the centre. Public transport runs from 0500 to midnight. There are special hire taxi ranks around the centre including outside the National Theatre, the Garden City and Oasis Nakumatt shopping malls, the Old and New taxi parks and you can usually flag down one passing by. The minimum fare is about US$4 for a short trip and US$15 to the closer suburbs. *Matatus* patrol the streets and cost as little as US$0.50 for a short ride; simply stand on the side of the road in the direction you want to go and wait for a driver to stop, honk, or raise his hand or eyebrows at you. To catch a *matatu* out of the city centre, you'll need to go into a taxi park (see above).

A convenient and cheap way of travelling about town (especially in rush hour) is to use a *boda-boda* (motorbike taxi), which are available everywhere and cost from US$1 for a short ride. However, bear in mind that the accident rate involving *boda-bodas* and other vehicles is particularly high in Kampala, as are the levels of traffic fumes likely to be inhaled.

Safety
During the day you can walk around Kampala safely, but it goes without saying, that if you have a camera hanging from your neck, an obviously expensive watch, jewellery or a money belt showing, then you are very vulnerable to theft. With all its hills and

valleys, the roads can be a bit confusing so try not to look lost; ask for directions or jump on a *boda-boda*. Be vigilant at night, when it is advised to always take a taxi. Kabalagala (Kampala's lively nightlife district) is relatively safe, but can get rowdy, particularly around the bars on Muyenga Road. These are fun places to visit and are certainly real

1 Greater Kampala

eye-openers, but it is best to visit in a group and don't take anything valuable with you or accept any food or drink from strangers as it may be drugged and used to facilitate a robbery. Men should be aware that they are likely to be approached by prostitutes in many of Kampala's late-night bars.

➡ **Kampala maps**
1 Greater Kampala, page 40
2 Kampala centre, page 44

200 metres
200 yards

Where to stay
Cassia Lodge **3** *F6*
Kabira Country Club **4** *A6*
Kampala Backpackers Hostel
 & Campsite **1** *E1*
Kenrock **10** *E6*
Lagoon Resort **5** *F6*
Lake Victoria Serena Resort
 & Spa **11** *F3*
Le Petit Village **6** *E5*
Namirembe Guest House **7** *D2*
Red Chilli Hideaway **8** *C6*
Speke Resort & Munyonyo
 Commonwealth Resort **9** *F6*

Restaurants
The Bay **15** *F6*
Café Javas **2** *D2*
Café Kawa & Wine Garage **6** *E6*
Café Roma **12** *E6*
Cayenne Restaurant & Lounge **3** *A6*
Ethiopian Village **4** *E6*
Fasika **5** *F5*
Le Château **9** *E5*
Le Petit Bistro **10** *F6*
Little Donkey **7** *E6*

Bars & clubs
Capital Pub **14** *E6*
Club Silk **16** *C6*
Club Venom **8** *E5*
Da Posh Bar **17** *E6*
Flamin' Chicken **19** *E5*
Fuego Cocktails & Restaurant **11** *E6*
Jakob's Lounge **12** *E6*
Miki's Pub **1** *F6*

Tourist information

Uganda Tourism ① *42 Windsor Cres, Kololo, T0414-342196, www.visituganda.com, Mon-Fri 0800-1700, Sat 0945-1300,* have very helpful staff. There is also a desk at Entebbe International Airport (page 38) and at the Garden City Shopping Mall on Yusuf Lule Road (page 63). The **Uganda Wildlife Authority (UWA)** ① *main office, 7 Kira Rd, between the British High Commission and the Uganda Museum, Kamwokya, T0414-355000, www.ugandawildlife.org, Mon-Fri 0800-1300 and 1400-1700, Sat 0900-1300,* controls all Uganda's national parks and game reserves. Arrange to pay for and collect permits to see the gorillas in Bwindi and Mgahinga and book *banda* accommodation in the national parks and game reserves. The **Kampala Backpackers Hostel and Campsite** (see page 55) and **Red Chilli Hideaway** (see page 56) are also excellent sources of up-to-date information.

Background

Early days

The name Kampala came from the luganda word *mpala* meaning a type of antelope, which, it is said, the Buganda chiefs used to keep on a hill near the Kabaka's Palace in Mengo. The name 'Hill of the Mpala' was given specifically to the hill on which Captain Fredrick Lord Lugard, a British administrator, established his fort in December 1890. At the fort, also an administrative post, Lugard hoisted the Imperial British East African Company flag in 1890, which in 1893 was replaced by the Union Jack. The Fort at Kampala Hill, as it became known (now Old Kampala Hill), attracted several hundred people and a small township developed.

Traders erected shops at the base of the hill, and by 1900 the confines of the fort had become too small for administrative purposes and it was decided that the colonial offices and government residences that were in Kampala (at this time most offices were at Entebbe) should be moved to Nakesero Hill. The shops and other commercial premises followed.

Kampala grew and the town spread, like Rome, over the surrounding seven hills. These historical hills are Rubaga, Namirembe (Mengo), Makerere, Kololo, Kibuli, Kampala (Old Kampala) and Mulago. On top of three of these hills, Rubaga, Namirembe and Kibuli, places of worship were built: Catholic, Protestant and Muslim respectively.

Modern Kampala

In 1906 Kampala was declared a township, and the railway joining it with the coast reached Kampala in 1931. In 1949 it was raised to municipality status, in 1962 it became a city and, in October of the same year, it was declared the capital. The city has continued to grow and now covers 23 hills over an area of nearly 200 sq km (administered as the Greater Kampala area).

Like the rest of Uganda, Kampala suffered enormously in the post-Independence upheavals. Prior to these years Kampala had developed into a green city; it was spacious and well laid out and had evolved into the cultural and educational centre of East Africa. But during the civil war years, under Obote and Amin, Kampala suffered heavily, many buildings were destroyed and the infrastructure completely broke down. But since the beginning of the 1990s, buildings have been renovated and new ones are being built all the time with a number of imaginatively designed skyscrapers dominating the skyline. Kampala has gradually smartened itself up into a modern and fairly prosperous African city, not too dissimilar to Nairobi or Dar es Salaam. Also, given that it is on the road that traverses Kenya on its journey from East Africa's most important port at Mombasa, Kampala has risen as a commercial hub serving other countries like the Democratic Republic of Congo and South Sudan.

On the eve of Independence in 1962, the city's population numbered about 137,000. Today it is one of the fastest-growing cities in Africa with a population of around 1.7 million. This is bolstered by commuters coming in from the outlying areas for work, to make an estimated daytime population of around 3 million. But because the population is growing so rapidly, in some aspects the infrastructure has been pushed to its limits; no more so than on the streets that were initially designed for only about one-third of the current population – today Kampala is as famous for its horrendously grid-locked traffic as it is for its legendary seven hills.

City centre → *For listings, see pages 54-68.*

A pleasant way to spend a day would be to walk around the city centre; there are plenty of places to stop to have a cooling drink and something to eat. Given the traffic, it is, in fact, much quicker to get between most of the sights below on foot than by vehicle. But if time is short or if walking gets tiring, you can always jump on a *boda-boda*.

Parliament buildings

The complex was built during the colonial era and was opened in 1958 and is located on the acacia-lined Parliament Avenue (the road that has undergone the most name changes in Kampala; it has been Obote Avenue twice and this is the third time it has been Parliament Avenue). At the entrance is the **Independence Arch**; the first Prime Minister of Uganda, Apollo Milton Obote, laid the Arch's foundation stone on 5 October 1962, just a few days before Uganda's first Independence celebrations on 9 October. Often perched on the plain white archway are what must be one of the world's ugliest and most sinister-looking birds, the marabou stork, which can be seen scavenging all over the city. The white building with the clocktower further up the hill is the Kampala City Council's **City Hall**. The pleasant Parliament Gardens separate the two and are the location of the **Stride Monument**. Built by a team of 11 sculptors, it was unveiled by Queen Elizabeth II in commemoration of Uganda hosting the Commonwealth Heads of Government Meeting (CHOGM) in November 2007. Depicting a husband, wife and son (who is holding a book) striding forward, the copper statue symbolizes the commonwealth of countries developing together as a family.

National Theatre

① *2-6 De Winton Rd, T0414-25 4567, www.ugandanationalculturalcentre.org.*

Part of the **Uganda National Cultural Centre** (the other component is the Nommo Gallery, see page 46), the National Theatre is located on De Winton Road at the junction of Siad Barre Avenue. It took three years to build and was opened in 1959 by the then Governor of Uganda, Sir Frederick Crawford. It is a curious building and is faced with a whole series of interconnected concrete circles. The main auditorium seats 380 people and there's also a TV recording studio that sometimes doubles up as a cinema. Check the website, the noticeboard outside or local press to see what's on. See also page 62.

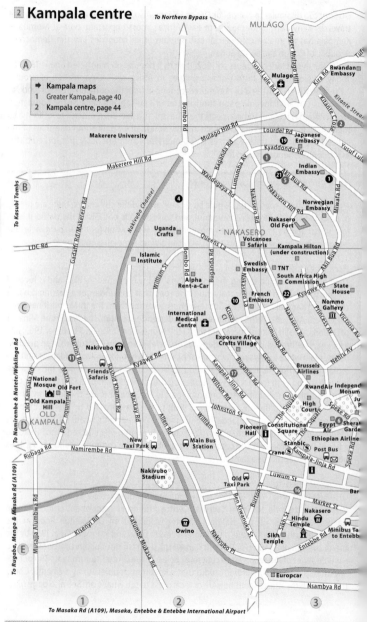

2 Kampala centre

➡ **Kampala maps**
1 Greater Kampala, page 40
2 Kampala centre, page 44

To Bukoto, Naguru & Northern Bypass

The Acacia Mall

Banana Boat

KISIMENTI

Windsor Life Loop Rd

British Embassy & Council

Uganda Museum

Athina Club

Mabua Rd

KOLOLO

John Babiha (Acacia) Av

Windsor Cres

Uganda Tourism

The Surgery

Elgon Terrace Rd

Upper Kololo Terr

Adrift Adventure Co

Irish Embassy

Uganda Golf Club

Kitante Stream

Kololo Airstrip

Independence Park

Lower Kololo Terr

Goethe-Zentrum & Alliance Française

Mackinnon Rd

Katonga Rd

Kagera Rd

Golf Course Rd

Tanzanian High Commission

Kyadondo Rd

Prince Charles Dr

Yusuf Lule Rd

Turkish Airlines

Garden City Shopping Mall

Dundas Rd

British Airways Citibank

Kampala Club

Kintu/Siad Barre Rd

Gordon Dr

Clement Hill Rd

DHL

Easy Coach & Queens Coach

Gulf Air

Waimpewo Av

Hannington Rd

AKA Gallery

Nakumatt Oasis Shopping Mall
Centenary Park

Nile Av

International Conference Centre

Immigration

Jinja Rd

Stride Monument

Kintu/Siad Barre Rd

Apollo Kaggwa Rd

Uganda Arts & Crafts

National Village

Kampala Coach

CENTRE

Sylcon Tours & Travel

City Hall

Parliament

De Winton Rd

Modern Coast Express & Mash Bus Services

Sixth St

Seventh St

Eighth St

Eagle Air

Independence Arch

King George VI Way

Kampala Casino

Christ the King

Hertz

Air Uganda, Kenya Airways & KLM

African Pearl Safaris

Nkrumah Rd

Nasser Rd

Roseberry La

Nakivubo Channel

By-Pass Rd

River Kay Unga

To Lugogo, Port Bell

To Bugolobi

To Muyenga, Kabalagala, Kansanga, Ggaba Rd, Lake Victoria & Munyonyo

To Ggaba Rd, Kabalagala, Muyenga, Kansanga, Lake Victoria & Munyonyo

N

200 metres
200 yards

Where to stay

Emin Pasha 1 *B3*
Fairway 4 *B4*
Golf Course 3 *C5*
Grand Imperial 6 *D3*
Humura Resort 2 *A3*
Kampala Serena 9 *C4*
Mamba Point
 Guesthouse 5 *B3*
Metropole 7 *B4*
New City Annex 8 *D5*
Protea Hotel
 Kampala 10 *B5*
Shangri La 12 *C3*
Sheraton 13 *D4*
Speke 14 *D4*
Tourist 16 *E3*
Tuhende Safari
 Lodge 11 *C1*

Restaurants

Arirang 1 *B3*
The Bistro 2 *A4*
Café Pap 3 *D4*
Café Javas 4 *B2 & A4*
Fang Fang 5 *D4*
Faze 2 22 *C3*
Food Court at
 Garden City 7 *C5*
Haandi 8 *D4*
Il Patio 10 *C2*
Khana Khazana 6 *B4*
The Lawns 11 *B6*
Mamba Point
 Italian 21 *B3*
Masala Chaat
 House 9 *D5*
Mish Mash 17 *B4*
The Pub 12 *D5*
Tamarai 18 *B5*
Yujo 19 *B3*

Bars & clubs

Bubbles O'Leary's 13 *A4*
Boda Boda 20 *C5*
Iguana & Gusto 15 *A4*
Rouge Lounge 17 *D2*

Railway station

South of the centre, off the Kampala–Jinja road, the solid, colonial-style railway station was completed in 1928. The Uganda Railway was built by the British and work on the line started at Mombasa, in the Kenya colony, in 1896 and reached Kisumu, on the eastern shores of Lake Victoria, in 1901. In 1931, the line finally reached Kampala. Although most of the line is in present-day Kenya, the original purpose of the project was to provide a link to transport raw materials out of, and manufactured British goods into, the Uganda Protectorate – hence the name, the Uganda Railway. On the Uganda side, the railway line covers 190 km from Kampala to the Kenyan border, and 8 km between Kampala and Port Bell. The railway had its glory days but, by the mid-1970s, traffic declined, finances came under stress and the condition of railway infrastructure deteriorated. Today, only sporadic freight services use it and, with no passenger trains running, the railway station is rather sad looking.

Sheraton Gardens

These used to be known as the Jubilee Gardens but are now kept in superb condition by the **Sheraton Kampala Hotel** (see page 54). They originally commemorated George V's jubilee and there is a bust of the king in the gardens. They are now fenced within the Sheraton complex, but visitors can still enjoy them by going through the hotel and having a drink in the gardens or a delicious breakfast buffet on the terrace at the hotel's **Victoria Breakfast Room**.

Just outside the gardens, at the top of Speke Road, is the impressive **Independence Monument**, which was unveiled by Obote on 5 October 1962, on the same day he laid the foundation stone for the Independence Arch at Parliament (see above). The monument was sculpted by Gregory Maloba, one of Uganda's first professional sculptors. He was actually a Kenyan but studied and taught art at the Makerere University from 1939 to 1965. The 6-m statue depicts a mother with bandages around her legs and waist unwrapping and lifting a child with arms held aloft. The child beckons the sky in triumphant jubilation, while its mother seems to ponder the future. It is said to signify a newborn country let free from the bondages of colonization. But as it was funded by the British colonial government, some historians believe its significance was that Britain had done her part of raising the child, and that it was now up to its people to take it to further heights.

A couple of metres east of the Independence Monument is the **Sir Edward Mutesa II Monument**. His full name was Edward Frederick William David Walugembe Mutebi Luwangula Mutesa and he was the 35th of the Buganda kings and the first President of Uganda (1963-1966); he was often simply known as King Freddie. Also referred to as the Presidential Monument, the statue was unveiled in 2007 by President Museveni. Mutesa is dressed in military fatigue and the memorial is said to represent his tireless efforts in fighting for Uganda's Independence. Mutesa died in 1969 in the UK after he was forced into exile by Obote.

Nommo Gallery

ⓘ *4 Victoria Av, next to the State Lodge, T0414-234475, www.ugandanationalcultural centre.org, Mon-Fri 0900-1700, Sat-Sun 0900-1500, free.*

This small building, once a private house set in spacious grounds, has housed Uganda's national art gallery since 1964, displaying artwork by local artists and those from other parts of East Africa. Exhibitions are advertised in the local press. There is a shop attached with both artworks and crafts for sale, and a small restaurant serves snacks.

Nakasero Old Fort

Nakasero Hill is dominated by the soon-to-be **Kampala Hilton Hotel**, which is being built on a 5.7-ha site that was previously occupied by the state's television stations. When completed it will be 24 storeys high and the tallest building in Kampala. But this accolade is expected to be short-lived, as construction of the 34-storey **Kampala Intercontinental Hotel** is also being planned on a site adjacent to Nile Avenue.

Also on top of Nakasero Hill is Nakasero Old Fort, which, despite its interesting history, has been reduced to little more that dilapidated brick walls covered in weeds, though the rifle slits are still visible. It was built as a temporary garrison in 1900 when Lugard left Fort Lugard in Old Kampala. Later it served as a prison and a police store among other things. During a drought at the end of the 1930s, the Old Fort became a distribution centre, where people would go with baskets to fetch food. And so it came to be known as the hill that people ascended with a basket (*akasero*), after which Nakasero Hill got its name.

Sadly, part of the wall has been knocked down to create space for the Hilton, and the remaining walls are currently closed to the public.

Market area

At the foot of Nakasero Hill, and just below the Kampala–Jinja road on and around Market Street, is the frenetic **Nakasero Market**. Believed to date back to 1895, the market is divided into two areas: one, where fresh produce is sold, is partially covered with a rusty corrugated-iron roof, and is the best and most colourful fruit and vegetable market in Kampala. The other is located in a neglected but perfectly functional colonial building with balconies known as Market Mansion, where electronics, hardware, clothes and a few tourist curios are on sale. Just to the south of Nakasero Market are two temples: one Sikh (the **Kampala Singh Sabha Gurudwara** on Sikh Street) and one Hindu (around the corner on Snay Bin Amir Street).

A little further west, the area around the Nakivubo Stadium is known as **Owino Market** (confusingly also known as St Balikuddembe Market). The Municipal Market was established here in 1971, but was later affectionately renamed by vendors after an old man called Owino who roasted maize and sweet potatoes here. Today the market sells all manner of goods, from food and spices to pots, pans and bed sheets. There is also a large second-hand clothes section where you may find cheap designer clothes. Any repairs or alterations can be done for you while you wait. Covering more than 7 ha, Owino is considered the biggest open market in Uganda. It's estimated to have more than 50,000 vendors, 70% of whom are women, and at least 300,000 customers visit each day. Both markets are close to the Old and New taxi parks and are absolute hives of activity as shoppers race to catch their *matatus* clutching their purchases. As with all markets, they can get very congested so watch out for pickpockets and do not carry anything valuable with you.

West of the centre → *For listings, see pages 54–68.*

Old Kampala Hill

Christened by the Bristish 'Hill of the Mpala' (hence the city's name, Kampala), today the hill is referred to as Old Kampala Hill or simply as Old Kampala. Captain Lugard built a fort on here in 1890 and it was the Imperial British East African Company's administrative headquarters until the company collapsed in 1893. Then, in 1905, the colonial office transferred the headquarters of the Uganda Protectorate from the fort to Entebbe. Most of the buildings were destroyed during the Amin years, when the land was donated to the Uganda Muslim Supreme Council, and for a number of years, all that remained of the old fort was a small block house. But even this was demolished in 2002; a replica was built just to the east to make room for the National Mosque (see below). Disappointingly, the original building was not dismantled systematically to enable reuse of the materials, so the replica has different brickwork and there's presently no access as it lies within the private grounds of the mosque.

The **National Mosque** ① *Old Kampala Rd, main entrance opposite the Old Kampala Secondary School, T0772-853077*, now dominates Old Kampala Hill. It is an impressive structure with several ornamental arches and copper domes and it sits on a 5-ha plot encircled by the Old Kampala and Matia Mulumba roads. Construction of the mosque started in 1972 after the Amin government formed the Uganda Muslim Supreme Council, but came to a standstill in 1976. It wasn't until 2001 when the Mufti of Uganda, Sheikh Shaban Ramadhan Mubaje, approached Libyan President Colonel Gaddafi to ask for financial assistance to complete it. The Libyans provided the funds and groundwork began again in 2002, when the old unfinished mosque, and the remains of the old fort, were demolished. The new mosque was officially opened and inaugurated in 2008 by the late Colonel Gaddafi himself, in an event that was attended by several African heads of state. For a while it was called Gaddafi National Mosque but was renamed in 2013 almost two years after the Libyan leader was killed. With a capacity of around 35,000 people, it is the biggest mosque in Uganda.

Muslims are welcome in the mosque at any time and the minaret is open to the general public outside of prayer times – call in at the office to get permission to climb the 304 stairs to the top; worth it for the views across the city. It goes without saying that visitors should dress modestly, and women should wear loose-fitting clothes and cover their heads. Scarves are available to borrow at the entrance. The area around the mosque is where many of the Asian population lived before expulsion by Amin, and still features many fine colonial Asian and European buildings among the more modern high-rise apartment blocks.

Kasubi Tombs
① *5 km west from the city centre on Kasubi Hill, Masiro Rd, off Hoima Rd, Nakulabye. By matatu, get off at the Kasubi Market at the junction with Hoima Rd and Kimera Rd and walk 500 m uphill on Masiro Rd. Daily 0800-1800, US$4 which includes a 30-min guided tour.*
In March 2010 the main buildings of the Kasubi Tombs, burial place of the Bugandan Kabakas or kings, caught fire and were reduced to ashes. Many artefacts were destroyed in the conflagration but the actual remains of the kings were saved by the caretakers. The tombs are a World Heritage Site and in late 2010 UNESCO approved emergency funds to support their restoration at an estimated cost of US$1 million. Since then, there have been successful fundraising efforts from the Buganda Kingdom and the government, among other donors. Reconstruction work of a replica of the former tombs using mud, reeds and wattle started in January 2013. But then there was a setback in June 2013 when another mysterious fire gutted one of the other huts, destroying traditional regalia that were rescued from the first fire more than three years earlier.

Nevertheless, while there isn't much to look at physically, you can still visit. The tombs remain an important spiritual and political site to the Baganda, and informative guides explain both the history and culture of the people. Despite the main tomb being a covered construction site, the other, smaller thatched buildings and the site itself help give a context to the stories. Hopefully the restoration is sympathetically completed and the tombs are replicated accurately.

Before the fires, the site contained the tombs of Muteesa I (1856-1884), Mwanga II (1884-1897), Sir Daudi Chwa (1897-1939) and Edward Muteesa II (1939-1966). Mwanga II was exiled to the Seychelles in 1899; he died there in 1903 and his body was returned to Uganda and buried at Kasubi in 1910. Muteesa II was removed from his position soon after Independence during the Obote I regime and died three years later in 1969 in London. His body was returned to Uganda in 1971 and buried at Kasubi in an attempt by Amin to appease the Baganda.

The tombs were constructed reflecting the typical Ganda architectural style of a large circular house, topped by a domed, thatched roof. The thatch was supported by 50 rings, each made by a different Bugandan clan. There were several buildings of similar construction surrounding the main tomb (many of which still remain), which were traditionally homes to the widows and granddaughters of the former kings and they were charged with the responsibility of looking after the tombs. Originally an outer fence that was over 6 km in length enclosed more than 500 houses. Before the tombs were destroyed, many of the artefacts of the kings, including spears, drums, furniture and a stuffed pet leopard, reputed to have been owned by Muteesa I, were on display.

Wamala Tombs

① *13 km along the Kampala–Hoima road, 30 mins' drive northwest of Kampala. After 6.8 km take the right turning to Nansana Town and at the Nansana Trading Centre turn right along the rough murram road for 1.5 km. The hilltop tomb is visible from a distance. Daily 0900-1700. US$2.*

Set on a hilltop in beautiful surroundings, this is the site of the palace and sacred burial ground of Kabaka Suuna II (d 1856), who was the son of Kabaka Kamanya and the first Kabaka to receive the Arab slave traders. He was a despotic ruler, reputed to have had 148 wives and over 200 children. Around the central platform spears and shields can be seen and a bark-cloth screen hides the mythical eternal forest to where he went for everlasting life. Although larger and similar in design to the Kasubi Tombs, there are no inner or outer enclosures. The main tomb is in disrepair with a broken down thatched roof that reputedly supports a large bat colony. Nearby is the Tomb of Nnamasole Kanyange, Kabaka Suuna's mother, who was buried on an adjacent hilltop.

Namirembe Cathedral

① *Approximately 1.5 km west of the city centre off Natete/Wakiliga Rd. Follow Willis Rd up the hill past Namirembe Guest House and there is either a footpath on the left or, if driving, continue on around the hill on Tucker Rd to the top. Daily 0700-1700, free, but donations are welcome.*

This brick-red Anglican Cathedral, also known as St Paul's Cathedral, has an impressive dome and is visible from much of Kampala. It's located at the top of Namirembe Hill (Mengo) offering spectacular views. Namirembe means 'mother of peace'.

The original church built in 1890 was made of bamboo poles, grass thatch and reed work by local craftsmen. It was relocated shortly afterwards as it was built in a swampy area. The second church was also short-lived. Built in 1891 the roof blew off in a thunderstorm the following year. The third church seating 4000 people was built between 1894 and 1895 with traditional African materials but dismantled due to termite infestation in 1900. A replacement building was begun in 1901 and completed in 1904. This was made of earth-baked bricks and thatch, but the roof was destroyed by lightning just six years later. The fifth building was constructed between 1915 and 1919 with the tiled roof that can be seen today. Particularly interesting is the graveyard where Sir Albert Ruskin Cook, who was the first to diagnose sleeping sickness in East Africa and established Mengo Hospital, and his wife Lady Katherine, who started midwifery training in Uganda, are buried. Also here are the remains of Bishop Hannington, who was murdered in 1885 (see box, page 105).

The cathedral has beautiful stained-glass windows, and an interesting history, including a small piece of St Paul's Cathedral in London and a piece of the Berlin Wall cemented into the wall near the altar. A guide is available. The congregation is called to the service by the beating of drums and by bells, audible if staying at **Namirembe Guest House** (see page 55).

Bulange

ⓘ *Off Natete/Wakiliga Rd, opposite the junction with Sentema Rd, passed on the way to Rubaga Cathedral (see page 51), T0414-421166, www.buganda.or.ug. Office Mon-Fri 0900-1700, visitors are permitted into the grounds at any time and maybe allowed inside if there is no official business on – ask at the entrance.*

This complex houses the Bugandan Parliament (the *Lukiiko* in Lugandan) and the kingdom's administration offices. Before it was constructed, members of the Lukiiko used to sit in the same spot under a grass-thatched shelter, until a brick building was constructed in 1903. As the Kabaka's government expanded, there was need to create a bigger Lukiiko, and in 1953, under the reign of Ssekabaka Muteesa II (and while he was in exile in Scotland), construction began on the present structure, which was completed in 1958. In 1966, Amin's government occupied and turned Bulange into the Uganda army headquarters, and it was finally handed back to the kingdom in 1993.

The Bulange is an imposing building and typical of colonial-era architecture with a large central spire flanked by two smaller ones. Inside, the main feature is the **Lukiiko Hall** that has no upper floors because traditionally nobody sits above the Kabaka's head. The symbols of the 50 clans are prominently depicted on the walls in the foyer, and at the base of the entrance steps is a large statue of King Ronald Muwenda Mutebi II. There are giant tortoises in the grounds, and you will probably be told that the oldest is 500 years old whilst the youngest is a mere stripling of 300.

Kabaka's Palace and Lake

From Bulange, a 1.6-km straight road known as Kabaka Njagala Road (meaning 'the-king-loves-me' road) runs southeast to the Kabaka's Palace, which today crosses busy Rugaba Road. Legend dictates that the Kabaka must only travel in a straight line to ensure there is no obstacle in the king's spirits' way. About halfway along Kabaka Njagala Road is a roundabout which is gated and locked. It is reserved solely for the use of the Kabaka's motorcade so he doesn't have to go around a corner.

At the southern end of the road on Mengo Hill, the Kabaka's Palace (also called Mengo Palace) faces Bulange on the opposite side of the valley. Within the complex of many buildings is the Kabaka's official residence called Twekobe. It's a handsome building with a cupola in classical style surrounded by high walls and beautiful gardens and was built in 1885 during Kabaka Danieri Mwanga II's reign. At the main gate is a fireplace called Kyoto Ggombolola, where a fire is kept alight at all times and is only extinguished when the king dies.

The palace was shelled by Amin on Obote's orders in 1966 when Kabaka Edward Mutesa was exiled. Later, Amin built underground torture and execution chambers here, which were used by his soldiers for their appalling deeds during their terror reign from 1971 to 1979. Just a short walk from Twekobe, the surprisingly simple but eerily evil concrete cave-like structures are still here today and reputedly could hold up to 500 people at a time. When Amin ordered people to the chambers, they were blindfolded and stuffed into the back of large trucks. Then, the drivers would drive for hours, but in reality were driving around the palace in circles, and when the prisoners arrived at the chambers, they would have no idea that they were in fact on the palace grounds. The captives were imprisoned there to die, and the long hallway to the chambers was filled with water about 30 cm deep, which had an electric charge running through it. Allegedly many jumped into the water to electrocute themselves to make the inevitable quicker. Graffiti that can still be made out on the walls describe some of the horrors enacted.

The soldiers moved out in 1993 and the palace was returned to the Buganda. One of the conditions of the Kabaka's return was that his role would be purely ceremonial and cultural, without any political function, and the kingdom has been a constitutional monarchy since then. No visitors are permitted inside the palace but you can walk up to the walls of the compound and the caretakers who are permanently at the entrance may allow you to visit the torture chambers on the hill.

The Kabaka's Lake lies at the bottom of the hill and was also built by Kabaka Danieri Mwanga II from about 1885 to 1888. The original plan was to create a channel which was to take him by canoe between the palace and his lodge in Munyonyo on Lake Victoria; a distance of about 13 km. He was also reputedly known to love swimming and fishing. Unfortunately, the Kabaka died before the channel was completed, hence the stand-alone lake. It covers about 2 sq km and the average depth is about 60 m. It's fed by underground springs and, as a result, the water level has hardly ever fluctuated since it was made. It's possible to walk around most of the lakeshore on a dirt road, which is also used for cattle grazing and by small-scale car-washing enterprises. The two tiny islands in the centre attract a wide variety of birds, including an estimated 5000 cattle egrets (*Bubulcus ibis*).

Rubaga Cathedral of the Sacred Heart
① *On Rubaga Hill, Mutesa Rd, about 500 m south of Natete/Wakiliga Rd, Mon-Sat 1000-1700, Sun 0700-1700, free, but donations are welcome.*
Rather confusingly a number of signs refer to this building as Lubaga Cathedral and it also known as St Mary's Catholic Cathedral. It was built by the White Fathers between 1914 and 1925, and restored for the visit of Pope John Paul II to Uganda on 1993. It's a huge cathedral with two sets of steeple bells, one for everyday use and the other solely reserved to proclaim the death of a pope. Inside are the remains of the first African Catholic Bishop and the first African Archbishop of Kampala Diocese, Joseph Kiwánuka, who held the position from 1960 until his death in 1966.

North of the centre → *For listings, see pages 54-68.*

Uganda Museum
① *5-7 Kira Rd, Kololo, T0414-232707, www.ugandamuseums.ug. Daily 1000-1800, US$2, children 5-16 US$1, camera US$2, video camera US$4.*
Founded in 1908 on the site of the Old Fort on Old Kampala Hill, the Uganda Museum moved to the present site in Kololo in 1954. In late 2010 plans were announced to demolish the museum and replace it with a 60-storey tower block of government offices. However, these plans have been delayed indefinitely amidst significant protest. In the

meantime the museum has a neglected feel about it and could definitely do with a bit of a spruce up, but it is mildly diverting for anyone who has an interest in Uganda's pre-colonial history.

Displays include a number of artefacts from archaeological sites from around the country, with exhibitions of Stone and Iron Age finds, and fossil materials from the Albertine Rift Region. The ethnographic section has models of dwellings, settlements and hunting scenes, wood carvings, metalwork, leather craft, pottery, traditional weaponry and a large and impressive canoe. The museum is also home to a collection of musical instruments including many drums, which visitors are allowed to play. The first printing press used in Uganda, a movable variety, is on display. It was imported by Reverend Alexander Mackay, an Anglican Church missionary, and used to print catechism lessons and the Bible in Uganda.

Bahá'í Temple
① *Off Gayaza Rd, 6 km out of Kampala on Kikaya Hill. Open daily for prayers 0830-1730.*
The Bahá'í Temple, also known as the Uganda House of Worship, was built between 1958 and 1962 and is the only temple of the Bahá'í religion in Africa. The nine-sided temple has bright coloured windows of amber, green and blue, topped by a large 37-m-high dome and is surrounded by 30 ha of beautifully manicured gardens. Founded by Baha'u'llah (1817-1892) in Iran in 1844, followers of the Bahá'í religion believe that every religious manifestation forms a successive chapter in the revelation of God and all the world's major religions form a progressive process by which God reveals His will to humanity. People of all faiths are therefore welcome to visit this temple for prayer and meditation at any time. A wonderful view of the temple can be seen from the end of Kira Road in Kampala, just beyond the Uganda Museum to the left. From the temple itself there are excellent views of Kampala and the surrounding countryside.

Uganda Martyrs' Shrine Namugongo
① *13 km northeast from Kampala off the Namugongo Rd, turn north off the Kampala–Jinja road opposite the Mandela National Stadium, T0312-274581, www.ugandamartyrsshrine. org.ug. Daily 0600-2000, free.*
Also known as the Namugongo Martyrs' Shrine, this is the site where 22 Ugandan Christian converts (Catholic and Anglican) were burnt to death on the orders of Kabaka Mwanga II on 3 June 1886. Although Mwanga had appeared to like and support the European missionaries as a young prince, his attitude towards Christianity changed when he became Kabaka. He believed that the converts in his royal court had diverted their loyalty to some other authority and that their allegiance at all cost could no longer be counted on. On the visit of Pope Paul VI to Uganda in 1969, the victims were canonized and are now regarded as saints in the Catholic Church. Since then the shrine has been an important site for Ugandan Christians.

There is a Catholic Church on the site, the **Basilica of the Uganda Martyrs**, which was consecrated by the pope on his visit in 1969. It's in the shape of a traditional conical Baganda hut with 22 copper pillars representing the 22 martyrs. Below the altar is the spot where Charles Lwanga, the leader of the Catholics, was burnt to death. He was in fact a page in the royal household and had been close to Mwanga. In the middle of the complex is the Uganda Martyrs Lake and Pavilion where Mass is celebrated on Martyrs' Day (3 June), which is a public holiday in Uganda.

Kibuli Mosque

ⓘ *3 km southeast of the city centre off Prince Badru Kakungulu Rd and next to Kibuli Muslim Hospital. Mon-Fri 0800-1800, Sat 0900-1500, Sun 0900-1400. Guided tours can be arranged for a donation outside of prayer times.*

On Kibuli Hill this attractive mosque is surrounded by palm and mango trees. The land was given to Muslim settlers in the mid-19th century when a mosque was built but later fell into disrepair. The foundation stone for the current building was laid by the Aga Khan (Prince Aly Khan) in 1941 and he returned 10 years later for the opening ceremony. There are spectacular views of Kampala from the minaret.

Kabalagala and Muyenga

Kabalagala is a lively area, 6 km southeast of central Kampala at the junction of Ggaba Road, Nsambya Road and Muyenga Road. It derives its name from a locally made pancake, made of sweet bananas, cassava flour and spiced with peppers. According to legend, residents of Kabalagala used to make the tasty pancakes, which then drew a lot of people to the area and the name stuck. Today roasted meat is the more common snack for sale from stalls along the sides of the road and the area has a large number of restaurants and bars attracting many tourists and residents; many of the establishments are open 24 hours, seven days a week. The **American Embassy** is located nearby on the Ggaba Road.

The adjacent district to the east is the more affluent suburb of Muyenga on and around **Muyenga Hill**, which, at 1306 m, is one of Kampala's highest points and there are lovely views of the city to the north and Lake Victoria to the south. The suburb is often called **Tank Hill** after the water reservoirs on the summit. The **International Hospital** is located here, along with a few good restaurants and shops, and it's a popular residential area for NGO workers and expats.

Munyonyo

If you follow Ggaba Road from Kabalagala and Muyenga, it eventually reaches Murchison Bay on Lake Victoria. In a fabulous location on the lakeshore, Munyonyo is 13 km southeast of Kampala, or a 30-minute drive if the traffic is kind, and regular *matatus* depart from the Old Taxi Park in the city centre. Although nothing remains of it, in 1871 a hunting lodge was built here for Kabaka Muteesa I where he could indulge in some of his favourite pastimes: canoeing on the lake and hunting for hippos. Today it's the most peaceful suburb of Kampala with lush views of the lake from Munyonyo Hill, spacious houses and apartments, and the **Speke Resort** and the adjoining **Munyonyo Commonwealth Resort** (see Where to stay, page 56). Both these resorts have a commanding position on the lakeshore and permit day visitors (US$10, children under 16 US$5; the swimming pools are open 0800-1830), to swim, enjoy the beach and restaurants, plus horseriding and boat trips are on offer, and it's a refreshing excursion from the city centre.

For hotel and restaurant price codes and other relevant information, see pages 16-20.

◐ Where to stay

City centre *p43, map p44*

$$$$ Kampala Serena Hotel, Kintu/Siad Barre Rd, T0414-309000, www.serena hotels.com. Once the notorious **Nile Hotel** on Nakasero Hill where Amin's secret service thugs were based, this reopened as the Serena in 2006. It has a slick, luxury atmosphere, although its gardens are no match for the **Sheraton**, with 152 rooms, 3 restaurants, 2 bars, large pool, roof terrace, Moorish-themed spa and helipad.

$$$$-$$$ Emin Pasha Hotel, 27 Akii Bua Rd, Nakasero, T0414-236977, www. eminpasha.com. Boutique hotel with 20 tastefully decorated a/c rooms and suites converted from a gracious 1930s colonial house with wide verandas in nearly 1 ha of rambling, mature gardens with a pool. The **Fez Brasserie ($$$)** offers outside dining with excellent food, service and a good selection of wine.

$$$$-$$$ Sheraton Kampala Hotel, Ternan Av, T0414-420000, www.starwood hotels.com. A 15-storey Kampala landmark with lovely city views and 233 a/c rooms and suites with balconies set within the 4 ha of the **Sheraton Gardens** (see page 46). Pool, gym, good lobby coffee bar, the **Paradise Grill** offers international cuisine and the **Equator Bar** has a wide selection of cocktails and is open until 0500. Rates vary from US$250-2500 per room.

$$$ Golf Course Hotel, 64-86 Yusuf Lule Rd, T0414-563500, www.golfcoursehotel. com. Situated beside the Uganda Golf Club and the Garden City Shopping Mall overlooking the west side of the city, this offers a choice of 3 rooftop 'executive pyramids' (penthouses with a shared swimming pool), 6 apartments or 105 a/c rooms. Use of the golf club is included

plus there's a revolving restaurant with panoramic city views, a steakhouse, 24-hr coffee shop, pool and gym.

$$$ Grand Imperial Hotel, 6 Nile Av, T0414-311048, www.imperialhotels.co.ug. Built in the 1930s, it may feel old-fashioned to some and it could do with a little modernization, but it retains a degree of faded colonial charm and is very central, with 103 a/c rooms, 2 restaurants, bar, ballroom, pool and shopping arcade.

$$$ Humura Resort, 3 Kitante Close, Kololo, T0414-700040, www.humura uganda.com. A professionally run mid-range choice with 18 spacious a/c rooms in natural tones, with cool tiled floors, Wi-Fi and DSTV. The public areas are decorated with carefully chosen African art, and there's a pool, gym, garden bar and restaurant.

$$$ Protea Hotel Kampala, 4 Upper Kololo Terrace, Kololo, T0414-550000, www.proteahotels.com. Among the best for modern luxury, part of the efficient South African hotel chain, with 59 a/c rooms and 11 suites, restaurant and bar and gym. The front-facing rooms offer wonderful views of Kololo.

$$$-$$ Mamba Point Guesthouse, 22 Akii Bua Rd, Nakasero, T0312-563000, www.mamba-point.com. An alternative to the large hotels in a peaceful part of Nakasero with 6 modern and neat rooms with Wi-Fi and DSTV arranged around a lawned garden with pool. Attached is the good Italian restaurant of the same name (see Restaurants, page 58), which can also deliver pizzas and other dishes to the rooms.

$$ Fairway Hotel,1-2 Kafu Rd, T0414-259571, www.fairwayhotel.co.ug. Although a series of concrete blocks built in 1969, this is a pleasant hotel set in attractive grounds opposite the golf course. 110 rooms, most with balconies, pool, gym, 2 restaurants, bar and an attractive terrace under palms where a barbecue is held most evenings.

$$ Metropole Hotel, 51-53 Windsor Crescent, Kololo, T0414-391000, www.metropolekampala.com. Sensibly priced modern hotel in a striking pink-and-blue glass 5-floor block with a vast lobby and great views over the golf course. 60 neat a/c rooms, gym, bar, an Oriental restaurant, barbecue grill and 24-hr coffee shop. Doubles from US$140.

$$ Speke Hotel, 7-9 Nile Av, T0414-259221-4, www.spekehotel.com. Built in the 1920s, this popular hotel is the oldest in town and has attractive decor with portraits of explorer John Manning Speke. 50 a/c rooms, some with balconies, plus Indian and Italian restaurants and a fine terrace overlooking Speke Av. The **Rock Garden**, however (see Bars and clubs, page 60), can get very noisy, so ask for a room at the rear.

$$-$ Shangri La Hotel, 8-10 Ternan Av, T0414-250366, www.shangri-la.co.ug. Positioned behind the **Sheraton** in the grounds of the **Kampala Club**, the 12 simple but good-value rooms here have DSTV and used to be where members from out of town used to stay. Guests can use the club's facilities like the bar, gym, pool, badminton and tennis courts, and there's an attached Chinese restaurant.

$ New City Annex Hotel, 7 De Winton Rd, T0414-254132, ncahotel@gmail.com. Centrally located above a row of shops opposite Uganda Arts & Crafts Village and close to the long-distance bus offices. The 31 rooms are sparse but have nets and fans and the shared bathrooms are clean with hot water. Restaurant for local food are in a thatched compound around the back. Double/twin US$18, triple US$20.

$ Tourist Hotel, 9 Market St, T0414-251471/2, www.touristhotel.net. Overlooking Nakasero Market this haphazard concrete block doesn't look much from outside and it's up 3 flights of stairs, but the 70 rooms are spacious, spotless and secure with TV and Wi-Fi. Close to the taxi parks, affordable

restaurant and bar, friendly staff and good value from US$40 for a double B&B.

West of the centre *p47, map p40*
$ Kampala Backpackers Hostel and Campsite, Natete/Wakiliga Rd, Kikandwa Hill just past Mengo, 2 km from the city. centre, T0414-274767, www.backpackers.co.ug. A Kampala institution that has been evolving for more than 20 years and is centred around an old colonial house in over 1 ha of rambling gardens. The downside is there are intermittent problems with power and water. Accommodation is in 19 rooms with or without bathrooms (from US$22-30), cheaper grass-thatched *bandas* (US$20), more than 60 dorm beds in 8 dorms (US$8-12), and plenty of space for camping (US$6). Vast bar area, restaurant serving daily specials, burgers and pizzas, kitchen for self-catering, laundry and Wi-Fi. An excellent place to get travel information and make bookings, including gorilla permits, and they organize day trips for whitewater rafting at Bujagali, safaris to Murchison Falls National Park and Rwenzori climbs. They also own **Trekkers Hostel** near Kasese (see page 197).

$ Namirembe Guest House, 1085 Willis Rd, Namirembe, T0414-273778, www.namirembe-guesthouse.com. Run by the Church of Uganda and high on Namirembe Hill just below St Paul's Cathedral, this has fantastic views of Kampala. 40 spotless rooms with fans, most with balconies, the nicer ones are in the new block and some have 5 beds at around US$25 per person. Restaurant and nice thatched café but no alcohol.

$ Tuhende Safari Lodge, 8 Martini Rd, Old Kampala Hill, T0772-468360, www.tuhendesafarilodge.com. A long-standing favourite with budget travellers in an old colonial Asian-style building in Old Kampala and not too far from the taxi parks. 10 basic but clean rooms with 1 shared bathroom per 2 rooms, doubles US$30, or US$10 per person in a 4-bed room. The street-side restaurant is superb – barbecued tilapia fish, chicken or steak for less than US$4 – while there's a good supermarket a few doors along.

North of the centre *p51, map p40*

$$$ Kabira Country Club, 63 Old Kira Rd, Bukoto, T0312-227222, www. kabiracountryclub.com. Good for families with 95 a/c rooms; doubles, apartments and cottages with 2-3 bedrooms and kitchenettes, arranged around a massive laned swimming pool in gardens full of giant palms. Decor is fairly ordinary but good facilities including gym, squash and tennis courts, bar, coffee shop and restaurant. Doubles from US$150.

South and east of the centre *p53, map p40*

$$$$-$$$ Lake Victoria Serena Resort & Spa, Kigo Rd, off Kampala–Entebbe Rd, 15 km south of the city centre, T0417-121000, www.serenahotels.com. Opened in 2009, with 124 rooms and suites in mock-Tuscan villas spread around beautiful gardens, this offers all the amenities expected of a 5-star luxury resort and is in a commanding position on Lake Victoria. The architecture is super impressive with glass atriums, marble terraces and mosaic frescoes. A frequent contender as Uganda's best hotel and deservedly so. Rates US$250-1000.
$ Red Chilli Hideaway, 13-23 Bukasa Hill View Rd, Butabika, 10 km east of the city centre, T0312-202903, T0772-509150, www. redchillihideaway.com. This hugely popular backpackers has recently moved to bigger and better purpose-built premises in Butabika, with 28 rooms and 36 dorm beds. To get here, catch a *matatu* from the Old Taxi Park to Butabika and get off at Butabika Hospital. The Hideaway is 500 m from the hospital down the 2nd turning on the right. Otherwise phone ahead to book a place on the free shuttle bus that runs 3 times a day between the Hideaway and the Oasis

Nakumatt Shopping Mall (page 64). Facilities include a 16-m pool, restaurant serving barbecues and pizza, bar, free Wi-Fi, laundry, travel desk and luggage store. En suite twins/doubles (US$40), with shared bathrooms (US$30), dorms (US$10) and **campsite** with hot showers and kitchen facilities (US$7 per person). Also runs the **Red Chilli Rest Camp** at Murchison Falls (page 238) and offers scheduled good-value safaris to the falls and to Queen Elizabeth and Kidepo Valley national parks.

Kabalagala and Muyenga *p53, map p40*

$$$ Le Petit Village, 1273 Ggaba Rd, Kabalagala, T0312-265530, www. lepetitvillage.net. Next to the American Embassy and Belgian-owned, this is considered the best boutique hotel in Kampala. It has 12 delightful a/c thatched suites with elegant safari-style decor, DSTV, Wi-Fi and patios clustered around a swimming pool. Also well known for **Le Château** restaurant with its patisserie and delicatessen (see Restaurants, page 59).
$ Hotel Kenrock, Barnabas Rd, Muyenga, T0312-333377, www.hotelkenrock.com. A deservedly popular budget option in a good location for nightlife. 26 rooms with fans, tiled floors, Wi-Fi and reliable hot water. Restaurant and bar with garden tables and an excellent Italian supermarket across the road. Room sizes vary but start from US$20 for a small single.

Munyonyo *p53, map p40*

$$$$-$$$ Speke Resort, Wavamunno Rd, T0414-227111, www.spekeresort.com. Lakeside resort set in 36 ha of attractive landscaped grounds with its own marina and 449 spacious and comfortable rooms in cottages, apartments or studios. Activities include horse riding, boat trips and there's an Olympic-size pool and several restaurants. From US$160 for a double with a lavish breakfast buffet, excellent value considering its location and standards.

Day visitors are welcome. On the same property and under the same management, is **Munyonyo Commonwealth Resort** (T0417-716000, www.munyonyocommon wealth.com), which is an additional wing of 59 palatial presidential suites built for the 2007 Commonwealth Heads of Government Meeting and now often used for conferences.

$$$ Cassia Lodge, Buziga Hill, T0755-77 7002, www.cassislodge.com. Belgium-run and in a commanding position on the top of Buziga Hill, this has simply stunning views of both Lake Victoria and Kampala – the best of all the Kampala hotels. 20 rooms with balconies or patios, a pool in lush gardens, and excellent restaurant with outside terrace that is worth visiting for lunch even if not staying.

$$$ Lagoon Resort, opposite Munyonyo on the eastern side of Murchison Bay, T0775-78 7291, www.ug-lagoonresort.com. Set in 4 ha of established trees, this peaceful offshore resort is a 40-min boat ride from the jetty next to **Speke Resort**. Just 6 comfortable thatch and canvas *bandas* built on stilts, the glass-fronted restaurant has lake views, and they can organize fishing excursions. Pre-booked day visitors are welcome for around US$60 per person for the return boat ride, a swim in the pool and lunch.

❼ Restaurants

City centre *p43, map p44*
$$$ Il Patio, at Mayfair Casino, Kisozi Close, off Kyagwe Rd (near the French Embassy), T0414-258448, www.myfrgroup.com. Daily 1200-2230. Italian restaurant with elegant decor of marble pillars, quality upholstery and table linen and there's a canopied lobby and pretty garden. A pricy but excellent menu of thin-based pizza, creamy pasta sauces, veal and prawns, and fine Italian wines. Reservations recommended.
$$$ Khana Khazana, 20 John Babiiha (Acacia), Av Kololo, T0414-233049. Tue-Sun

1200-1500, 1900-2230. Considered the best Indian restaurant in Kampala in an old colonial residential villa with lovely outdoor tables in the flowering garden. Great breads and appetizers, rich North Indian curries and some interesting desserts. Good winelist or try a mango *lassi*.
$$$ The Lawns, 34 Impala Av, off Upper Kololo Terrace, Kololo, T0414-250337, www.thelawns.co.ug. Mon-Sat 1300-2400, Sun 1300-2200. Excellent and inventive continental menu specializing in game meat, including impala, ostrich and crocodile – the uninitiated can try a platter. Good wines and superb service, and, as the names suggests, outside tables are dotted around spacious lawns.
$$$ Yujo, 4 Kyadondo Rd, Nakasero, near the Japanese Embassy, T0794-2892856. Mon-Sat 1200-1500, 1800-2230. All the classic dishes you'd expect from a good Japanese restaurant, including sushi and sashimi, miso soup, teriyaki, tempura and *katsu* curry in elegant Japanese decor with an *izakaya* area where seats are at low tables. Lunchtime bento boxes are around US$14.
$$$-$$ Faze 2, 10 Nakasero Rd, Nakasero, T0772-345808. Mon-Thu 1200-2300, Fri-Sat 1200-0100. Upmarket al-fresco dining in a large tropical garden, good Indian tandoori food and popular for melt-in-the-mouth steaks and ribs, also has its own butchery where you can buy quality pork, beef and poultry (they supply many 5-star hotels in town). Has another branch in Entebbe (page 76).
$$$-$$ Haandi, 1st floor, Commercial Plaza, 7 Kampala–Jinja Rd, T0414-346283, www. haandi-restaurants.com. Daily 1230-1430, 1930-2230. This fine Indian restaurant started in Nairobi in 1991 and today has branches in Kampala and London. Quality cuisine cooked from scratch by a team of North Indian chefs in a glass-fronted kitchen and beautifully presented in copper bowls.
$$ Fang Fang, 1st floor, Communications House, 1 Colville St, T0414-344806,

www.fangfang.co.ug. Mon-Sat 1200-1530, 1730-2230, Sun 1200-1430. Popular Chinese restaurant run by one of the longest-standing Chinese families in Kampala, serving a wide range of generous dishes. Eat in the large indoor restaurant with red-lantern type decor, or outside on the airy veranda.

$$ Mamba Point Italian, 22 Akii Bua Rd, Nakasero, next to the **Mamba Point Guesthouse** (see Where to stay, page 54), T0772-243225. Daily 1200-2230. With a pleasant terrace surrounded by potted plants, offers favourites like antipasti, bruschetta and tiramisu, plus Italian twists on Nile perch and tilapia. The cheeses, hams, capers, anchovies and olives are imported and there's a good choice of Italian wine.

$$ Mish Mash, 28 John Babiiha (Acacia) Av, Kololo, T0794-010101, www.mishmash uganda.com. Sun-Fri 1200-2300, Fri-Sat 1100-0200. There is indeed a mish-mash of entertainment at this constantly evolving venue, including a restaurant serving anything from baguettes and nachos to bangers and mash and Nile perch, a late night bar, stage for live music and movie screenings, kids' playground, art gallery, quality craft shop and Sat farmers' market, and all set in lush mature gardens. Check the website or their Facebook page to see what's on.

$$ Tamarai, 14 Lower Kololo Terrace, Kololo, T0755-791790. Daily 1100-2230. Good choice for Thai food, plus some Chinese and Indonesian dishes, in traditional decor of giant Buddha's and carved elephants. The lovely tea lounge has luxurious cushioned couches and more than 15 types of fruit, green and black teas to choose from.

$$-$ Arirang, 15 Kyaddondo Rd, Nakasero, next to the Indian Embassy, T0414-346777. Daily 1100-2200. Kampala's only Korean restaurant is in a plain cavernous dining room but with a long menu of authentic beef, pork, poultry, seafood and vegetarian

dishes. Try the mixed meat soup-based hotpot with dumplings that can be shared by the whole table.

$$-$ The Bistro, 5 Cooper Rd, Kololo, T0757-247876. Mon-Sat 0700-2200, Sun 0900-1600. In the Kisimenti Shopping Centre with fat leather couches and pleasant terrace, serves all-day breakfasts, light lunches, and the tapas menu is popular in the evening. Happy hour (1600-1900) is called 'Gin o'clock' because of their inventive gin cocktails.

$ Food Court at Garden City Shopping Mall, Yusuf Lule Rd (see Shopping, page 63). Daily 1100-2200. Zero ambience but fast inexpensive meals in a/c with a choice of pizza, Thai, Lebanese, Indian, Chinese, chicken and burgers and chips, and it's next to the **Cineplex** cinema. There's a similar food court at **Oasis Nakumatt Shopping Mall** next door.

$ Masala Chaat House, 3 De Winton Rd, opposite the **Uganda Arts and Crafts Market** and **National Theatre**, T0414-236487. Daily 0930-2200. 'Chaat' means Indian snack and this is a cheap and tiny cafeteria with about 10 tables. Indians eat here which is always a good sign. The *uttapams* (a fried batter and topped like a pizza) and *dosas* (rice pancakes stuffed with the likes of lentils or chutney) are recommended. Also sells tasty Indian sweets like *jalebis* and coconut *burfi*.

$ The Pub, De Winton Rd. Daily 1100-late. A small sports bar opposite the National Theatre's rear entrance by the Uganda Arts and Crafts Market. The dining room is hidden away at the back. Primarily known for serving the Ugandan traditional dish *ekigere*, cow hoof cooked in an aromatic sauce, although their chicken stew is good too. Noisy and crowded during football matches.

Cafés
Café Javas, Oasis Nakumatt Shopping Mall (see Shopping, page 64), 42 Bombo Rd, 32-36 Namirembe Rd, 9 Kira Rd, www.cafejavas.co.ug. Daily 0600-2300.

This swish, trendy coffee shop chain with Wi-Fi and a/c has branches sprouting up all over Kampala. Offers great meals in famously giant portions to accompany fine Kenyan coffee and also sells bags of beans. **Café Pap**, 13 Parliament Av, T0414-254570, www.cafepap.com. Mon-Sat 0730-2300, Sun 0930-2300. Centrally located and popular with office workers, light meals include breakfasts, burgers, crunchy salads and Danish pastries. There's another branch at the entrance of the **Uchumi Supermarket** at the Garden City Shopping Mall.

North of the centre p51, map p40
$$-$ Cayenne Restaurant and Lounge, 1213 Kira Rd, 200 m east of the **Kabira Country Club**, Bukoto, T0792-200555, www.cayennekampala.com. Mon 1700-2400, Tue-Sun 1200-late. A sprawling complex with a relaxed pub-style atmosphere and outside tables around a swimming pool. The menu ranges from fish and chips and T-bone steak to Indian butter chicken and Thai green curry. Doubles up as a nightclub popular with expats.

Kabalagala and Muyenga p53, map p40
$$$ Le Château, at Le Petit Village hotel (see Where to stay, page 56), 1273 Ggaba Rd, Kabalagala. Mon-Sat 0700-2300, Sun 0800-2200. Going strong since 1994, this serves fine, beautifully presented continental food, lovingly prepared by the Belgian owner. Save room for the waffles. The stylish thatched complex also has a superb French-style patisserie with a menu of coffee and light meals, a delicatessen and wine shop.
$$ Café Roma, 689 Tank Hill Rd, Muyenga, T0772-501 847. Tue-Sat 1200-2230, Sun 1200-1600. This informal garden restaurant is a gathering point for Italian expats in the Muyenga area. Serves pizza and pasta, a few adventurous mains like steak with gorgonzola, and a pork roast on Sun lunch. Decent wines, and good pistachio ice-cream and tiramisu.

$$ Le Petit Bistro, opposite Barclay's Bank, Ggaba Rd, Kabalagala, T0414-267789. Daily 1200-2300. Next to traffic with rickety furniture and renowned for its slow service, but it has a well-priced and highly rated French-oriented menu that includes superlative steaks and even duck and rabbit if they have it, and there's a French/Belgium bakery on site.
$$-$ Little Donkey, 555 Kisugu Rd, off St Barnabas Rd, Muyenga, T0414-692827. Lunch Tue-Fri 1230-1430, dinner Mon-Sat 1700-2200. About 100 m from the International Hospital, a tiny and colourful Mexican restaurant with rooftop terrace and surprisingly authentic tacos, quesadillas, enchiladas and burritos and you can't go wrong with guacamole made from a Ugandan avocado. A pitcher of margarita costs around US$15.
$ Ethiopian Village, Muyenga Rd, Kabalagala, T0414-510378, www.ethiopian villagerestaurant.com. Daily 1100-late. Sit either on the terrace or in small, unlit traditional *bandas*, hence 'the village'. They serve excellent Ethiopian food and wonderful coffee, accompanied by a smoking brazier of incense. There is a plaque commemorating the bomb attacks that claimed scores of lives in the restaurant during the 2010 World Cup final.
$ Fasika, corner of Ggaba and Muyenga roads, Kabalagala, T0414-510441. Daily 0930-2400. Another atmospheric and very authentic Ethiopian restaurant with shaded garden seating, serving *injera* with delicious *wats* (thick stews), plus Western steaks and chicken. A main course is little more than US$4. On Tue and Sat nights the famous Ethiopian coffee ceremony is performed by a waitress in traditional dress.

Cafés
Café Kawa, 2133 Tank Hill Rd, Muyenga, T0703-700776. Daily 0700-2200. Good coffee shop with Wi-Fi, light meals (the baguettes and salads are especially good), and it's attached to the **Wine Garage**

(0900-2400), which sells probably Kampala's best choice of French, Spanish, Australian and South African wines and has a wine bar for tastings open until midnight.

Munyonyo *p53, map p40*

All the Munyonyo hotels have excellent restaurants with views over the lake and diners are able to use other facilities like swimming pools (see Where to stay, page 56).
$$$-$$ The Bay, next to Speke Resort, follow signs from Wavamunno Rd, T0772-304745, www.thebaykampala.com. Daily except Tue 1300-2300. A wonderful garden setting for both families and romantic couples, with stunning views and a bonfire and sofas to watch the sunset. The menu features anything from pizza and burgers to grilled prawns and local tilapia fish. Offers boat rides and fishing and the restaurant will cook the catch.

🎵 Bars and clubs

City centre *p43, maps p40 and p44*

Boda Boda, Garden City Shopping Mall, Yusuf Lule Rd, T0781-579754. Daily 1100-0300. Modern bar on the rooftop/4th floor of the mall with views over the golf course from the palm-decked balcony, stylish leather and rattan furnishings, chilled music and sometimes live jazz.
Bubbles O'Learys, 30 Windsor Cres, Kitante, T0312-263815. Mon-Thu 1100-0200, Fri-Sat 1100-0400, Sun 1100-2400. An Irish pub with typical green and white decor but unfortunately no Guinness. A fun and popular expat hangout, with garden terrace, large screen for sports, dance floor and predictable pop music.
Club Silk, 15-17 1st St, Industrial Area, south of the Kampala–Jinja road, not far from Centenary Park, T0414-250907, www.clubsilk.co.ug. Tue and Thu 1900-0600, Fri and Sat 2100-0600. Probably the most commercial nightclub in Uganda in a massive factory conversion.

Several cavernous bars and dance floors downstairs, and quieter lounges upstairs. International DJs play a variety of music, and it gets seriously busy at weekends.
Iguana & Gusto, 8 Bukoto Rd, behind the new Acacia Mall, Kisimenti, T0777-667909. Tue-Sat 1700-0600. **Iguana** is the upstairs club with interesting music that varies every night. Downstairs **Gusto** is a little tamer with a café-like atmosphere and opens earlier from 1000 and serves food like pizzas, burgers and tapas.
Rock Garden, at Speke Hotel, 7-9 Nile Av (see Where to stay, page 55). 1000-0200. A little seedy and very loud, but popular, with circular bar, open-air dance floor, recognizable music and pool tables. You can eat at the hotel's restaurants.
Rouge Lounge, EM Plaza Building, 2 Kampala Rd, T0774-789782. Mon-Sat 1800-0500. Classic 70s-style swanky nightclub, with mirrored walls, low lighting, comfortable lounge seating, attracting an upmarket crowd. It has a reputation for premiering new DJs and dance music acts.

Kabalagala *p53, map p40*

Muyenga Road in Kabalagala is well known for its strip of raucous bars and many are open 24 hrs. The area has plenty of energy and makes for a fun night out. However, be wary of petty theft and men can expect to be approached by pushy prostitutes (who may also give women a bit of playful aggro if they see them as competition!).
Capital Pub, Muyenga Rd, T0414-269676. Daily 24 hrs. Pub/disco that is a Kabalagala institution. The dance floor is open air, with a raised thatched roof, **and** is packed from 2300 almost every night. The music varies from heavy Ugandan dance hall to Cliff Richard, often mixed together. At the back there is a relatively quiet sports room with pool tables and a giant TV screen for football.
Club Venom, Tirupati Mazima Mall, near the American Embassy, Ggaba Rd, Kabalagala, T0759-011230, www.venomkampala.com. Tue-Sat 2000-0400. A stylish nightclub

above Uchumi Supermarket and popular with the well heeled. Multi-coloured dance floor, themed nights and attached to a microbrewery so a variety of beers on tap are served in tankers and pitchers.

Da Posh Bar, Muyenga Rd. Daily 24 hrs. One of the many densely packed bars along this stretch of Muyenga Rd recognizable by its tangled Christmas lights hanging in trees over the patio and kitsch red decor. Similar set-ups nearby include **Timelezz** and **JB's Pub**.

Flamin' Chicken, 1351 Ggaba Rd, close to the junction with Muyenga Rd, T0781-444880. Mon-Thu and Sun 1200-2400, Fri-Sat 1200-0200. Relaxed open-air and (oddly) Iranian-run bar serving barbecued chicken as well as excellent lamb burgers and kebabs. There are authentic shisha pipes and a great view of the busy thoroughfare.

Fuego Cocktails & Restaurant, Zimwe Rd, off Kisugi Church Rd, north of the junction with Muyenga Rd, T0774-456 9028, www.fuegorestauranguganda.com. Daily 0900-0400. Pleasant garden setting among giant trees, fully stocked bar that stays open very late. The interesting menu features Ugandan, continental and Eritrean cuisine, including *nyama choma* (grilled meat) and the Sun brunch with live music is popular.

Jakob's Lounge, Muyenga Rd, T0784-760007. Daily 1200-2400, happy hour 1500-1800. One of the more sophisticated nightspots on Muyenga Rd with excellent views of the chaotic street life from the 2nd-floor balcony. Reasonable food includes bagels, Tex-Mex and burgers and you can try a cheekily named cocktail like Sex in Kampala or the Kabalagala Kiss.

Munyonyo *p53, map p40*
Miki's Pub, Wavamuno Rd, 1 km after the turn-off from Ggaba Rd towards Speke Resort, T0414-501461. Daily 1100-2400. Popular for its out-of-town location, great pizzas, barbecued pork, chicken and chips, and cocktails. Typical pub atmosphere, relaxing garden tables and it livens up in the evening with DJs and pool competitions.

☻ Entertainment

The informative free bimonthly publication *The Eye* (www.theeye.co.ug) lists what's on in Kampala, and is widely available from hotels and bookshops. Also see the *New Vision*, both the daily newspaper and online (www.newvision.co.ug), for listings and reviews.

Casinos

Kampala's casinos have slot machines and gaming tables for roulette, poker and black jack. None of them are especially plush, but they are venues for late-night eating and drinking to accompany a flutter.

Casino Simba, Garden City Shopping Mall, Yusuf Lule Rd, T0414-340371, www.pashainternational.com. Mon-Thu and Sun 1000-0400, Fri and Sat 1000-0600.

Kampala Casino, 2nd floor of Pan Africa House, 2 Kimathi Av, T0414-343628, www.kampalacasino.com. Daily 1200-0600.

Mayfair Casino, Kisozi Close, off Kyagwe Rd (near the French Embassy), Nakasero, T0414-234983, www.myfrgroup.com. Daily 1200-0600.

Pyramids Casino and Restaurant, 7 Yusuf Lule Rd, T0414-234840, www.pyramids.co.ug. Mon-Sat 0900-0600.

Cinemas

International releases are shown in modern multi-screen complexes with kiosks for snacks and drinks. Expect to pay US$6-8 for a ticket.

Cinema Magic, Metroplex Shopping Mall, Northern Bypass, Naalya, approximately 12 km northeast of the city centre, T0414-240092, www.metroplexmall.com. Mon-Fri 1400-2200, Sat-Sun 1000-2200.

Cineplex, 3rd floor, Garden City Shopping Mall, T0312-261415, and 1st floor, Oasis Nakumatt Shopping Mall, next to **Garden City**, both on Yusuf Lule Rd, T0312-261440, www.cineplexuganda.com. Daily 1100-2130.

Cricket

Lugogo Cricket Oval (also known as **Lugogo Stadium**), Jinja Rd. Exceptional location in a natural amphitheatre that was originally a quarry. Holds regular cricket games on Sun between local clubs. Europeans, Indians and Africans all participate. Check local press for details of fixtures.

Cultural centres

Alliance Française, 6 Mackinnon Rd, Nakasero, T0414-344490, **www.afkampala. org**. Offers films, art exhibitions and literary readings. Along with the Ugandan-German Cultural Society (see below), it makes sterling efforts to promote Ugandan folk and jazz music.

British Council, 4 Windsor Loop Rd, off Kira Rd, **Kamwokya**, T0414-560800, www.britishcouncil.ug. Excellent facilities, with films, concerts and talks, a library and all UK newspapers.

Goethe-Zentrum (**German** Institute), 6 Mackinnon Rd, Nakasero, T0414-533410, www.goethe.de. Promotes German culture through similar cultural activities as the Alliance Française, which is at the same address.

Football

Mandela National Stadium, Kireka, about 10 km east of the city on the Jinja road opposite the turning to the Northern Bypass, T0312-111027, www.mandelastadium.co.ug. Football is the most popular sport in Uganda. As well as international matches by the Ugandan national team, 'The Cranes', there are also league matches at this 40,000-seater stadium. Even if you're not a great football fan, you'll find the occasion fun. Check the website or local press for fixtures.

Theatre

National Theatre, 2-6 De Winton Rd, T0414-25 4567, www.ugandanational culturalcentre.org. Box office Mon-Fri 0830-1230 and 1400-1645, Sat 0830-1200, also open 30 mins before each performance. In addition to the stage shows on in the main auditorium Fri-Sun, there are occasional mid-week events like comedy nights or jam sessions with local bands. Check the website, the noticeboard outside or local press to see what's on. See also page 43.

Ndere Centre, Ntinda, junction of Northern Bypass and Kisaasi–Kira Rd, T0312-291936, www.ndere.com. A purpose-built cultural centre that is home to an internationally renowned 60-strong dance troupe that performs in an open-air auditorium on Wed and Fri at 1900, and Sun at 1800, US$15, children (under 16) US$7.50. The 2-hr show includes many traditional Ugandan dances and songs accompanied by various indigenous percussion, string and wind instruments. The centre is set in a large flowering garden where there's a kids' playground and a restaurant that's open daily from 1230 and stays open on the evenings of the performances when it offers a barbecue. Highly recommended and entertaining for all ages.

O Shopping

Art galleries

Afriart Gallery, 57 Kenneth Dale Dr, off Kira Rd, Kamwokya, T0414-375455, www.afriartgallery.org. Mon-Sat 0900-1800. Renowned Ugandan artist Daudi Karungi's gallery hosts an unusual selection of **contemporary** work by Ugandan artists, and it also sells art books and ceramics. Check for hidden gems from previous exhibitions tucked away in the storerooms. AKA Gallery (formerly Tulifanya Gallery), 28 Hannington Rd, T0414-254183, www. akagalleryuganda.com. Tue-Fri 1000-1700, Sat 1000-1600. This small but charming art gallery features East African artists and exhibitions change at least once a month. It's particularly involved in promoting new young artists and there are group exhibitions usually Aug-Sep.

Ujuzi Art Studios, Bukoto–Kisasi Rd (60 m before the turning to Kisu/Kabiri International School, adjacent to Bukoto Market), Bukoto, T0414-532252, www.paulo akiiki.com. Mon-Sat 0800-1800, Sun 1200-1800. Small gallery with unusual fine art collection, including abstract paintings and wooden sculptures by the talented Paulo Akiiki who frequently exhibits overseas.

Bookshops

Aristoc Booklex, city centre at 23 Kampala–Jinja Rd (opposite **Steers** restaurant), T0414-253 112, and 2nd floor, Garden City Shopping Mall, Yusuf Lule Rd, T0414-253112/3, www.aristocbooklex.com. Mon-Sat 0800-1900, Sun 0900-1400. The best bookshop in Kampala with a comprehensive range of international novels, plus useful city maps including the *A-Z Kampala*.

Crafts and curios

Banana Boat, www.bananaboat.co.ug. There are 3 franchises: **Craft and Gift Shop**, ground floor, Garden City Shopping Mall, Yusuf Lule Rd, T0414-525190, Mon-Sat 0930-1900, Sun 1030-1600; **Tribal Arts and Crafts**, 23 Cooper Rd, Kisementi, T0414-232885, Mon-Sat 0930-1900; **African Crafts and Interiors**, Lugogo Shopping Mall (see below), T0414-222363, Mon-Sat 0930-1900, Sun 0930-1500. Each of these quality shops sells interesting tourist goods hand picked from the markets or commissioned from popular workshops. They include handmade paper, recycled glass, batiks, jewellery, clothing and carvings.

Exposure Africa Crafts Village, 15 Buganda Rd, Nakersero, www.sewa crafts.org. Mon-Sat 0900-1800, Sun 1000-1600. A good selection of crafts made almost wholly from recycled materials, including jewellery, metal, glass and fabric, and the project supports disadvantaged women's groups. There are more than 30 stalls and bargaining is welcomed.

Uganda Arts & Crafts Village (also known as the **African Crafts Village**), behind the National Theatre, De Winton Rd. Mon-Sat 0900-1900, Sun 1000-1600. A compound of small shops and kiosks built in a semicircle, selling batiks, prints, carved folding chairs, wooden sculptures, bark-cloth, jewellery and antique masks, all reasonably priced and bargaining is possible especially if trade is slow.

Uganda Crafts, 32-36 Bombo Rd, T0414-250077, www.ugandacrafts2000ltd.org. Mon-Fri 0900-1800, Sat 0900-1700, Sun 1000-1600. The largest craft shop in Uganda with a range of handmade products from all over East Africa made by women's groups, disabled people and those living with HIV/AIDS. Prices are fixed and the quality is excellent.

Shopping malls

Opening hours are listed for shops: restaurants and other facilities open later in the evening. Kampala's most prestigious shopping mall was being built at the time of writing: **The Acacia Mall** on John Babiha (Acacia) Av in Kololo, www.theacaciamall. com, will cover 35,000 sq m of retail space when finished.

Garden City Shopping Mall, Yusuf Lule Rd, T0414-258906. Mon-Sat 0830-2000, Sun 0900-1600. This red-brick modern shopping mall – the first multi-storey mall to be built in Kampala – has banks with ATMs, a branch of the excellent bookstore, **Aristoc Booklex** (see above), some interesting souvenir and clothes shops, a large electronics store, an **Uchumi** supermarket, a **Woolworths** (South African clothes and homeware store), several decent cafés, and a food court on the 3rd floor (see page 58). For entertainment, it also has a cinema and a casino (see page 61).

Lugogo Shopping Mall, Lugogo ByPass Rd, about 3 km east of the city centre off the Kampala–Jinja Rd. Mon-Sat 0800-2000, Sun 0900-1500. The 2 large anchor stores here are **Shoprite Supermarket** and **Game** (a South African department store that sells just about everything), plus there are small individual shops and cafés.

Metroplex Shopping Mall, Northern Bypass, Naalya, approximately 12 km northeast of the city centre, follow the Northern Bypass east through Bukoto and Kiwaatule to Naalya, T0414-240092, www.metroplexmall.com. Mon-Sat 0900-2100, Sun 1000-1700. Currently the largest and newest of Kampala's malls but some distance from the city centre in the upmarket suburb of Naalya. It has a number of South African chains including **Shoprite** and **Woolworths**, a food court and Cinema Magic (page 61).

Oasis Nakumatt Shopping Mall, Yusuf Lule Rd, T0414-348040. Mon-Sat 0830-2000, Sun 0900-1600. Next to and a little more enclosed than **Garden City Shopping Mall** (see above), and very usefully with a branch of **Nakumatt Supermarket** that is open 24 hrs, plus boutiques, a couple of good coffee shops, and another cinema. On the 1st floor is **Media Hub**, T0312-261415-6, which sells CDs, DVDs, games and magazines as well as electronics including mobile phones and games consoles.

☼ What to do

Climbing and trekking
Mountain Club of Uganda, info@mcu.ug, www.mcu.ug. Meets on the 1st Thu of the month at 1900 at the Athina Club, 30 Windsor Cres, Kololo. It's quite a social event, anyone is welcome and there's the opportunity to ask members advice on trekking in Uganda.

Golf
Palm Valley Golf & Country Club, 20 km south of Kampala on the Kampala–Entebbe road near the Akright Estates, T0782-519021, www.palmvalleygolf.co.ug. Part of a timeshare development, this new 9-hole course with 18 tees features water features and large bunkers and there's a pleasant club house with restaurant and bar. Expect

to pay in the region of US$25 for a round.
Uganda Golf Club, Yusuf Lule Rd, opposite the Fairway Hotel (page 54), T0414-233911, www.ugandagolfclub. com. Established in 1908, this 18-hole par-72 course lies in the heart of the city centre and is gloriously lush with gentle hills and the Kitante Stream running through it. Visitors can play for around US$50 plus US$5 for a caddy.

Swimming
Most large hotels accept visitors for a daily fee of around US$6-10, and many of the nicest have poolside restaurants and bars. Try the **Sheraton** (page 54), where the giant pool is circular with an island in the middle and towels and lockers are included in the fee; **Speke Resort** (page 56), which has an Olympic-size pool for serious swimmers; or the **Kabira Country Club** (page 56), which has an additional kids' pool and playground and day visitors can also use the gym.

Tour operators
Adrift, 14 York Terrace, Kololo, T0312-237438, www.adrift.ug. Specialists in whitewater rafting, bungee jumping and jet boating at Bujagali, near Jinja (page 93). The popular day trip for rafting and other activities picks up in Kampala from the **Kampala Backpackers Hostel & Campsite** (0700), the **Sheraton** (0730), **Nandos Restaurant** on the Kampala–Jinja road (0745) and the **Red Chillli Hideaway** (0800). Will also collect from other Kampala or Jinja hotels by arrangement. **Nile River Explorers** and **Nalubale Rafting** based at Bujagali (page 100) also offer the same transport arrangements. Bookings are essential.
Afri Tours and Travel, Fairway Hotel (page 54), 1 Kafu Rd, T0414-233596, www.afritourstravel.com. Specialize in safari planning, hotel and lodge bookings.
Africa Adventure Travellers, T0414-597257, www.adventure-travellers.com. Good-value

safaris from 1-day Ngamba Island visits to 11-day gorillas and game parks.

African Pearl Safaris, 2nd floor, Station House, 3 Kampala–Jinja Rd, T0414-233566, www.africanpearlsafaris.com. Well-established firm offering trips to the gorillas, parks and other parts of Uganda.

Let's Go Travel, 1st floor, Garden City Shopping Mall, Yusuf Lule Rd, T0414-346667, www.ugandaletsgotravel.com. Long-established company offering safaris and hotel and lodge bookings. Also has a desk in the arrivals hall of Entebbe International Airport.

Gorilla Tours, T0414-200221, www.gorillatours.com. Mid-range operator offering scheduled and tailor-made gorilla and chimpanzee tours and runs the **Airport Guesthouse** in Entebbe (page 76) and the **Travellers Rest Hotel** in Kisoro (page 166).

Pearl of Africa Tours & Travel, Oasis Nakumatt Shopping Mall, Yusuf Lule Rd, T0414-340533, www.pearlofafricatours.com. Offers a wide range of tours including a useful half-day city tour of Kampala if you're short of time, plus day trips to Jinja.

Prime Safaris, T0414-532162, www.primeugandasafaris.com. Good range of affordable safaris and gorilla trips from 3 days to 3 weeks and will tailor to budgets using lodges or camping.

Rwenzori Trekking Services, T077-411 4499 (Kampala), T077-611 4442 (Kilembe in the Rwenzoris), www.rwenzoritrekking.com. Reliable Rwenzori climbs of various duration and difficulty and can organize extensions to the parks.

Uganda Bicycle Tours, T0787-016688, www.ugandabicycle.com. Enjoyable 4- to 5-hr bike tours on the eastern side of Murchison Bay to experience rural village life along the lakeshore, and the guides will take you to a market and school. From US$40 including the boat crossing from Ggaba.

Ugandan Safari Company, T0414-251182, www.safariuganda.com. Run **Apoka Safari Lodge**, see page 244, and **Semliki Safari Lodge**, see page 213, and also organizes tailor-made safaris.

Volcanoes Safaris, 27 Lumumba Av, Nakersero, T0414-346464, T0312-263823, www.volcanoessafaris.com. Gorilla and chimpanzee safari specialists using their own beautifully designed and eco-friendly upmarket lodges: **Bwindi Lodge** (page 165), **Mount Gahinga Safari Lodge** (page 168), and **Kyambura Gorge Lodge** (page 186), as well as **Virunga Lodge** in Rwanda. A typical safari would spend at least a couple of days at each to do both the primate activities and visit community-based and conservation initiatives.

Walter's Boda-Boda Tours, T0791-880106, www.walterstours.com. Enterprising Walter and his team offer fun city tours by *boda-boda* to all the main sights or you can tell them where you'd like to go. The excellent drivers/guides have good knowledge of Kampala's history and can help with bargaining at the markets and curio shops and take you for a traditional Ugandan lunch. From around US$30 for half a day, excluding entry fees.

Wild Frontiers, T0414-321479, www.wild frontiers.co.ug. Arrange wildlife safaris throughout Uganda, as well as operators for boat cruises and fishing safaris at Murchison Falls (see page 238 for their details there), and on Lake Victoria (see page 77 for the Entebbe office).

☉ Transport

Air

Entebbe International Airport is 40 km south of Kampala and 3 km from Entebbe's town centre. For details of the airport see page 38; for international airlines serving Uganda, see Essentials, page 9; and for Getting around by air, see Essentials, page 13.

Airline offices **Air Uganda**, Jubilee Insurance Building, 14 Parliament Av, T0412-165555, airport, T0414-321485, www.air-uganda.com. **British Airways**, Centre Court, 4 Ternan Av, Nakasero, T0414-257414-6, www.britishairways.com. **Brussels Airlines**, Rwenzori House, 1 Lumumba Av, Nakasero, T0414-234200, www.brusselsairlines.com. **Egypt Air**, 11 Grand Imperial Arcade, Speke Rd, T0414-233960, airport, T0414-320698, www.egyptair.com. **Emirates**, FCN Building, Kimathi Av, T0417-710444, www.emirates. com. **Ethiopian Airlines**, United Assurance Building, Kimathi Av, T0414-345577, airport, T0414-321130, www.flyethiopian.com. **Fly Uganda**, Kampala Aeroclub, Kajjansi Airfield, Kampala–Entebbe road, 17 km south of Kampala and 23 km north of Entebbe, T0772-712557, www.flyuganda.

com. **Gulf Air**, 1st floor, Garden City Shopping Mall, Yusuf Lule Rd, T0414-346666, www.gulfair.com. **Kenya Airways**, Jubilee Insurance Building, 14 Parliament Av, T0312-360000, airport, T0414-320234, www.kenya-airways.com. **KLM**, Jubilee Insurance Building, 14 Parliament Av, T0414-338001, airport, T0414-323715, www.klm.com. **RwandAir**, Rwenzori Courts, 27 Lumumba Av, Nakasero, T0414-344851, www.rwandair.com. **South Africa Airways**, Suite 14, Workers House, 1 Pilkington Rd, T0414-345772-5, airport, T0414-322219, www.flysaa.com. **Turkish Airlines**, 3rd floor, Ruth Towers, 15A Clement Hill Rd, T0414-253433-36, airport, T0414-322260, www.turkishairlines.com.

Bus

Long distance The main long-distance bus station is between the Old and New taxi parks near the Nakivubo Stadium. Buses from Kampala to the other major towns in Uganda generally leave every couple of hours between 0600 and 1400 and there are numerous companies. Destinations include Fort Portal (4 hrs), Hoima (3 hrs), Kabale (5 hrs), Kasese (5 hrs), Kisoro (8 hrs), Masaka (2 hrs), Mbale (4 hrs) and Mbarara (4 hrs). The nearer towns of Entebbe (37 km) and Jinja (78 km) are mostly served by *matatus* (see below).

By far the most reliable bus service is the **Post Bus**, T0414-255511, ww.ugapost.co.ug, which is well driven with some luggage space and runs to a fixed timetable. Post Buses stop at all the post offices on their routes and the time it takes to load and unload mail doesn't add much to the journey time. They run Mon-Sat and all services depart at 0800 from the Kampala main post office on Kampala–Jinja road, near its junction with Speke Rd. Get there by at least 0700 to buy a ticket as you can't pre-book. The routes are: Kampala–**Gulu**; Kampala–**Kabale** via Masaka and Mbarara; Kampala–**Kasese** via Fort Portal; Kampala–**Hoima** via Masindi; and Kampala–**Lira** via

Mbale and Soroti. Naturally the routes run in reverse and most depart from the post offices at the end or their routes at 0800 again and you need to enquire at the local post offices en route to ask when they expect them to arrive and depart. Fares vary depending on destination but these fares will give some idea of what you can expect to pay: **Fort Portal** US$7; **Gulu** US$7.50; **Hoima** US$5; **Kabale** US$8; **Masaka** US$4; **Masindi** US$4; **Mbarara** US$6; **Soroti** US$8; **Tororo** US$6.

International Kenya: The journey to **Nairobi** via either the Busia or Malaba borders (see Border crossing, page 106), takes a scheduled 12 hrs, but could be nearer 15 hrs and fares range from US$25 to US$40. The buses also stop at Kenyan's western towns of **Eldoret** (6½ hrs) and **Nakuru** (9 hrs), and some of the companies also offer connecting services from Nairobi to **Mombasa**. Easy Coach (lower ground floor, Oasis Nakumatt Shopping Mall, Yusuf Lule Rd, T0772-657561, www.easycoach. co.ke) departs Kampala at 0700, 1400 and 1800; departs Nairobi at 0700 and 1900. Also has an additional service between Kampala and **Kisumu** on Lake Victoria in Kenya. Kampala Coach (Kampala–Jinja road, opposite the Shell petrol station, T0776-773355) departs Kampala at 1000; departs Nairobi 0600. **Modern Coast Express** (opposite the National Theatre, De Winton Rd, T0779-557089, www.modern coastexpress.com) departs Kampala 0800, 1200 and 1800; departs Nairobi 0700, 1900 and 2000. **Mash Bus Services** (opposite the National Theatre, De Winton Rd, T0713-111557) departs Kampala 1800, 1930; departs Nairobi 0700 and 1930. **Queens Coach** (lower ground floor, Oasis Nakumatt Shopping Mall, Yusuf Lule Rd, T0759-002010, www.queenscoach.com) departs from both Kampala and Nairobi at 0800.

Rwanda: The Katuna (Uganda) and Gatuna (Rwanda) border is between Kabale and Kigali (see Border crossing, page 141). Jaguar Executive Coaches (30-32 Namirembe Rd, between **Café Javas** and the **Kobil** petrol station, T0414-237798), and **Kampala Coach** (see above), both have 4-5 daily services (some overnight) between Kampala and Kigali (8-9 hrs; US$9-12). There's a time difference – Rwanda is 1 hr ahead of Uganda.

Tanzania: How you get to Tanzania from Uganda depends on where you're going. For **Arusha** and the game parks in the Northern Circuit such as the Serengeti or the Ngorongoro Crater, or **Moshi** for Mount Kilimanjaro, it is by far easier and quicker to go via Nairobi in Kenya. For the western side of Lake Victoria in Tanzania, there are services between Kampala and **Bukoba** via the border at **Mutukula** (see Border crossing, page 124, 5-6 hrs; US$10-12). Several companies go from the main bus station or try **Friends Safaris**, Rashid Hamis Rd, T0712-555540. The first of 3-4 departures from Kampala is at 1100 and they depart from Bukoba at 0700-1000.

Car hire

For information about car hire and driving in Uganda, see Essentials, pages 14 and 15. The companies listed below offer a variety of vehicles including saloon cars, 4WDs and minibuses.

Alpha Rent-a-Car, EMKA House, 3-5 Bombo Rd, Nakasero,T0414-344332, www.alpharentals.co.ug.

Car Hire Kampala, 1001 Ggaba Rd, next to the American Embassy, Kabalagala, T0758-582097, www.carhirekampala.com.

Europcar, 1-11 Nsambya Rd, T0414-237211, airport T0711-115169, www.europcar.com.

Expedient Car Hire, Capital Shopper's Centre, New Port Bell Rd, Nakawa, about 5 km east of the city centre, T0778-673889, www.expedientcarhire.com.

Hertz, Communications House, 1 Colville St, T0414-347192, airport, T0772-450460, www.hertzuganda.com.

Roadtrip Uganda, Valley Drive, off Grace Musoke Rd, north of Old Kira Rd, Bukuto, T0773-363012, www.roadtripuganda.com.

Sylcon Tours & Travel, 59 Katazamiti Rd, off New Port Bell Rd, Nakawa, about 5 km east of the city centre, T0414-222409, www.sylcontours.com.

Uganda Self-Drive, Najja Shopping Centre, Kampala–Entebbe road, about 5 km south of the city centre and 1.5 km south of the Kibuye roundabout/the junction with the Masaka road, T0772-552950, www.ugandaselfdrive.com.

Viva Safaris, 1st floor, Airways House, 6 Colville St, T0312-100065, www.vivasafaris.net.

Matatus

Matatus also cover the longer distances from Kampala and depart when full but they stop off on the way and therefore take much longer than buses. They arrive and depart at the Old Taxi Park on Ben Kiwanuka St and the New Taxi Park, opposite the stadium in Namirembe Rd, 400 m away, with the bus station in between. The busier **Old Taxi Park** serves **Jinja** and towns in eastern Uganda, while the **New Taxi Park** serves **Masaka**, **Fort Portal** and other western and northern destinations. *Matatus* for **Entebbe** leave from both parks. Additionally, other *matatu* parks include **Nakawa Taxi Park** on the Kampala–Jinja road near the junction with New Port Bell Rd, for the east; and **Natete Taxi Park** on the Masaka road about 1 km east of the junction with the Northern Bypass, for the west and north. *Matatus* from closer places like Jinja and Entebbe also stop and pick up at various places on the main roads in and out of the city. These taxi parks might

seem chaotic at first, but surprisingly there is a significant level of organization and vehicles are parked together according to their destination.

🛈 Directory

Embassies and consulates For a full list of foreign representatives in Kampala, visit http://embassy.goabroad.com. **Immigration** 75 Jinja Rd, T0414-595 945, www.immigration.go.ug. Mon-Fri 0800-1630. **Medical services** There are several hospitals but the quality of care varies. These are the best private hospitals in Kampala: **International Hospital Kampala (IHK)**, St Barnabas Rd (off Tank Hill Rd), Muyenga, which also operates the **International Medical Center (IMC)**, KPC Building, Bombo Rd, Nakasero, enquiries T0312-200400, 24-hr emergencies 0772-200400, www.img.co.ug. **The Surgery**, 2 John Babiiha (Acacia) Av, Kololo, enquires T0772-756003, 24-hr emergencies T0752-756003, www.thesurgeryuganda.org. This is a medical and travel clinic popular with expats and Uganda's specialist hospital for tropical diseases. **Post** Kampala's main post office is on the Kampala–Jinja road, on the corner of Speke Rd, T0414-255511, www.ugapost.co.ug. Mon-Fri 0830-1700, Sat 0830-1300. This is also where the **Post Bus** departs from (see page 14). To send anything of value, use a courier. The post office is the agent for **EMS Courier Services**. **DHL**, 18 Clement Hill Rd, T0312-210006, www.dhl.co.ug. **TNT**, 24 Nakasero Rd, Nakasero, T0414-343942, www.tnt.com.

Entebbe and around

Prior to Independence in 1962, Entebbe, 37 km south of Kampala, was the colonial administrative capital of Uganda. It's a rather pretty town on hilly terrain along the northwestern shoreline of Lake Victoria, virtually on the equator. With a population of about 80,000, the pace of life is far less frenetic than Kampala, and it's a popular area for middle-class Ugandans to set up home. Although most visitors just pass through it on their way from the airport, Entebbe has several worthwhile sights, including the well laid out Botanical Gardens and the Uganda Wildlife Education Centre (UWEC). Both are of great interest to birdwatchers with a diverse array of over 250 forest and shorebirds. On Ngamba Island, 23 km offshore, visitors can observe orphaned chimpanzees living in a heavily forested sanctuary.
▸▸ *For listings, see pages 75-78.*

Arriving in Entebbe → *Phone code: 0414. Colour map 2, B4.*

Getting there
Air Entebbe International Airport is 3 km from Entebbe's town centre and 37 km from Kampala. For details of the airport, see page 38. A taxi from the airport to hotels in Entebbe costs in the region of US$4-6.

Matatu There is a continuous stream of *matatus* to Entebbe from various places in Kampala including the Old and New taxi parks, and the junction of Entebbe and Nasser roads in Nakasero. A special hire taxi will cost in the region of US$30-35 between Entebbe and Kampala; these are mostly the airport taxis which are white with a yellow band across the side.

Traffic is very busy along the Kampala–Entebbe road. Outside rush hour, it takes around 1½ hours. Rush hours are generally Monday-Friday 0700-0900 from Entebbe to Kampala, and 1630 to as late as 2000 in the opposite direction, when it could easily take two to 2½ hours. Another obstacle to the free flow of traffic is that there are frequent official convoys on their way to and from Kampala and the airport or State House, and traffic is obliged to pull onto the side of the road and stop to allow these convoys to pass. A new four-lane highway (expected to be called the Entebbe–Kampala Expressway) is currently under construction. It will join up with Kampala's Northern Bypass and the Masaka road to the west of the city centre.

Background

Entebbe, meaning 'a seat' in the Luganda language, was the place where an 18th-century Baganda chief sat to adjudicate legal cases. It first became a British colonial administrative and commercial centre in 1893 when Sir Gerald Portal, a colonial commissioner, used it as a base. From 1894 to 1962 the city was the administrative capital of the British Uganda Protectorate before it moved to Kampala. Entebbe is still the site of the fine State House, the official residence of the president, although today there's also another one on Nakasero Hill in Kampala, and most of the presidents since Independence have used them interchangeably.

Entebbe is perhaps best known as the home of Uganda's main international airoprt, which was first opened in 1929. It became infamous in 1976 when an **Air France** plane flying from Israel to Paris via Athens, was hijacked, diverted to Entebbe and forced to land there by a group of Palestinian and German militia. The 100 Jewish passengers on board were held hostage as demands were made for the release of prisoners held in Israeli jails. Ugandan soldiers and the hijackers were then taken completely by surprise when three Hercules transport planes landed after a 3500-km trip from Israel, and about 200 elite Israeli paratroopers stormed the airport building. During the raid 20 Ugandan soldiers and all seven hijackers died along with three of the hostages. Additionally, 11 Ugandan war planes (which amounted to a quarter of the Uganda Air Force) and much of the airport were destroyed. It was repaired and today the new domestic terminal, built in 2007, sits on the site of the original building where the incident took place.

Places in Entebbe → *For listings, see pages 75-78.*

Colonial Entebbe

At the turn of the 19th century the colonialists built their administrative centre at Entebbe and some government offices are still located here. Walking along the criss-cross of lanes between the main road and the lake shore there are a number of beautiful old buildings to be seen. One relic from former times is the **cannon** in the square in front of the Entebbe Club, captured from the Germans during the First World War. It bears the maker's number, name and date: 103, Krupp of Essen, 1917. The gun now sits on a plinth and is surrounded by fountains (not always working). Standing alongside the gun are the statues of two modern camouflaged soldiers peering through binoculars across Lake Victoria.

Botanical Gardens

① *Berkeley Rd, T0414-320638. Daily 0900-1800. US$4, plus US$2 for a camera (if declared) and US$2 for a vehicle.*

Covering 40 ha with a 1.5-km stretch of lakeshore, the gardens were established in 1898 when Entebbe was the seat of the British Uganda Protectorate. They were originally used as a research ground for the introduction of various crop species and ornamental plants to Uganda. Those of foreign origin such as cocoa, coffee, tea and rubber were introduced and evaluated to see how well they would thrive in Uganda's climate and soils. Many did thrive and became main cash crops of the country. At one time the gardens had a collection of 2500 plant species, but the number dwindled to the present 350-400 due to neglect during the period of the country's political turmoil, and there has been little attempt to redevelop it as a centre for research and education. Nevertheless, it's a lovely well-established garden and a fantastic spot for birdwatching; some trees still have their original metal labels on them. The gardens' claim to fame is that the first Johnny Weismuller *Tarzan* film was shot here.

There are few actual paths so visitors can wander where they like through the open woodland, patches of tropical rainforest, spacious lawns and along the beach. Watch out for the dragon spiders (so named because they catch dragonflies), which are pretty big and weave enormous webs. There is a troupe of black-and-white colobus monkeys here, as well as green vervet that can be seen playing on the grass in the early morning and at dusk. Keen twitchers will be well rewarded, and the tall trees near the main entrance are the favourite day-roost of a pair of Verreaux's eagle owls; key garden birds include orange-tufted and red-chested sunbirds, black-and-white casqued hornbill, splendid starling and several species of weaver. Along the lakeshore look for the long-tailed cormorant, black-headed heron, giant and pied kingfishers, as well as various terns, storks and ducks.

There is a small café and picnic area by the lake, which is a popular swimming spot at weekends and holidays – usually with lots of noise and, sadly, litter. Some tourists have complained about informal guides appearing and demanding high rates for tours of the gardens: if you are approached make sure you negotiate a price before engaging

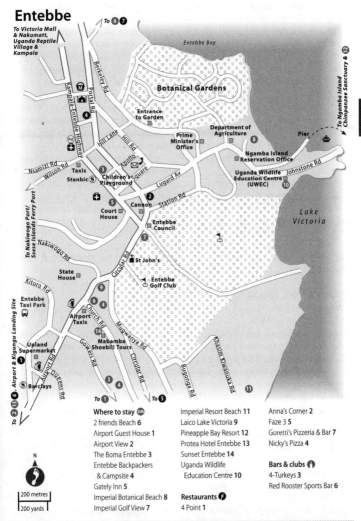

Entebbe

Where to stay 🛏
2 friends Beach **6**
Airport Guest House **1**
Airport View **2**
The Boma Entebbe **3**
Entebbe Backpackers
& Campsite **4**
Gately Inn **5**
Imperial Botanical Beach **8**
Imperial Golf View **7**

Imperial Resort Beach **11**
Laico Lake Victoria **9**
Pineapple Bay Resort **12**
Protea Hotel Entebbe **13**
Sunset Entebbe **14**
Uganda Wildlife
Education Centre **10**

Restaurants 🍴
4 Point **1**

Anna's Corner **2**
Faze 3 **5**
Goretti's Pizzeria & Bar **7**
Nicky's Pizza **4**

Bars & clubs 🍸
4-Turkeys **3**
Red Rooster Sports Bar **6**

Shoebill storks and Mabamba Swamp

The rare shoebill stork (*Balaeniceps rex*) is arguably Africa's most sought-after bird sighting, and is the species that attracts the biggest number of birdwatchers to Uganda. With a global population of at most 8000 individuals, the species is considered 'vulnerable' and is thinly distributed where it does exist. It's a prehistoric-looking bird with affinities somewhere between a pelican and a stork, with plumage that is an anonymous battleship grey. The size of a large heron, it stands up to 152 cm tall, weighs 4-7 kg and has a wingspan of up to 260 cm. But it's most distinctive feature is its enormous bill in the shape of a shoe, albeit one with a hook, that is in fact rather like a cobbler's blank in appearance.

The shoebill, a master of ambush, lurks in the shallows standing motionless waiting for its prey. These can be mudfish, frogs, baby crocs or water snakes – anything that fits the bill – and then it lunges forward with a speed that belies its size. It's a solitary creature, and a breeding pair will only meet up during the breeding season (usually April to June), when they engage in a bill-clacking courtship prior to mating. Shoebills prefer swamps and in particular papyrus. Given that 17% of Uganda is covered by freshwater lakes, rivers and swamps, it's one of the best countries in Africa to see the stork. Murchison Falls National Park and areas around Lake Albert are favourite habitats but, closer to Kampala and Entebbe, Mabamba Swamp is considered Uganda's most reliable place to seek the shoebill.

Covering over 16,000 ha of the marshy northern shores of Lake Victoria and stretching through the long, narrow Mabamba Bay fringed with papyrus, Mabamba Swamp is a Ramsar site and a Birdlife International Important Bird Area.

their services, and try to establish that they do actually know something about the plants and birds.

Uganda Wildlife Education Centre (UWEC)
ⓘ *Johnstone Rd, T0414-320520, www.uweczoo.org. Daily 0900-1800, last admission 1700. US$15, children (3-14), US$8.*

An animal orphanage was originally established at Entebbe in 1952 by the colonial government to offer sanctuary to young animals found abandoned or venerable in the wild. Gradually by the 1960s it had developed into a zoo with non-indigenous species like tigers and bears and became significantly rundown over the years. It was then redeveloped in 1994 as a conservation and education centre, and a captive breeding centre for endangered animals. Even though it is still locally referred to as Entebbe Zoo (and if getting a *boda-boda* from the town centre you'll still need to ask the driver for the 'zoo'), this is far from correct. Today it houses only indigenous species in as natural environments as possible, and again all the animals have been rescued from poachers, the illegal pet trade or accidents. Many – especially reptiles and grey parrots – have been confiscated from smugglers at the airport. The chimpanzees are worth going to see here if you're not visiting them elsewhere in Uganda and the playful population of 11 live on a forested island surrounded by a moat

The centre replicates the country's ecological zones in miniature, such as savannah, wetlands and tropical forest. There is a pair of resident shoebill storks (see box, above),

At any one time, it's thought to be home to over 190,000 birds and, along with the shoebill, it supports more than 75% of the global population of blue swallows and three globally threatened birds: the papyrus gonolek, pallid harrier and papyrus yellow warbler.

Visitors can arrange a 1½-hour excursion by canoe into the swamp for around US$15 per boat, plus a US$5 per person conservation fee. By road, the swamps are located 52 km southwest of Kampala, and 35 km west of Entebbe, and the closest village is Kasanje. From Kampala, after 30 km turn left off the Masaka road just before reaching Mpigi and then it's 12 km to Kasanje. After that, follow the road around for about 10 km to Mabamba Bay. You can get a *matatu* from Kampala's New Taxi Park to Kasanje, and then take a *boda-boda* to Mabamba Bay. From Entebbe follow the Kampala–Entebbe road for 13 km up to Kisubi and

take a left turn to Nakawuka, then another left turn to Kasanje, from where again it's 10 km to the jetty where the canoes depart into Mabamba. **Note**: once off the main highways these are dirt roads.

Without your own transport, **Mabamba Shoebill Tours** (Sunset Entebbe Motel at 25 Church Road, Entebbe, T0772-646777, www.shoebill mabamba.com) organize a four-hour guided excursion into the swamps. Departing from Entebbe, it includes a short boat ride across Nakiwago Bay (with great views of Entebbe and the airport) and the canoe ride in the swamp. Although sightings are never guaranteed, shoebills are usually spotted within just 10 or 20 minutes. The cost is US$160 for one to three people, US$200 for three to six people, and so on; you can contact them to see if you can join an exisiting group. Pickups from Kampala cost extra. Book by 1700 the day before.

a few lions, as well as leopard, chimpanzee, white rhino, hyena, waterbuck, impala, giant forest hog, ostrich, crested cranes (Uganda's national bird) and several varieties of monkeys and reptiles. There's an interesting zone displaying medicinal plants with excellent explanatory plaques and a 1-km forest trail, where you can see monkeys, birds and butterflies. Also here is a lakeside café, accommodation (see page 76) and a good craft and book shop.

Ngamba Island Chimpanzee Sanctuary
ⓘ *Reservations office, 24 Lugard Av, Entebbe, T0414-320662, www.ngambaisland.com. Half-day visits by a 45-min speedboat ride start at US$110 per person; full-day visits by a 90-min traditional Ssese canoe ride (weather dependent) from US$110 per person. Rates are based on 4 people; the price increases for 1-3 people. Feeding times from the visitor platform are 1100 and 1430 so boats are scheduled to arrive on the island 30 mins before. A maximum of 25 people are permitted at each feeding time, so booking in advance is essential.*
About 23 km southeast of Entebbe lies Ngamba Island, west of Kome Island in Lake Victoria. A chimpanzee sanctuary was established here in 1998 by the **Chimpanzee Sanctuary and Wildlife Conservation Trust** (**CSWCT**), formed from the Jane Goodall Institute, Born Free Foundation, Uganda Wildlife Education Centre Trust, International Fund for Animal Welfare and the Zoological Parks Board of New South Wales, Australia. Ngamba Island is approximately 45 ha in size, and is covered with indigenous tropical rainforest that is an ideal habitat for the chimpanzees.

Originally 19 chimpanzees were relocated here from Isinga Island, Queen Elizabeth National Park, and the Uganda Wildlife Education Centre, Entebbe. Today their numbers have risen to 48 orphans, mainly rescued from smugglers or illegal pets. Orphaned or captured chimpanzees cannot be released back into the wild as they are likely to be rejected, injured or killed by other chimpanzees. Ngamba Island offers them a sanctuary that closely resembles life in the wild and an alternative for visitors to view the chimpanzees in their forest habitats in western Uganda. Numbers are equally divided between males and females, and the chimpanzees have the freedom of the island, which they share with water monitor lizards, hippos, otters and a large variety of birds including fish eagles and kingfishers. The adult females are given a contraceptive implant, inhibiting reproduction but not other social interaction.

Day visits include an overview of the project and observing the supplementary feeding of the chimps from the visitor platform. Sun protection is strongly advised; insect repellent, sandals, a sweater and a torch (if staying overnight) are also recommended. Visitors are not allowed to bring their own food and drinks to the island but refreshments are available to buy and a buffet lunch is included in the price of a full-day trip. The lake crossing can be rough if it's windy (more common in June and July), and a change of clothes may be necessary. On the slower boat trip, if the weather is favourable, the boatman may stop and offer passengers the opportunity of jumping overboard for a quick swim at the equator, so bring swimming gear and a towel.

There is also the option to stay overnight when additional programs are on offer, including one-to-one interaction known as 'Caregiver-For-A-Day', or early-morning walks with the chimps. Accommodation is in comfortable two-person safari tents on elevated platforms and rates are full board (check the website for details). **Note**: overnight visitors who are to have any interaction with the chimps, must have had certain vaccinations (like gorillas, chimps can easily contract illnesses from humans).

Uganda Reptile Village
① *Abaita-Ababiri, 2 km north of Entebbe on the Kampala–Entebbe Highway, turn off at the Petro City fuel station and follow signs for 4 km, T0782-349583, www.reptiles.ug. Daily 0800-1800, US$6 per person, which includes a guide.*

The Reptile Village was established in 2002 to educate local people about the ecology of snakes, and the role they play in the environment, so as to stop people from automatically killing any snake they see. It also offers a snake removal service for local citizens who find an unwanted reptile in their house or on their property. It's home to the largest collection of poisonous snakes in the country, 14 species in all, including cobras, vipers, mambas, boom slang, twig and vine snakes. Non-venomous snakes are also on display: the python, house snake and green tree snake may be handled, and in addition there are tortoises, chameleons and monitor lizards. It's very popular with visiting school children. A 3-km channel has been cut through a pretty wetland area and is a nice walk to observe wild birds and monkeys.

Kigungu Landing Site
Located on Tunnel Road about 5 km from town off the Airport Road is the place where the first Catholic Missionaries to Uganda, Reverend Father Simon Lourdel and Brother Amans of the Society of White Fathers, landed on 17 February 1879. There is a small brick church marking the spot, a memorial plaque and painted statues commemorating these venerable missionaries.

For hotel and restaurant price codes and other relevant information, see pages 16-20.

● Where to stay

Entebbe *p69, map p71*
All accommodation in Entebbe arranges airport transfers; some are complementary at least 1-way or expect to pay around US$10.

$$$$ Pineapple Bay Resort, Bulago Island, reservations with **Wild Places**, T0414-251182, www.wildplacesafrica.com. This 200-ha island, 16 km from Entebbe and 7 km north of Ngamba Island, is accessed by charter flight from Entebbe, or 45-min speedboat from Entebbe or Munyonyo (see page 53). A luxury hideaway with 8 large chalets, some for families, swimming pool, pretty sandy beach, activities include fishing for Nile perch, birdwatching and you walk all over the forested island on a network of trails. Very remote and peaceful with stunning lake views.

$$$ Gately Inn, 2 Portal Rd, T0414-321313, www.gatelyinn.com. A pleasant and exceptionally friendly mid-range option with a relaxed guesthouse atmosphere. The 11 well-appointed rooms are in the main house or cottages in lovely gardens with DSTV and good hot showers. Restaurant serves a bistro-style and Thai menu, has sofas for relaxing and there's an excellent craft shop.

$$$ Laico Lake Victoria, Circular Rd, T0414-351600, www.laicohotels.com. Refurbished ex-government hotel in wonderful gardens with ancient trees and great lake views. Grand entrance, opulent furnishings, 144 large comfortable a/c rooms, Wi-Fi throughout, lovely pool with bar, gym, sauna and massages available.

$$$ Protea Hotel Entebbe, 36-40 Sebugwawo Drive, off Airport Rd, T0312-207500, www.proteahotels.com. Just 1 km from the airport and currently the best hotel in Entebbe, newly built with 73 stylish rooms, large pool, restaurant and set right on the beach with sweeping lake and sunset views. Top-rate service and quality from South Africa's **Protea** chain.

$$$-$$ Airport View Hotel, 34 Kiwafu Close, T0312-261751, www.airportview hoteluganda.com. Located in Kitoro 3 km from the airport, welcoming with 12 large modern rooms with Wi-Fi and DSTV. Restaurant offers a varied menu, pleasant bar, nice gardens with both airport and lake views. They are well used to early departures/late arrivals from the airport and offer the likes of early breakfasts and day rooms.

$$$-$$ Imperial Golf View Hotel, Circular Rd, T0417-304000, www.imperialhotels. co.ug. Adjacent to the golf course with great lake views, 86 modern rooms and good restaurant, this is by far the best of the 3 **Imperial** hotels in Entebbe; the others are the **Imperial Resort Beach Hotel** and the **Imperial Botanical Beach Hotel**, which, despite having fantastic beachside locations, are truly ugly concrete blocks with 100+ old-fashioned rooms and geared to the conference market. Rates for all are in the US$120-200 range.

$$ 2 Friends Beach Hotel, 3 Nambi Rd, T0772-236608, www.2friendshotel.com. Just north of the Botanical Gardens, this Norwegian-run stylish guesthouse has a lovely location opposite the beach and 16 arty individually decorated rooms with fantastic modern art on the wall, DSTV, free Wi-Fi, verandas and lake views, excellent food including beach barbecues, lovely pool and bar area surrounded by palms. The welcoming family also runs the **2 Friends Guesthouse** in Jinja (page 91).

$$ The Boma Entebbe, 20A Gowers Rd, T0772-467929, www.boma.co.ug. Converted from a 1940s colonial home, this quiet, family-run guesthouse in lovely grounds offers 16 excellent-value rooms with verandas. Restaurant offers home-made food, ice cream (recommended) and there's a well-stocked bar and pool.

$ Airport Guesthouse, 17 Mugula Rd, T0414-200221, www.gorillatours.com. 10 comfortable rooms, set in beautiful gardens with patio, delicious food, Wi-Fi and pleasant, helpful staff. Superb value from US$60 for a double and also an excellent gorilla tours enterprise.

$ Entebbe Backpackers and Campsite, aka **Frank's Place**, 33-35 Church Rd, T0414-320432, www.entebbebackpackers.com. Long-established backpackers situated just behind the **Laico Lake Victoria**, with 16 en suite rooms and cottages sleeping 2-4 (from US$20), an 8-bed dorm (US$8 per person) and camping (from US$4 per person) with your own or pre-erected tents, all set in a lovely garden under mango and guava trees heavy with fruit. Restaurant has a reasonably priced à la carte menu, or you can use the kitchen, lounge with DSTV and fully stocked bar.

$ Sunset Entebbe, 25 Church Rd, T0414-323502, www.sunsetentebbe.com. With helpful staff and 13 rooms set in a neat colonial bungalow, Wi-Fi, and leafy garden, this quiet motel-style place is great value. Double/twin from US$45, triple US$80, quad US$100 and rates include a generous buffet breakfast.

$ Uganda Wildlife Education Centre (UWEC), see page 72. A unique place to stay with 11 basic stone and thatch en suite *bandas* within the UWEC premises, some right next to the enclosures and with complementary nocturnal vocalizations from the lions and hyenas. Eat in the restaurant before 1900 or you can go out to town and a guard will escort you back to the accommodation. From US$60 for a double and rates include 24-hr entry to the centre.

🍴 Restaurants

Entebbe *p69, map p71*

$$$-$$ Faze 3, 6 Circular Rd, T0414-598080. Daily 1200-2300. Branch of the popular **Faze 2** restaurant in Kampala, and one of the best places to eat in Entebbe. Great lake views from the terrace, long menu of continental food, well known for its steaks (it also has a butchery on the premises). Live music every Fri evening.

$$-$ 4 Point, Kitoro Rd, near Barclays Bank, T0414-378826. Daily 1100-late. Popular with expats and UN workers, with a mixed menu from excellent Indian curries thanks to the Indian owners, to generous burgers and tilapia and chips. Large premises with grass-thatched roof and outdoor terrace.

$$-$ Goretti's Pizzeria & Bar, Nambi Rd, T0772-308887. Daily 0800-2200. Opposite **2 Friends** and right on the beach with waves lapping up to the tables. Relaxing outdoor place under palms with thatched bar and barbecue grill/pizza oven, long menu of pizzas, imported ingredients include salami and mozzarella, mains like tilapia fish prepared in numerous ways, such as pan-fried with lemon butter, or try the whole barbecued chicken to share.

$ Anna's Corner, Station Rd, near Gately Inn, T0772-505619. Daily 0900-2100. Lovely café/early evening restaurant with tables under gazebos in the garden, meals include breakfasts, hot and cold sandwiches, burgers and pastas, good veggie options, great coffee from Uganda, Burundi and Kenya, normal or iced. The **Lake Spa** is also here, T0414-695469, 0900-2100, for massages, manis, pedis and facials.

$ Nicky's Pizza, 19 Portal Rd, T0776-441234. Daily 1000-2400. Informal and relaxed with reasonable wood-fired pizzas from a giant oven, other dishes include fish and chicken and chips, gardens tables and the long bar has a dartboard and pool table.

🍸 Bars and clubs

Entebbe *p69, map p71*

4 Turkeys Pub, Kampala–Entebbe Highway, opposite Stanbic Bank, T0782-402335. Daily 1000-late. British-style pub, very popular, lively venue with TV for sports and pool tables. The menu offers snacks such as chicken wings, burgers and some Chinese dishes.

Red Rooster Sports Bar, 3 Church Rd. Daily 1100-late. Fun, loud bar run by an expat with red and black modern decor, loads of sports memorabilia and photos on the wall, large garden, average food includes grills like steaks, chicken and pork.

🛍 Shopping

Entebbe *p69, map p71*

The best range of crafts, which are beautifully presented and packaged, is at **Gately Inn** (see Where to stay, page 75) and the shop is open daily 0900-2100. The quality items are sourced from Uganda, Kenya and Zimbabwe. They also sell the nicely illustrated range of Uganda Maps (see page 16).

A large **Nakumatt** supermarket (0830-2200) has opened on the Kampala–Entebbe road about 1 km north of the centre near the Total petrol station. It's part of the Victoria Mall development, Entebbe's first modern mall, and also has a pharmacy, forex bureau and cafés.

Upland Supermarket, Kitoro Rd, near Barclays Bank, T0414-321880. Mon-Fri 0800-2000, Sat-Sun 0800-1700. Small but well-stocked supermarket, some imported goods including wine, plus it has a bakery so you could make up a picnic here to take the Botanical Gardens.

⏺ What to do

Entebbe *p69, map p71*
Golf

Entebbe Golf Club, Circular Rd, T0414-322067. This was the 1st golf course in East Africa, built in 1901 in a glorious position, and still popular. Non-members can play a round for about US$30 for 18 holes and you can rent clubs and hire a knowledgeable caddy. Spectators can watch from the club house which has a good veranda restaurant.

Swimming

Most of the large hotels allow day visitors to use their pools for around US$5 per day. The nicest is the massive pool at the **Laico Lake Victoria Hotel**, which has elevated diving boards, a separate kids' pool, a café and Wi-Fi. There are also good pools at the **Imperial Resort Beach Hotel** and the **Imperial Botanical Beach Hotel**, which also have stretches of white sandy private beaches with sun loungers (although swimming in the lake is inadvisable because of bilharzia). Very usefully these hotels will store luggage for the day if you are paying entry fee or having lunch, so the option is to come down from Kampala, spend the day in Entebbe to see the sights before a late flight.

Tour operators

Wild Frontiers, office at the Uganda Wildlife Education Centre (page 72), T0772-502155, Kampala T0414-321479, www.wildfrontiers.co.ug. Sunset and birdwatching boat cruises on Lake Victoria from US$35-75 depending on numbers and duration, plus fishing safaris for Nile perch from US$125 per person for half a day. They can also arrange boat transfers to the Ssese Islands as well as Murchison Falls boat cruises and fishing (see page 238 for their details there) and wildlife safaris throughout Uganda.

⊖ Transport

Entebbe *p69, map p71*

The Entebbe Taxi Park is 1 km south of the town centre in Kitoro, off Airport Rd. Fares are US$1.50-2 to and from **Kampala**. If you're heading from Entebbe towards the west of the country; either towards **Fort Portal** or **Masaka** and beyond, there's no need to go right into central Kampala to swap vehicles. Instead take a *matatu* from Entebbe to the Natete Taxi Park (or vice versa), which is 8 km west of Kampala on the Masaka road.

To get to the Ssese Islands, the Entebbe–**Lutoboka** (on **Buggala Island**) ferry service goes from Nakiwogo port, to the west of Entebbe. To get to **Nakiwogo**, turn off the Kampala–Entebbe Rd at Wilson St, also known as Nsamizi Rd, on to Nakiwogo Rd for 3 km. For details of the ferry, see page 129.

Contents

Jinja, Mount Elgon & the east

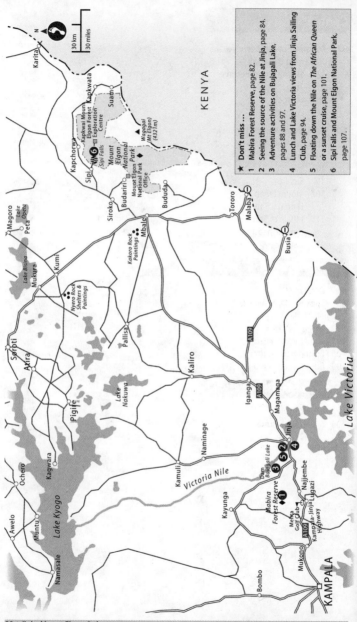

★ **Don't miss ...**

1 Mabira Forest Reserve, page 82.
2 Seeing the source of the Nile at Jinja, page 84.
3 Adventure activities on Bujagali Lake, pages 88 and 97.
4 Lunch and Lake Victoria views from Jinja Sailing Club, page 94.
5 Floating down the Nile on *The African Queen* or a sunset cruise, page 101.
6 Sipi Falls and Mount Elgon National Park, page 107.

The east of Uganda receives a relatively large number of visitors in addition to those passing through on their way to and from Kenya. The excellent Kampala–Jinja Highway is a busy road, with several towns and trading centres along the way. It first passes through Mabira Forest, where the huge trees, darkening the sunlight, tower over the road before it emerges once more into the brightness of sugarcane fields.

Less than two hours from the capital, Jinja is a very popular destination and one of the highlights of a visit to Uganda for activity-inspired travellers. First, spend a little time looking for the ripples of the Ripon Falls, the source of the River Nile, before going to the beautiful Bujagali area a little further north. Here the Nile flows through the newly created Bujagali Lake and, although a new dam has submerged the once-raging Bujagali Falls, the river downstream still offers some of the best whitewater rafting in Africa and there are countless other outdoor adventures to try.

Interest in climbing Mount Elgon (that straddles the Kenyan border) is increasing and many are taking the opportunity of exploring the caldera with its fascinating plant life. New access roads and trails have been developed enhancing the region, and the highest peaks can in fact only be reached from the Ugandan side. Exploring the gentle slopes and impressive caves in the foothills of Mount Elgon is an alternative activity for travellers who do not wish to climb the extinct volcano. Also here, the Sipi Falls are magnificent, and posters of them are seen all over Uganda. Good accommodation makes for a relaxing break in this pretty highland region.

Mabira Forest Reserve, Jinja and Bujagali

Mabira Forest contains more than 300 varieties of tree, several varieties of monkey, over 300 mainly forest bird species, and is also famed for its clouds of glorious butterflies. Areas of primary and secondary forest can be explored on foot or by bicycle via an extensive trail network.

The fabled River Nile, Africa's longest river, begins its epic journey northwards at the attractive town of Jinja, Uganda's second city. Jinja suffered badly under the Amin regime but some fine Asian-influenced architecture dating from the colonial era survives. Nearby are what were the impressive Bujagali Falls. But these have recently been submerged by a new dam, which has left in their place a picturesque lake of the same name. However, the whitewater rapids remain beyond the dam wall and the Bujagali area continues as Uganda's most exciting centre for adventure sports including rafting, kayaking, jet-boating, bungee jumping or exploring the countryside on quad bikes. More sedate activities are available such as horse riding, fishing, birdwatching, cycling or guided village walks.
▶▶ *For listing, see pages 91-102.*

Mabira Forest Reserve → *Colour map 2, B5.*

Arriving at Mabira Forest Reserve
The reserve is located 500 m north of Najjembe village on the Kampala–Jinja Road (A109), 55 km east of Kampala and 26 km west of Jinja. Open daily 0700-1900, US$8, children (6-16) US$4. Entry includes a guide but an extra tip of around US$15 per guide is usual. The visitor centre sells crafts, maps and bird books.

Visiting Mabira Forest Reserve
Mabira Forest straddles the Kampala–Jinja Highway and is an easy excursion from Kampala or Jinja. By *matatu* between both, get off at Najjembe village and walk the last 500 m through the forest to the visitor centre, which is in a lovely sunny glade and has picnicking facilities in traditional umbrella-thatched shelters. Wandering through both primary and secondary forest teeming with butterflies, birds and monkeys is the main attraction. From the visitor centre there are 10 looping trails and either guided or self-guided walks take one to four hours. If you are out to see the monkeys, it's best to go in the morning or during the late afternoon when the heat of the day has passed.

Mabira, technically a moist semi-deciduous forest, covers 306 sq km and ranges in height from 1070 m to 1340 m. Much is secondary forest, having been heavily influenced by human activity until the late 1980s. It was first leased in 1900 to the Mabira Forest (Uganda) Rubber Company, but the cost of clearing the dense forest around individual rubber trees was too high and the plantation was abandoned. It was declared a forest reserve in 1932 but over the years poor management practices increasing population pressure resulted in extensive encroachment into the reserve. A further threat to the forest was a government proposal in 2006 to allow almost a quarter of the area to be cleared for sugar plantations. A protest rally in Kampala in May 2007 resulted in at least three fatalities and, given the scale of the opposition, the proposal was dropped later that year. The reserve is now under the jurisdiction of the **National Forest Authority (NFA)**, with increasing collaboration from the local communities.

Mabira has an enormous biodiversity and the figures speak for themselves: 315 bird species, 312 tree species, 218 species of butterfly, 97 species of moth, 40 species of mammal, including the red-tailed, black-and-white colobus and vervet monkeys, and the grey-cheeked mangabey, as well as more than 20 species of shrew and rodent.

The large moth fauna here is quite typical of a large forest on the Victoria Lake crescent. The 97 recorded species, include seven range-restricted, three hawkmoth and four rare forest silkmoth species. Mabira has extremely rich butterfly fauna and supports species seldom found in Uganda, including several species with 'novel' distribution patterns and limited ranges. The bird community at Mabira Forest is especially rich, and, of the 300-odd species present, more than 50 can be viewed just from the picnic area next to the visitor centre. Almost half the species are strictly forest-dependent, and many rare birds have been recorded, including the blue swallow, the papyrus gonolek and the Nahan francolin. Other species present and seldom seen elsewhere in Uganda are the tit hylia, purple-throated cuckoo shrike and the grey apalis. Mabira is especially valuable for its lowland species as well; for example, the white-bellied kingfisher and the blue-crested flycatcher. Of the mammals, the normally elusive red-tailed monkey is fairly common and seen more often than black-and-white colobus. Blue duiker and bush-pigs are present but are rarely seen. Of the trees, the famous 'strangler fig', *Ficus nantalensis*, is widely present in the forest and is the source of the fibre for the bark-cloth that is traditional material to central Uganda.

Jinja → *For listing, see pages 91-102. Phone code: 0434. Colour map 2, B5.*

Jinja is at the head of Napoleon Gulf, at the northern end of Lake Victoria, on the east bank of the Victoria Nile. It would probably be a fairly nondescript town if it were not famous for being the source of the Nile; the point at which the great river exits Lake Victoria and commences its 6695-km journey to the Mediterranean. Practically everything to do with the town is connected to the river: electricity production, brewing and tourism being its main sources of income.

Jinja suffered severely during the bad times, particularly when all Asians were expelled from Uganda by Amin in 1972 as the town had a high Indian population. But it is now a pretty and vibrant place covering a wide area and, with an estimated population of 120,000, is Uganda's second largest urban space after Kampala. The shops in the main streets are well maintained and, as you walk through the town, you will see the old colonial and Asian bungalows in their spacious gardens, many of which have been renovated. The section popular with tourists is around Main Street, where there is a grid street pattern, home to most of the shops, cafés, restaurants, banks and internet cafés, while the garden suburbs to the west and south have some reasonable accommodation options.

Arriving in Jinja
Getting there and around Jinja lies on the A109 82 km east of Kampala and 128 km west of Tororo. The journey from Kampala to Jinja takes around two hours by bus or *matatu*. To get to hotels in Jinja and around directly from Entebbe International Airport (120 km), the airport shuttle bus companies (page 38) charge around US$85 for one to three people and US$110 for four or five. The whitewater rafting and other activity companies at Bujagali (8 km north of Jinja) offer their clients free daily transfers from Kampala. An alternative route from Kampala is to go 22 km from the city to Mukono on the A109 and

head northeast for 50 km on the good tarred road to Kayunga. This loops around the top of Mabira Forest Reserve; just before Kayunga there's a fork and the road goes southeast for 48 km to Jinja past the Bujagali resorts on the west bank of the Nile. This is roughly 30 km longer than the A109 but is a favorable alternative if traffic is heavy on the main road (which it often is). From Kenya, the long-distance buses that ply the route between Nairobi, Nakuru and Eldoret and Kampala stop in Jinja. Once in town, there are plenty of special hire taxis, *matatus* and *boda-bodas* to get around. ▸▸ *See Transport, page 100.*

Background

Jinja is a Lugandan word meaning 'stone', and the name is thought to have originated because the area around the Ripon Falls was where the river could be breached over large flat rocks. For the original inhabitants, the location was a crossing point for trade, migration and a launch for boats. The town of Jinja was founded in 1901 by the British as an administrative centre for the Busoga region. It was around this time that a lake steamer service operated between Jinja and Port Florence (today's Kisumu in Kenya), the port that became the terminus of the railway from Mombasa on the coast. This railway access led to the establishment of cotton and sugar plantations (both export crops that thrived in the climate), and Jinja grew in size. By 1906 a street pattern had been laid out and Indian traders moved in from around 1910. Also in 1910, Winston Churchill passed through the region on his epic journey down the Nile, after which he advocated the idea of a dam to harness the power of the Nile and help Uganda's economy develop.

The Owen Falls Dam opened in 1954 and the Ripon Falls (and its flat rocks) were submerged. Thanks to the dam and the power generated from its hydroelectric Nalubaale Power Station, Jinja was the manufacturing heart of Uganda between 1954 and the early 1970s. But Amin expelled the Indians – who ran many of the industries – from Uganda, Jinja fell into economic decline. However, since the 1990s, many businesses (Indian or otherwise) have been re-established in Jinja, and today the Kakira Sugar Works is one of the largest sugar producers in East Africa (sugar plantations flank the town on all sides). Economically the town has also benefited from its location on the main road that runs from Mombasa to Kampala and cities in the other landlocked countries of East Africa.

Source of the Nile

Although Lake Victoria has many feeder rivers and streams, which makes any claim to being the true source of the Nile highly contentious in modern times, the lake was considered to be the source of the White Nile by the early explorers and is still celebrated as such today. The second tributary, the Blue Nile, emerges from Lake Tana in Ethiopia and joins the White Nile in Khartoum, Sudan. The White Nile is longer, so it's from Jinja that the mighty river begins its 6695-km journey through four countries – Uganda, South Sudan, Sudan and Egypt – on a course that takes the water on a three-month journey from Lake Victoria to the Mediterranean.

The source of the Nile was originally designated at the site of the Ripon Falls. These were submerged during the construction of the Owen Falls Dam in 1954, although ripples can still be seen from the picnic areas overlooking the river on both the east and west banks. The islets and rocks recorded by Speke (see box, page 86) also disappeared when the dam was built.

Confusingly, there are two places facing each other across the river where you can see the source of the Nile. On the west bank, 3 km from Jinja, is the **Speke Memorial and**

Jinja

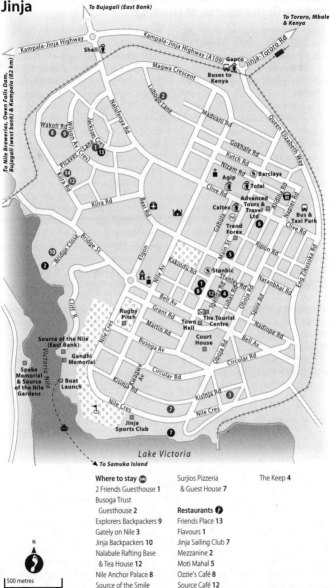

Where to stay 🏠
2 Friends Guesthouse **1**
Busoga Trust
  Guesthouse **2**
Explorers Backpackers **9**
Gately on Nile **3**
Jinja Backpackers **10**
Nalabale Rafting Base
  & Tea House **12**
Nile Anchor Palace **8**
Source of the Smile
  Guesthouse **14**

Surjios Pizzeria
  & Guest House **7**

Restaurants 🍴
Friends Place **13**
Flavours **1**
Jinja Sailing Club **7**
Mezzanine **2**
Moti Mahal **5**
Ozzie's Café **8**
Source Café **12**
Space Café **6**

The Keep **4**

Speke and the source of the Nile

John Hanning Speke was an officer of the British army in the East India Company, and in 1854 he eagerly joined an expedition to explore East Africa under the command of Captain Richard Burton. While in Berbera in Somaliland, the explorers were involved in a fierce battle with tribesmen and both were wounded, Speke almost fatally. Rightly or wrongly, Speke believed that Burton had questioned his courage during this incident, and it went on to bother him for the rest of his life and caused a growing hostility between the two men. Nevertheless, Speke joined Burton on another expedition to East Africa in 1856 organized by the Royal Geographical Society. The goal was supposedly to follow up rumours that there was a great lake in the interior, the so-called Sea of Ujiji, but in reality the search was on for the source of the Nile.

The expedition departed from Zanzibar and in February 1858, they discovered Lake Tanganyika. After three months exploring the lake, both Burton and Speke became ill and the expedition started back towards the coast. However, they had heard tell of another huge

lake to the north of Tanganyika. Speke, who had by now recovered, set off in command of a small party and in August 1858 came upon what he later described as "a vast expanse" of "the pale-blue waters" of the northern lake. He named it Lake Victoria after his queen and believed, correctly, that it was the source of the Nile. But Burton wouldn't accept Speke's claim to have discovered the Nile's source, for which he felt there was no convincing evidence. He believed that the true source was more likely to be 'his' Lake Tanganyika. However, Speke got back to England before Burton in 1859, and announced that he had found the source of the Nile. Burton felt belittled and was infuriated by Speke's account of the expedition.

The Royal Geographical Society sent Speke back to Africa to substantiate his Nile claims. The expedition left the coast in September 1860, but there were delays because of complications in negotiations with the local rulers whose territories the expedition had to pass through and with the Arab traders from whom it needed supplies. Finally, in February 1862, the powerful king of Buganda (Mutesa I)

Source of the Nile Gardens ⓘ *daily 0600-1830, US$4, children (under 16) US$2, car US$1, to get there, take a boda-boda over the dam wall towards Kampala, then turn left just before Nile Breweries and go along Nalufenya Rd, then several turnings make it a little complicated but ask the way and the gardens are on the river side of the railway line.* Many people consider this setting on the west bank to be much more atmospheric than the other side, and it is lovely to sit on the lawns in the shade listening to the birds and watching the swirling river below. A plaque mounted on a small rock known as the **Speke Memorial** indicates the spot where Speke stood when he first sighted the source of the Nile on 28 July 1862. There are faded information boards including a drawing of the falls before they were submerged. It's a popular place for picnics and weddings, and you can negotiate to camp in the well-maintained gardens – a formal campsite with bathrooms is presently being built. On the eastern bank, easier to access from the town by *boda-boda* or a 30-minute walk on Cliff Road is the other **'Source of the Nile' venture** ⓘ *daily 0600-1830, US$5.* However, the little park here is not as appealing as the gardens on the other side, with surly staff, vendors selling overpriced souvenirs, and a dilapidated bar. To see the allowed Speke to proceed to the point on Lake Victoria where a great river issued from the lake. He reached what he named Ripon Falls (after Lord Ripon, president of the Royal Geographical Society) on 28 July 1862 and became the first European to see the source of the Nile.

Back in London, he published his books *The Journal of the Discovery of the Source of the Nile*, in 1863 and, in 1864, *What Led to the Discovery of the Source of the Nile*, about the earlier expedition. Unfortunately for him, both books were badly edited and appeared inaccurate and disagreeably boastful. Burton was still refusing to admit that Speke had discovered the source of the Nile. He claimed that, because Speke had not followed the river from the place it flowed out of Lake Victoria to Gondokoro (the limit of navigability of the Nile, which is today in South Sudan), he could not be sure they were the same river.

The two men were at loggerheads and a debate between them was scheduled at the British Association for the Advancement of Science for 16 September 1864. It was dubbed 'the Nile duel' by the Royal Geographical Society. But Speke went partridge shooting in Wiltshire the day before, climbed over a wall with his gun cocked and tragically shot himself. His death was probably an accident, but rumours spread that he had committed suicide because he was too scared to face Burton in debate. He was 37 when he died. It took another 13 years (4 April 1875) before Henry Morton Stanley's epic circumnavigation of Lake Victoria finally proved Speke had been correct and that Lake Victoria was indeed the source of the Nile.

Speke recorded the moment of his discovery by saying:
"Most beautiful was the scene, nothing could surpass it! It was the very perfection of the kind of effect aimed at in a highly kept park; with a magnificent stream from 600 to 700 yds wide, dotted with islets and rocks, the former occupied by fishermens' huts, the latter by terns and crocodiles basking in the sun, flowing between fine high grassy banks, with rich trees and plantains in the background. The expedition had now performed its functions; old Father Nile without any doubt rises in the Victoria Nyanza."

spot designated as the source of the Nile, you need to take a short boat ride by motorized canoe to a tiny rocky island in the river, which sits in the small remaining eddies of the Ripon Falls. It's overpriced and you'll have to negotiate hard (roughly US$15-20 for the 30-minute excursion for up to four people). The actual 'source' is pretty disappointing, just a few bubbles coming to the surface, but it's good for birdwatching and, once on the island, the unabashed touristy thing to do is to sit on the piece of cement in the middle and put your left hand in Lake Victoria and your right hand in the River Nile. The boats will drop you on the other side at the Source of the Nile Gardens if you want to visit both sites, though entry fees apply.

Another attraction in the east bank gardens is the **Gandhi Memorial**, dedicated to Mahatma Gandhi. Although he never visited Uganda, the bronze bust commemorates Gandhi's decision to have a portion of his ashes sprinkled in the Nile here in 1948. The memorial was put up by the Hindu community in Uganda and unveiled in 1997 by Indian Prime Minister Gujral accompanied by President Museveni. Gandhi spent 21 years of his illustrious career in Africa where he championed the rights of the downtrodden and

Owen Falls Dam

The 831-m-long and 31-m-high Owen Falls Dam was constructed in 1954 and was officially opened by Queen Elizabeth II. It completely submerged both the Owen Falls, 4 km upstream from Lake Victoria, and the Ripon Falls, the point at which the river leaves Lake Victoria – the source of the Nile. It was later renamed **Nalubaale**, which is the Luganda name for Lake Victoria, but is still commonly known by the old name. Its hydroelectric Nalubaale Power Station was the major source of electricity in Uganda and a good part of Kenya for many years. During the turmoil of the Amin period a group of dedicated engineers managed to keep the generators going almost without interruption. While it still generates electricity, its volume has been superseded by the new US$800 million **Bujagali Hydroelectric Power Station**, 9.7 km upstream, immediately north of the former location of the Bujagali Falls. This became operational and was officially inaugurated in October 2012 by Ugandan President Museveni and His Highness Aga Khan IV in the presence of African politicians and investors. Today the **Nalubaale Bridge** that spans the top of Owen Falls Dam forms a spectacular gateway to Jinja. It is one of only two road crossings over the Nile in Uganda; the other is Karuma Bridge at the southeastern corner of Murchison Falls National Park. If you're crossing the dam in a vehicle, try and get a seat on the appropriate side (left if you are heading east) in order to get a good view of the Nile below.

marginalized communities. It was his wish that some of his ashes be sprinkled in the Nile, perhaps to cement his long-lasting relationship with the continent.

Unveiled on the same day in 1997 by Guiral and Museveni, in the compound of the **Hindu Temple** on Bell Avenue, is a full-figure statue of Gandhi. He is holding a stick in the right hand and a book in the left, while sporting his famously simple traditional Indian *dhoti* and shawl. On 2 October, Gandhi's birthday, Jinja's Hindu community pays homage to their country's founding father by visiting both the memorial and statue and presenting flowers.

Bujagali → For listing, see pages 91-102.

About 9 km downstream from the Owen Falls Dam are what were the Bujagali Falls. This was a spectacular tiered waterfall of about 1 km of raging whitewater flowing down a cataract and splitting the Nile into several channels separated by rocky outcrops of forest-clad islands. Since the new **Bujagali Hyrdoelectric Power Station** and its dam were built 3 km downstream, the river has been diverted through the turbines of the dam and some of the rapids disappeared. The river flattened out, and the site of the falls has now become what is commonly referred to as **Bujagali Lake**. The river is actually no wider or higher than it was; a reservoir is not needed for the new dam as Lake Victoria serves that purpose, and the water simply passes through Owen Falls Dam and on through Bujagali Dam. The name Bujagali Lake would probably stick more easily if it were not for the celebrated association of **Bujagali Falls** as being one of Africa's top spots for whitewater rafting and other adventure activities. And in fact it still is; the falls may have gone but it remains an impossibly pretty spot fringed with woodland full of birds and monkeys, there's a great choice of accommodation for all budgets. Rafting and kayaking trips now start below the new dam and extend into the section that was originally reserved for two-day trips, and there are numerous other things to do. Indeed, some of the activities, such as fishing, birdwatching and sunset cruises, have been developed around the newly formed lake. So Bujagali is still very much on the tourist circuit and it remains one of Uganda's most popular destinations. How long you stay, rather depends on how much you want to do.

Arriving in Bujagali

Getting there The site of the former falls (now Bujagali Lake) is roughly 8 km north of Jinja. All rafting companies offer return transfers from Kampala and Jinja, and if you're under your own steam, a long day visit from Kampala or Entebbe by private or public

Bujagali

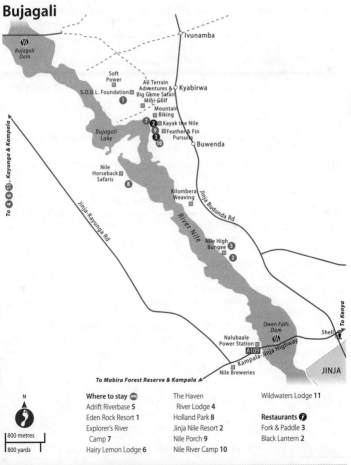

Where to stay	The Haven	Wildwaters Lodge 11
Adrift Riverbase 5	River Lodge 4	
Eden Rock Resort 1	Holland Park 8	**Restaurants**
Explorer's River	Jinja Nile Resort 2	Fork & Paddle 3
Camp 7	Nile Porch 9	Black Lantern 2
Hairy Lemon Lodge 6	Nile River Camp 10	

N
800 metres
800 yards

transport is possible. The accommodation and tourist activities are either on the east or west bank of the Nile.

For the east bank, turn north of the Kampala–Jinja Highway at the Shell roundabout (where the Shell petrol station is), and continue for a further 7 km along the Jinja–Budonda road, passing the turn-off to **Jinja Nile Resort** along the way. The sealed road changes to murram. Watch out for speed bumps, children, cyclists and unlit vehicles. Pass through Buwenda village, across a small valley and, as you climb out, take a well-signposted left-hand turn at Kyabirwa village for 500 m to the river.

The facilities on the west bank are accessed by a tarred road. Turn north off the Kampala–Jinja Highway at the roundabout opposite Nile Breweries on the western side of the Owen Falls Dam. *Boda-bodas* and special hire taxis are always available from this and the Shell roundabout (see above).

An alternative route from Kampala is to go 22 km from the city to Mukono on the Kampala–Jinja Highway and head northeast for 50 km on the good tarred road to Kayunga. This loops around the top of **Mabira Forest Reserve**, and just before Kayunga there's a fork and the road goes southeast for 48 km to Jinja, past the Bujagali resorts on the west bank. *Matatus* from Kampala go to Kayunga, where you can swap on to one going to Jinja. **Note**: the rafting companies use this route for their return journeys from Jinja to Kampala as they pick up their rafting clients from the river at the finishing points near Kayunga.

Background

It is said that the falls were named after a 15th-century spiritual leader called Mandwa Budhagali. After 1954, when construction work on the Owens Falls Dam was completed and the Ripon Falls were submerged, and as the population of Jinja grew, people seeking a day out beside the Nile started to visit Bujagali Falls. Until the end of Uganda's civil war, there were still large populations of crocodile and hippo; sadly there are none today, but it is still a hotspot for many species of endemic and migratory birds. Then, when overland trucks started visiting Uganda from the 1980s, it became a tradition to overnight at the falls on the way to Kampala and beyond. After 1996 (when **Adrift** and **Nile River Explorers** started up), this section of the Nile became very popular for whitewater rafting. The first major rapid was Bujagali Falls – a short sharp cascade dropping 4 m, which entitled the river to have a Grade V rafting status – before going through a 28-km series of furious whitewater interspersed with calm stretches and finishing with the 'Bad Place' at Itanda Falls. Over the years numerous other activity operations developed to cater to these young and adventurous travellers, and budget *bandas* and campsites provided the first tourist accommodation. These are now highly developed in commanding riverside locations, and there are also a clutch of upmarket resorts making the most of the scenic first 20 km or so of the Nile. With a climate that has an average temperature of 27°C, and water temperature year round of 23°C, it is an ideal location for outdoor adventures.

For hotel and restaurant price codes and other relevant information, see pages 16-20.

Where to stay

Mabira Forest Reserve *p82*

$$$ The Rain Forest Lodge, 2 km south of Najjembe on the opposite of the Kampala–Jinja Highway to the visitor centre, reservations Kampala T0414-258273, www.geolodges.com. Built of natural materials with 12 spacious timber cottages nestling in forest glades with balconies looking directly into the canopy of trees, an elevated restaurant and bar and swimming pool. It's a popular weekend retreat from Kampala.

$ Little Kingston da Global Village, Buikwe Rd, Najjembe, T0712-536133. This friendly and cheap Belgian/Ugandan guesthouse offers 4 double/twin rooms (US$10), a 4-bed dorm (US$4 per person) plus camping (US$2 per person) with shared toilets and (cold) showers, all set in a pretty gated garden. The restaurant/bar favours reggae music and has Wi-Fi.

$ Mabira Forest Camp, also known as **Griffin Falls Campsite**, near Wasswa Village, 10 km north of Lugazi on the Kampala–Jinja Highway and 11 km west of Najjembe and the visitor centre, T0751-949368, www.mabiraforestcamp. com. Community-run camp in the west of the forest and accessed from Lugazi; you can get a *boda-boda* for the last 10 km through sugar plantations. This is much quieter experience than the facilities at Najjembe, where there is a constant traffic drone. A clutch of huts and a campsite are in a lovely forest glade, simple accommodation with beds and nets and local buffet meals can be provided. Self-contained doubles US$25, tent or dorm bed US$10 per person, camping US$6 per person. Guided forest walks to the pretty Griffin Falls take about 1 hr, and mountain bikes are for hire. The Mabira Forest entry permit (page 82) is additional.

$ Mabira Forest Tourism Centre, near the visitor centre, T0712-487173. The **National Forestry Authority (NFA)** offers a campsite and 3 simple *bandas* sleeping 2-4. Outside toilets, and a bucket of hot water can be provided for washing. There's firewood for cooking, or a local cook can provide meals or cook your own food at reasonable rates; but order well ahead of time. Alternatively, you can eat at **Little Kingston da Global Village**, and Najjembe is famous for its delicious grilled chicken that's bought on the roadside. Doubles US$8 and a *banda* US$10, camping US$3; forest permits are extra.

Jinja *p83, map p85*

$$$-$$ Gately on Nile, 34 Kisinja Rd, T0434-122400, www.gatelyonnile.com. The sister property to the **Gately Inn** in Entebbe (page 75), this is centred around a beautiful refurbished old colonial house set in 1.6 ha of stunning grounds. The cheaper of the 9 rooms are in the main house, while the more expensive are in spacious double-storey cottages with expansive lake views, balconies/terraces, stone showers and kitchenettes. The restaurant (page 94) is worth visiting even if staying elsewhere.

$$ 2 Friends Guesthouse, 6 Jackson Cres, T0783-160804, www.2friends.info. One of Jinja's best and most stylish guesthouses, 18 comfortable rooms either in the main house or by the poolside with touches of contemporary African decor, lush tropical gardens enhanced by sculptures and an excellent restaurant (see page 94). Deservedly popular and under the same Norwegian ownership as **2 Friends Beach Hotel** in Entebbe (page 75).

$$ Source of the Smile Guest House, 39 Kiira Rd, T0783-842021, www.sourceof thesmile.com. Well-regarded option with eclectic arty decor of lanterns, mosaics and colourful fabrics, and another enterprise of the extended Norwegian family that runs 2 Friends. The 11 rooms have terraces and fans, thatched outdoor bar/lounge, pool and Wi-Fi. Breakfast included and other meals can be delivered from Friends Place restaurant if you don't want to go out.

$$ Surjios Pizzeria & Guest House, 24 Kisinja Rd, T0772-500400, www.surjios. com. A former presidential lodge, now a guesthouse with good river and lake views from the patio, 23 rooms in the main house or nicer newer block with balconies, pool, TV lounge and Wi-Fi. As the name suggests, they serve excellent pizzas cooked in wood-fired oven in the garden; non-guests are welcome (1230-1430 and 1730-2130).

$ Busogo Trust Guest House, 18 Lubogo Lane, T0772-653306, www.busogatrust. co.uk. Late colonial house c1950, a 10 min-walk from town, 3 8-bed dorms and 7 en suite double/twins, attractive garden with a barbecue, rates include breakfast and there's a kitchen for self-catering. Popular with NGOs. Profits go towards the purposeful Busogo Trust charity that provide water wells, hygiene and sanitation education to rural villages.

$ Explorers Backpackers, run by Nile River Explorers (page 100), 41 Wilson Av, T0772-422373, www.raftafrica.com. Excellent set-up in a comfortable house with a lovely garden with hammocks, bar, free tea and coffee until 1000, inexpensive meals, pool table, Wi-Fi, DSTV, hot showers and laundry facilities. Free Kampala–Jinja shuttle, must be pre-booked. Deals can be done on accommodation if you are rafting with them. They can help organize gorilla permits in Uganda and Rwanda and other bookings such as Ngamba (Chimp) Island. Doubles US$30, dorm US$12 per person, camping US$7 per person.

$ Jinja Backpackers, 8 Bridge Close, T0775-860876, www.jinjabackpackers.com. Lively set-up with a large thatched bar serving coffee and muffins during the day and

Wi-Fi. Dorms US$10 per person, camping US$5 per person. The excellent **Mezzanine** restaurant is here (see page 94). They can organize sunset boat trips for US$15 to the Source of the Nile.

$ Nalubale Rafting Base & Tea House, 38 Kiira Rd, T0782-638938, www.nalubale rafting.com. A simpler place and smaller than the other budget options, in a sprawling 1950s house, home to Bujagali's **Nalubale Rafting** who offers a free night's accommodation if rafting with them. Snack menu (including tea), 24 dorm beds in 5 rooms (US$10 per person), or camping (US$5 per person). Affiliated with **Nile River Camp** at Bujagali which has better accommodation including rooms.

$ Nile Anchor Palace, 4 Wakoli Pl ace, T0712-600223, www.nileanchorpalace.com. An alternative to the backpackers and great value and exceptionally friendly set up in a lovely old restored colonial house not far from **Explorers**. The 18 rooms are simply decorated but spacious and airy, the ones in the newer block have balconies, Wi-Fi and good breakfasts. Doubles/twins from US$40 and an extra bed is US$20.

Bujagali *p88, map p89*
East bank of the Nile
There are 2 main centres on the eastern side: the first is **Adrift's Riverbase** and **Jinja Nile Resort**, approximately 4 km from the Shell roundabout in Jinja; the second, larger centre is at Bujagali Lake, 5 km further along the same road.

$$$ Jinja Nile Resort, 4 km from Jinja, T0434-122190, www.madahotels.com. A large sprawling development in 8 ha of gardens with spectacular views across the river and its lush mid-stream islands. There are 140 cottages with private balconies. Ttry for a downriver outlook, otherwise the Owen Falls Dam 1 km away spoils the view a bit. Facilities include 4 restaurants with fairly expensive buffets, 4 bars, a sauna, gym, tennis, squash, pool and 'chip & putt' golf. Popular weekend retreat from Kampala and conference venue. Non-guests can use the pool for the day for US$4 and eat at the pool bar.

$$ Nile Porch, 8 km from Jinja, T0782-321541, www.nileporch.com. A mid-range and quiet option with 8 very comfortable thatched-roof safari tents with river-facing verandas and 2 family 2-bed cottages sleeping 5 and overlooking the neat swimming pool. All furnished with locally sourced furniture and set in leafy gardens with decorative ponds. There's a boat for birding and fishing excursions and the excellent **Black Lantern** restaurant (see page 95). This is the base for **Soft Power Education**, a charity that offers volunteer opportunities (see page 99).

$$-$ Eden Rock Resort, 8 km from Jinja, T0434-131476, www.edenrocknile.com. Set slightly back from the river so no expansive views but the advantage is a lovely swimming pool and wonderful tropical gardens. 20 thatched and stone *bandas* (from US$40), some with lofts for children; also bunks for dorms (US$8 per person) and camping on a shady lawn (US$5 per person). Quiet and friendly, food includes excellent grilled tilapia fish, and it's over the road from **Explorers River Camp** (see below) if you're in a party mood.

$ Adrift Riverbase, 4 km from Jinja, T0312-237438, www.adrift.ug. Previously the **Nile High Camp** (the bungee jump here is still called the **Nile High Bungee**, see page 97). Well-organized, popular budget venue on a little cliff behind the Jinja Nile Resort, with great river views and an all-day clifftop bar and restaurant showing videos of the day's rafting action. Offers 8 safari tents and 3 wooden chalets from US$50, 36 dorm beds US$10 per person, and camping on lush lawns US$5 per person. **Adrift**, the first company to raft the Nile, offers a variety of whitewater rafting trips (page 100) and a free Kampala–Jinja shuttle.

$ Explorers River Camp, 8 km from Jinja, T0772-422373, www.raftafrica.com. Run by **Nile River Explorers** (see page 100 for rafting options). Wonderfully positioned overlooking the expanse of the river, with fabulous views, and a fantastic spot to watch the sun set. Accommodation comprises en suite twin rooms (US$50), safari tents nestling on the terraces (US$25-30), dorms (from US$12 per person) and a campsite (US$7 per person), plus the liveliest bar in Bujagali (**Fork & Paddle**, see Restaurants, below), free Wi-Fi, laundry and a little sandy beach and jetty for swimming in the Nile. Free Kampala–Jinja shuttle. Very popular, booking advised.

$ Nile River Camp, 8 km from Jinja, T0776-900450, www.camponthenile.com. Owned by **Nile Porch** next door, and the base for **Nalubale Rafting**, with 10 twin/double safari-style tents with river views (US$54), dorms (US$12 per person), and the campsite (US$6 per person), which is especially nice with levelled-off sites on the hillside. Large open bar area with DSTV and Wi-Fi, the menu includes home-baked bread and barbecues, mountain bikes for hire, a rope-swing over the river, and swimming pool that non-guests can use for US$4 a day. Free Kampala–Jinja shuttle.

West bank of the Nile

The places on the west bank are listed with their distance from Jinja, but they can be just as easily reached on the back road from Kampala via Kayunga, see page 90 for these directions.

$$$$ Wildwaters Lodge, 26 km from Jinja, the jetty and car park is 3 km down a murram road from Kangulumira, reservations T0312-37438, lodge 0772-237400, www.wild-uganda.com. Owned by Adrift and in a sublime location perched on granite rocks on the 6.5 ha mid-stream Muyanja Island by Kalagala Falls. with rapids roaring all around. 10 elevated luxury suites nestle in the rainforest with amazing river views and are linked by raised wooden walkways to the restaurant, bar and library. There's a lovely swimming pool carved out of rocks, and activities include fishing and guided walks as well as the usual Bujagali adventures. Most guests get here by the free Adrift Kampala–Jinja shuttle. Day visitors are welcome for the short canoe ride and use of the pool for a US$25 fee, lunch extra. There are plans underway to build the **Kalagala Falls Tented Camp**, with 16 safari tents overlooking the falls (**$$$**) with its own facilities, and a **campsite** (**$**); check with **Adrift** for progress. *The African Queen* is also based here (see box, page 101).

$$$ The Haven River Lodge, 20 km from Jinja, T0702-905959, www.thehaven-uganda.com. A peaceful lodge located on a bluff that overlooks the first rapids of the river where rafting now starts. 8 *bandas* or cottages and 1 lovely honeymoon suite with terraces, restaurant, bar and Wi-Fi. They rent out canoes, mountain bikes and fishing tackle, and you can camp (**$**) at a pretty site on the river with your own tent or they provide tents with mattresses and bedding. Campers can eat at the lodge.

$$ Holland Park, 5 km from Jinja, T0782-507788, www.hollandparkuganda.com. The only self-catering accommodation at Bujagali with sweeping views of the new lake from a grassy hill, 3 double-storey chalets sleeping 4 and 1 double safari tent, very well equipped including towels, and there's a swimming pool. Close to **Nile Horseback Safaris** (page 98) and, if you don't want to cook, the boatman will take you across the river to the **Black Lantern Restaurant** (page 95).

$$-$ Hairy Lemon, 38 km from Jinja, T077-282 8338. From the Jinja–Katunga road, turn off at the village of Nazigo for 8 km, at the end park at the house with all the flowers, walk down the hill and summon the boatman by banging on the tyre rim; the last canoe leaves for the island at 1800. It's about 1 hr from Jinja so from Kampala use the back road via Katunga. This beautiful secluded island close to the new rafting takeout point is only accessed by boat, and as all supplies are ferried across.

Advanced booking is essential. Popular with international kayakers on long stays and families from Kampala, it's basic and maybe too quiet for some but has a laid-back vibe with a cushion-strewn outdoor lounge, small beach for swimming, and buffet meals in the outdoor restaurant and bar. 8 twin/double/family *bandas* (from US$60 per person), dorms (from US$38 per person), camping (US$30 per person) Rates include tea, coffee and 3 wholesome meals a day.

🍴 Restaurants

Jinja *p83, map p85*
Thanks to Jinja having such a touristy vibe and international community, there are plenty of restaurants and cafés for quality international food. For cheap eats there are numerous local eating houses along Main St and around the market.

$$$ Gately on Nile Restaurant, see Where to stay, page 91. Daily 0700-2100. Serves excellent continental and authentic Thai food in beautiful lush gardens; try and get a table in one of the private gazebos. Sensibly priced winelist and efficient friendly service.

$$$-$$ Friends Place (formerly 2 Friends Restaurant), next to the guesthouse of the same name, 6 Jackson Cres, T0772-984821. Daily 1100-2300. Outdoor thatched restaurant with a varied menu including grills, fish, steaks, pizzas, Indian and local dishes, and small but decent winelist. The lovely bar has relaxing tables under palm trees with Wi-Fi.

$$$-$$ Jinja Sailing Club, 1-5 Pier Rd, T0434-420222. Daily 1230-2300. Jinja's newest offering in a fantastic lakeside location and recently rebuilt by Masara who run **Mweya Safari Lodge** in QENP and lodges at Murchison Falls. Formal indoor restaurant and tables on the grass next to the water. Excellent fish, Indian dishes and rich desserts. Staff wear jaunty sailor uniforms.

$$ Mezzanine Restaurant and Bar, at Jinja Backpackers (see page 92), T0774-730659, www.mezzanine-jinja.com. Daily 1100-2300. A picturesque setting with river views from the upstairs floor (hence the name), great for a sundowner, well known for its fish and also offers pizzas, wraps, salads and burgers and caters well for vegetarians. Popular with the rafting fraternity so can sometimes be in a party mood.

$$-$ Flavours, 12 Main St, T0776-263333, www.enjoyflavours.com. Tue-Sun 0830-2130. Offers filling mains, sandwiches and burgers, coffee, smoothies, wine and beer, and there's Wi-Fi and a book exchange. Shows movies on a big screen in the garden every Wed at 2000 and interesting modern paintings and sculptures by local artists are for sale.

$ Moti Mahal, 46 Iganga Rd, T0718-357199. Daily 1200-2130. Bare decor with plastic tables, but swift and friendly service and tasty North Indian food; caters well for vegetarians. A main dish with unlimited rice and naan bread can be as little as US$10 and they give a free ice cream after every meal.

Cafés
The Keep, 12 Iganga Rd, T0788-073649. Daily 0800-2200. Named because of its mock-castle exterior and run by a pleasant American couple serving good espresso coffee, delicious milkshakes, a range of wholesome meals and famous for its American-inspired bagels and brownies. Outdoor tables and Wi-Fi. Profits go to a Christian charity.

Ozzie's Café, Main St, opposite **Source Café**. 0800-1800, Fri and Sat until 2100. Lively venue offering Western dishes such as burgers, pizzas, pasta, full English breakfast, milkshakes and cakes at reasonable prices. Popular with the many expats around Jinja. Service can be slow though.

Source Café, 20 Main St, T0434-412 0911, www.source.co.ug. Mon-Sat 0800-1900. Serves coffees, juices, home-made cakes and light meals in a 1920s house with pavement tables. Also has a gift shop

selling cards and batiks and has internet facilities. Profits go to poverty alleviation projects in the region.

Space Café, 49 Lubas Rd, T0434-121183. Mon-Thu and Sun 0700-2200, Fri and Sat until 2400. Another café/bar that's open late with international dishes such as burgers, pizzas, pasta, full English breakfasts, milkshakes and cakes at reasonable prices. Popular with the many expats around Jinja.

Bujagali *p88, map p89*
East bank of the Nile
All the places to stay have great restaurants in river locations. Around the turn-off at Kyabirwa village down to **Nile River Explorers** and the other places are a number of stalls and *duki* (small shops) selling souvenirs and street snacks including the famous 'Bujagali Rolex' – a *chapatti* stuffed with an omelet and avocado.

$$$-$$ Black Lantern, attached to the **Nile Porch** (page 93). Daily 0730-2130. Wonderful location high above the Nile under a large thatched roof with a spacious veranda overlooking the newly formed lake. Famous for its 1-kg servings of pork spare ribs but also offers a great range of international dishes, full English breakfasts and the grilled tilapia fish from the river is very tasty. Must make a reservation if not staying.

$ Fork & Paddle, **Explorers River Camp** (see page 93). Daily 0800-late. A lively bar with food, music and videos of the day's rafting adventures. Food on offer includes burgers, chips, baked potatoes, steak rolls, vegetarian meals and desserts. The well-stocked bar has a huge choice of drinks with guaranteed cold beers.

O Shopping

Jinja *p83, map p85*
There are several small supermarkets scattered along Main St and Clive Rd. Compared to Kampala's frenetic markets, Jinja's main market near the taxi park is

relaxed and fairly orderly and worth a look, with occasional great second-hand clothing finds. The **Source Café** craft shop has a wide selection of local and imported crafts and there are curio stalls along Main St and at the Source of the Nile on the eastern bank.

Bujagali *p88, map p89*
Kilombera Weaving, east bank of the Nile, 5.5 km from Jinja, T0782-306602. Mon-Fri 0900-1700, Sat 0900-1200. A local cooperative that produces lovely colourful 100% cotton woven items including bedspreads, tablemats and *kikoys*, and items made from *kikoys* like bags, hammocks, picnic blankets and baby-slings. You can watch the women at work on the traditional looms. **Kilombera** is the name of a local weaver bird and for the male to find a mate it must spend hours weaving an intricate nest to attract a female. If you get a *boda-boda* here from Jinja or Bujagali, make sure it waits for you for the return journey.

☉ What to do

Jinja *p83, map p85*
Fishing
Jinja Fishing Safaris, T0773-236005, or book through **Nile River Explorers** (page 100). Has a 32-ft boat and all equipment for fishing for Nile perch in Lake Victoria. Half day from US$60 including snacks, full day from US$120 including lunch at the **Jinja Sailing Club** (page 94). Also offers trips downstream at Bujagali for casting from the riverbank.

Golf
Jinja Golf Club, Nile Cres, T0774-787289. This 9-hole/18-tee course was established in 1912 and enjoys views of the Nile and Lake Victoria. When it first opened there was a famous rule allowing a free drop of the ball if it came to rest in a hippo's footprint; fortunately for golfers, there are no hippos anywhere near Jinja these days. US$20 for a round with a caddy and golf

club rental is US$6. Anyone can use the open-air swimming pool here for US$2.
Mehta Golf Club, in Lugazi on the Kampala–Jinja Highway, 35 km west of Jinja and 11 km west of Mabira Forest Reserve, T0703-666308. A private hilly 9-hole/14-tee course in an exceptionally scenic spot surrounded by sugar plantations and owned by the sugar company, but visitors are welcome and the club holds tournaments including the **Mehta Open**. Costs around US$10 to play and there's excellent Indian food available in the clubhouse, which featured in the movie *The Last King of Scotland*.

Mountain biking
Explorers Biking Safaris, at Explorers Backpackers (page 92), T0782-862088, www.explorersbikingsafaris.com. Mountain bikes can be hired for around US$15 for half a day, US$25 full day, helmets provided. Guided trips can be arranged including a 4- to 6-hr tour to **Mabira Forest Reserve** (page 82), US$45-60 including lunch. Longer bike safaris go to some of the national parks; the UWA have permitted bike riding in **Lake Mburo** (with an armed ranger), for example, and up to the trailheads at **Bwindi**. 5- to 17-day trips can be arranged with a support vehicle that carries bikes and passengers on the long straight roads and allows for biking along the dirt roads. Discuss with Nash what you would like to do.

Tour operators
Advanced Tours & Travel Ltd, 28/30 Clive Rd, T0434-120457, T071-246 3474 (mob), www.advancedtours.ug. An agent for other tour operators for gorilla, chimp and park safaris and can organizes tailor-made packages with transport and accommodation. Also offers well-priced car hire (see Transport, page 101).
Safari Wildz, T0775-201119, www.safari wildz.com. Jinja-based and New Zealand-

owned tour operator offering small-group scheduled and tailor-made tours to the gorillas, chimps and parks from 3-10 days. Departures from Jinja, Kampala or Entebbe. All budgets from camping to luxury lodges. The excellent staff will talk through ideas about what you'd like to do.

The Tourist Centre, 2 Main St, in the Post Office building, T0434-122758, www. touristcentresafaris.com. Owned by an ex-mayor of Jinja, this enterprising tour operator was established in 1996, long before the town actually had any tourists, so naturally has always been keen to promote the region. It offers day tours of Jinja and Kampala, and an interesting half-day cultural tour that walks through villages and farms on the edge of town. Also books Bujagali activities and organizes multi-day safaris to the gorillas and game parks. Plus car hire and is the agent for **Easy Coach** for buses to Kenya (see Transport, page 101).

Bujagali *p88, map p89*
All activities on the east and west banks of the Nile can be booked directly, at all the accommodation in Bujagali, most of the accommodation in Jinja, at the **Kampala Backpackers Hostel and Campsite** (page 55) and **Red Chilli Hideaway** (page 56) in Kampala, at **The Tourist Centre** in Jinja (see above) and, if you are visiting on an organized tour, by your tour operator. Look out for special deals and combos; for example, if booked together, whitewater rafting can be combined with bungee jumping, jet boating, kayaking or a sunset cruise, and considerable discounts are available. Additionally, the 3 rafting companies (**Adrift**, **Nile River Explorers** and **Nalubale Rafting**) have their own accommodation in Jinja or Bujagali or both, and when booking rafting and other activity trips, offer 1 free night's accommodation in a dorm, or 2 nights' camping, or a discount in rooms or safari tents. All 3 rafting companies also offer their clients free shuttles from Kampala.

Birdwatching
With around 225 bird species recorded in the area, this is a rewarding pursuit that can be combined with any of the river activities, or can be enjoyed from the terrace of your lodge. Since the new dam has submerged the rapids, there has been a slight change in habitat for birds at Bujagali and there has been a marked increase in the number of water birds attracted to the peaceful shores. Whereas previously the noise from the falls used to drown out any birdsong, birds can now be heard clearly across the flat water, making it easier to spot them. Species present include open-billed stork, great cormorant, African fish eagle, green-backed and purple heron and several species of kingfisher. Rare birds include the rock pratincole and white-backed night heron.

Feather & Fin Pursuits, Nile River Camp, T0772-900451, www.ffp.ug. 2-hr guided birdwatching cruises from US$40 per person, which can be combined with lunch at the **Black Lantern** (page 95). Fun and educational and great for experienced or novice birders and children. Binoculars are supplied.

Holland Park (page 94) on the west bank, but can pick up from other places along the river. Organizes 2-hr guided boat trips for US$120 for up to 8 people that go down as far as Bujagali Dam. Worth getting a group together.

Bungee jumping
Nile High Bungee, at Adrift Riverbase (page 93). For the intrepid or foolhardy (depending on your viewpoint), this 44-m jump is from a 12-m cantilevered tower on top of a 32-m cliff over the Nile. There's also the option of being dipped headfirst into the river prior to the first bounce and you can jump during full moon: US$115, single or tandem. Minimum age 13.

Golf
Big Game Safari Mini-Golf, All Terrain Adventures (see quad biking below),

opposite **Explorers River Camp**, T0772-377185, www.atadventures.com. Daily 0800-1700, US$5. Kitsch and over the top but adults and children will have lots of fun for 1-2 hrs. The 10-hole crazy golf course has a big game theme with a life-size statue of an animal at each – putt the ball through the legs of a hippo or fangs of a python.

Fishing

Many of the places to stay rent out rods and tackle.
Feather & Fin Pursuits (see above) offers half and full-day fishing by boat from **Nile River Camp** for Nile perch, catfish and tilapia from US$50.

Horse riding

Nile Horseback Safaris, on the west bank 9 km from Jinja, turn right at Naminya village for 1 km along a dirt road towards the river; if the road is wet go via **Holland Park** (page 94), T0774-101196, www.nilehorsebacksafaris.com. Offers pleasant rides along the riverbank on well-schooled horses suitable for all abilities. Rides all depart at 1000 and 1400: 1 hr US$40, 2 hrs US$60, 3 hrs US$80. On Fri and Sat there's an additional 1½-hr sunset safari at 1600 for US$55, which includes a boat transfer from **Adrift Riverbase** or **Explorers River Camp** on the east bank. There are also guided pony rides for children aged 3-10 years. The popular overnight excursion goes for 15 km north along the river to **The Haven River Lodge** (page 94). Once there there's time to relax at the lodge before returning the next day on a different route through part of the **Mabira Forest Reserve** (page 82). Prices for this start at US$265 per person if you camp in a pre-erected tent at the **Haven** (more if you choose *banda* accommodation) and include all meals.

Jet boating

Wild Nile Jet, Adrift (see page 93). Since Bujagali Falls were submerged this has been moved to **Adrift**'s rafting launch base below the dam near Kalagala Falls and **Wildwaters Lodge**. **Adrift** provide transport. The 12-seater 450 horsepower boat was imported from New Zealand and offers an exhilarating 30-min ride through the rapids with a few 360° turns and rock 'buzzing'. You are firmly strapped in with life jackets but expect to get wet. US$75, children (under 12) US$50 (minimum age 5). *The African Queen* (see box, page 101) is also based at **Wildwaters** for Nile cruises.

Kayaking

Kayak the Nile, Explorers River Camp, T0772-880322, www.kayakthenile.com. Like rafting, whitewater kayaking has moved downstream below the dam. 1-day tandem trips with a guide including refreshments and transport to the launch site near Kalagala Falls costs US$140. Minimum age 16. Multi-day trips and coaching can be arranged for experienced whitewater kayakers. Now that Bujagali Lake is there, gentler options from **Explorers River Camp** include 2-hr guided paddles in 2-person canoes with drinks (especially popular for sunset), US$30 per person; a full-day kayaking lesson that includes some action in smaller rapids, US$115; or rent your own kayak for US$20 per hr.

Mountain biking

Mountain bikes can be hired from **Explorers River Camp** (page 93) and **Nile River Camp** (page 93) for leisurely rides through the villages along the east bank. Expect to pay around US$15 for half a day, US$25 full day, helmets provided. Guided trips can be arranged including a 2-hr Bujagali tour, US$30, and a more challenging 4- to 6-hr tour to Mabira **Forest Reserve** (page 82), US$45-60 including lunch. See also **Explorers Biking Safaris** in Jinja (page 96).

Nile cruises

Bujagali's whitewater may have gone but in its place is the serene and incredibly beautiful Bujagali Lake, surrounded by forests full of birds and monkeys. Aside from more specialist boat trips for guided fishing and birdwatching, all accommodation can arrange relaxing cruises; ideal to enjoy a sunset over the Nile with a cold drink and perhaps an onboard barbecue. Prices start from US$25, US$30-45 with food. Children under 12 half price.

Quad biking

All Terrain Adventures, opposite Explorers River Camp, T0772-377185, www.atadventures.com. Exciting quad-bike safaris through the lush countryside around Bujagali and along the river. Tuition is given on practice circuits riding mini quads before you graduate to the bigger bikes. Protective clothing, helmets, overalls, boots, gloves and eye protection are supplied. A small donation is made to the local councils of the villages visited en route. 1-4 hrs plus practice costs US$45-110, full day US$185 including lunch, twilight safari at 1700 including a traditional Ugandan banquet in Kyabirwa village, US$80. The team at All Terrain Adventures also run **Africa Smart Rider**, an advanced motorcycle training facility at affordable prices with discounts for Ugandan citizens to help reduce the high rate of accidents. It's aimed at local *boda-boda* drivers and international overlanders on motorbikes, and if you've never ridden before (or never on dirt), this is a unique place to learn.

Stand-up paddle boarding

This is one of the new sports made possible by the formation of Bujagali Lake. No experience necessary, it's lots of fun, a good all-round body workout and, since you're standing at full height, it's an excellent way to enjoy the scenery. Boards and paddles can be rented for US$20 for 3 hrs from **Explorers River Camp** and **Nile River Camp** (page 93).

Voluntary work

Given the number of international visitors that have passed through Bujagali over the years, a couple of very worthwhile projects for 'Voluntourism' have been established, and this is an ideal way to spend some extra time while doing Bujagali's numerous activities.

Soft Power Education, www.softpower education.com, or book through **Nile River Camp** (page 93), **Nile Porch** (page 93), **Explorers River Camp** (page 93) or **Black Lantern restaurant** (page 95). Established here in 1999 by an ex-overland truck crew **Soft Power Education** now operates the **Amagezi Education Centre**, the **Endowoza Arts Centre** and the **Soft Power Medical Centre** at Kyabirwa village in Bujagali. They have helped thousands of children in the area to get better education and healthcare. Volunteers can give a day or more of their travels to visit the projects and join in, and the work is tailored to suit the capabilities of each volunteer. The project leader will designate a task for the day; anything from teaching art and nursery rhymes to painting or laying a floor. A voluntary contribution is required, a minimum of US$25 for a day which includes a local lunch, but more is appreciated, all of which is invested into the projects.

S.O.U.L. Foundation (Supporting Opportunities for Ugandans to Learn), www.souluganda.org. Founded in 2009 by US former backpackers who had visited Bujagali Falls. This is an option for volunteers to sign up for 1- to 4-week placements in and around the Kyabirwa village. The programs are mainly teaching from pre-primary to healthcare and computer skills, but work can be arranged depending on skills and other projects, include poultry and fish farming. Volunteer fees start from US$500 per week.

Walking

A good way of learning more about rural life is to join a village walk. Knowledgeable villagers escort you around Bujagali and show agricultural production, building techniques and point out different plants and animals. The lifestyle and traditions of the villagers are all carefully explained. **Nile River Explorers** organize the walk and they depart from **Explorers River Camp** (page 93) at any time during the day. Allow at least 2-3 hrs. US$7 per person includes local lunch.

Whitewater rafting

Whitewater rafting started at Bujagali Falls in 1996 and while the construction of the Bujagali Dam has moved the goalposts somewhat for this popular activity, rafting now operates on the rapids below the dam wall. The launch site is off the Kayunga road, 15 km north of the turn-off opposite **Nile Breweries**, on the western bank. All trips include transport from Kampala, Jinja and the Bujagali lodges on both banks, plus breakfast, snacks like fruit and biscuits while rafting, and either lunch on an island or a barbecue at the end on the riverbank near the departure point. The full day route now covers 30 km and there are 8 major rapids, 2 of which are Grade V, and calm stretches of water in between to swim and enjoy the river. No experience is necessary and there is the option of paddling as a team or riding in an oar raft with the guide. Full day US$125, half day US$115.

Minimum age 15. DVDs, photos and the obligatory 'been there, done that' T-shirt are for sale afterwards. There are also 2-day rafting trips, with an overnight at **Hairy Lemon** (page 94) and the 2nd day covers another 15 km of river with fewer rapids but lovely scenery, from US$200.

Adrift, Adrift Riverbase, Bujagali (page 93), T0772-237483, Kampala office T0312-237438, www.adrift.ug.

Nalubale Rafting, Nalubale Rafting Base & Tea House, Jinja (page 92), **Nile River Camp**, Bujagali (page 93), T0782-638938, www.nalubalerafting.com.

Nile River Explorers (**NRE**), Explorers Backpackers, Jinja (page 92), **Explorers River Camp**, Bujagali (page 93), T0772-422373, www.raftafrica.com.

⊖ Transport

Jinja p83, map p85
Bus and matatu

Vehicles between **Kampala** and Jinja, 2 hrs, US$3.50. The bus and taxi park in Jinja is clustered around Clive and Napier roads near the market, but vehicles will drop off at the roundabouts north of town on the Kampala–Jinja Highway. From Jinja to other towns in eastern Uganda such as **Tororo** and **Mbale**, vehicles go from the bus and taxi park. From Kenya, the long-distance buses that ply the route between **Nairobi**,

The African Queen

Adapted from the 1935 novel by CS Forester, and directed by John Huston, *The African Queen* is a 1951 adventure movie starring Humphrey Bogart as Charlie Allnut, the slovenly, gin-swilling captain of a small steamship called *The African Queen*, which shipped supplies to small East African villages during the First World War. Katharine Hepburn played Rose Sayer, the prim sister of a British missionary, Reverend Samuel Sayer (played by Robert Morley). When Germans invaded in 1915 and Samuel dies, Allnut offers to take Rose back to civilization. She can't tolerate his drinking or bad manners, and he isn't crazy about her imperious, judgmental attitude. However, it does not take long before their passionate dislike turns to love, and together the disparate duo work to ensure their survival on the treacherous waters and devise an ingenious way to destroy a German gunboat. Hepburn was nominated for an Academy Award as Best Supporting Actor for the movie, while Bogart did win the Best Actor award – his only Oscar.

The African Queen was filmed in many locations including Shepperton Studios in the UK, Biondo, the Ruiki River and Ponthierville Falls in the Belgium Congo (now the DRC), and Kabalega Falls, Lake Albert, Murchison Falls and Port Butiaba in Uganda. The cast and crew endured sickness and spartan living conditions during their time on location. To show her disgust with the amount of alcohol that John Huston and Humphrey Bogart consumed in real life during filming, Katharine Hepburn drank only water. As a result, she suffered a severe bout of dysentery. In fact, just about everyone in the film crew came down with dysentery except Bogart and Huston. Bogart explained, "all we ate was baked beans, canned asparagus and drank Scotch whiskey. Whenever a fly bit me or Huston it dropped dead". Lauren Bacall famously ventured along for the filming in Africa to be with her husband Humphrey Bogart, which also marked the beginning of her life-long friendship with Katharine Hepburn.

There were actually two identical *African Queens*, which saved on some of the logistical problems of moving the boat scenes between the various locations. One was restored in 1983 and taken to Florida in the USA where it is today used for tourist cruises in the Florida Quays. The other was fully restored by **Adrift** in 2013 and now offers cruises on the Nile from **Wildwaters Lodge** (page 93). Contact **Adrift** (www.adrift. ug) or **Wildwaters Lodge** (www.wild-uganda.com) for details and options, but expect to pay around US$90 for a two-hour cruise. Transfers can be arranged if you're not staying there.

Nakuru and **Eldoret** and **Kampala** stop in Jinja at the Gapco petrol station on the roundabout on the Kampala–Jinja Highway (A109). It is imperative that you inform the bus driver that you want to get off the bus in Jinja so your luggage can be put in the hold last. You can get on the Kampala–Kenya bus in Jinja if it is not already full. The buses get to Jinja roughly 1¼ hrs after they leave Kampala. For contact details and departure times of the bus companies see Kampala Transport, page 66. In Jinja, **The Tourist Centre** (page 97) is the agent for **Easy Coach** and you can book at their office on Main St or at the **Easy Coach** office on the Gapco roundabout.

Car hire

Both **Advanced Tours & Travel Ltd**, and **The Tourist Centre** (see Tour operators, page 97) can arrange car hire with or without a driver. Rates vary and are generally dependent on a limited mileage of around 120 km per day so may only be suitable for travel around Jinja, but they are mostly cheap and start from US$30 a day for a self-drive saloon car.

Bujagali *p88, map p89*

At Jinja there are plenty of special hire taxis and *boda-bodas* at the Shell roundabout (for the east bank), and the roundabout opposite Nile Breweries on the western side of the Owen Falls Dam (for the west bank). If coming from Kampala via Kayunga (see Getting there, page 90, for this route), *matatus* from Kampala go to Kayunga, where you can swap to one going to Jinja via the west bank. Most visitors use the pre-booked free shuttle buses provided by the rafting companies from either Kampala or Jinja.

To Kenya, Mount Elgon and the northeast

From Jinja, the A109 road to Kenya continues first northeast and then swings east. About 20 km from Jinja the road goes through the small market town of Magamaga and then, after another 5 km or so, there is a road off to the right. Here you'll come to the little village of Buluba, where Bishop Hannington was murdered in 1885 (see box, page 105). After another 15 km you will pass through the town of Iganga, the district headquarters. Here is the turn-off to the attractive mountain foothills town of Mbale, the access town to the Mount Elgon National Park, while the A109 continues to the two border crossings with Kenya: Malaba and Busia. Mount Elgon, an extinct shield volcano, with an enormous intact caldera, bestrides the Kenyan border. Mount Wagagai at 4321 m is the tallest peak, the fourth highest mountain in East Africa. It has gradual slopes up to the peaks on the crater rim, which means that even non-mountaineers can climb it. The foothills are an excellent hiking area, very beautiful and virtually untouched by tourists, and offer great trekking, cave exploration and varied montane flora. To the north are the magnificent 100-m-high Sipi Falls, an area famous for Bugisu Arabica coffee production.

North of Mbale, there are routes into northeast Uganda and once off the foothills of the mountains, you will notice the terrain becomes drier and dustier and the temperatures rapidly become warmer. The northeast is a sparsely populated and little-visited region with few attractions or amenities, but it is possible to go via the principal town of Soroti and then either to Kidepo Valley National Park in the extreme northeast, or to the northern towns of Lira and Gulu. ▸▸ For listing, see pages 113-116.

Iganga to Kenya → Phone code: 0434. Colour map 2, B6.

This sleepy little town, 44 km east of Jinja, has wide streets bordered by shops and houses with broad verandas. Most people just pass through in transit and there are few facilities other than a clutch of basic board and lodgings and street stalls for local food. However, Iganga is the junction town for the Mbale road from the Kampala direction, and the largest settlement between Jinja and where the road splits to go to the two border crossings with Kenya. From Iganga the A109 continues east for 60 km to the junction with the Busia road, and it's another 33 km to the **Busia** border post. From the same junction the A109 continues to **Tororo** and then on to the **Malaba** border post. Generally, Malaba is the most commonly used border for trucks and is very congested with heavy vehicles. However, if you're heading to the Ugandan side of Mount Elgon before going to Kenya, it makes sense to use the Malaba crossing. If you are in your own vehicle it may be better to cross at Busia, as it is less commercial and is the most popular border with buses between the two countries. (See Border crossing, page 106). The roads to both these borders are fair, but have the usual occasional pot holes and you will pass through fairly typical Ugandan scenery: clusters of small huts surrounded by farmland, as well as areas of verdant bush and elephant grass with the occasional anthill. There are also many mango trees in this part of Uganda and during the season their fruit can be bought on the roadside.

Tororo → For listing, see pages 113-116. Phone code: 0454. Colour map 1, C5.

Situated in the far east of Uganda, Tororo is 4 km north of the A109 and 10 km from the Malaba border with Kenya, but few people pass through as most travellers use the border crossing at Busia. Built during the colonial period in the late 1940s, **Tororo Cement**

Limited made an important contribution to the development of Uganda as it took away the necessity of importing cement from Kenya. It functioned well until Amin's time. As everything in Uganda began to fall apart so did the cement works, its roof eventually collapsing under the weight of the cement dust. Now, however, the operation is up and running again, but Tororo has failed to capture its former prosperity and remains a backwater town. Tororo's major claim to fame is the rock named after it, which can be seen from miles around. Known locally as **Morukatipe**, it's a forested volcanic plug that rises to about 1800 m above sea level. It is possible to climb and the views of the countryside from the top are fantastic; however, contrary to some reports, Lake Victoria cannot be seen. There are steps and ladders to help you get to the summit, and the climb takes about an hour. Another claim to fame is Tororo's very high frequency of spectacular thunderstorms.

Mbale → *For listing, see pages 113-116. Phone code: 0454. Colour map 1, C5.*
Population approximately 95,000.

Mbale is located 245 km northeast of Kampala on the good tarred road via Iganga (105 km); there's another road from Tororo (55 km) in the south. In the foothills of Mount Elgon, the town has an altitude of 1200 m, giving it a comfortable climate. Mbale shows clearly the Asian influence on towns in Uganda; in particular, many of the buildings have the distinctive veranda that is seen all over East Africa, and the pink clock tower on the main roundabout is the most distinctive landmark. It is a pleasant, bustling market town that teems with bicycles and *boda-bodas*. For visitors, it is the springboard for visiting the Mount Elgon National Park and Sipi Falls and there is a good choice of accommodation

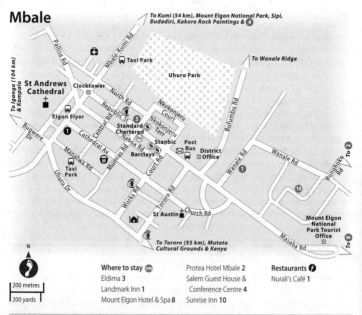

Mbale

To Kumi (54 km), Mount Elgon National Park, Sipi, Budadiri, Kakoro Rock Paintings & **④**

To Iganga (104 km) & Kampala

To Wanale Ridge

St Andrews Cathedral

Clocktower

Uhuru Park

Taxi Park

Mbale-Kumi Rd

Pallisa Rd

North Rd

Republic Rd

Nkonjeru Court

Nkonjeru Terr

Elgon Flyer

Bugwere Dr

Central Av

Cathedral Av

Standard Chartered

Maboa Rd

Stanbic

Barclays

Post Bus

District Office

Burtumbu Rd

Wanale Rd

Wanale Rd

Bungholo Rd

To **②**

Masawa Rd

Taxi Park

Uhuru Dr

Munias Rd

Court Rd

Works Rd

Tororo Rd

St Austin

Church Rd

To Tororo (55 km), Mutoto Cultural Grounds & Kenya

Mount Elgon National Park Tourist Office

Masaba Rd

To **⑧**

⑩

N

200 metres
200 yards

Where to stay
Eldima **3**
Landmark Inn **1**
Mount Elgon Hotel & Spa **8**

Protea Hotel Mbale **2**
Salem Guest House & Conference Centre **4**
Sunrise Inn **10**

Restaurants 🍴
Nurali's Café **1**

Bishop Hannington

Coming from Kampala, a little beyond Jinja on the right, is Buluba, where Bishop Hannington, consecrated in 1884 as the first Bishop of the Diocese of Eastern Equatorial Africa, met his death. Hannington kept a detailed diary during his journeys and it is through this, and stories from the survivors, that we know what happened.

James Hannington had first visited East Africa in 1882 as the leader of a party of reinforcements for the Victoria Nyanza Mission in Uganda. He had suffered severely from dysentery and had been forced to return to Britain. However, after being made bishop, he planned his return to Africa. At this time the route into Uganda was from Zanzibar, through what is now Tanzania, to the south of Lake Victoria. In 1883 a new route was tried, through Kenya, via Busoga, to the north of the lake. This route through Masai country was more direct and climatic conditions were not as harsh.

Arriving on the East African coast in January 1885, Hannington planned to use the Masai route. On hearing this, the missionaries in Buganda informed him that the current political situation in Buganda was such that entering by the 'back door', through Busoga, was extremely dangerous. However, the warning arrived about two weeks after Hannington had set off.

Hannington's only real mistake was that he did not stick to his plans as set out in a letter to the missionaries in Buganda. He told them that he would go overland as far as Kavirondo on Lake Victoria, where the mission boat would meet him, and that he would enter Buganda by boat. This would mean he would avoid entering Uganda through Busoga, which was so sensitive. Mwanga, the son of King Mutesa I, had been told that those entering Buganda from the east (that is, Busoga) would destroy the Kingdom of Buganda and the missionaries in Buganda had assured Mwanga that the Bishop would not enter via that route. So when he did, it appeared as a calculated deceit.

In March 1890 a boy who had been with Hannington arrived in the camp of Jackson, another missionary who was on his way to Uganda. The boy had with him a skull (its lower jaw bone missing), identified as belonging to Hannington by its gold teeth. He also had the soles of Hannington's boots, a hot water bottle and the lid of an Army and Navy canteen.

The remains eventually found their way to Kampala and on 31 December 1892 they were buried on Namirembe Hill.

and plenty of shops to stock up on provisions. The superb Wanale Ridge towers above town, and on a clear day the peaks of Mount Elgon can be seen.

Arriving in Mbale

Tourist offices Uganda Wildlife Authority (UWA) ① *19-21 Masaba Rd, T0454-435035, www.ugandawildlife.org, Mon-Fri 0800-1300 and 1400-1700, Sat 0900-1300*, is also called the **Mount Elgon National Park Tourist Office**, close to the **Mount Elgon Hotel**, and provides information about climbing Mount Elgon. There are maps as well as up-to-date advice, and anyone planning to climb the mountain is advised to visit the office before travelling to the park and the trailheads at Budadiri, Kapkwai or Kapkwata. Information and booking can also be arranged at the **UWA** head office in Kampala (page 42), the **UWA** office in Budadiri (page 108) and at the **Forest Exploration Centre at Kapkwai** (page 109). However, only the Mbale office rents out equipment – tents cost around

Border crossing: Uganda–Kenya

Malaba and Busia

The two border crossings between Uganda and Kenya are roughly 45 km apart. Both Malaba and Busia, together with their sister towns of the same name on the Kenyan side, are dusty nondescript border towns, with huge numbers of trucks and buses and even more motorcycles and bicycles crowding the roads on either side of the immigration and customs offices. But both borders are open 24 hours; and procedures are quick and efficient.

Visas for both countries are available at the border, as is third-party insurance for drivers. Remember, because of the East Africa customs agreement, you are permitted to travel between Uganda, Tanzania and Kenya on single-entry visas without getting re-entry visas for each of these countries, as long as the visas you have are valid. For more information on visas between the East African countries, see box, page 33.

Buses between Kampala and Jinja and Nairobi via Eldoret and Nakuru use the Busia border. If you are in your own vehicle at either border you will be badgered by touts offering to sell relevant forms or escort you through the procedures for a fee. Ignore them; all forms are available inside the border buildings where you will be told what to do. Be wary of petty thieves – lock everything up and make sure anything on the outside of the vehicle is tied down. There are banks with ATMs on both sides of the border at both Malaba and Busia.

In total, Kampala to Malaba is 220 km, and Kampala to Busia is 210 km. Malaba is on the A109, 10 km east of Tororo. Once in Kenya the road turns into the A104 and from the border it's 128 km east to Eldoret via Webuye. Busia is 33 km southeast of the A109 and, once in Kenya, the road becomes the B1 and it's 153 km to Kisumu on Kenya's side of Lake Victoria, or 157 km to Eldoret.

There is no accommodation in Malaba so it's best to stay in Tororo on the Ugandan side (see Where to stay, page 113) or push on to Eldoret or other destinations in Western Kenya on the Kenyan side (see the *Footprint Kenya Handbook*). Other than some pretty dire board and lodgings, there is little choice of accommodation in Busia and nicer places are on the Kenyan side of town. Try the Hotel Itoya ($), T(+254) 020-207 1840, www.hotelitoya.com, which is smart modern block on the left just after the border with comfortable rooms with TV and Wi-Fi, restaurant and bar.

US$5 per day and sleeping bags US$2 per day. This office can also organize transport to the trailheads.

Wanale Ridge

Above Mbale is a large 150- to 260-m-high rock named Wanale Ridge or Cliffs, also known locally as **Nkokonjeru**, which means 'the white rock'. It is a spur of Mount Elgon, and several waterfalls course down its rock face. Idi Amin once planned to build a huge international hotel and conference centre here. The building began with the construction of the 20-km road from Mbale up to the top of the rock, but that was as far as it got and the complex itself was never built. When the road was made is was a smooth highway; it's now badly rutted but you can drive or hike up and there are wonderful views. It is sometimes possible to see the peregrine falcons, hawk eagles and rock kestrels that nest on the rock. Alternatively, you can paraglide off the top; see What to do, page 115.

Kakoro rock paintings

There are two sets of rock paintings in eastern Uganda. The Nyero rock paintings, near the town of Kumi (see page 111), are the more impressive.The Kakoro rock paintings, although less spectacular as they are being worn away by local children and by animals moving to graze, are easier to reach. The paintings, about 20 km from Mbale, are located on a *koppie* near the village of Kabwangasi in an area of scrubland surrounded by plantations of sweet potato and cassava. There is no accommodation but the local people are happy to talk to visitors about the rock paintings. There are two sites with red paintings, including some concentric circles on the south and west sides of a rock pillar at the southern end of the hill. On the underside of a rock ledge there is a third example of rock art in white pigment, but the subject matter is unidentifiable. The paintings are thought to be the work of hunter-gatherers who lived in this region 2000 years ago.

The site can be reached by travelling north from Mbale towards Kumi to the village of Nakaloke, then turning west to the village of Kabwangasi, from which there is a track to the paintings. Take a *matatu* from Mbale to Nakatoke, then a *boda-boda* to Kakoro. Alternatively, it's possible to drive all the way to the site in a 4WD.

Sipi Falls → *For listing, see pages 113-116. Altitude: 1750 m. Colour map 1, C5.*

The Sipi Falls are 60 km northeast of Mbale on the slopes of Mount Elgon. The waterfall and the surrounding area are very pretty and it is a pleasant place to spend a few days unwinding, especially before tackling the Elgon climb. At an altitude of 1750 m you can expect some refreshingly chilly nights as well as ample sweeping views of the mountain and over the plains of eastern and northern Uganda. There is in fact a series of four waterfalls on a 7-km stretch of the Sipi River, not just the main one featured in most of the promotional pictures. This main one, however, drops for almost 100 m, is the most accessible of the four, and is where the accommodation and campsites are located. The others can be reached via a network of local trails, but the walking is not easy and a reasonable level of fitness is required. It's advisable to take a guide; you may well be pounced on by would-be guides around the village and main falls, but it's advisable to organize one at your hotel.

The Sipi River is named after the *sep*; an indigenous local medicinal plant that grows on the river banks and resembles a wild banana. The translucent green frond is used for treating measles and fever. The Sipi Falls area is particularly famous for locally grown Bugisu Arabica coffee, which only grows at an altitude of between 1600 and 1900 m. You are likely to see coffee plantations on small-scale farms using family labour.

Arriving at Sipi Falls

Getting there From Mbale follow the Kumi road for 6 km, then turn right on to the road to Moroto. After 5 km is the turn-off to Budadiri (for the Mount Elgon National Park) and then it's roughly another 28 km to the next right-hand fork towards Kapchorwa on the road to Suam. The village of **Sipi** and the Sipi Falls is 15 km before Kapchorwa. In total it is 60 km or a 1½ hours' drive from Mbale and the route is tarred all the way.

Mount Elgon National Park → *For listing, see pages 113-116.*

Straddling the Uganda/Kenya border, roughly 120 km northeast of Lake Victoria as the crow flies, Mount Elgon is the eighth highest mountain in Africa and has the largest surface area of any extinct volcano in the world. It is believed to have first erupted about 24 million years ago and last erupted 10 million years ago, so is the oldest volcanic mountain in East Africa. Its base covers a staggering area of around 4000 sq km, and it rises through a series of gradual slopes punctuated by steep cliffs to a height of 4321 m at Wagagai Peak, which lies on the Ugandan side of the mountain. It is named after the Elgeyo tribe, who once lived in huge caves on the south side of the mountain. It's protected by national parks in both Uganda and Kenya, creating an extensive trans-boundary conservation region that is an important water catchment area supplying several millions of people in the region.

Elgon's upper slopes are cloaked in tropical montane forest, while above this lies a vast tract of Afro-Alpine moorland, and this unique vegetation extends over the caldera, a collapsed crater covering over 40 sq km at the top of the mountain. Endemic flora includes the giant lobelia, giant heather and giant groundsel, and wild flowers abound. Mammals include tree hyrax, bush pig, buffalo, blue monkey, baboon and black-and-white colobus monkeys. There are more than 300 species of bird and frequent sightings of the casqued hornbill, the crowned eagle, Ross's touraco and the lammergeier.

Arriving in Mount Elgon National Park

Getting there Dirt roads lead off the tarred Mbale–Suam road via Kapchorwa to reach the three trailheads (starting points) to the mountain's peaks; **Budadiri** for the Sasa Trail; **Kapkwai** for the Sisi Trail; and **Kapkwata** for the Piswa Trail. They are well signposted.

Budadiri is a small trading centre about 30 km or 45 minutes northeast of Mbale on the western boundary of the park. It is the trailhead for the **Sasa Trail**, the most popular climb up the mountain. There's another Uganda Wildlife Authority's **Mount Elgon National Park Office** here which can organize porters and guides. Budadiri can be reached by taking the Mbale–Kumi road north of Mbale and then taking the right-hand fork on to the Mbale–Suam road. After 5 km take another right turn passing through the villages of Bulwalasi and Bugusege to Budadiri. *Matatus* go directly to Budadiri from the Kumi Road taxi park in Mbale.

Climbing Mount Elgon

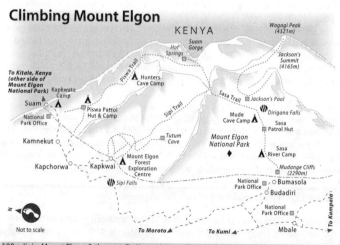

Bugisu circumcision

The Bugisu have a strong belief in their rites and the ceremony of circumcision is an important part of the life cycle. All men must undergo circumcision, and males who die before this has been done will be circumcised before they are buried, in order to complete their life on earth.

Circumcision takes place every other year – on years ending with an even number – and is performed on young men aged between 14 and 25. The circumcision season is said to be marked by the appearance of a strange bird whose singing marks the beginning of the preparations. The elders gather under the clan tree, which is said to be older than the memory of man itself. They then begin training the candidates for the rituals, which last three days.

On the first day the young man is smeared with sorghum paste all over the body. He wears the traditional dress of animal skins and a head dress, puts three heavy bangles on each leg and then visits his relatives, singing and dancing. The songs he sings are mainly praising his forefathers and the gods. Every so often he stops and leaps high in the air.

On the second day his hair is cut and he is allowed to bathe – the last opportunity before the ceremony proper begins. This symbolizes the death of the past and of what he has been, and a new beginning.

The white sorghum paste is again smeared on his body. The singing and dancing continues and this evening is one of great celebration amongst the people of the village.

On the morning of the circumcision the young man wakes at first light and is again smeared with sorghum paste. He then sets off to visit his maternal uncles, who give him gifts of cows or goats, which are part of the bride price paid by his father. Later in the day he is taken down to the river by the men who wash him thoroughly from the waist to the knees. He is then brought at a slow pace to the ground that is traditionally used for these ceremonies. On the ground is a Y-shaped stick, which he picks up and holds behind his head. The circumcision itself is over fairly quickly and a whistle is blown to announce that the candidate has been successful. Occasionally it happens that a man will try to run away, but this is looked upon as the epitome of disgrace and cowardice.

Traditionally, once a man has been circumcised he can sit in on tribal meetings and participate in decision making, and is also allowed to marry. Only once he has been through what is known as the pain of the knife can he be called a man, and it is said that, just like birth and death, it can only be done once in a lifetime.

Kapkwai is roughly 65 km or two hours northeast of Mbale just inside the national park boundary and is the trailhead for the Sipi Trail. The Uganda Wildlife Authority's office here is known as the **Mount Elgon Forest Exploration Centre**, and is also the best place to come for day walks for those not wanting to ascend the summit as several trails radiate from the centre. To reach Kapkwai from Mbale, go 50 km to Sipi on the Mbale–Saum road and then, 6 km beyond Sipi towards Kapchorwa, turn right for 6 km to the centre. Alternatively, take a *matatu* from Mbale to Sipi, and then it's roughly a 90-minute, 4-km walk cross-country to the centre, but you'll need to pick up a guide to show you the way.

Kapkwata is the trailhead for the **Piswa Trail** and the turn-off is 44 km beyond Sipi via Kapchorwa and about 40 km before Suam on the Kenyan border. It takes some two hours to get to from Mbale. Any *matatu* from Mbale, Sipi or Kapchorwa to Suam will drop off at the village. There are few facilities here but pre-arranged guides and porters will meet climbers at the patrol hut on the trail into the park.

Tourist information   Uganda Wildlife Authority ⓘ *www.ugandawildlife.org*. Park entry US$25, children (under 12) US$5, guided walk fees are US$15 per person for up to four hours. Climbing costs US$90 per person per day which includes park entry and guide. Fees for porters, US$10 per day per porter, and camping, US$6 per person per night, are extra.

Best time to visit Mount Elgon National Park can be visited at any time of year, but the period to avoid is during the long rains, which are in April and May, when the trails become slippery, slow and tedious. The dry seasons (June-August and November-March) are best, especially in the spring months of November and December when the wildflowers are in bloom.

Climbing Mount Elgon

Mount Elgon has gradual slopes up to the peaks on the crater rim, and offers a satisfying trek that doesn't require expert skills or equipment. In fact, a climb on Elgon's deserted moorlands unveils a magnificent and uncluttered wilderness without the summit-oriented approach common to many mountains such as Kilimanjaro or Mount Kenya. This is because the ultimate goal is not the final ascent to the 4321-m **Wagagai Peak**, but the descent into the vast **caldera** once there. Trekkers will be well rewarded by the volcanic foothills, cliffs, caves, gorges and waterfalls along with panoramic views across the wide plains below. Additionally, while hikers need to be reasonably fit, there's less of a risk of altitude sickness associated with climbing higher mountains, and the cost is significantly lower.

For organizing a climb, facilities are better on the Ugandan side than the Kenyan side (and Wagagai is in Uganda). The **Uganda Wildlife Authority**'s offices in Mbale, Budadiri and Kapkwai can give you maps and make suggestions to suit your requirements and organize guides and porters. Porters help carry up to 18 kg of your gear as well as setting up/takinging down camp, collecting water and firewood (though bringing a camping stove is more sustainable) and cooking. You need to bring food, warm clothing, rain gear, hiking boots, tent and sleeping bag, although tents and sleeping bags can be hired through the office in Mbale.

The climb itself is straightforward and can be accomplished easily by non-mountaineers. The trail is steep in places but it is possible to reach the caldera and return to the trailhead within four days of setting off and walking at a comfortable pace. With an extra two days you could also reach **Jackson's Summit** on the highest point, **Wagagai**, or visit the hot springs at the head of the **Suam Gorge**. The most direct route to the peaks is the **Sasa Trail** (four days), accessed from Budadiri. It is quite steep in places with a climb of 1600 m on the first day. The **Sipi Trail** (seven days) starts at the Mount Elgon Forest Exploration Centre, Kapkwai, and this route includes a visit to Tatum cave. The **Piswa Trail** (seven days) starts from Kapkwata, and is longer but gentler. The **Sasa–Piswa** trails or **Sasa–Sipi** trails can be combined.

Foothills of Mount Elgon

If you are less ambitious there are many alternative walks, ranging from easy hikes to harder climbs, and you may spot blue and black-and-white colobus monkeys and rare birds in the forests. **Numagabwe Cave** is about an 8-km hike from Budadiri, and is a shrine where local people perform rituals of circumcision during the year (see box, page 109). The entrance to the cave is very narrow and leads into a large chamber inhabited by bats and small birds. There are also three interconnecting circular day walks from the **Mount Elgon Forest Exploration Centre** at Kapkwai, ranging from 3 km to 14 km. The most rewarding is the 7-km **Bamboo Trail** to **Kapkwai Cave** that can be combined with the 3-km **Ridge Loop** that goes to the beautiful **Chebonet Falls** and a superb viewpoint looking up at the brooding mountain.

Mbale to Soroti and the northeast → *For listing, see pages 113-116. Colour map 1, C5.*

A main feature of travel into the northeast is not so much the beauty of its scenery, which is breathtaking at times, but more that it gives you a glimpse of Uganda's history, from the Arab slave traders of centuries ago, through the colonial era, and the last few decades of civil unrest. Between 1986 and 2006 the northeast of Uganda was terrorized by rebels from the Lord's Resistance Army (LRA) and most of the population was forced to move into internally displaced people's camps for security. In 2006 the rebels were driven out of the country and over the subsequent years much reconstruction progress has been made in the regional towns. It's safe to travel in this region these days and on this route from Mbale you can get to Kidepo Valley National Park (page 242). However, this is not the preferred route and it's quicker to go from Kampala via Gulu on much better roads. Kampala, via Mbale, Soroti, Moroto, Kotido and Kabong is roughly 800 km and takes at least 13-15 hours. For the other routes to Kidepo, see page 242.

Nyero rock paintings → *Colour map 1, C5.*
ⓘ *US$4.*
Located in dry, rocky attractive scenery, **Kumi** is 62 km northwest of Mbale on the road between Mbale and Soroti. The principal attraction of this rather backwater town are the Nyero rock paintings, which are 10 km due west of the town along the Ngora road and can be visited on a day trip from Mbale or on the way to Soroti. If you don't have your own transport, you can rent a motorbike *boda-boda* from Kumi. It's possible to walk here although the intense heat discourages it.

The site consists of three painted shelters close to each other. Believed to be between 300 and 1000 years old, the paintings are in red and white pigment and are mainly of geometric shapes.

Nyero site No 1 is a small shelter formed by an overhanging rock. The white-pigmented drawings are of concentric circles, plus some elongated shapes, sometimes described as acacia pods. The main site, **Nyero 2**, has a vertical rock face with an overhang that has helped to preserve the paintings from the elements and the concentric circles dominate in varying shades of red pigment. Linear motifs, again thought to resemble acacia pods or possibly a boat containing a couple of people, can also be identified. At the top of the rock face are some very weathered marks, said to resemble zebras. **Nyero 3** is a short distance away behind the other sites. It contains the painting that has been described as looking like an enormous star or a sunburst, best viewed by lying down underneath it. This white-pigmented painting is a series of concentric circles with lines drawn at right angles to the external circle. This pattern is repeated nearby with red pigment but it is much fainter.

The surrounding area is covered with smooth boulders, many adorned by sunbathing monkeys. Occasionally, reptiles can also be seen basking on the rocks, mostly during the afternoon. Paving stones mark a path between the sites, but become very slippery in wet weather. It is possible to climb some of the surrounding rocks for lovely views of low-lying hills to the west past Ngora. The cool breeze is pleasant and tall trees offer welcome shade.

Soroti → *Colour map 1, C4.*

Soroti is the administrative centre of Soroti District in Eastern Uganda and is 48 km northwest of Kumi and 104 km from Mbale. The Mbale–Soroti road is tarred but is in a poor state and littered with potholes. Although not that far north (293 km or five hours' drive from Kampala), there is something about Soroti that gives it a northerly feeling. It is a hot, airless town with a frontier atmosphere and is situated north of Lake Kyoga on virtually flat plains, with a few rocky outcrops visible. The most spectacular of these is **Soroti Rock**, a volcanic plug resembling the one at Tororo (see page 103). It's a striking granite formation that towers above town offering good views across to Lake Kyoga from the pinnacle.

The town's architecture reflects its multicultural history. The Asian influence is most apparent along the main streets, the mosques decorated with crenellated projections and delicate minarets. On the other side of the airport is a municipal cemetery where there are many graves with Arabic inscriptions. There are also some rather run-down English-style houses, which were built during the colonial period. Soroti has a good market, where the ingenuity of the local people at refashioning scrap metal to make cooking pots and other household items from the remains of cars and metal drums is to be much admired.

In the summer of 2003 Soroti was attacked by soldiers from the Lord's Resistance Army (LRA). Before then previous attacks by the LRA had been centred on districts in northern Uganda. The attack on Soroti was seen by the Ugandan government as an escalation in the threat posed by the LRA because of Soroti Airport's strategic military importance. Fierce gun battles between the LRA and government troops forced the LRA back into the northern countryside.

Even though there are no scheduled flights, **Soroti Airport** has the third longest paved runway in Uganda, measuring 1800 m and is capable of handling jets the size of Boeing 737s. It was originally built as a training school for the **British Overseas Airways Corporation** during the colonial days to train their pilots in tropical flying techniques. It was later used by the **East African Flying Academy** to train pilots from the East African Community (Uganda, Kenya and Tanzania), which became defunct in 1977. Today, the airport is home **Soroti Flying School**, although its official name is the East African Civil Aviation Academy.

From Soroti the road continues to Lira, 122 km, and this section has been resurfaced. For information on Lira, Gulu and the other towns in the north see pages 239-242. Alternatively, you can veer off at Soroti to Moroto and take the northeasterly approach to Kidepo Valley National Park (page 242).

Moroto → *Colour map 1, B6.*

Kampala to Moroto via Soroti is 500 km, a journey that can be done in a day, but is not for the faint hearted. The drive from Soroti to Moroto (178 km) is mainly through acacia thorn bush. Every so often you will see a herd of scrawny goats being looked after by a couple of young boys, or perhaps some cattle with some Karamajong guarding them. Most of the time it is very hot and dusty but at certain times of the year there are the most fantastic thunderstorms and the road can become very muddy in the wet. Occasionally there are stands of borassus palms which were originally planted to mark the route of Arab traders. Moroto itself is a dusty nondescript town overshadowed by Mount Moroto, which reaches a height of 3400 m and is one of the chain of extinct volcanoes that border

Kenya and begin with Mount Elgon. The **Moroto Hotel** (page 115) is the only reason to stop, whether or not you stay here (although there's nowhere else).

The alternative eastern route from Mbale to Moroto is via **Nakapiripirit** to the north of Mount Elgon but, although it is about 60 km shorter than via the route via Soroti, it's a long arduous journey on rocky hilly roads and a 4WD is essential. To continue from Moroto to Kidepo Valley National Park, you need to head north via Kotido and Kaabong; it's a journey of about 250 km on dry dusty dirt roads.

◉ To Kenya, Mount Elgon and the northeast listings

For hotel and restaurant price codes and other relevant information, see pages 16-20.

◉ Where to stay

Tororo *p103*

$ Hotel Meritoria, 10-12 Rock Crescent Rd, T0776-585536, www.hotelmeritoria.com. The best option if you have to overnight in Tororo. This newly built motel-style place in the centre of town has 18 decent-sized rooms with DSTV and reasonable food, including barbecues, salads, sandwiches and tilapia fish. The upstairs open-air thatched bar has great views of Tororo Rock.
$ Rock Classic Hotel, on the A109, 4 km south of town and 8 km before the border, near the Caltex petrol station, T0454-448012. Set in gardens, behind the golf course, this vast hotel has 100+ rooms, the slightly better ones are in the newer block but that isn't saying much as everything is pretty tired. Nevertheless, rates include an English cooked breakfast, there's a swimming pool, snack bar, restaurant and friendly staff. You can negotiate to camp in the gardens.

Mbale *p104, map p104*

Most hotels are in the pleasant suburb known as the **Senior Quarters** (favoured by Europeans during the colonial period) about 2 km to the east of the centre. It's about a 30-min walk or take a *boda-boda*.
$$$ Protea Hotel Mbale, 50 Bungokho Rd, T0454-433 920, www.proteahotels.com. Mbale's newest and best offering, managed by the quality South African chain **Protea**, is a modern glass block with large swimming pool, palm-filled gardens, outdoor and inside bars, smart 1st restaurant, and impressive lobby. It's aimed at the conference market so could be full or eerily empty. All 74 a/c rooms have balconies facing Wanale Ridge.
$$$-$$ Mount Elgon Hotel & Spa, 30 Masaba Rd, near the national park office, T0454-433454, www.mountelgonhotel. com. Dating from the 1950s and last renovated in 2006, this hotel has a grand colonial façade and commanding views of Wanale Ridge. 30 large rooms with DSTV, a/c or fans, pool in extensive gardens, sauna, steam room and massages available. There are simpler and cheaper rooms in the annex across the road. Given that it's owned by Italians, the restaurant serves authentic pizza and pasta, and there's excellent coffee in the bar.
$ Hotel Eldima, 35 Republic St, T07 87-762484, www.hoteleldima.com. Friendly budget option in a central location opposite the police station, multi-storeyed over a restaurant with 25 clean, tiled en suite rooms, good views over town. Doubles from US$14 include breakfast. The restaurant serves mostly local food plus the likes of burger and chips.
$ Landmark Inn, Wanale Rd, T0454-433880. Charmingly dilapidated Mangalore tiled, colonial house with a pillared terrace overlooking the lush, large mature garden, and only 3 spacious double en suite rooms, 2 with patio balconies. Camping available in garden. The restaurant serves excellent Indian food in a garden setting. Doubles from US$14.

$ Salem Guest House & Conference Centre, 12 km northwest of town on the road to Kolonyi, T0772-505595, www.saleminternational.org. Salem Foundation is a Christian NGO and all profits go towards the running of a local health centre and children's home. Rural accommodation is in 1-, 2- or 3-bed *bandas*, mostly en suite, or there are camping facilities in the leafy gardens. Wholesome meals and beers are available, and they can arrange hire of drivers and guides for Mt Elgon National Park, Sipi Falls and Nyero rock paintings.

$ Sunrise Inn, 45 Nakhupa Rd, T0454-433090. Lovely garden and good, clean, attractive accommodation with DSTV and fans. The restaurant serves excellent Western and some interesting regional local dishes, among the best in Mbale. There's a pretty outdoor eating area and rates include a tasty and filling buffet breakfast. Camping available in the grounds. Doubles from US$30.

Sipi Falls p107

$$$-$ Sipi River Lodge, 2 km past Sipi village, T0751-79 6109, www.sipiriverlodge.com. Easily one of the most pleasant places to stay east of Jinja in 7 ha of beautiful grounds along the Sipi River beside the middle waterfall, with well-priced accommodation and plenty of activities making it warrant at least a couple of nights. Accommodation is in 2 luxury double/twin cottages, a family cottage sleeping up to 7, 2 double *bandas* and a dormitory for up to 5. Rates are full board, so a bunk costs from US$60 per person but includes all meals plus afternoon tea on the veranda. The main house has comfy sofas, a dining room with an open fire in the evenings and a good library. Can organize coffee tours, archery, hiking, rock climbing, abseiling and trout fishing.

$$ Sipi Falls Resort, T0752-529040. Originally built in the 1950s as a 2-room holiday home for the governor and officials during the colonial period. Now has 5 basic

but comfortable en suite bamboo and thatched *bandas*, restaurant and bar with terrace and garden, limited menu but good food like chicken or tilapia with chips/rice and tasty French toast for breakfast. The highlight is its location right next to the roaring main falls.

$$-$ Lacam Lodge, 50 m past the police post, 150 m from the main Sipi Falls, T0752-29 2554, www.lacamlodge.co.uk. Set on a steep hillside with 6 comfortable en suite log cabins, each with 2 double beds, thatched roofs and verandas, plus cheaper huts with shared bathrooms and there's a campsite on a grassy terrace. All rates are full board, with excellent home-grown food in the attractive restaurant and bar with fantastic views of the Sipi River valley.

$ The Crow's Nest, signposted left just before Sipi Trading Centre, T0772-687924. Built in the 1990s by Peace Corps volunteers, this popular budget choice has spectacular views across to the main falls, as well as views of 2 smaller falls, and a quiet, laid-back atmosphere. Accommodation is in simple double log cabins with corrugated-iron roofs (US$20), 4-bed dorm (US$10 per person) and camping (US$2per person). Reasonable and very cheap food, packed lunches for hikes can be organized, free tea and coffee and there's a bar. Interesting village walks can be arranged with a local guide.

Mount Elgon National Park p107
Budadiri

$ Rose's Last Chance, opposite the Uganda Wildlife Authority office, T045-36172, T0772-623206, www.roseslastchance.yolasite.com. A simple and friendly community-run place to stay if you are making Budadiri a staging post for the climb up Mt Elgon; they can also point you in the right direction with a packed lunch on local hikes. Offers 7 single/double rooms (US$8/12), 20 dorm beds (US$6 per person), or camping (US$5 per person), all with shared bathrooms, warm bucket baths available. Breakfast included, restaurant and bar, secure parking for a small fee while on the climb. Also rents out tents, bags, sleeping mats, boots and raincoats.

Kapkwai
$ Uganda Wildlife Authority Camp, Mbale office, T0454-433170, www. ugandawildlife.org. There is a small, under-used campsite with 4 *bandas*, long-drop toilets and bucket showers, next to the Mount Elgon Forest Exploration Centre. Single/double US$16/20, camping US$8 per person, but as it's just inside the park boundary, park entry fees apply if you stay overnight. Simple basic food and warm beers and sodas are available at the **Bamboo Grove Canteen** and guests can use the cooking facilities. Usually used on the night before climbing the Sipi Trail.

Kapkwata
$ Uganda Wildlife Authority Kapkwata Guesthouse, 500 m from the village at the park entrance, Mbale office, T0454-433170, www.ugandawildlife.org. Very basic, there are just 3 bare rooms here attached to the park office, 2 with twin beds and the other with 6 bunks, expect to pay around US$8 per person, camping US$5 per person, but its outside the park so no park fees apply. Bring bedding and everything with you, you can cook over a fire or eat basic meals in the village.

Nyero rock paintings *p111*
Kumi
$ Kumi Hotel, 6 Malera Rd, T0772-434380, www.kumihotel.com. The best of a poor choice in town with 20 clean en suite rooms in a concrete block with TV and fans, green lawned gardens, secure parking, small restaurant with limited but adequate menu.

Soroti *p112*
$ Akello Hotel, T0776-995501, www.akello hotel.co.ug. The best of the bunch and only built in 2012 so everything is very fresh, with 81 comfortable a/c rooms with DSTV and reliable hot showers. Doubles US$50,

cheaper rooms with shared bathrooms go from US$20. Primarily built for use by trainee pilots at the Soroti Flying School (it's the only place with views of the runway from the balconies). Restaurant, bar and good breakfast buffet. If for any reason this is full, try the **Soroti Hotel** on Serere Rd, about 1 km from the town centre, or the **Golden Ark Hotel** on the Mbale–Soroti road, both in the same price range but not as good.

Moroto *p112*
$ Moroto Hotel, 3 km from town towards Mount Moroto, T0751-493000, www. morotohotel.com. Quite a find for such a remote region and, although old, it's well maintained with 40 en suite rooms in the main block or newer garden chalets with DSTV and Wi-Fi (though power and water are hit and miss). There's a restaurant, bar and secure parking. You can camp here and have use of a bathroom. They can organize local guides for walks up and around the mountain.

🍴 Restaurants

Mbale *p104, map p104*
All the places to stay have surprisingly good restaurants and are open to non-guests. There are plenty of snack bars and *nyama choma* joints around Republic St in the centre of town.
$ Nurali's Café, 7 Cathedral Av, T0714-470602. Daily 0800-2200. Well regarded for its authentic Indian food although there are some Western dishes, and a plate of meat or paneer tikka masala with naan bread and rice costs little more than US$5. Good mountain views from the upstairs terrace bar but the TVs are on most of the time (showing football and Indian movies) so can be a little noisy.

⏰ What to do

Mbale *p104, map p104*
Fly Mamia Afrika, T0785-748719, www. flymamiafrika.com. The only paragliding

outfit in Uganda, American Adam Robinson can organize tandem paragliding from the top of Wanale Ridge and landing in a school playing field in Mbale. Flights last 15 mins to 1 hr depending on the wind and drop for just over 500 m. Rates usually include accommodation and meals; contact to discuss packages from Kampala.

Sipi Falls *p107*
Rob's Rolling Rock, T0776-963078, or book through the **Sipi River Lodge**. This local company trained by Italian climbers offers 25-m abseils next to Sipi Falls from US$35, and guided rock climbing on a series of bolts in the cliff face adjacent to the falls from US$30 (beginners can try). Helmets are provided.

✹ Festivals

Mbale *p104, map p104*
If you are here during even-numbered years you may see some local festivities of the Imbalu people, as well as the mass circumcision ceremonies of the Bugisu and Sebei people (see page 109). The official 1st day of the circumcision season is on 1 Aug, when there is a celebration at the Mutoto Cultural Grounds just outside Mbale. There is a signposted turning to the east about 1 km south of Mbale on the Tororo–Mbale road. Everyone is welcome. The festivities reach a climax in Dec and involve singing, dancing, drumming and general merrymaking.

⊖ Transport

Tororo *p103*
Bus and matatu
The bus and taxi park is next to the market on the Mbale–Tororo road. *Matatus* run to and from **Kampala**'s Old Taxi Park and take about 4 hrs, US$5; to/from **Jinja** 2 hrs, US$3. Regular *matatus* go to **Mbale** (1 hr) and **Busia** (40 mins). The **Post Bus** (see page 14) stops in Tororo on its Kampala–Lira route.

Mbale *p104, map p104*
The shortest route from **Kampala** to Mbale is via the tarmac road from **Iganga** on the Jinja–Tororo (A109) road, which is 245 km and takes 4 hrs or less.

The **Elgon Flyer**, Soroti–Mbale Rd, just south of the clock tower, Mbale T0200-900323, Kampala T0200-900323, www.elgonflyer. com, has several daily services between **Kampala** and Mbale (4 hrs, US$4). The **Post Bus** (see page 14) stops at the Mbale post office on Republic St on its Kampala–Lira route, but note it goes to Tororo first and not by the quicker direct route from Iganga, so takes about 6 hrs from Kampala.

There are 2 taxi parks in Mbale. *Matatus* from the Kumi Rd Taxi Park, which is on the Soroti–Mbale Rd northeast of the clock tower, go north and east to **Kumi** (1 hr), **Soroti** (2½ hrs), **Sipi** (1 hr), **Kapchorwa** (2 hrs) and **Budadiri** (45 mins). *Matatus* from the Manafwa Rd taxi park go to **Kampala** (4 hrs), **Jinja** (2 hrs), **Iganga** (2 hrs), **Tororo** (1 hr), **Busia** (1 hr 40 mins) and places south.

Mbale to Soroti and the northeast *p111*
The **Post Bus** (see page 14) stops at both **Kumi** and **Soroti** on its **Kampala–Lira** route, and there are other buses from **Kampala** (5 hrs, US$11). Frequent *matatus* link Mbale and **Soroti** (2½ hrs) via **Kumi** (1 hr). *Matatus* very infrequently go from Soroti to Moroto (up to 5 hrs).

⊙ Directory

Mbale *p104, map p104*
Medical services Mbale Regional Referral Hospital, Pallisa Rd, T0454-433193. Open 24 hrs, the largest public hospital in the region.

Contents

Footprint features

Border crossings

Sseses, Bwindi & the south

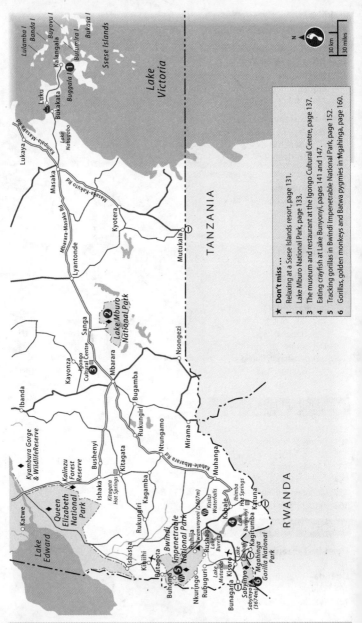

★ Don't miss ...

1 Relaxing at a Ssese Islands resort, page 131.
2 Lake Mburo National Park, page 133.
3 The museum and restaurant at the Igongo Cultural Centre, page 137.
4 Eating crayfish at Lake Bunyonyi, pages 141 and 147.
5 Tracking gorillas in Bwindi Impenetrable National Park, page 152.
6 Gorillas, golden monkeys and Batwa pygmies in Mgahinga, page 160.

The southwest region is the country's most popular destination, simply because few people visit Uganda without going to see the mountain gorillas. This fascinating but highly endangered species live in spectacular tropical rainforest, sheltered by mountain peaks and steep valleys. They can be tracked through the dense undergrowth and enormous trees at Bwindi Impenetrable National Park or Mgahinga Gorilla National Park, and seeing the gorillas in their natural habitat is rightly rated as one of Africa's top wildlife encounters.

On the way to this magical corner of Uganda, there are several distractions along the road from Kampala. Accessed from Masaka, the 84 lush, tropical Ssese Islands are heavily forested with waterfalls, and teem with birds including kingfishers, grey parrots and fish eagles. There are empty beaches, friendly islanders and trekking and fishing are popular activities.

About midway between Kampala and the gorillas, Lake Mburo National Park offers safaris and boat rides in tranquil surroundings of rolling hills and lush grass-covered valleys. Beyond Mbarara, the road forks southwest to Kabale and nearby picturesque Lake Bunyonyi. Dotted with tiny islands, this irregularly shaped lake is surrounded by lush terraced hillsides and is a haven for birds, and there are several laid-back resorts to relax at.

From Kabale the road continues to the friendly market town of Kisoro in the extreme southwest, close to the borders with the Rwanda and the Democratic Republic of Congo (DRC). This region is dominated by views of the dramatic Virunga Volcanoes that straddle the three countries; the access points into the mountains are in the vicinity of Kabale and Kisoro. Activities include delightful forest walks, tracking golden monkeys or challenging volcano climbs. But it is gorilla tracking at Bwindi or Mgahinga that is the undisputed highlight of the southwest.

Kampala to Masaka

The road immediately out of Kampala can be hectic, especially in the mornings as it passes through Natete, with its endless trading stores and matatu stops. But once out of the city, as the road lies just inland from Lake Victoria, the landscape alternates between fertile, well-watered fields and swampy areas with small patches of forest. About 40 km out of Kampala is Mpigi and, if you are hoping to buy any traditional musical instruments (particularly drums), this is the place to do so. There are drum-makers and their stalls on the side of the road. Mpigi is also the closest place to buy provisions for the nearby Mpanga Forest Reserve. Unlike the Mabira Forest on the Jinja road, only a very small patch of the Mpanga Forest Reserve is visible so watch out for the signs carefully. The reserve is an excellent day trip from Kampala. Further on is Masaka, a major hub for traffic to Tanzania and the Ssese Islands if travelling from the west.
▸▸ *For listing, see pages 126-128.*

Mpanga Forest Reserve → *For listing, see pages 126-128. Colour map 2, B4.*

Mpanga is a 450-ha lowland forest reserve about an hour's drive and 36 km from the capital. This remnant of the Guineo-Congolian rainforest, dating from the Pleistocene period 15,000 years ago, was gazetted for protection in 1951, when research plots were delineated within the forest to establish the productivity of indigenous forest trees. The main attractions are the mighty trees with their knotted roots, as well as monkeys, birds and over 180 varieties of butterflies. The most easily viewed mammals are the red-tailed monkey, flying squirrel and bushbuck. Over 200 bird species have been recorded here including the African pied hornbill, the great blue turaco and the black-and-white-casqued hornbill. The forest is contiguous with a papyrus swamp where the rare shoebill stork can be spotted (see box, page 72). The forest provides five types of timber used in drum-making. The Buganda royal drum-makers are in the nearby village of **Mpambire** on the Kampala–Masaka road about 3 km after the forest turn-off. Apart from drums, the few roadside stalls here sell wooden stools, woven baskets and mats to passing tourists on their way southwest.

Arriving at Mpanga Forest Reserve
Getting there The main Kampala–Masaka road bisects the forest. The turn-off 5 km after Mpigi is well signposted, and there is an 800-m murram track from the highway to the reception office. Take public transport from the New Taxi Park in Kampala to Mpigi, and then a *boda-boda* to the reserve. Alternatively, any *matatu* between Kampala and Masaka will drop off at the Mpanga turn-off.

Park information The entry fee for foreigners is listed as US$15 per day, with guided walks at US$15 per person. However, despite this listed tariff, foreign visitors are generally charged the local US$2 entrance fee and another US$2 guided forest walk fee.

Trails
Three trails have been marked. The **Base Line Trail** traverses the forest to a papyrus swamp 3 km away on the west side. The trail crosses a couple of streams with drifts of butterflies to be seen in the clearings. The 1-km **Butterfly Loop** takes less than 30 minutes and involves some scrambling over fallen trees and struggling through thick

Drums of Buganda

There is a saying in Luganda that goes *Tezirawa ngumba* which means 'They are not beaten without a reason'. In modern times you are most likely to hear drums being played at traditional weddings, funerals, and particularly in rural areas. Drums are often played on occasions of celebration, too, such as the Kabaka's coronation.

Although drums are frequently thought of as being merely musical instruments, they in fact have a wide range of uses. In the past there were literally hundreds of different beats for the drums and each rhythm was known and had a definite meaning; for example, a certain dance taking place, a call to war, a fire alarm or the news that a certain chief was passing. As a person heard the drum it was their duty to repeat the message so that within a few minutes the message could pass over many miles.

Traditionally, the drums belonged to the Kabaka and when he presented a chief with a position of office he bestowed upon him a drum. This is why the playing of the drums was an important part of the ceremonies involved in the crowning of the Kabaka – once he had 'tuned' the drums no one else was allowed to play them.

Kiganda (as Buganda culture is known) has drums of two kinds – the first is made of a hollowed block of wood, tapering towards the base, with skins stretched over the head and base. The skins are laced with thongs of hide. They are named according to their size and use, and the important ones are also given names individually. The other type, seen more rarely nowadays, is known as *ngalabi* and exists in various sizes. Also made of hollowed-out wood, it is long and slender, tapering gradually and then widening out again to form the base on which the drum stands. The top is covered with a skin – usually that of a type of water lizard – which is pegged on.

The bottom of the drum is left open. These drums are particularly attractive and large ones may be as much as 140 cm high.

In the past the ceremonies of the Baganda court were closely tied to the use of a large number of drums belonging to the Kabaka. Each drum or group of drums was named and men were specifically appointed to take up residence at the Lubiri (the Baganda palace) for the sole purpose of beating drums.

The range of drums used in the past was enormous – each was made slightly differently of varying sizes with different decorations. Each type served a distinct purpose and was played in a slightly different way, often by a specific clan. Examples of names include Nakawanguzu, which means the 'Conqueror'. This drum was played when the Kabaka had been successful in his attacks on surrounding tribes. The Kyejo was used when the Kabaka executed troublemakers as a warning to others. The Makumbi warned people to cultivate their banana gardens or risk having their hands cut off. The Va-mu-lugudo, meaning 'get out of the way', was used when the wives of the Kabaka were out walking; no one was allowed to be on the road in front of them, so the drummer went ahead to warn people to stand aside.

Drums are also associated with chieftainships, with each chief having his drum bestowed with his office by the Kabaka. The various clans of Baganda also had their own drums and particular drum beats. Selected clans were responsible for the making, beating, maintenance and safekeeping of the drums – different clans for each particular drum type.

There is a splendid collection of drums at the Uganda Museum in Kampala (see page 51). Drum-making can be seen in the village of Mpambire near the Mpanga Forest Reserve (see page 120).

vegetation. Tracks of both bush-babies and leopards are reported but, alas, the mammals themselves are rarely seen. The **Hornbill Trail** follows a 5-km loop taking about three hours along streams with exotic fungi, butterflies, birds and monkeys all on view.

Mpanga Forest Reserve to Masaka

Croc Camp ① *T0712-844944, www.ugandacrocs.com*, is the first distraction along this road after the Mpanga Forest Reserve, 66 km southwest of Kampala on the shores of Lake Victoria. It's the tourist component of **Uganda Crocs Ltd**, which farms young Nile crocodiles for their skins and meat. It also serves as a rescue centre and works closely with the **Uganda Wildlife Authority** (UWA), who has moved some particularly troublesome large crocodiles from villages along the Nile and other rivers. The camp has a pleasant location on a small beach on the lake and you can pull in to see the crocs in the ponds (for a small fee) and for lunch. Croc steaks are (naturally) on the menu as well as good fish and chips. See Where to stay, page 126, for details of accommodation in the cottages here.

Just after Buwama and 72 km from Kampala, you cross the **equator**, which is marked by large concrete circles on either side of the road. It is a Uganda must-do to pull over for a photo standing within the circle with one foot on the south and the other on the north, as many visitors have done since the circles were erected in the 1950s. Shops sell papyrus mats, trays and baskets and equator-themed souvenirs, like T-shirts. There are a couple of roadside restaurants serving snacks, cold drinks and coffee (see page 127). For a tip, you can also watch local entrepreneurs with jugs and bowls demonstrate how water swirls in opposite directions in the northern and southern hemispheres. (Uganda's other equator markers are located in the Kasese district within the Queen Elizabeth National Park, 420 km southwest of Kampala.) From the equator, the road then crosses the Katonga River, which links Lake Victoria and Lake George.

As you approach Lukaya, you will see roadside stands selling fresh and smoked fish, and you may spot pelicans and herons in the broad swamps. There is a weighbridge for heavy vehicles at Luyaka, where trucks and *matatus* are weighed, and as a result there are lots of street vendors milling around; look out for some good grilled chicken on sticks for sale.

From here onwards goats, sheep and Ankole cattle with their long horns (see box, page 138) are seen grazing along the roadside. The vegetation also changes, from papyrus grass in the swamps, to plantations of banana (*matoke*), coffee, cassava, mango and papaya. There are large termite mounds on either side of the road, some 2 m tall and 1.5 m in diameter at the base. Masaka is 30 minutes past Lukaya.

Masaka → *For listing, see pages 126-128. Phone code: 0481. Colour map 2, B3.*

Masaka is a pretty town, built on the side of a hill, but it's fairly unremarkable and most people just pass through. It is a stopping-off point for the Ssese Islands and an important road junction to the west for Kabale and Kisoro, northwest to Kasese and south to Tanzania. For a while it was the country's second largest town after Kampala but it was largely destroyed during the Tanzanian invasion of 1979. Today, with a population of around 75,000, it is considered Uganda's eighth largest town and it prospers on agriculture – bananas, tomatoes, avocados and pineapples thrive in this region – and the streets are crowded by bicycles with incredulous towers of fresh produce strapped to their panniers.

The name Masaka was thought to have derived from when the Ankole people migrated to the area from their kingdom in present-day Mbarara in search of food. They

Masaka

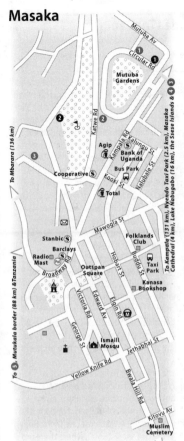

To Mbarara (136 km)
To Matukala border (88 km) & Tanzania
To Kampala (131 km), Nyendo Taxi Park (2.5 km), Masaka Cathedral (4 km), Lake Nabugabo (16 km), the Ssese Islands & Kalangu
To Bukakata (39 km), for Ferry to Ssese Islands

Where to stay
Brovad **1**
Croc Camp **4**
Golf Lane **2**
Masaka Backpackers'
  Cottage & Campsite **5**
Zebra **3**

Restaurants
Café Frikadellen **1**
Plot 99 Coffeehouse
  & Lounge **2**

Bars & Clubs
Club Ambience **3**

200 metres
200 yards

found millet, which in their language was called *omugisha*. When they asked the local Baganda people for it, the Baganda couldn't pronounce *omugisha*, and instead called it Masaka.

Arriving in Masaka

Getting there The 131-km trip from Kampala to Masaka takes around two to three hours, depending on traffic. There are frequent *matatus* from the New Taxi Park and the Natete Taxi Park and buses from the central bus station in Kampala. If continuing to the Ssese Islands the same day, make sure you get to Masaka by lunchtime. See Transport, page 128.

Masaka Cathedral

ⓘ *Kituvo Cathedral Rd, off Kampala Rd, 4 km northeast of town, Mon-Sat 1000-1700, Sun 0700-1700, free, but donations are welcome.*
The Masaka township began life in the 1900s, and in 1909 a small church was built in the village of Kituvo, now a suburb of Masaka. Less than two decades later, the congregation had grown and the modest thatched building was replaced by the larger red-brick Masaka Cathedral (also referred to as the **Cathedral of Kitovu**). The major event in the building's religious history occurred in 1939, when Joseph Kiwánuka arrived to preside over the Kituvo congregation. Born in central Uganda, he was the first sub-Saharan African Catholic bishop and was ordained in 1939 by Pope Pius XII in the Basilica of St Peter in Rome. Because of this appointment, the cathedral also became the first autonomous African Catholic church. Kiwánuka served in Masaka until 1961 when he then became Archbishop at the Rubaga Cathedral of the Sacred Heart in Kampala (page 51) until his death in 1966. He was buried at Rubaga.

Decades of harsh weather and seismic activity caused Masaka Cathedral to become structurally unstable in the 1990s; in particular the roof was sagging dangerously. The building was nominated

Border crossing: Uganda–Tanzania

Mutukula

The Mutukula border (0600-1800) is 217 km southwest of Kampala and 88 km south of Masaka. The section of road from Masaka has been recently surfaced, as has the 82-km road from the border to Bukoba, the nearest town on the Tanzanian side on the shores of Lake Victoria. These new roads have made the journey much easier and quicker than it once was and, with the border crossing, it now takes around five or six hours to cover the 299 km between Kampala and Bukoba. There are over-the-border buses between Kampala and Bukoba via Masaka. Alternatively, you can get to the border and Bukoba by short *matatu* hops – Kampala–Masaka, Masaka–Mutukula, and Mutukula–Bukoba.

Visas for both countries are available at the border. Remember, because of the East Africa customs agreement, you are permitted to travel between Uganda, Tanzania and Kenya on single-entry visas without getting re-entry visas for each of these countries, as long as the visas you have are valid. For more information on visas between the East African countries, see box, page 33. If you're in your own vehicle allow plenty of time to process the paperwork (between 30 minutes and two hours) and remember the border closes at 1800. There is a branch of Stanbic Bank on the Ugandan side of the border but the nearest banks with ATMs are in Masaka and Bukoba.

There is no accommodation in Mutukula and the nearest on the Tanzania side is in Bukoba. The best of a limited choice is the (**$$**) **Walkgard Westland Hotel**, 3 km southwest of Bukoba on the slopes of Kashuru Hill, overlooking the lake, T+255 (0)28-222 0935, www.walkgard.com, which has 42 comfortable rooms with balconies, swimming pool and a reasonable restaurant. Budget travellers and overlanders should head to the (**$**) **Kioyera Backpackers Campsite**, Jamhuri St, T+255 (0)28-222 0203, www.kiroyeratours.co.tz, which has a shady campsite right on the beach, you can rent a tent or a thatched domed *banda*, and there are reliable hot showers, a bar and restaurant.

Bukoba lies in the extreme northwest of Tanzania and is in fact a lot closer to Kampala than Dar es Salaam or any of the major tourist places in Tanzania. As a result, a little forward planning is needed to get from Bukoba to anywhere else if you choose to enter Tanzania from Uganda. There are a number of transport options: the Tanzanian airline **Precision Air** (www.precisionairtz.com) has at least one flight a day between Bukoba and Mwanza (on the south shore of Lake Victoria), where there are onward flights to Dar es Salaam and then on to other destinations in Tanzania; there are buses between Bukoba and Mwanza around the south of the lake (eight to 10 hours); and the third option of getting between the two is the overnight ferry across the lake. These depart on Monday, Wednesday and Friday from Bukoba to Mwanza, and on Sunday, Tuesday and Thursday from Mwanza to Bukoba, both leaving at 2100 and taking 11-12 hours, but check the schedule locally. For more information see the *Footprint Tanzania Handbook*.

to the New York-based **World Monument Fund**'s watch-list and, with considerable fund-raising efforts, in 1998 the entire roof and tower were repaired and steel was introduced into the cathedral's skeleton to improve long-term stability. Today it's an impressive red-brick building set in manicured gardens and attracting a congregation of around 5000. Its other claim to fame is that it has the only pipe-organ in Uganda.

An easy excursion from Masaka, or a detour on the way to the Ssese Islands (page 129), Lake Nabugabo is a shallow, oval, freshwater lake, 8.2 km by 5 km, separated from the western shore of Lake Victoria, 3 km distant, by an arm of the Lwamunda swamp and a sandbar. It's estimated to have developed about 3700 years ago, and is thought to have been formed by strong winds developing the sandbar. The northern shore is forested and there are sandy beaches on the eastern edge. Because of the mineral content of the lake, it is claimed that bilharzia does not occur here and this has made it popular for swimming.

It's a very peaceful place to relax and to watch birds, either along the shores of the lake or from a small fishing boat. In 2004 Lake Nabugabo was declared a Ramsar wetland site; almost 300 plant species have been identified and over 180 bird species confirmed, including the shoebill stork (see box, page 72), kingfishers and crested cranes, along with important migratory birds such as the blue swallow.

The lake was popular with expats during the colonial period, among other reasons because of the supposed absence of crocodiles. One report of a crocodile seen in 1932 was dismissed, but when a dog was snatched while swimming in the lake in 1946, a meticulous search was made. So much for no crocodiles: in a period of three months a total of 10 crocodiles were seen and shot in the lake. These included a particularly large 4.5-m-long male thought to be around 30 years old. The lake was cleared of crocodiles with the aim of making it safe for swimmers. However, after exceptionally heavy rains later that year flooded the land between the Lake Nabugabo and Lake Victoria, crocodiles reappeared. It is doubtful whether there are currently crocodiles in Lake Nabugabo, but you might want to check with local residents before you dive in.

Arriving at Lake Nabugabo
Getting there Lake Nabugabo is 16 km from Masaka, 6 km east of the Masaka–Bukakata road. From Masaka you can get the bus or *matatus* to Bukakata (page 128), for the ferry to the Ssese Islands (page 129), which go past the clearly signposted turning to Lake Nabugabo. From there you have to walk the last 6 km or you may be lucky to flag down a *boda-boda*. The easiest is to get a special hire taxi from Masaka directly to the lake's resorts (US$8-10), which takes about 30 minutes.

⊙ Kampala to Masaka listings

For hotel and restaurant price codes and other relevant information, see pages 16-20.

⊙ Where to stay

Mpanga Forest Reserve *p120*
$ The simple accommodation, campsite, barbecue, picnic and latrine facilities are near the office, and there's another picnic site in a forest glade about 100 m from the start of the Base Line Trail. There are 2 rooms in a double-storey *banda*, and another double room attached to the National Forest Authority's buildings. But it's very basic, only beds and mosquito nets, so bring all bedding and food, though water and firewood are available and basic meals can be pre-ordered with considerable notice from the caretaker. A bed is US$10 per person, and camping US$2 per person.

Mpanga Forest Reserve to Masaka *p122*
$ Croc Camp, Kampala–Masaka Rd, 66 km southwest of Kampala, T0712-844944, www.ugandacrocs.com. A pleasant lakeside resort at this crocodile farm. 5 simple A-frame brick cottages (from US$40) and campsite (US$5 per person) in lovely grounds, open-air bar and restaurant with lake views, fishing from local canoes can be arranged, birdwatchers may spot the crested crane in the grounds.

Masaka *p122, map p123*
$$ Golf Lane Hotel, 1 Kinanina Rd, T0392-200 669/70, www.golflanehotel.com. On Kizungu Hill, the highest point in Masaka and overlooking the golf course, the **Golf Lane Hotel** is a business hotel in the former mansion of ex-Vice-President Muwanga. It has modern wings, 78 well-appointed rooms and 7 suites, with DSTV and great balcony views. There's a bar, restaurant, gym and pool.

$$-$ Hotel Brovad, 6 Circular Rd, T0772-425666, www.hotelbrovad.com. In a plain white block, this is functional rather than charming, and has 125 rooms, some triples, with DSTV and slightly dated furnishings, but there's a comfortable bar with terrace and the restaurant is very good, especially the authentic Indian food.

$ Hotel Zebra, Baines Terr, T 0481-420936. Located on a crescent uphill north of the post office, and aimed at the conference market with 100+ rooms with DSTV. Despite being fairly new, there have been reports of poor cleanliness. However, it has a pleasant terrace and garden overlooking Nyabajuzzi Valley, a papyrus wetland area that attracts a lot of birds, and the bar and restaurant has a varied menu and a good-value buffet lunch on Sun.

$ Masaka Backpackers' Cottage and Campsite, 4 km from Masaka, on the Bukoba–Kakuto road, Nyendo, T0752-619389, www.masakabackpackers.webklik.nl. Well positioned on a semi-rural hilly site overlooking banana plantations with singles/doubles (US$10/18), dorms (US$7 per person) and camping (US$4 per person), also has 2 tents for hire. Cooking facilities or tasty food prepared to order, well-stocked fridge for beers and sodas, lounge with DSTV. Can organize transport to Lake Nabugabo. To get here take a special hire taxi or *boda-boda* to Kirimya, disembark at Kasanvu and follow the signs.

Lake Nabugabo *p125*
The 3 simple lake resorts are within a few hundred metres of each other at the end of the lake's access road from the Masaka–Bukakata Rd. Day visitors are welcome for around US$3 per person.

$$-$ Nabugabo Holiday Centre, T0772-433332, www.nabugabo.com. Previously the **Church of Uganda Guesthouse**, built in 1926 as a holiday resort and conference centre for the missionaries of the Church of

Uganda, who also run **Namirembe Guest House**, Kampala (see page 55). Has 4 twin or family cottages (from US$46), full board or B&B but alcohol-free, and there's a pretty campsite (US$8 per person, tent hire US$10-14). Canoes can be hired for birdwatching and fishing.

$ Lake Nabugabo Terrace View Beach, T0785-570398, www.lake-nabugabo.net. The terrace title comes from the fact that this resort lies on a slightly raised sandbank on the lakeshore, where there are 6 2-bed en suite thatched *bandas*, simple furnishings but fairly new so the tiled bathrooms are good, or you can camp. Restaurant and bar for basic meals like grilled tilapia fish, beers and sodas with pleasant outdoor tables, electricity is from a generator that operates 1900-2200.

$ Sand Beach Resort, T0772-416047. The place to be if you want a lively atmosphere and it gets very busy on the weekends and holidays with families from Masaka and beyond. Although not a lot of sand is found on the lakeshore, it's a good place to swim, especially for children, because the water has a shallow gradient. There are 8 en suite smallish doubles in cottages (from US$40), or you can camp (US$4 per person) on the lawns next to the lake. Restaurant, bar and activities include boat rides, and (oddly) donkey rides for children.

❼ Restaurants

Mpanga Forest Reserve to Masaka
p122

$ AidChild's Equation Café & Gallery, on the Kampala–Masaka Rd on the equator. Daily 0700-1900. An outlet of the NGO **AidChild**, a US-based charity involved with HIV/AIDS concerns in Uganda. The pleasant café offers home-made muffins, filled pancakes and hot meals of chicken or sausage and chips. The gallery and shop is stocked with some interesting fair-trade souvenirs, although they are pricey compared to the other stalls at the equator.

$ Uganda Equator Line Restaurant, on the Kampala–Masaka Rd on the equator, T0702-653223. Daily 0630-2030. This place is literally 'on the equator' and has been strategically built over the yellow line on the ground and is 5 m from the concrete circle on the west side of the road; some tables inside straddle the yellow line. There's an interesting map on the wall showing the countries the equator passes through. Serves drinks, snacks, English breakfasts, local dishes and good grilled tilapia fish, which you'll see for sale at the side of the road between here and Masaka, plus cakes, chocolate and souvenirs.

Masaka *p122, map p123*
The hotels offer decent enough food and additionally Masaka has 2 excellent expat-run cafés that are deservedly popular with Masaka's NGO community.

$$-$ Plot 99 Coffeehouse & Lounge, Hill Rd, near **Golf Lane Hotel**, T0700-151649. Mon, Wed andThu 1200-2200 (closed Tue), Fri-Sun 1000-2200. Friendly Belgium set-up with outdoor pergola and terrace with great views over town. Good Western-style menu including burgers, tapas and pizza, plus coffees, herbal teas, fresh juices, cold beers, and possibly the best chocolate cupcakes in Uganda. Also has Wi-Fi and offers massages and facials.

$ Café Frikadellen, 1 Mutuba Gardens, T0792-081010. Daily 0900-1930, Fri until 2200. Danish-run in the same compound as **Uganda Childcare** and a little tricky to find as it's down a dusty dirt road but most *boda-boda* drivers know it. This lovely café serves Western dishes – the cinnamon buns and pancakes for breakfast are great, as are the toasted sandwiches and *frikadellens* (meatballs) for lunch. There's a barbecue (US$10-12) on Fri from 1800; phone or pop in earlier to book if possible. Shaded outdoor or indoor seating and Wi-Fi. The profits go to support local schools.

🍷 Bars and clubs

Kampala to Masaka *p120*
Club Ambiance, Ddiba St, off the Kampala
Rd. Wed-Sat 2000-0400. Busy at the
weekends, this has a flashy 3-storey glass
exterior outside, and a seedy disco with
several bars inside.

🚌 Transport

Masaka *p122, map p123*
The main taxi and bus parks are in the
centre on or around Buddu St. There are
frequent direct buses and *matatus* to and
from **Kampala** (2-3 hrs) and **Mbarara**
(2 hrs), both US$4. Vehicles from Kampala
west to Mbarara, **Kabale** and **Kasese** (and
vice versa) go via Masaka but not all of
them go into town. Some stop at the Total
petrol station on the Masaka–Mbarara
Bypass Rd, 6 km north of the centre. The
Post Bus (see page 14) between Kampala
and Kabale stops in Masaka, and the post
office is in the centre of town on Hill Rd
close to Stanbic Bank.

Matatus leave frequently for **Bukakata**,
40 km away, for the ferry to the Ssese
Islands. You can also catch these and get
off after 12 km at the turning to **Lake
Nabugabo** (page 125). Bukakata vehicles
depart from the Nyendo taxi park on the
junction with the Kampala–Masaka Rd
and the Bukakata road, 2.5 km northeast
of Masaka's centre and a short hop by a
town *matatu* or *boda-boda*. Alternatively,
if travelling by bus or *matatu* from
Kampala straight to the Ssese Islands,
you can get off at Nyendo and not go
into Masaka at all. Make sure you get to
Masaka by lunchtime if you are going
to the islands the same day. There is
usually 1 *matatu*, 1 hr, US$4, from Nyendo
to Bukakata to connect to each ferry
departure/arrival (see page 130 for
details of the ferry). Additionally, there
is 1 daily bus service from the main bus
station in Masaka at around 1400, which
connects with the 1600 ferry, and arrives
in **Kalangala** (the main town on Buggala
Island) at about 1900, US$6. It leaves
Kalangala on its return journey at around
0630-0730.

To get to **Tanzania** via the **Mutukula**
border, 88 km from Masaka, the Kampala–
Bukoba buses (see Transport, Kampala,
page 66) get to Masaka at about
1230-1330 (1½ hrs-2 hrs after leaving
Kampala), and arrive in Bukoba 1600-1700.
Alternatively, only marginally cheaper and
much slower, take one of the frequent
matatus in the morning from Masaka
to **Kyotera** (1 hr), the small town about
halfway between Masaka and the border,
and then take another *matatu* to Mutukula
(1-1½ hrs, but more sporadic). You need to
get to the border by about 1600 to allow
time for the administrative procedures to
be completed as it closes at 1800. Another
matatu (*dala-dala* in Tanzania), to Bukoba
(82 km) should take around 1½-2 hrs,
but you may need to wait for some time
before one fills up to depart. See also
Border crossing box, page 124.

Uganda Wildlife

Practically everyone travelling around Uganda will come into contact with animals at some time during their stay, and the country's unique wildlife is its biggest draw. It may not have the vast herds of plains game you'll find in neighbouring Kenya and Tanzania, even though several of the savannah parks (like Queen Elizabeth, Murchison Falls, Lake Mburo and Kidepo Valley) do have some of the larger mammals safari-goers expect to see. However, Uganda has one the densest and most varied populations of primates in the whole of Africa, and one of the country's greatest attractions is tracking habituated groups of these primates, such as the mountain gorillas and chimpanzees, through beautiful tangled forests. Uganda is also world famous for its rich and colourful birdlife and, with 1060 species, it has well over half of Africa's total number of birds. This is a quick photographic guide to some of the more fascinating animals and birds you may encounter.

■ **Hippopotamus** *Hippopotamus amphibius*. A large beast with short stubby legs that can weigh up to four tonnes but is agile and fast on land. During the day it rests in water, rising every few minutes to snort and blow at the surface, because its skin

Below: Hippopotamus in the Kazinga Channel

Above: Rothschild giraffe
Right: Common zebra
Below: Leopard

would dry up if not kept damp and its body temperature needs to be regulated. At night hippos graze on land; they need up to 60 kg of grass every day, so have to forage far.

■ **Rothschild giraffe** *Giraffa camelopardalis rothschildi*. Yellowish-buff with patchwork of brownish marks and jagged edges, a mature male can be over 5 m tall; both male and female have horns. Found throughout Africa, the subspecies in Uganda is the Rothschild giraffe, also known as the Ugandan giraffe, seen in Murchison Falls and Kidepo.

■ **Common/Burchell's zebra** *Equus burchelli*. Stocky horse-like bodies, manes of short, erect hair, coats are black and white striped that are a form of camouflage which breaks up the outline of the body. They form herds, sometimes with antelope, and can be seen in Murchison Falls and Lake Mburo.

iii

■ **Leopard** *Panthera pardus*. Found in varied habitats ranging from forest to open savannah, generally nocturnal, hunting at night or before the sun comes up to avoid the heat. Well camouflaged, its spots, typically dark rosettes with a tawny-yellow middle, merge into foliage or blend well into less sparse grassland. Present in all forested parks in Uganda, but seldom spotted amongst the dense trees.

■ **Elephant** *Loxodonta africana*. The largest land mammal weighing up to six tonnes with an average shoulder height of 3-4 m, form groups led by a female matriarch. Although populations in Uganda suffered terribly during Uganda's strife years, numbers are increasing rapidly to the present 5000 country-wide; two-thirds are in Queen Elizabeth National Park. The smaller **African forest elephant** (*Loxodonta africana cyclotis*) is present in Bwindi Impenetrable and Kibale national parks.

■ **Buffalo** *Syncerus caffer*. A robust species with black-brown coat and large curved horns, a shoulder height of 1-1.7 m, weight of 500-900 kg, a long stocky body, and short, thickset legs. More likely to be seen on open plains but equally at home in dense forest and in Uganda often seen wallowing with hippo on the edge of lakes and rivers.

Left: Elephant
Below: Buffalo

■ **Lion** *Panthera leo*. The largest of the big cats in Africa with weights of around 250 kg for a male. Found on open savannah, they are sociable animals living in prides of up to 30 animals. The females do the hunting, being smaller, swifter and more agile than the males; they prey mostly on large antelope or buffalo. Colouration varies from light buff to yellowish, reddish or dark brown, the underparts are generally lighter and the tail tuft is black.

■ **Vervet monkey** *Chlorocebus pygerythrus*, 39-43 cm. A smallish primate, one of the most recognized monkeys in Africa and often seen at campsites and lodges. Brown body with a white underbelly and black face ringed by white fur; males have blue abdominal regions. Spends the day foraging on the ground and sleeps at night in trees.

■ **Chimpanzee** *Pan troglodytes*, 1.2-1.7 m tall. A primate that is the closest living relative to a human being, with black-brown fur, human-like fingers and toes. It weighs as much as 70 kg, uses tools, has a complex structure of communicating and displays emotions, including laughing out loud. Generally vegetarian but also known to eat smaller monkeys. Lives in forests in western Uganda where several communities have been habituated.

■ **Olive baboon** *Papio anubis*. A large heavily built primate weighing up to 40 kg, olive brown or greyish in colour, the adult male has a well-developed mane. Often found in acacia grassland or in rocks, and is sociable, living in groups called troops. The female is often seen with young clinging to

Top: Vervet monkey
Middle: Olive baboon
Bottom: Black-and-white colobus monkey

her. In some areas they have become very used to the presence of man and can be a nuisance; be careful, they have a nasty bite.

■ **Black-and-white colobus monkey** *Colobus guereza*. A striking-looking primate with black fur and a long white tuft running from the shoulders to the end of its long tail. Newborns are completely white. Extremely agile and can jump 30 m. Colobus means 'mutilated' in Greek, as, unlike other primates, they don't have thumbs.

■ **Mountain gorilla** *Gorilla beringei beringei*, 1.5-1.8 m. Highly endangered and the world's largest primate weighing 204-227 kg. Lives in family groups led by mature males called 'silverbacks' because of the silver hair on their backs. Newborn gorillas are tiny, weighing about 2.5 kg. A female's gestation period and mothering behaviour is similar to that of humans. Lives at altitudes of 2200–4300 m and spends most of the day foraging for shoots and leaves.

■ **Defassa waterbuck** *Kobus ellipsiprymnus defassa*, 122-137 cm. A subspecies of the common waterbuck and found in all Uganda's savannah parks. Has a shaggy grey-brown coat, rounded ears, white patches above the eyes and on its rump. Males have long, gently curving horns which are heavily ringed. Despite its name, it's not an aquatic animal, but it does take refuge in water to escape predators, and its coat emits an oily secretion for waterproofing.

■ **Greater kudu** *Tragelaphus strepsiceros*, 140-153 cm. A slender elegant antelope, its colour varies from greyish to fawn with several vertical white stripes down the sides of the body. Horns long and spreading, with two or three twists (male only). Distinctive thick fringe of hair running from the chin down the neck. It prefers fairly thick bush, sometimes in quite dry areas, but in Uganda it is rare and only found in Kidepo Valley National Park.

■ **Topi** *Damaliscus korrigum*, 122-127 cm. Has a striking reddish-brown coat that is glossy, even iridescent in bright sunlight, with distinct black patches on the face, as well as upper forelegs, hips and thighs, making the legs look as if they are encased in stockings. Both sexes have thick, heavily ringed, lyre-shaped horns. Seen in Uganda's savannah parks.

■ **Jackson's hartebeest** *Alcelaphus buselaphus*, 127-132 cm. Has a long, narrow horse-like face and rather comical expression. The shoulders are much higher than the rump giving it a very sloped-back appearance. Short horns that differ from any other antelope, as they are on a bony pedicel; a backward extension of the skull which forms a base.

■ **Eland** *Taurotragus oryx*, 175-183 cm. The largest of the antelope, cow-like in appearance with a noticeable dewlap and shortish spiral horns (both sexes). Greyish to fawn, sometimes with rufous tinge and narrow white stripes down side of body. Travels large distances in search of food and can eat tough woody bushes and thorny plants.

Opposite top: Mountain gorilla
Opposite middle: Defassa waterbuck
Opposite bottom left: Topi
Opposite bottom right: Jackson's hartebeest

■ **Sitatunga** *Tragelaphus spekii eurycerus*, 80-120 cm. A good swimmer and semi-aquatic, with shaggy fawn-coloured coat, and unique splayed hooves that allows it to negotiate the vegetated marshy terrain that it favours. Males have long twisted horns. Present throughout Uganda, but shy and well camouflaged so seldom seen.

■ **Ugandan kob** *Kobus kob thomasi*, 100-115 cm. An animal depicted on Uganda's coat-of-arms and common in Queen Elizabeth and Murchison Falls national parks, but not unique to Uganda at it's also found in parts of the DRC and South Sudan. Coat is reddish-brown with white rings around each eye, and a white chevron on the throat. Lyre-shaped, ringed, short, thick horns (male only). Live in groups of either females and calves or just males.

■ **Bushbuck** *Tragelaphus scriptus*, 76-92 cm. Shaggy coat with white spots and stripes on

Top: Ugandan kob
Above: Bushbuck

the side and back and two white, crescent-shaped marks on the neck. Short horns (male only), slightly spiral. High rump gives characteristic crouch. White underside of tail is noticeable when running. Occurs in thick bush, often near water, in pairs or singly.

■ **Günther's dikdik** *Madoqua guentheri*, 36-41 cm. So small it cannot be mistaken, it is greyish brown, often washed with rufous. Legs are thin and stick-like. Slightly elongated snout and a conspicuous tuft of hair on the top of the head. Straight, small horns (male only).

■ **Grant's gazelle** *Gazella granti*, 81-99 cm. Has a coat that is a beige orange on the back with a white belly, and has lyre-shaped horns which are stout at the base and clearly ringed. Fond of open grassy plains, it is extremely fast and can run up to 80 km per hour.

■ **Common duiker** *Sylvicapra grimmia*, 58 cm. Also known as the grey or bush duiker, grey-fawn in colour with darker rump and pale colour on the underside. Its dark muzzle and prominent ears are divided by straight, upright, narrow pointed horns. Of 21 species of duiker, this is the only one found in open grasslands; it is usually associated with a forested environment.

■ **Oribi** *Ourebia ourebi*, 61 cm. Slender and delicate looking with a longish neck and a sandy to brownish-fawn coat. It has oval-shaped ears, a patch of bare skin just below each ear, and short, straight horns with a few rings at their base (male only). Lives in small groups or as a pair and is never far from water.

■ **Impala** *Aepyceros melampus*, 92-107 cm. Has a bright rufous-coloured coat with a

Top: Grant's gazelle
Above: Oribi

Above left: Impala
Above right: Side-striped jackal
Left: Warthog
Opposite page: Bush pig

white abdomen flanked by black stripes, a white 'eyebrow' and chin and white hair inside its ears. It has long lyre-shaped horns (male only). Above the heels of the hind legs is a tuft of thick black bristles (unique to impala), which are easy to see as the animal runs in graceful leaps. Found in herds of 15 to 20, it likes open grassland usually close to water.

■ **Spotted hyena** *Crocuta crocuta*, 69-91 cm. A large scavenger, its high shoulders and low back give it a characteristic appearance. Brownish, with dark spots and a large head, the hyena is an aggressive creature that has been known to attack live animals and will occasionally try to steal a kill from lions. It always looks dirty because of its habit of lying in muddy pools to keep cool and alleviate irritation from parasites.

■ **Side-striped jackal** *Canis adustus*, 41-46 cm. A dog-like carnivore with a long muzzle, bushy tail and pointed ears, greyish-fawn fur with a darker stripe along the side. A well-known plains scavenger, the jackal can be seen in most parks, often near lion kills, but is also common on farmland.

■ **Warthog** *Phacochoerus aethiopicus*, 63-85 cm. A common and comical plains animal and member of the pig family. Grey and almost hairless, with large head, tusks and wart-like growths on its face; these are thought to protect the eyes as it sweeps sideways with its tusks, digging up roots and tubers. It often kneels on its forelegs when eating, and when startled will run at speed with tail held straight up in the air followed by its young.

■ **Bush pig** *Potamochoerus porcus*, 66-100 cm. Larger than a warthog and prefers forest environments. Compact body with short legs, rounded back, long tufted tail and elongated snout. Coat colour is extremely variable from blond, or pale red, to a dark brown or near-black. Omnivorous and highly adaptable, it eats anything from roots and fungi, to eggs and small mammals. In Uganda can be seen following monkeys and feeding on their discarded fruits.

 **Rock hyrax** *Heterohyrax brucei*. Looks a bit like a large grey-brown guinea pig and lives in colonies amongst boulders and on rocky hillsides, protecting itself from predators like eagles and leopards by darting into rock crevices. The structure of the ear is similar to that found in whales, its molar teeth look like those of a rhinoceros, two pouches in the stomach resemble a condition found in birds, and the arrangement of the bones of the forelimb are like those of the elephant.

 **Banded mongoose** *Mungos mungo*. An entertaining small mammal with large head, short, muscular limbs and long tail (almost as long as the rest of the body). The abdominal part of the body is higher and rounder than the breast area.

Greyish brown fur with several dark brown to black horizontal bars across the back. Makes dens for shelter including in termite mounds.

■ **Spotted-necked otter** *Hydrictis maculicollis*, 71 to 76 cm from nose to rump. Has a sleek tale and webbed paws used for swimming, reddish to chocolate-brown fur marked with creamy or white blotches over the chest and throat. Broad head with short muzzle, small rounded ears and a hairless nose pad. In Uganda it is frequently seen fishing in Lake Victoria and Lake Bunyonyi.

■ **Nile crocodile** *Crocodylus niloticus*. Lives in lakes, rivers and swamps, and is the second largest reptile in the world after the saltwater crocodile. Has four short, splayed legs, long tail, scaly hide, powerful jaws and is a fast swimmer and runner. A fierce predator and capable of taking almost any animal within its sight; an attack is sudden and unpredictable. The largest crocodiles in Uganda, and possibly in Africa, are in the Nile at Murchison Falls National Park where they reach lengths of 6 m and weights of 700 kg.

■ **Nile monitor lizard**, *Varanus niloticus*. About 120-160 cm in length with muscular greyish-brown bodies, greenish-yellow rosette-like spots, strong legs, powerful jaws and sharp claws used for digging or tearing at prey. The name derives from the way it stands on hind legs to monitor the surroundings. Its favourite food is crocodile eggs.

■ **Chameleon** *Chamaeleonidae*. Small, common reptile seen all over Uganda with long, worm-like tongue that can suddenly extend for a distance greater than the length of its own body to catch insects. Eyes are set on prominent cones, and each moves independently so that while one is seeing where the next foothold is, the other is looking around for food. Best known for its ability to change colour depending on its surroundings.

Below: Nile monitor lizard
Bottom: Nile crocodile

Ugandan birds

From the scenic shores of Uganda's many great lakes to the lush forests of the Albertine Rift Valley and the banks of the mighty Nile, Uganda has an astonishingly rich diversity of habitats for birds. These include open savannah, montane and equatorial rainforests, rivers, swamps, freshwater and saline lakes. Uganda has an enviable bird list of 1060 species, which constitutes 67% of Africa's total number of bird species and 11.1% of the world's total population. Murchison Falls National Park (page 232) has a recorded 450 species, while Queen Elizabeth National Park (page 174) has more than 610 species, making these two parks among the most prolific protected areas to be found anywhere on earth. Additionally, with a checklist of 346 species, Bwindi Impenetrable National Park (page 150) is believed to hold the greatest number of forest bird species anywhere in Africa, with Budongo Forest Reserve (page 227) and its 340 species coming a close second.

Uganda has 33 Important Bird Areas covering some 7% of the country; also known as IBAs, these are areas recognized by BirdLife International as being globally important habitats for the conservation of birds. (In Africa, there are over 1230 IBAs and over there are 10,000 worldwide.) In Uganda, many of these are in the protected areas (national parks and reserves) but not restricted to them. For example, Mabamba Bay (page 72), Lake Nabugabo (page 125),

Below: Shoebill
Bottom: Turaco
Opposite page: Marabou stork

and Lutoboka Point in the Ssese Islands (page 131) are also listed as IBAs.

There are so many good birdwatching sites in Uganda that the special interest of each individual birder will to a large extent determine the places to visit. Birdwatching in Uganda is good all year round. But the best time is generally from late May to mid-September, when birds are at their most abundant as it is the main fruiting season in most of the forests and seeds are plentiful in the open areas. But other months have their advantages too: for example the Palearctic migrants arrive in October and head back in March; intra-African migrants arrive in July and start leaving in December; and the main nesting season in Bwindi and Mgahinga (key sites for the Albertine Rift endemics) is April to June.

Of the many species, there are three large and conspicuous birds worth mentioning – they could perhaps be considered the principal characters of Uganda's star-studded avian show. A massive grey bird with a staring yellow eye and broad bill and the most prized species to look for is the rare, prehistoric-looking shoebill stork (*Balaeniceps rex*) (see page 72). It is a tall bird, 110-152 cm high, weighs 4-7 kg and has a wingspan of 230-260 cm. It inhabits most of Uganda's papyrus swamps and is the single species that attracts the biggest number of birdwatchers to Uganda.

Keep an eye out for the beautiful grey-crowned crane (*Balearica regulorum*), also known as the crested crane, which is an elegant bird measuring up to 1 m tall, 3.5 kg in weight and with a wingspan of 2 m. It has a black head with red and white patches on its face and a brilliantly golden crest – the same colours as the Ugandan flag (red, yellow and black); it is the country's national bird and features on its coat-of-arms.

Finally, an unmissable bird and the largest and ugliest of them all, the marabou stork (*Leptoptilos crumeniferus*) measures up to 1.5 m in height, 9 kg in weight, and has a wingspan of up to 3.7 m. It's an intelligent, bare-headed (and bare-faced) scavenging stork that is known to follow vultures and scavenge off the remains of large predator kills. Thanks to its enormous bill and dagger-like jaws, even hyenas are wary of approaching it. This large, hulking bird is present all over Uganda, and is just as likely to be seen in the car park of Entebbe International Airport as it is in the parks and reserves. Kampala is an unusual haven for marabous, and they are often seen picking their way through the rotten mess of rubbish dumps looking for anything edible. They also use Kampala's high-rise buildings as roosts; the story goes that they only moved into the city during the time when Idi Amin's murderous troops enjoyed throwing victims off tall buildings – it is said the corpses were left for the marabous to dismember...

Ssese Islands

This collection of islands (sometimes spelt Sese or Ssesse) is situated in the northwestern part of Lake Victoria and is an increasingly popular tourist destination. There are 84 attractive islands in the group. All the islands are hilly and the smaller islands remain fringed with dense rainforest, containing 240 bird species, several species of monkey and the occasional large snake. The islands are also suited to those keen on walking or sport fishing. Being quite remote, they have retained an easy-going atmosphere. Buggala Island's Lukoboka Bay is where most tourist hotels are found along the white sandy beaches.

Early in the 20th century the Ssese Islands were depopulated following a widespread outbreak of sleeping sickness. After 15 years some people began to drift back again, but there were few settlers until the period of civil unrest during the 1980s, when the remoteness of the islands offered safety against the insurgents. As a result of the low population numbers the islands were not marred by development. Regrettably deforestation now scars great tracts of land with an estimated 40% of forests felled on Buggala Island. Cash crops like palm oil plantations have been planted and industrial vessels over-fishing Lake Victoria have created a crisis for local fishermen. ▶ *For listing, see pages 131-132.*

Arriving on the Ssese Islands → *Phone code: 0481. Colour map 2, B/C4.*

Getting there
There are a few ways of reaching the Sseses. One option is to go on the Entebbe–Kalangala (on Buggala Island) ferry from Nakiwogo port, on the western side of the Entebbe peninsula. To get to Nakiwogo from Entebbe, turn off the Kampala–Entebbe road at Wilson Street, also known as Nsamizi Road, on to Nakiwogo Road for 3 km. The ferry leaves Nakiwogo at

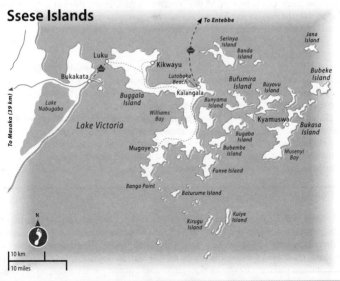

Ssese Islands

1400 and Kalangala at 0800 daily and takes 3½ to four hours. There are two types of ticket: 'business class' costs US$8 (padded seats with headrests and tables), and 'economy class' US$6 (wooden benches). Drinks and snacks are available from a little bar. The ferry also takes vehicles – normally about eight cars, but fewer if a lorry is taking up most of the room. Vehicle rates are determined by their length, US$25-30 one way. It's also possible to leave your car at Nakiwogo for a couple of days while you're on the islands and pay for an *askari* (security guard). **Note**: The Entebbe–Kalangala ferry service can be disrupted as a result of mechanical problems or political wranglings and it has been known to be out of operation for a couple of months at a time. It was running at the time of writing, but it's essential to double-check the situation before your arrival by asking your intended place to stay in either Entebbe or on the islands; they should be able to find out for you.

The other option for getting to the Sseses from Entebbe (although not recommended) is to take a **lake taxi** (motorized Ssese canoe). These cost as little as US$2 and leave from the **Kasenyi fish terminal**, which is 5 km north of Entebbe off the Kampala–Entebbe Highway. Crossing times to Banda and Buggala islands are roughly four to six hours over 50- to 60-km distances, and the boats usually stop at other islands picking up and dropping off fish, cargo and people. However, the canoes are moored 20 m offshore through bilharzia-infested viscous mud, they are often overcrowded, the provision of life-jackets is not guaranteed; and the possibility of capsizing is a real occurrence…need we go on?

The best, most reliable option is the free **Bukakata–Luku ferry** between Bukakata on the mainland 40 km east of Masaka, and Luku on Buggala Island, 34 km west of Kalangala. The ferry leaves Bukakata Monday-Saturday at 0900, 1200 and 1600 and Sunday 0900 and 1600. The crossing takes 50 minutes and they return from Luku after a turnaround time of no more than 30 minutes (estimate that their departures from Luka are an hour after they depart from Bukakata to be on the safe side). It's possible to take a car if you're willing to squeeze it on, and the roll-on roll-off pontoon is large enough to take the daily bus from Kampala (page 66). Adherence to this timetable is fluid, so get there at least an hour before the scheduled departure time, especially if you want to get a vehicle on board.▸▸ *For details of buses and matatus from Masaka to Bukakata, see Masaka Transport, page 128.*

Getting around
Once off the ferry, transport along the 34-km stretch of road between Luku and Kalangala is in the way of infrequent and crowded pick-up vans, which can take well over an hour as goods are offloaded at every stop. Other than the few pick-up vans, the best way to see the islands is on foot, by *boda-boda* or by hiring a bicycle.

To get between the islands, fishermen operate informal lake taxis, which are motorized Ssese canoes. These operate in just the same way as public transport on the roads: they are either shared with a fixed price between destinations and generally depart when full, which in the case of canoes can be perilously overloaded, or you can arrange a 'special hire' boat just for you and have to agree on a price first.

The islands → *For listing, see pages 131-132.*

The Ssese Islands vary in size from less than 1 ha, to the over 40-km long Buggala Island, the largest in the archipelago. About 50% of the 84 islands are uninhabited, but temporary fishing camps are sometimes seen on the shores of these as the fishermen follow the seasonal changes in the lake. The islands are hilly with an undulating terrain and, in the uncultivated parts, the forests are home to around 240 bird species, including hornbills, kingfishers and weavers, the ubiquitous vervet monkey, the occasional large snake, and millions of lake flies. There are beautiful walks around the islands through the forests, and you can visit caves full of bats and fishing villages. You can also make a boat trip to see parts of the islands inaccessible on foot, where birds nest freely and otters roll in the water. It's rare to see crocodiles or hippos, which have been frightened away to the more isolated areas of the lake, but hippos are still found near Mulabana, at the south of Buggala Island. It can be difficult to resist swimming in Lake Victoria on a sunny day, but in many places, there is a risk of bilharzia, although many resorts claim otherwise.

Buggala Island

Just over 40 km long, Buggala Island (sometimes spelt Bugala) is the largest in the archipelago and has about 50 km of red soil roads. The best way to explore is on foot or by bicycle, available for hire from most beach resorts. Its main towns are Kalangala – also the name of the district or spelt Kalengala – and Luku, which are linked by *matatu*. All around are wonderful views of the lake and of the other islands, some forested, cultivated or a mixture of both. Pineapple and the ever-expanding palm oil tree farms dominate the south of the island. Kalangala is on the northern shores of the island on a ridge about 200 m above the lake. With a population of around 5000, it is the administrative centre of the Sseses and has one long main street with the district offices, a post office, a branch of Stanbic Bank (no ATM), and a colourful market that naturally sells an abundance of fish and fruit. For visitors, the main attraction is Lutoboka Beach that curves around the bay of the same name below town on both sides of the ferry terminal, and is where the resorts are located. The power supply on the island is sporadic, and is only available in the resorts that have generators; these are usually only switched on from 1900 to 2200. However, the government is in the process of electrifying the island.

Other islands

Most visitors stick to Buggala Island, but provided you are flexible you can explore the other islands too. The second largest island, **Bukasa**, is particularly attractive, as it has a smaller population, is more forested and has a wider range of wildlife. There are two beautiful beaches on the island as well as a waterfall. **Bufumira Island** can be easily visited from Kalangala for the day, as can many of the uninhabited islands. The verdant **Banda Island,** a remote, beautiful, small island in the north of the archipelago, gets a fair share of visitors thanks to its long-established backpacker resort (see Where to stay, page 132).

Ssese Islands listings

For hotel and restaurant price codes and other relevant information, see pages 16-20.

☻ Where to stay

Buggala Island *p131*
The following are along Lutoboka Beach at Kalangala. When you get off the Entebbe–Kalangala ferry there are signposts to the resorts. If you come from the other direction via Luku and arrive on Kalangala's main

street, it's a 1-km walk or *boda-boda* ride from the top of the hill to Lutoboka Beach.
$$ Brovad Sands Lodge, reservations Kampala T0701-367970, www.ssese islandsresorthotel.com. The Ssese's newest offering that opened in 2013/2014, located at the northern end of the beach between Mirembe Resort Beach and Islands Club, a 30-min walk from the ferry or they'll pick you up. At the time of writing there were a few 'teething' issues but improvements

are expected when the lodge is completely finished. Accommodation is in neat thatched cottages arranged on terraces with lake views, restaurant and bar, activities include canoe and fishing trips.

$$-$ Mirembe Resort Beach, reservations Entebbe T0392-772703, hotel T0782-528651, www.miremberesort.com. Next to **Brovad Sands Lodge** a 25-min walk from the ferry or they'll pick you up. Comfortable accommodation is in rooms, *bandas* or chalets with DSTV and Wi-Fi, or there's a shady campsite (US$10 per person). The lovely restaurant with sunset views offers a varied à la carte menu. Activities include boat rides to other islands, fishing, volleyball, guided forest walks and they rent out bikes.

$$-$ Pearl Gardens Beach, reservations Kampala T0414-349107, hotel T0772-372164, www.pearlgardensbeach.com. A 2.5-ha site with a narrow beach strip, next to the fishing village and ferry terminal. This is not as peaceful as the other places and has a reputation as the Ssese's party resort with very loud music and a DJ at night on the beach (which unfortunately can encroach on the other resorts), drawing a crowd of university students from Kampala at weekends, holidays and at the end of exams; it may not be for everybody but outside of these times it's quiet and relaxing. Accommodation is in 9 wooden *bandas* sleeping 4-6, 14 twin/doubles or you can hire tents in the sprawling campsite in the forest. Rates vary from US$7 per person for camping with own tent to US$80 for an executive double. Restaurant, nightly barbecuess, 3 bars, volleyball and canoe rides.

$$-$ Ssese Islands Beach Hotel, reservations Kampala T0414-220065, hotel T0772-408244, www.sseseislandsbeachhotel.com. Situated at the top end of the island at Lutoboka Point, a 15-min walk from the ferry or they'll pick you up, this is the nicest and widest stretch of white sandy beach and is more remote and private than the other resorts. There are 13 neat cottages with balconies overlooking the lake or forest,

restaurant with a long menu and bar with pool table. Doubles (from US$60), camping on the beach (US$4 per person).

$ Islands Club Ssese, T077-250 4027. Next to **Brovad Sands Lodge**, a 30-min walk from the ferry, with well-maintained gardens and a clean, white sandy beach. Several wooden chalets for 2-4 people, a bit dark and dated but hot water in the fully tiled showers, good meals include excellent tilapia fish. Fishing trips can be arranged. Doubles from US$40.

$ Panorama Cottages, T0772-406371. A peaceful friendly place 500 m uphill from the ferry in a pretty forest clearing with lots of vervet monkeys around. 18 large cottages (US$30-60), the cheaper ones don't have hot water but buckets are arranged, and camping, tents provided (US$4 per person). Food is plentiful and includes nightly curries but takes a while to come.

Banda Island *p131*

$ Banda Island Resort, T0772-222777, www.bandaisland.biz. Remote and impossibly relaxed long-established backpackers place on a beautiful beach where you're likely to stay 1-2 weeks. Simple thatched beach chalets and bunks in *bandas* or mattresses in tents. The food is excellent and low-key activities include exploring the island, chilling in hammocks or playing volleyball and backgammon. Beach cabin (US$35 per person), dorm/tent (US$33 per person), camping with own tent (US$27 per person), which include all meals and tea and coffee. No electricity, but lanterns and campfires make it very atmospheric. It's important to text/SMS ahead as the mobile reception is variable. To get here from the ferry at Kalangala, either take a lake taxi or organize a special hire boat which should cost in the region of US$60 for up to 6 people. From Entebbe, it's possible to take the lake taxis from Kasenyi fish terminal (not recommended, see page 130); a better alternative is to organize a special hire boat with a boatman recommended by the resort from around US$130 for up to 6 – contact them in advance to make arrangements.

The southwest

Heading west of Masaka the countryside gradually gets drier and more hilly and the population more sparse as you move into Ankole, home to pastoralists. Lake Mburo National Park lies south of the main road, four hours' drive from Kampala, where animals can be observed on a game drive or lake cruise, or on foot and horseback. Mbarara, the heart of the former Ankole Kingdom and the next major town, has few tourist attractions. But the road here divides with one branch travelling northwest to Queen Elizabeth National Park via Ishaka, while the road southwest passes through Ntungamo. The far southwest of Uganda is very beautiful with many lakes, crops grown on terraced hillsides and dramatic volcanic mountains where gorillas can be tracked along steep-sided ravines. Kabale, is the largest town in this region, and close by is charming Lake Bunyonyi, one of Uganda's most popular tourist destinations. ▶▶ *For listing, see pages 142-149.*

Lake Mburo National Park → *For listing, see pages 142-149. Colour map 2, C2.*

The 260-sq-km Lake Mburo National Park has a pleasant landscape of open plains, acacia grasslands, riverine woodland and marshes, and within the park boundary are five lakes, which are best viewed from the Kazuma lookout point. The eastern sector can be explored on a network of tracks, while there are horse trails around Mihingo Lodge, and boat rides are on offer on Lake Mburo to see the birds and hippos. Another great attraction is that it is possible to walk around the park, with an armed ranger, rather than having to tour in a vehicle, so it's quite possible to get close to plains game like zebra, warthog and impala.

Arriving in Lake Mburo National Park

Getting there The two well-signposted entrance gates into the park, Nshara Gate and Sanga Gate, are both reached from the Masaka–Mbarara road. The park is roughly (depending on which gate is used) 90 km west of Masaka, about 1½ hours, and 40 km east of Mbarara, which takes less than an hour. From Kampala it is 230 km, about four hours. Coming from Masaka, the Nshara Gate turn-off is on the left, 13 km past the village of Lyantonde. The park gate is a further 8 km along an unsealed track. The Sanga Gate, coming from Masaka, is down a left turn at the Sanga trading centre, 27 km past Lyantonde and about 33 km before Mbarara. From here the park gate is 13 km, also on a poor, unsealed track that is particularly difficult September-January during the rains, when a 4WD is essential. It is about a 20-minute drive from either gate to the central area where the Rwonyo park headquarters, the Rwonyo Rest Camp, the restaurant and the jetty for boat trips are located. Travelling by *matatu* from Masaka or Kampala, ask to get off at Lyantonde; from Mbarara, get off at Sanga, and then get a special hire taxi for around US$20, or a *boda-boda* for US$7, to take you to the park gates. However, there is then the issue of getting to the accommodation as any passing tour operator going into the park is unlikely to give non-paying passengers a lift. Nevertheless, it is possible to arrange with the lodges to be picked up from the gates or from Lyantonde or Sanga.

Park information Uganda Wildlife Authority (UWA) ① *T0392-711346, www.uganda wildlife.org, daily 0630-1930.* Park entry fees US$40, children (5-15) US$20; foreign-registered vehicles: saloon car US$50, 4WD US$150 per 24 hours; Uganda-registered vehicles: saloon car US$8, 4WD US$12, per 24 hours.

Background

Historically, the area around Lake Mburo was grazing land for the Ankole people (called Banyankole) and a hunting ground for the Ankole royalty. During the colonial years it was gazetted as a controlled hunting area in 1933 and then was upgraded to a game reserve in 1963. The Banyankole continued to graze their cattle in the reserve until it was upgraded to national park status in 1983 under Obote's government, which meant pastoralists were evicted from the park. Reportedly, this decision was in part intended to weaken the Banyankole, who supported anti-Obote rebels. As the evicted pastoralists were not compensated for lost grazing land or assisted with resettling, many remained hostile to the park's formation. In 1985, when Obote's regime was ousted, these previous residents re-occupied the park, expelling the staff, and destroying infrastructure. The Museveni government re-gazetted the park in 1986, but agreed to only demarcate 40% of the original, and allowed local people to graze their livestock and fish in the lakes. The last people moved out of Lake Mburo National Park in 1997, and were financially compensated, and 20% of park fees still today go towards funding community projects such as building clinics and schools around the park boundary. Nevertheless, this forced resettlement remains a controversial issue. On a good note for the national park, however, the natural environment has flourished undisturbed since 1997 and as a result wildlife populations have increased dramatically. With **Uganda Wildlife Authority**'s management and the establishment of lodges, Lake Mburo has become a popular halfway stop for tourists between Kampala and Uganda's western parks.

Lake Mburo National Park

Where to stay 🛌
Arcadia Cottages **1**
Lake Mburo Camp **2**
Mburo Safari Lodge **5**
Mihingo Lodge **3**

Rwakobo Rock **6**
Rwonyo Rest Camp **4**

Campsites ⛺
Campsite 1

Campsite 2
Campsite 3

Restaurants 🍴
UWA Lakeside **1**

Flora and fauna

Most of the park is covered in acacia woodland while narrow bands of lush riparian woodland line the lakes. Together with 13 other lakes in the area, Lake Mburo forms part of a 50-km-long wetland system linked by a papyrus swamp. Five of these lakes lie within the park's borders. Animals found here include impala, zebra, topi, oribi, eland, klipspringer, buffalo, Defassa waterbuck, reedbuck, warthog, hyena and jackal but no elephants. Baboons and vervets are commonly seen and the lake contains hippos and crocodiles, while buffaloes can often be found in the marshes. Lions, leopards and roan antelopes are present but are rarely seen. The sitatunga, a swamp-dwelling antelope, with its elongated hooves and flexible toe joints, is well adapted for living in the papyrus swamp but they is very shy and, again, hardly ever seen. There are more than 350 species of bird including the shoebill stork (see box, page 72), crested crane (Uganda's national bird and emblem), saddlebill stork and Abyssinian ground hornbill. Lake Mburo attracts a wide range of waterbirds, including pied and malachite kingfishers, African fish eagles, pelicans, herons and cormorants.

Mbarara and around → *For listing, see pages 142-149. Phone code: 0485. Colour map 2, B2.*

The countryside becomes flatter towards Mbarara with more banana plantations as the acacia shrubs recede. There are lots of Ankole cattle grazing (see box, page 138). Mbarara is a busy town that has greatly expanded in recent years and the current population is put at about 110,000. Since the Masaka bypass was built it is now the first major town you come to when travelling southwest from Kampala. It is a crossroads for travellers heading towards the Queen Elizabeth National Park, Lake Mburo National Park, the Rwenzori Mountains and Kabale in the southwest.

Arriving in Mbarara

Getting there Mbarara is located 136 km from Masaka, 298 km from Kampala and 140 km from Kabale on the continuous Mbarara–Masaka and Kabale–Mbarara road. A bypass is being planned that will go around the north of town linking the two. This is expected to decongest Mbarara by rerouting trucks destined for and coming from Rwanda and the DRC. Heading northwest, there is the good road from Mbarara to Ishaka, Kasese and Fort Portal. The access points to the Queen Elizabeth National Park are between Ishaka and Kasese (see page 174 for a description of this route). Given that Mbarara is a major junction, there are frequent buses to and from all these destinations. ⏭ *See also Transport, page 149.*

Background

The name Mbarara is derived from the Ankole word for their cattle's favourite type of grass, *emburara*. The town was named by the British when they founded an administrative post here in 1911. It grew quickly into a commercial centre as Asian traders settled here from 1950, and it was declared a municipality in 1973. The surrounding region was part of the historical Ankole Kingdom, a pastoralist monarchy that was thought to have been founded in the 1500s. The kingdom had a highly sophisticated centralized administration system headed by the Omugabe (king), assisted by a prime minister who in turn appointed local chiefs. The kingdom became defunct when, in 1967, the four traditional Ugandan monarchies were abolished by the government under the new constitution of Obote (the others were Buganda, Toro and Bunyoro). Despite the other three monarchies being restored by the Museveni government in 1993, the Ankole Kingdom was not; in fact, the offer was declined by the Ankole people (Banyankole). This was attributed to the

Mbarara

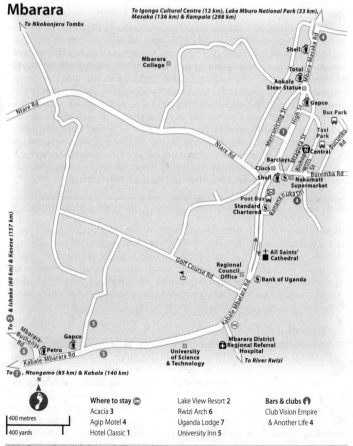

To Igongo Cultural Centre (12 km), Lake Mburo National Park (33 km), Masaka (136 km) & Kampala (298 km)

To Nkokonjeru Tombs

Mbarara College

To 2 & Ishaka (60 km) & Kasese (157 km)

Ntare Rd

Shell

Total

Ankole Steer Statue

Gapco

Bus Park

Taxi Park

Central

Mercanting St

High St

Magura St

Bishopric Willis St

Buremba Rd

Barclays

Clock

Shell

Nakumatt Supermarket

Post Bus

Standard Chartered

Banana Nuka Dr

All Saints' Cathedral

Golf Course Rd

Regional Council Office

Bank of Uganda

Kabale Mbarara Rd

Mbarara-Bushenyi Rd

Gapco

Petro

Mbarara District Regional Referral Hospital

University of Science & Technology

To River Rwizi

To 7, Ntungamo (85 km) & Kabale (140 km)

N

400 metres
400 yards

Where to stay		Bars & clubs
Acacia 3	Lake View Resort 2	Club Vision Empire
Agip Motel 4	Rwizi Arch 6	& Another Life 4
Hotel Classic 1	Uganda Lodge 7	
University Inn 5		

fact that the former Ankole Kingdom had had a rigid almost caste-like social structure and many Banyankole did not want its return. Indeed as early as 1971 when Amin raised a debate about restoring the monarchies, a group of Ankole elders signed a petition against a resurrection saying it would halt "our stated goal of freedom and progress".

As a result, the Ankole Kingdom properties in and around Mbarara have all fallen into disrepair. These include the Palace of the Omugabe and its administration buildings, located on Kamukuzi Hill on the outskirts of town. Today it is no more than a crumbling mound of bricks which has been mostly cleared to make way for gardens and telecommunication masts. Three and a half kilometres northwest of Mbarara are the Nkokonjeru Tombs at Kakika, the burial place of the last two Omugabe of Ankole: Kahaya II who died in 1944, and Gasyonga II who died in 1982 and wasn't replaced. You can visit, but there's nothing really to see, and the two plain concrete-slab tombs are inside a lone almost derelict colonial-style house full of bats. Despite all of this, many traditionalist Ankole people in the Mbarara region still recognize and celebrate their ancestry. To learn more, a visit to the Igongo Cultural Centre (below) is highly recommended.

Places in Mbarara
This area is renowned for Ankole cattle (see box, page 138), and in fact processes more milk than any other part of Uganda; just before you enter the town centre you will see in the middle of a roundabout a statue of a steer with impressive horns. The huge Coca Cola bottling plant is close by, which makes for an interesting cultural juxtaposition. The town is home to the **Mbarara University of Science and Technology (MUST)**, one of Uganda's six universities and this, together with the regional offices and the Bank of Uganda regional building, tends to split the town into two. The town centre is in the west, where the central market and taxi and bus parks are located on and around Bishop Willis Street (named after the first white man to encounter the Ankole people).

There is not much of architectural interest although the **Library** on Main Street is an old colonial single-storey building, with a well-sheltered courtyard with foliage in front, which has unfortunately been allowed to deteriorate. The **Aga Khan School**, just on the eastern edge of town, is an impressive building combining neoclassical and Indian architectural styles. There are three arches at the front with double mock columns. Portico windows face the building and above the main entrance are crossed flags and the date of construction (1948).

Igongo Cultural Centre
① *12 km north on the Mbarara–Masaka Rd, T0392-722828, www.igongo.co.ug; museum 0800-2100, US$4, restaurant 0700-2300.*
Opened in 2011, the main attraction of this multi-faceted venue is the museum. There's another fine statue of an Ankole steer with magnificent horns at the entrance. Inside exhibits are well laid out and trace the history and lifestyles of the southwestern Ugandan ethnic groups, including the Ankole people. A great Banyankole saying: "no cows, no banana plantation, no wife" is explained in interesting detail by the excellent guides. There are mock-ups of traditional huts with life-size statues of people tending cooking pots or making jewellery. There's also an interesting topographic relief map of Uganda showing the lakes, rivers and national parks, and an excellent display of currency in Uganda from cowrie shells to rupees during the colonial years and today's bank notes – look out for those with Obote and Amin's faces on and notice how rapidly the currency devalued during the troubled years in the 1980s. Also exhibited is a display of the lineage

Ankole cattle

These very large cattle, weighing up to 700 kg, are famous throughout the country for their enormous white horns. Some have horns that reach lengths of 2.4 m which are so heavy that the animals are unable to raise their heads, or else their heads are constantly leaning to one side. As the cattle sleep together at night, with the calves in the centre of the group for protection, the horns of the adults serve as formidable weapons against any intruders. The cattle are highly prized by pastoralist groups in southwest Uganda as the terrain is characterized by endless rolling hills that are ideal for grazing, the cattle adapt well to the climate, are resistant to most diseases and produce high milk yields. Traditionally they provide meat, milk, ghee and hides, are used as currency; marriages are cemented with the payment of a dowry in the form of cattle. They are especially revered by the Nshenyi people around Ntungamo. When 100 head of cattle is accumulated, a bell is put around the neck of the beast with the biggest horns to demonstrate the owner's achievement and status. They are also highly valued by the people of the former Ankole Kingdom around Mbarara. Those with the whitest and longest horns belonged to the king and were considered sacred. As a result, the breed is often referred to as the 'Cattle of Kings'.

of all Uganda's traditional kingdoms, replicas of the royal Buganda drums which now live in the National Museum in Kampala (page 51) and in the garden the guides will explain the medicinal uses of the plants and trees.

The superb **craft and bookshop**, an outlet for Uganda's **Fountain Publishers** (www.fountainpublishers.co.ug), one of the centre's sponsors, complements the cultural theme with a wide range of books on all things Ugandan by Ugandans. Additionally there are a number of books on Rwanda, including the 1994 genocide, plus the range of **Uganda Maps** (see page 16). The crafts are not cheap, but are specific to the cultural groups in the region and include decorated beaded gourds (used as milk pots) and drums made from Ankole hides. The **restaurant** serves an excellent lunchtime buffet (1100-1600; US$8 per person) of traditional dishes of millet bread, *matoke* and ghee, chicken, goat and vegetables, along with a local drink made from sorghum. There is also a menu of good Western dishes – including Ankole steaks – plus cold beers and sodas, great café lattes and cappuccinos, and plenty of gardens tables at which to enjoy them.

Kabale → *For listing, see pages 142-149. Phone code: 0486. Colour map 2, C1.*

The road from Mbarara to Kabale is good, passing through pastoral areas, a mix of dry plains and undulating countryside. Some of the views are simply stunning: Ankole cattle grazing in hedged fields, with hills denuded of trees in the far distance. The first town of any notable size is **Ntungamo**, 85 km from Mbarara. Lots of shops now line the bypass road around the west of town, and there are several simple lodgings and eating places. The old Kabale–Kasese road from Ntungamo leads 52 km north to Ishaka and by the time you read this will have been completely tarred. The access points to the Queen Elizabeth National Park (page 174) are between Ishaka and Kasese. At Kitagata, 32 km north of Ntungamo, are the **Kitagata Hot Springs**; two adjacent clear sulphur-rich pools with temperatures as hot as 80°C. They are used by local people suffering from rheumatism and arthritis, and you can jump in for a soothing splash if you are passing by. They are clearly signposted.

Back on the main road, shortly before you reach Kabale, the terrain changes and becomes greener, more hilly and increasingly dramatic with steep slopes. Parts are densely forested while most of the hillsides are heavily populated and intensively cultivated in terraced fields which give this part of Uganda its distinctive character.

With a population of around 45,000, Kabale is the largest town in the Kigezi District, and is the major trading centre for the southwest. Thanks to its marvellously fertile terrain, the fresh food market is a must see, with narrow passages full of wooden stalls piled high with colourful fruit, vegetables, beans, grains and nuts. Kabale is also where the Kampala road from the north joins the roads to Rwanda and the DRC and, with its dusty streets lined with goods sheds, precariously overloaded haulage trucks, fuel

Kabale

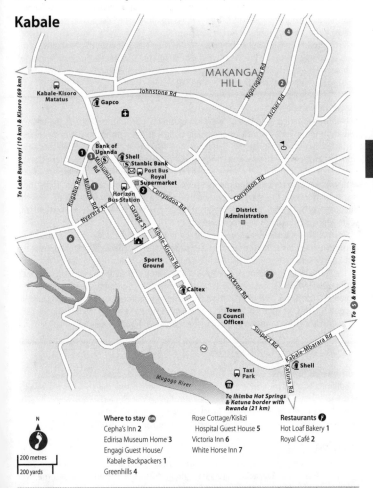

N
200 metres
200 yards

Where to stay 🛏
Cepha's Inn **2**
Edirisa Museum Home **3**
Engagi Guest House/
Kabale Backpackers **1**
Greenhills **4**

Rose Cottage/Kislizi
 Hospital Guest House **5**
Victoria Inn **6**
White Horse Inn **7**

Restaurants 🍴
Hot Loaf Bakery **1**
Royal Café **2**

stations and roadside mechanics, it takes on a distinct frontier-town feel. It is one of the highest towns in Uganda at 2000 m above sea level. Average daytime temperatures are around 18 °C and can fall to 10°C at night. Early in the morning the valleys are filled with mist. The area around Kabale is ideal for hikers; it's often described as the 'Little Switzerland' of Africa. Many travellers pass through here on their way to see the gorillas, although most choose to overnight at impossibly pretty Lake Bunyonyi (see page 141), just 10 km over the hill to the southwest.

Arriving in Kabale

Getting there Kabale is 402 km southwest of Kampala and 140 km from Mbarara. There are frequent buses from the central bus station in Kampala which take six or seven hours and stop at Mbarara on the way. Kabale is the terminus for the Post Bus on the Kampala–Kabale route. Regular *matatus* run to and from Kisoro, 69 km away, on a very twisty but beautiful road. The Katuna border post with Rwanda lies 21 km south of Kabale and the road continues on to the Rwandan capital of Kigali (see Border crossing box, opposite). Kabale has hundreds of *boda-bodas* to get about town, both motorbikes and traditional wobbly bicycles. ▸▸ *See also Transport, page 149.*

Places in Kabale

Kabale was founded in 1913 by the British. In the old part of the town, up the hill, you will find the government offices and many buildings dating back to the early colonial period, such as the hospital, the church and the White Horse Inn. The inn gets its name from the European settlers who rode their white horses on the hill. That other essential part of colonial life, the golf course, is also on the hill. Everything is spaciously laid out, with well-kept flower beds and mowed lawns in between. The newer part of the town is spread out along the main road, down in what used to be a swampy valley, with the buildings set back from the road. There are some attractive colonnades marked with the years when the buildings were completed.

Edirisa ① *www.edirisa.org, US$2, free if you're staying at the hostel,* is a small cultural museum at the **Edirisa Museum Home** (see page 144), a backpackers' hostel opposite the **Hot Loaf Bakery** in the middle of town. Originally it was built by a Bakiga elder who turned his traditional thatched homestead into a small museum of the Bakiga people. It was taken over in 2003 by **Edirisa**, a worthwhile local NGO involved in community development in the region. Edirisa means 'a window' in the Bakiga language. Inside are various cooking utensils like pots, gourds, weapons, drums, stools and a grain store, even a rat-catching mechanism. It's open most of the time and the staff at the hostel will show you around.

Around Kabale → *For listing, see pages 142-149.*

Ihimba Hot Springs

The Ihimba **Hot Springs** are 8 km south of Kabale towards Katuna; they are on the side of the road, partially obscured by a eucalyptus forest. You can either hire a bike or walk there. Many of the local people traditionally use the hot springs for soothing joint pains and may find the presence of tourists either amusing or embarrassing.

Kisiizi Waterfalls

These 27-m-high falls are near the village of Kisiizi, about 45 km north from Kabale. They lie on the Rushoma River which eventually drains into Lake Edward. At Kisiizi the river

Border crossing: Uganda–Rwanda

Katuna

The Katuna border (also known as Gatuna on the Rwandan side) lies 21 km south of Kabale and the road continues for 81 km to the Rwandan capital of Kigali. It's open 24 hours and is a major crossing for trucks that transit Uganda to Rwanda from Kenya's port Mombasa. Buses between Kampala and Kigali take eight or nine hours (see Kampala Transport, page 66). They stop in Kabale, from where they then take 2½ to three hours to Kigali. Alternatively, you can get a *matatu* from Kabale to Katuna (about one hour), and then another from Katuna to Kigali (about two hours). The nearest banks and ATMs are in Kabale and Kigali. You can change a small amount of money into Rwanda francs (RWF) for *matatu* fares with money-changers at the border, but most drivers also accept Uganda shillings for this journey. Visas for both countries are available (but always check with an embassy or high commission first), as is third-party insurance for drivers, and visas and vehicle costs can be paid with US dollars cash. Remember that traffic drives on the right in Rwanda so it's at the border that you swap over sides of the road, and that Rwanda is one hour ahead of Uganda. The other major border with Rwanda is Cyanika, 15 km south of Kisoro, which is the nearest option for seeing the gorillas in Rwanda's Volcanoes National Park (see page 163).

---

drops prettily into a canyon below and has been harnessed to provide electricity for the hospital and local communities. Historically, in the local Bakiga community, girls who got pregnant before marriage or in their youth would be thrown off the falls to meet their death. It was usually their elder brothers that committed the dastardly deed. The practice was discontinued when the Church of Uganda established a hospital here in 1958. To get here, follow the Kabale–Mbarara road for 32 km to Muhanga then take the left murram road for 33 km that leads to the falls and Kisiizi Hospital. It takes about two hours in a private vehicle, and there's one daily bus to and from Kabale. Keen hikers may enjoy this region and there are plenty of local tracks through the forests and farmland. You can stay overnight at the hospital's guest cottage (see Where to stay, page 145).

Lake Bunyonyi → *For listing, see pages 142-149. Altitude: 1840 m. Colour map 2, C1.*

Located in the hills 10 km by road above the town of Kabale, picturesque, irregularly shaped Lake Bunyonyi and her 29 tiny islands are undisputedly one of the most beautiful areas of Uganda. The lake, which shares its shores with Rwanda, is relatively young (around 10,000 years old), having been formed when a volcanic eruption blocked a river exit. It has an approximate surface area of 60 sq km and, despite popular belief, is not very deep, averaging about 40 m. The surrounding hillsides, as elsewhere in this region, are intensively cultivated in terraces in every shade of green imaginable. These vibrant colours accentuate the glassy water. It's a haven of peace and calm, broken only by the sounds of paddles dipping into the water or the soft banter of local fishermen as they glide by in their dugout canoes. It is one of the few lakes in the country that doesn't have hippos and crocs, and it is supposedly bilharzia-free – though watch out for leeches when swimming.

The forest groves, gardens and farms attract a wide diversity of birdlife; in fact 'Bunyonyi' means 'the place of many little birds'. Over 250 species have been recorded and some 50 can be seen within the first hour or two. Otters are frequently seen fishing in the lake, and nighttime brings with it a deafening chorus of frogs. On its southwest shores there are a number of villages, but most tourist facilities are clustered around the village of Rutinda and its nearest islands, on the eastern side of the lake. Rutinda itself is a tiny collection of thatched huts, and its community are farmers, fisherman or else work in the lodges. It comes alive on market days (Monday and Friday) when laden canoes arrive from all over the lake (including Rwanda) and 'stalls' are laid out on the ground around the jetty selling a colourful variety of fresh produce. Most visitors stop here en route to the gorillas and it's a very scenic spot to relax, swim, canoe or mountain bike.

Arriving at Lake Bunyonyi

Getting there On the road from Kabale towards Kisoro there is a turn-off after 1 km, and a signpost to Lake Bunyonyi on the left-hand side. You can get here from Kabale (10 km away) either on foot (2½ hours) or by hired bike (be prepared for a long hard slog up and a wonderful run down). Some of the accommodation at the lake will pick up from Kabale and a special hire taxi takes about 20 minutes, US$8. You can also take a motorbike *boda-boda* for around US$2, but do not even remotely consider this if it's at all wet as the dirt road can be very slippery. *Matatus* in small pick-up trucks go between Kabale's main market and Rutinda market for US$1 but only on Monday and Friday (market days at Rutinda). If you're driving yourself, the road is dirt but accessible all year round (it's a mandatory stop for overland trucks and other tour operators). Just take it slowly up and down the hill from Kabale – and stop at the top for the tremendous views of the lake – and exercise caution in the wet.

⊙ The southwest listings

For hotel and restaurant price codes and other relevant information, see pages 16-20.

⊖ Where to stay

Lake Mburo National Park *p133, map p134*

$$$$ Lake Mburo Camp, 3.5 km north of Rwonyo, reservations Kampala T0414-321552, www.kimbla-mantanauganda.com. A luxury tented camp and sister property to **Engagi Lodge** at Bwindi (page 165), on a lightly wooded ridge overlooking the lake. 9 spacious safari tents on raised wooden platforms, bar and dining room serving international fare, and sundowners are enjoyed next to a bonfire above the camp with sweeping views. Access is via the Sanga Gate; follow the Impala Track for 7 km then take the signposted left turning for 500 m.

$$$$ Mihingo Lodge, 18 km west of Rwonyo, T0752-410509, www.mihingo lodge.com. Upmarket, well-run lodge with 10 large, tented rooms on stilts in varied settings; some in riverine forest, others with a lake view and 4 wonderfully positioned on top of a *kopje* (small hill). The thatched dining room is west facing with panoramic views over the park, especially stunning at sunset. There's a rim-flow swimming pool and horseback safaris (see page 148). Located adjacent to but outside the park on its eastern flank, access is via the Nshara Gate, 8 km from the main road; follow the Zebra Track for 5 km then turn a sharp left along the Ruroko Track and the lodge is signposted from there.

$$$ Arcadia Cottages, 2 km south of Rwonyo, T0781-480105, www.arcadia cottages.net. This is a **Uganda Wildlife Authority** concession and is well positioned for walking safaris and boat trips organized at Rwonyo. 9 simple but comfortably furnished stone *bandas* set in acacia woodlands, though the concrete mock-log façades are a little odd. The open-sided bar and restaurant is a short distance away but you are accompanied by a ranger after dark. Sister property to the Lake Bunyonyi cottages of the same name (see page 146).

$$$ Rwakobo Rock, 17 km north of Rwonyo, T0755-211771, www.rwakoborock. com. Run by a friendly British couple, lying outside the park on the northeast boundary, and built, as the name suggests, on a rocky outcrop. 9 well-designed cottages with west-facing/sunset views, restaurant and bar with massive thatched roof. They organize mountain biking in and outside the park, night drives and cultural walks to an Ankole village, in addition to the usual safari activities. A deservedly popular set-up and you can get here easily by *boda-boda* or special hire taxi from the main road; 8 km and 1 km before Nshara Gate. You can also visit for lunch if you phone ahead.

$$$-$$ Mburo Safari Lodge, 20 km west of Rwonyo, reservations Kampala T0414-577997, www.mburosafarilodge.com. One of the least expensive options and just outside of the park boundary about 2 km from **Mihingo Lodge**. 15 thatched wooden chalets with rustic furnishings and balconies overlooking the valley below; some are for families/groups and have little kitchens, plus there's a grassy **campsite ($)** with hot showers. Open restaurant/bar, swimming pool, and a bonfire is lit in the evening. Directions are the same as for **Mihingo Lodge** (see above) and follow signposts.

$ Rwonyo Rest Camp, run by UWA, T0392-711346, www.ugandawildlife.org. Next to the park headquarters, set in a wooded glade where antelope and warthog wander through. Double and single *bandas*, a 4-bed family *banda* and double tents, rates from US$8 per person, but very basic (check doors lock and there are pillows), no lighting so bring torches, communal showers with hot water mornings and

evenings. You can self-cater in the simple thatched kitchen hut, and camp staff can arrange for your own food to be cooked for a small fee, but most people eat at the **Lakeside Restaurant** (see page 146).

Camping
There are 3 campsites (US$8 per person): **Campsite 1** is at Rwonyo Rest Camp (see above). The best is **Campsite 2**, 1 km from Rwonyo, just north of the boat jetty, in a wonderful position to view the wildlife. There is every chance of spotting hippo come out of the lake during the night so be very wary of walking around and be sure to carry a torch. **Campsite 3** is in another lakeside position to the south, off the Kigambira Loop track, but you'll need your own transport. Each campsite has pit latrines, tap, thatched shelter and fireplace. Again you can eat at the restaurant. It's also possible to camp at a level spot next to **Nshara Gate** (US$6 per person), where there's a toilet and you can eat at Rwakobo Rock, 1 km before the gate. You can then enter and pay to go into the park early the next morning.

Mbarara and around *p135, map p136*
By the time you read this the **Igongo Cultural Centre** (page 137) will have opened a newly built 52-room hotel. Reports welcome.

$$ Lake View Resort, 2 km west of the centre off the Mbarara–Bushenyi Rd, T0772-367972, www.lakeviewresorthotel. co.ug. This 70-room hotel is in pleasant surroundings on the western outskirts of town. A little shabby with indifferent service but comfortable, popular with tour groups and offering a good range of facilities including a pool, gym, sauna, massage and beauty salon, Wi-Fi, restaurant and bar. The man-made lake belonged to the Ankole king as the top of a hill nearby is where the palace used to be.

$$ Rwizi Arch Hotel, 3 km west of town at the junction with the Mbarara–Kabale Rd and Mbarara–Bushenyi Rd, T0485-421173, www.rwizihotels.com. A new hotel in a smart 4-storey bright white block with bay windows and red-tiled roof in lovely gardens with palm trees and fountains. The 32 a/c rooms with DSTV, Wi-Fi and fridge have balconies or are in motel-style chalets. The excellent restaurant (**$$**) has a long international menu including some Chinese dishes and is one of the best places to eat in town with candlelit tables and outside terrace.

$$-$ Agip Motel, on the Mbarara–Masaka Rd, opposite the Shell petrol station, 500 m before the Ankole steer statue, T0485-421615, www.agipmotelmbarara.com. Modern, comfortable and professionally managed, with 20 carpeted rooms with DSTV; pay a little more for one with a door to the garden and motel-style parking. There's a pleasant terrace restaurant and bar serving good Western and local food, worth coming even if not staying. Camping is available on a large, flat area behind the hotel, securely enclosed by a wall, with a barbecue area and ablution facilities (cold water), US$5 per person.

$ Acacia Hotel, 7 Mbarara–Kabale Rd, T0392-916391. A functional, friendly option in a neat brick block with 40 modern rooms with DSTV and Wi-Fi, from US$40 a double with a generous buffet breakfast, secure parking, restaurant and popular bar in nice landscaped grounds. However, it's very close to the road, so ask for a room at the back.

$ Hotel Classic, 57 High St, T0485-421131, www.hotelclassicafrica.com. Centrally located above some shops, so another potentially noisy option, especially first thing in the morning, but with 30 decent rooms with DSTV, and good value from US$35 a double/twin and US$8 for an extra bed. Restaurant serving international fare and bar with a first-floor balcony, a good place to watch the street life below.

$ Uganda Lodge, Ruhanga, Mbarara–Kabale Rd, 40 km west of Mbarara on the way to Ntungamo, T0774-768090 (mob), www.ugandalodge.com. Run by a UK charity, this lodge houses volunteers working on local projects or travellers can stay en route to the southwest. A rural spot surrounded by banana and eucalyptus trees, it can accommodate 20 people in rooms or en suite *bandas* (from US$8 per person), or you can camp (US$2 per person). Restaurant and bar, local excursions arranged. Contact them if you are interested in volunteering.

$ University Inn, 9 Kabale–Mbarara Rd, T0485-420334. Close to the university in a pleasant and peaceful wooded area offering 20 simple, comfortable rooms, though the water supply is variable. Grassy, secure campsite often used by overland trucks, so it's not uncommon to find a group of international travellers in the bar, which always has cold beers. The restaurant serves the likes of chicken and chips and a decent buffet breakfast. Doubles (US$25), camping (US$5 per person).

Kabale *p138, map p139*

$$ White Horse Inn, 25-27 Rwamafa Rd, T0772-444921, www.whitehorseinn-kabale.com. Set in 5-ha gardens on a hilltop overlooking the town near the golf course, this is the best hotel in Kabale and dates from 1922. The 41 rooms are in comfortable cottages with steep shingle roofs connected by walkways, and have DSTV and Wi-Fi. A little dated but at the time of writing it was being refurbished. Pleasant lounge and bar where the wonderful log-fire is welcome on a cool night, and the restaurant is the best place to eat in town.

$$-$ Cepha's Inn, 7-9 Archer Rd, Makanga Hill, T0486-422097, www.cephasinn.com. A reasonable if dated option set in manicured grounds bordering the golf course, with 33 rooms, some adjoining for families, with DSTV, a pool, sauna and gym, restaurant serving decent Western meals including burgers and pizzas, and friendly bar with pool table.

$ Edirisa Museum Home, Muhumiza Rd, T0752-558222, www.edirisa.org. The most interesting budget place to stay in Kabale and an excellent place to meet other travellers, just across the road from the **Hot Loaf Bakery**. Has a 10-bed dorm (US$5 per person), 1 double, 1 twin and 1 tiny single (from US$9 per person), shared bathrooms though water can be erratic. Restaurant menu includes pizza, burgers or *soup du jour*, and there's a gift shop and rooftop bar. **Edirisa** also organizes trekking and tours, see page 148, and for the museum, see page 140.

$ Engagi Guest House, 20 Muhuza Rd, T0772-959667, www.engagiexperience.net. Often referred to as **Kabale Backpackers** and home to **Engagi Safaris** (page 149), which can organize budget gorilla tours in Uganda and Rwanda. The blue house with a big pink gate has 4-bed dorms (US$5 per person) or simple doubles (US$15) in garden outbuildings, communal bathrooms with warm water and restaurant. The lively **Amazing Pub** has a pool table and DSTV and is popular in its own right with a street side entrance.

$ Greenhills Hotel, Ngorogoza Rd, Makanga Hill, T0772-605925, www.greenhills-hotel. com. Quiet and attractive hotel in a white hilltop compound with good views over town. 24 simple carpeted rooms, some have balconies, there's a pool, a restaurant serving some continental dishes and 2 bars with DSTV. Small doubles from US$45.

$ Victoria Inn, off Nyerere Av, signposted off the main road opposite the **Royal Supermarket**, T0486-423414. The best of the cheap local lodgings, a couple of blocks away from the main street so quiet, 20 en suite rooms, cold showers but buckets of hot water, small bar and restaurant, friendly staff. Doubles US$12 with breakfast. Buses to Kampala park up overnight on the same road so you can be first on the bus in the morning.

Camping

Most campers and overlanders head to the wonderfully scenic campsites at Lake Bunyonyi but both the **White Horse Inn** and **Cepha's Inn** offer camping in their lawned grounds, see above.

Kisiizi Waterfalls p140
$ Rose Cottage, or the **Kisiizi Hospital Guest House**, T0392-700806, www.kisiizi hospital.org.ug. The hospital is run by Church of Uganda and welcomes overnight visitors and proceeds go to the hospital. Simple accommodation is in the cottage or 2 *bandas* set in lovely flowering gardens from where there are peaceful views of the falls. Wholesome meals can be arranged. The little lounge has a surprisingly good library of books on Uganda.

Lake Bunyonyi p141
Be aware that power supplies, and consequently water, can be erratic at the lake as showers are pumped by electricity (when there isn't any, hot water is usually provided in buckets). The places on the islands offer free motorboat transfers and organize secure parking near the jetty at Rutinda.

$$$ Birdsnest @ Bunyonyi Resort, 1 km before Rutinda, T0754-252560, www. birdnestatbunyonyi.com. This has its origins in 1963 when Frank Kalimuzo, a high-ranking politician, built his home here and, as more and more people came to stay, it became an informal 4-room hotel. In retaliation to Kalimuzo's allegiance to the Obote government, Amin's soldiers arrested Kalimuzo (he was never seen again) and all but destroyed his home which remained a ruin for decades. In 2009, with the Kalimuzo family's blessing, Belgium investors restored it to this smart thatched lakeshore resort (the best option at Bunyonyi) in a stunning location on the first headland into the lake you reach when coming down the hill. 14 rooms with fresh brightly coloured decor, balconies and lake views, a fine restaurant serving fish and crayfish from the lake, plus treats like Belgium-style chips and bread, thatched bar next to the water and lovely large swimming pool. Day visitors are welcome for a meal and swim.

$$$-$$ Heritage Lodge, Ha' Buharo Island, 25 min by motorboat from Rutinda, reservations Kampala, T0312-265454, www.heritagelodgesuganda.com. On a secluded wooded island on the western fringe of the lake, 7 safari tents on raised platforms and 1 family cottage, but they are a little tired-looking so hence a tad overpriced. However, the pleasant open-sided lounge, bar and restaurant is enhanced by local artwork and look over gardens leading down to the lake and the food is plentiful and good.

$$ Arcadia Cottages, from Kabale turn left at the top of the hill before going down to Rutinda, T0782-424232, www.arcadiacottages.net. No-frills accommodation in 11 stone cottages with balconies, a restaurant and bar but poor attempts at international food and indifferent staff. However, given its position high on the hillside, it has possibly the best view of Bunyonyi, which looks almost map-like from this elevation. Also runs Arcadia Cottages in Lake Mburo National Park (page 142).

$$-$ Nature's Prime Island, Akarwa Island, 5 mins by motorboat from Rutinda, T0772-423215, www.naturesprimeisland.com. On a 1-ha island more or less opposite the Bunyonyi Overland Resort (see below). Peaceful resort with Scandinavian log cabins or safari tents on raised platforms under thatch. Restaurant and bar where a bonfire is lit in the evening, guides can be arranged for birdwatching on foot or by canoe.

$ Bunyonyi Overland Resort, Rutinda, T0793-930006, www.bunyonyioverland.com. The epicentre of tourism at Bunyonyi and professionally run in a beautiful location with a great range of facilities and activities. It's also lively, crowded and noisy, popular with overland trucks and backpackers, so could be just what you're looking for or the complete opposite. Accommodation is in 12 cottages and 2 family cottages with private bathrooms, 4 rooms and 10 safari tents on raised platforms with shared hot showers,

tents with bedding are available for hire or there's camping with your own tent on lovely grassy terraced sites along the lake. Rates range from US$60 for a double to US$8 per person for camping Small grocery and craft shop, bar with DSTV and Wi-Fi, restaurant with a long menu and cosy log fire, pontoon on the lake for swimming, mountain bike hire (US$10). Day visitors are welcome for US$2.

$ Bushara Island Camp, Bushara Island, 10 mins by motorboat from Rutinda, T0772-464584, www.busharaislandcamp.com. A forested 16-ha island with 10 rooms in en suite tents, cottages and a treehouse, each with a wood and stone deck and good hot showers. Doubles from US$40, US$10 per person in a quad, and you can pitch your own tent for US$6, but campers have to pay extra for the motorboat/canoe transfer (from US$3 by canoe). Day visitors are also welcome at the Swallows Restaurant for lunch of delicious crayfish curries and pizza.

$ Byoona Amagara Island Retreat, Itambira Island, 20 mins by motorboat from Rutinda, T0752-652788, www.lakebunyonyi.net. This non-profit project supports education and healthcare projects in the area and offers accommodation in 'geodomes' (semi-open thatched huts with mosquito nets and wooden decks), dorms, wooden cabins, cottages or pitch your own tent. Rates from US$35 for a double to US$8 per person camping. There's a central lodge, library, restaurant serving excellent food and a shop with locally made crafts and basic goods.

❶ Restaurants

Lake Mburo National Park *p133, map p134*

$ Lakeside Restaurant. Daily 0700-2130. Run by the UWA, this has reasonable local and Western dishes from around US$5 a meal but waiting times are horrendous. However, the bar offers an excellent hippo-viewing area. You're not allowed to walk unescorted from **Rwonyo Rest Camp** to the restaurant and have to be accompanied by an armed ranger. Non-guests can also eat at **Arcadia Cottages**, 2 km south of Rwonyo.

Mbarara and around *p135, map p136*
The hotels offer the best options for eating. If you are driving through stop at the **Igongo Cultural Centre** for lunch.

Kabale *p138, map p139*
There are few restaurants, but all the hotels provide meals.
$$-$ White Horse Inn (page 144). Daily 0700-2230. The nicest restaurant in town with a long, varied menu from toasted sandwiches to Lake Bunyonyi crayfish curry. Lovely views of the terraced hills from the patio or beautifully manicured gardens.
$ Hot Loaf Bakery, in the centre of town opposite **Edirisa**. Daily 0700-1630. A bit of a Kibale institution (backpackers and overland trucks have made a beeline here for years), sells excellent mini-pizzas chocolate doughnuts and cheese pies, but the bread rolls are the usual Ugandan yellow, sweet kind.
$ Royal Café, on the Kibale–Kisoro road next to, and owned by, the **Royal Supermarket**, T0751-585698. Daily 0700-1700. Serves really tasty Indian curries, plus steak and chicken sandwiches, soups and chips. Also has the best lattes and cappuccinos in town, and when it's operational, Wi-Fi. Watch the streetlife from the terrace tables.

Lake Bunyonyi *p141*
All the places to stay have restaurants. Non-guests can eat at those on the 'mainland' and **Bushara Island Camp,** which can be reached by canoe. The famous Lake Bunyonyi crayfish, which features on all menus, is in fact the Louisiana red swamp crayfish that was introduced to the lake in the 1970s and has thrived. It is quite delicious and is served in a number of different ways from salads to curries.

$ Lake View Coffee Shop, T0750-777434. Daily 0830-2300. This is located on the summit of the hill on the road from Kabale, 2 km before Rutinda and, as the name suggests, has stunning views from the broad wooden deck. This is in fact the first view you'll get of the lake and it's jaw-dropping. They serve Uganda coffees and teas, cold beers and sodas, and meals include fish and chips, some Indian curries and toasted sandwiches. You may have to wait as the generator is fired up, but it's a lovely spot to hang around and enjoy the tremendous scenery and the good gift shop.

🍸 Bars and clubs

Mbarara and around *p135, map p136*
Club Vision Empire and **Another Life**, 35 Banaunka Drive, T0772-444265. Wed, Fri-Sat, 2000-late. Mbarara is a university town so bars and nightclubs are popular. These 2 are adjoined with several entrances and bars and are surprisingly modern with 3 separate dance floors and DJs. There are a number of other bars along Banaunka Drive and Buremba Rd, just to the north.

🛍 Shopping

Mbarara and around *p135, map p136*
Nakumatt, Buremba Rd, T0485-420256, www.nakumatt.net. Mon-Sat 0800-2000, Sun 0800-1600. Opened in 2012, the swish Mbarara branch of this popular Kenyan supermarket chain covers more than 3700 sq m. It's the best outside of Kampala and offers anything you could possibly want to buy in southwest Uganda, from a bottle of water to a fridge. It's rather incredulous claim to fame is that it is the first **Nakumatt** to have a travellator (moving walkway). The other Kenyan chain, **Uchumi**, also has plans to open in Mbarara.

Kabale *p138, map p139*
Kabale's main market next to the taxi park has no shortage of fresh produce. There's a

good curio shop at **Edirisa**, which also has outlets at some of the lodges at Bunyonyi. **Royal Supermarket**, close to the post office on the Kibale–Kisoro road, T0751-585698. Daily 0700-1700. Sells many items that are hard to get in this part of Uganda, like frozen meat, cheese, wine, cereals, chocolate and toiletries. The **Royal Café** is also here.

☉ What to do

Lake Mburo National Park p133, map p134
Boat trips
The popular UWA motorboat trip on Lake Mburo leaves from the jetty by the **Lakeside Restaurant**, 1 km away from Rwonyo park headquarters and **Rest Camp**. Book and pay at the park headquarters, T0392-711346, before going down to the jetty. The 2-hr trip departs every 2 hrs 0800-1800 (subject to demand), minimum 4, maximum 8, US$15 per person. It's a relaxing excursion and there's a good chance of spotting African fish eagles and numerous other birds, hippos and the odd crocodile in the water, and buffalo and small antelope coming down to drink.

Game drives
All the lodges offer game drives in their own vehicles and at the more upmarket places these are included in the rates. Day game drives in the 4WD UWA park vehicles can be arranged at the Rwonyo park headquarters, T0392-711346, for those staying at **Rwonyo Rest Camp**, campsites or **Arcadia Cottages**, 2 hrs, minimum 4, maximum 8, US$20, children (5-15) US$10. They can be organized for any time, though early morning and late afternoon are the best times for game viewing. Night game drives depart 1830-1900, 2-3 hrs, US$30 per person. Your own high-powered torch is useful, as the UWA spotlights don't always function.

Horseback safaris
Mihingo Lodge, see page 142, has the concession to operate horseback safaris

in and around the park. It's a great way to explore the area's fauna and birdlife; the animals are far less shy of horses than of vehicles. The most popular is a 4-hr hack in the middle of the park along Warukiri Track and up to hilltop viewpoints and waterhole, and there is the option of bush breakfasts or sundowners. Catering for a range of horse-riding abilities, prices start from US$25 (30 mins) to US$200 (full day with breakfast and lunch). For experienced riders they can also organize an overnight safari with 1 night in a bush camp in the park (US$395).

Walking
Guided walks with an armed ranger through the woodland provide an opportunity to spot forest birds and mammals, while the hilltop routes reward visitors with spectacular views of the lakes. The lodges offer guided walks, or they can be arranged at, and depart from, the **Rwonyo park headquarters**, T0392-711346, 2-4 hrs, minimum 4, maximum 8 people, US$30 per person (no children under 15). Early morning and evening are best. One of the most rewarding is the 2-hr early-morning walk to the western side of **Lake Mburo**. At this time of day, you may encounter hyenas returning to their dens and hippos retreating to the lake. Of particular interest to birders is the 2-hr walk through **Rubanga Forest**, a closed canopied tropical forest that supports a large and diverse bird population. The 2-hr **night walks** with spotlight/torches usually depart 1900-2000, US$40 per person, and often include a visit to a salt lick near Rwonyo where animals are attracted to the salty rocks.

Kabale p138, map p139
Tour operators
Edirisa, at Edirisa Museum Home (page 144), T0752-558222, www.edirisa.org. Organizes a number of community-orientated tours including a half-day trip to Lake Bunyonyi which includes canoeing and visits to a school and traditional healer (US$35); 2- to 3-day canoe and hiking safaris

on and around the lake with nights spent camping with local families (from US$125); or there's a challenging but immensely enjoyable 5-day trekking and canoeing safari from Kabale all the way to Buhoma (Bwindi's park headquarters, page 152), through the beautiful hills and lakes either camping or staying at lodges (from US$580 per person for 2 people, US$390 per person for 4). You can download brochures from the website. **Engagi Safaris**, Engagi Guest House (see page 145), T0782-421519, www.engagi experience.net. If you haven't arranged a gorilla excursion before reaching Kabale, this tour operator will do their best if they can get permits. 1- to 2-day excursions to Bwindi, Mgahinga or to the Volcanoes National Park in Rwanda. The day tours are understandably long, departures are at 0400, but are doable if a little exhausting. Rates vary depending on group size and destination but start at around US$200 per day for vehicle, driver/ guide and lunch, but exclude gorilla permits (see page 6). Also rents out mountain bikes which are ideal for a day trip to Lake Bunyonyi.

⊕ Transport

Mbarara and around *p135, map p136*
Mbarara is a major crossroads and transport is plentiful. The bus and taxi parks are on and around Bishop Willis St near the market. Buses to **Kampala** are frequent (4 hrs, US$8) and during the day you shouldn't have to wait more than 30 mins for one. There are also *matatus* although many people avoid them as they drive particularly fast on the road to the capital. Buses and *matatus* to **Kabale** go from the bus and taxi parks, and also from the Shell petrol station near the post office (1½ hrs, US$4). There are also vehicles northwest to **Fort Portal** via **Kasese** on a newly improved road. The Post Bus (page 14) stops on Mbarara High St on its Kampala–Kabale route.

Kabale *p138, map p139*
Buses to **Kampala** depart frequently throughout the morning from 0600 until about 1300 (8 hrs, US$12). Or take the **Post Bus**, which leaves for Kampala from the post office near the Royal Supermarket Mon-Sat at 0800. It usually arrives in Kabale about 1600. There are also *matatus* to Kampala, which are a bit cheaper, usually leave about mid-morning and take about 1 hr less than the buses, although many people choose to avoid them as they drive particularly fast on the road to the capital.

Regular *matatus* link Kabale with **Kisoro**, 68 km to the west and, although the road is now tarred, it is still steep and windy and takes the best part of 2 hrs, US$4.50. Kisoro *matatus* go from the western end of town beyond the Gapco petrol station.

It's possible to get to **Kasese** or **Fort Portal** in a day, but it takes a lot of patience; take the bus to **Mbarara** and change there. There is 1 daily bus operated by **Horizon** opposite the Royal Supermarket, which goes to Fort Portal (292 km away), via Mbarara and Kasese; it's supposed to leave at 0700, but often goes earlier if it's full, 8½-9½ hrs. These bus arrangements may change as the shortcut road between Ntungamo and Ishaka will have been tarred by the time you read this cutting down the journey time.

Around Kabale *p140*
There's 1 daily bus to Kisiizi (for the Kisiizi Waterfalls) which departs Kabale at 1200 and returns from Kisiizi at 0700 the next morning. The better option are *matatus* which go between the 2 throughout the day and take 2 hrs.

⊕ Directory

Mbarara and around *p135, map p136*
Medical services Mbarara District Regional Referral Hospital, off the Kabale–Mbarara road, T0485-421806. As this is a teaching hospital, it's on the university campus; 24 hrs.

The far southwest: gorilla land

For many people, Uganda is synonymous with gorilla tracking. The gorillas are in the corner of the country where Uganda meets Rwanda and the DRC, the only three countries in which it is possible to visit mountain gorillas (Gorilla beringei beringei). The route here is mountainous and spectacular and, as the road winds from Kabale to Kisoro, there are glorious views of the Virunga Volcanoes, deep valleys, streams and lakes. It is around Kabale and Kisoro that you'll reach the access points to the gorilla tracking trailheads in Bwindi Impenetrable National Park and Mgahinga Gorilla National Park. Until a few hundred years ago when farmers began to clear land and grow crops around what is now Kisoro, the forests of Bwindi were contiguous with the forests of the Virunga Volcanoes. This explains why the gorillas live both in the Virungas at Mgahinga (and Rwanda and the DRC) and in the now-separated Bwindi. There are two ways of seeing the gorillas. The first is to organize transport, permits, accommodation, etc, yourself. The easier but expensive alternative is to go on an organized tour, arranged in Uganda or before you arrive. For details of how to get a gorilla permit, see Essentials, page 6. ▸▸ *For listing, see pages 164-170.*

Bwindi Impenetrable National Park → *For listing, see pages 164-170. Colour map 2, C1.*

A UNESCO World Heritage Site, **Bwindi Impenetrable National Park**, formerly known as the Bwindi Impenetrable Forest, is a magnificent, green swathe of dense rainforest on the steep ridges of the Western Rift Valley in southwest Uganda. In the local language Bwindi means 'a place of darkness' and the name refers to its dense vegetation, also reflected in the name 'Impenetrable Forest'. The name is certainly apt: it's a magical place of tangled vegetation draped over a deeply fissured landscape of steep, slippery valleys and high, draughty ridges. It is one of the most biologically diverse areas on earth, and covers 331 sq km over a series of hills ranging in heights of 1160-2607 m. Its unique and precious flora sustains roughly 400 mountain gorillas, the majority of the entire population of 880. Nine groups are habituated in Bwindi, and as eight permits are issued per day for each group, 72 people a day can go gorilla tracking, making Bwindi the most popular destination for this once-in-a-lifetime experience. Apart from gorilla tracking, there are a number of other guided hikes and trails within the park, plus some community-driven activities like village visits, which are great ways to fill in time while you wait for your pre-arranged date with the gorillas. ▸▸ *For details of gorilla permits, see Essentials, page 6.*

Arriving in Bwindi Impenetrable National Park

Getting there By road: Very broadly and depending on which sector you're heading to, Bwindi can be reached from Kabale to the southeast (two to three hours), from Kisoro to the south (two hours), from Kampala via Mbarara (eight to 10 hours), and from Queen Elizabeth National Park to the north (two to three hours). Now that there are nine habituated groups of mountain gorillas, gorilla tracking takes place in four locations in the park; **Buhoma** in the northwest, **Ruhija** in the east, **Nkuringo** in the southwest and **Rushaga** in the south. There are several approaches to the park as well as accommodation at each of these gorilla-tracking starting points (trailheads). Which of these you go to depends wholly on where your gorilla permit is allocated, and with which lodge your tour operator has made arrangements, although those who have organized their gorilla permits independently are most likely to go to Buhoma – the park headquarters and original gorilla tracking starting point, from where three of the groups can currently be visited. It's also Bwindi's main point of access for public transport as all buses arrive at and depart from Butogota, the nearest large village to Buhoma, 17 km away; *matutus* and *boda-bodas* link the two. How to reach Buhoma and the other three sectors is explained in more detail below.

By air: Aerolink ⓘ *T0317-333000, www.aerolinkuganda.com, see also Essentials, page 13)*, run one return scheduled flight Monday to Friday between Entebbe International Airport and the airstrip at **Kihihi** (40 km north of Buhoma); the plane also touches down at Kisoro airstrip on request. They operate the flight on demand, usually with a minimum of four passengers, and can also arrange charter flights. A special hire taxi from the airstrips to the lodges is then the option, or a tour operator will organize flights and transfers for a Bwindi fly-in package.

Background

Bwindi's forest is extremely old, which explains its extraordinary biological diversity. When most of Africa's forests disappeared during the last ice age (12,000-18,000 years ago), Bwindi was one of a few that survived. Consequently, its vegetation has been weaving itself into tangles for at least 25,000 years, and in the process it has accumulated a lengthy species list.

The park was first gazetted to the status of a forest reserve in 1932, then in 1964 as an animal sanctuary in order to give the mountain gorillas better protection. It was renamed the Impenetrable Central Forest Reserve and, from 1966, it was under the joint management of the Forest and the Game Departments. Then in 1991, along with Mgahinga Gorilla Reserve and Rwenzori Mountains Reserve, it was designated as a national park and was renamed Bwindi Impenetrable National Park. In 1994 it was inscribed as a UNESCO World Heritage Site and also came under the management of Uganda National Parks, since renamed **Uganda Wildlife Authority (UWA)**.

Gorilla tracking in Bwindi started in 1993 with one gorilla family called the Mubare group. Hardy overlanders and the most adventurous of early tour operators got to Bwindi on almost impassable roads on a journey that would take three to four days from Kampala; they would then camp in a basic clearing next to the Buhoma park gate, which had little more than a long-drop toilet and a stream to wash in, and wait – sometimes for days – until it was their turn for a gorilla permit (there was no pre-booking). News of the wonderful experience of being able to sit with a mountain gorilla family quickly spread and more and more tourists started flocking to Bwindi. Today 72 gorilla permits are allocated each day and there are numerous accommodation options catering for every budget. Ruhondeza, the silverback of the Mbuare group since gorilla tourism started at Bwindi in 1993, died a natural death at the age of 50 in 2012. His grave is near the park headquarters at Buhoma where there's a monument. He remains an icon for the UWA and the Bwindi communities, symbolizing what gorilla tourism has done for the region and Uganda as a whole.

Bwindi was the scene of a terrible tragedy in March 1999, when a force of 100-150 former Rwandan Interahamwe guerrillas crossed the border through the thick forest from the DRC and kidnapped 14 foreign tourists and a Ugandan guide from campsites next to the park headquarters. They eventually released six but murdered the remaining eight with machetes after forcing them to walk for some distance into the forest towards the DRC. The attack was reportedly intended to destabilize security in Uganda and frighten away tourist traffic from the park, depriving the Ugandan government of vital income; which it did, at least temporarily as Bwindi was forced to close for several months. The perpetrators were captured and there have been no incidents since then; the only reason the guide carries a gun while gorilla tracking is to protect against wildlife.

Best time to visit Bwindi can be visited throughout the year, but it can be cold, especially at night and first thing in the morning. Average temperatures are 7-20°C with the coldest months being June and July. Warm clothing is required, plus wet-weather gear, since Bwindi receives up to 2390 mm of rain annually. It can rain at any time, but the heaviest rainfall is concentrated during March and May and September to November. Instead of short tropical deluges, rain in Bwindi often falls as long hours of soft drizzle. There are low-season rates for gorilla permits during periods typically characterized by heavy rains. For details of gorilla permits, see Essentials, page 6.

Flora and fauna

Bwindi is a rainforest in every sense of the word, and is the source of five major rivers, which flow into Lake Edward. The forest has been estimated to have at least 120 species of mammal, of which 10 are primates. In addition to the gorillas, there are chimpanzees, the grey-cheeked mangabey, black-and-white colobus, red-tailed and vervet monkeys. Other species include giant forest hogs and bushbucks, although these are both rare and shy animals. A small group of forest elephants survive in the southeast section of the park, although again they are very rarely seen. The forest supports a huge range of birdlife, with 348 species, of which 23 are endemic to the local area. The plant and insect life is also phenomenal, with 220 butterfly varieties, and about 150 tree species as well as a wide range of ferns, orchids, mosses and lichens.

Gorilla tracking

① *Daily at 0800 sharp; late arrivals may lose their place. Permits US$600 including park entry. No under 15s. For details of getting gorilla permits, see Essentials, page 6).*
On each particular day, 72 individuals can visit the Bwindi gorillas, eight people for each of the nine habituated groups, and trips depart from **Buhoma**, **Ruhija**, **Nkuringo** and **Rushaga**. Until a few hundred years ago the Bwindi forest was contiguous with the forests of the Virunga Volcanoes, and continuous research on the Bwindi gorillas comparing them to Virunga population has shown that they have evolved slightly differently. One marked observation is that the Bwindi gorillas' diet is higher in fruit than that of the Virunga. They are more likely to climb trees and travel further each day to find fruit than the Virunga gorillas, who mostly feed on more easily found fibrous foods at ground level. As a result, Bwindi gorillas are much more likely to build their nests in trees rather than the undergrowth.

Buhoma

Buhoma is located to the northwest of the park and faces the dark, hilly forests of Bwindi. It was the first sector of the park to be developed, and is where the **UWA headquarters** ① *T0486-24121, www.ugandawildlife.org*, is based and is well served by accommodation, transport, little grocery shops and craft stalls as well as a community hospital. Most importantly, there are three habituated gorilla groups that can be tracked from here: **Habinyanja**, **Rushegura** and **Mubare** (Mubare being the oldest habituated gorilla group in Uganda, first visited by tourists in 1993).

Other activities at Buhoma include mountain biking and nature walks to waterfalls in the forest, and also community-run village walks for exploring the culture and lifestyle of the local Bakiga and Batwa people. There are at least a dozen accommodation choices here, and most are clustered just before the park gates, while a couple are beyond the gates within the park boundary, but you don't have to pay any park entry fees unless you want to go into the forest on walks.

Bwindi Impenetrable National Park

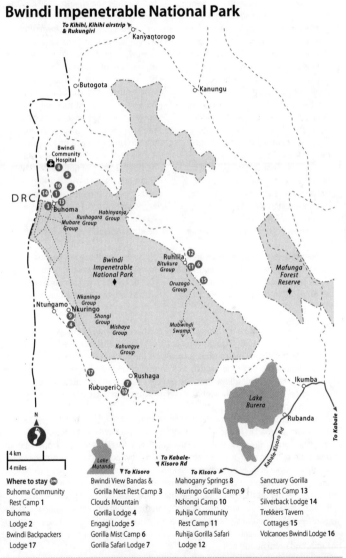

Where to stay
Buhoma Community
Rest Camp **1**
Buhoma
Lodge **2**
Bwindi Backpackers
Lodge **17**

Bwindi View Bandas &
Gorilla Nest Rest Camp **3**
Clouds Mountain
Gorilla Lodge **4**
Engagi Lodge **5**
Gorilla Mist Camp **6**
Gorilla Safari Lodge **7**

Mahogany Springs **8**
Nkuringo Gorilla Camp **9**
Nshongi Camp **10**
Ruhija Community
Rest Camp **11**
Ruhija Gorilla Safari
Lodge **12**

Sanctuary Gorilla
Forest Camp **13**
Silverback Lodge **14**
Trekkers Tavern
Cottages **15**
Volcanoes Bwindi Lodge **16**

Gorilla tracking rules

- As gorilla tracking starts at 0800 in the morning and you have to be at the park office by 0730, it is essential that you get to your accommodation near the trailhead the night before. If you are staying some distance away, confirm that your accommodation can arrange a transfer to get you there on time. If you're late, you lose your booking and do not get any money back.

- Gorilla tracking begins with a briefing where you meet your guides and trackers and the rest of the group. The chances of sighting the mountain gorillas are excellent and it's an immensely rewarding experience, but tracking lasts from a few hours to a full day and can be tough going. The heavily forested mountains have steep peaks and valleys covered in dense undergrowth, thorny trees, tangled vines and slippery floors laden with matted vegetation. Some slopes are so steep that you may well have to crawl. If you are going during the rainy season be prepared to get very wet and muddy.

- Wear sturdy walking shoes, a raincoat, and thick trousers and a long-sleeved top as protection against scratches; the gorillas are thoroughly used to people, so it makes little difference whether you wear bright or muted colours. You can borrow sturdy walking sticks at the park offices. Take plenty of water.

- If you're not very fit, consider taking a UWA porter, which can be arranged at the park offices or through your tour operator at US$15 per day. They will carry day packs and help negotiate the thick foliage and assist up hills, etc.

- A maximum number of eight visitors may visit a group of gorillas per day. This minimizes behavioral disturbance of the gorillas and the risk of their exposure to human-borne diseases. Always wash your hands before you head out. You will not be able to track if you have an infectious disease such as diarrhea or flu; do not pass off something contagious like a common cold with hay fever, for example. If at all possible, an alternate permit will

Getting there Butogota is the nearest village and transport hub 17 km south (but uphill) from Buhoma. To get to Butogota from Kabale (110 km, and about three to four hours), turn right at the clearly signposted turn-off on the Kabale–Kisoro road after 18 km, and then follow the dirt roads which fork to the left at the villages of Kanungu and Kanyantorogo and are all signposted. The dirt road is regularly maintained but you may need to engage 4WD when it's wet as it can be slippery in parts. *Matatus* run between Kabale and Butogota.

To get to Butogota from Kampala, the shortest route is to go first to Mbarara and then turn off the main road at Ntungamo (after 85 km) on to a newly tarred road to Rukungiri (45 km), then go on dirt roads via Kihiihi to Butogota. In total this route is around 455 km, of which about 70 km is on dirt, compared to 520 km, of which 110 km is on dirt, via Kabale. There are a couple of daily buses between Kampala and Butogota that take the route via Mbarara, Rukungiri and Kihihi, but the journey is long (about 10-11 hours), as the buses stop a lot; they depart from both Kampala and Butogota at 0500-0600, US$14-16.

Buhoma is roughly 160 km south of Mweya in the Queen Elizabeth National Park and the journey takes around three to four hours. The route goes via the southerly Ishasha sector of the Queen Elizabeth National Park, and then it's 65 km from the Ishasha Gate via Kihihi and on to Buhoma.

be arranged for you, or you will be refunded your money. Once with them you are not allowed within 7 m, and in case you want to cough or sneeze, cover your mouth and move away.

- The guides and trackers follow the scents and movements of the gorillas, usually using the previous night's nest as a starting point. They follow the flattened foliage and piles of dung that indicate in which direction the gorillas have headed. Once they are located it is hugely exciting – you might see a baby clambering up a tree, a female quietly munching on a branch, even a silverback pounding his chest. Your guide will immediately motion for the group to stay quiet and drop to the floor and this is when the one-hour permitted to stay with the gorillas commences.
- More of the members of the family will come into sight as they get used to their human audience and often move closer and stare back just as intensely and equally inquisitively.

You must stay in a tight group, keep voices low and flash photography is not permitted. Sometimes the gorillas charge; follow the guide's example and crouch down slowly, do not look the gorillas directly in the eyes and wait for the animals to pass.

- The maximum time you can spend with the gorillas is one hour. However, if the gorillas become agitated or nervous, the guide will finish the visit early. He will silently motion when the time is up, and gently lead the group away. The gorillas get on with their day-to-day business and the tired but immensely exhilarating and privileged group will descend back to the park gate.
- A guide and between three and six trackers will accompany each trip and a recommended tip for the one-day excursion is about US$20-40, which can be placed in the appropriate tip box at the park office for your gorilla group. Tips are usually given in Uganda shillings or US dollars cash.

Once in Butogota, *matatus* and *boda-bodas* go the 17 km to Buhoma; a special hire taxi costs about US$10; you may be able to hitch a ride from other tourists going to Buhoma in their own vehicles; or you could walk (about three hours).

Walks Several guided walks of the forest (US$15-30 per person) can be started from the park headquarters and gate and they depart at 0900 and 1415 (except the longer Ivi River Walk which has to be started at 0800). The reception at **Buhoma Community Rest Camp (BCRC)**, see Where to stay, page 165, near the park gate, takes bookings and organizes guides. The **Muyaga Waterfall Walk** is a return three-hour walk through the dense forest that culminates where the attractive Muyaga Falls plummet 33 m into a tangled gorge. The three-hour **Muzabajiro Loop Trail** is through forest to the slopes of the Rukubira Hill, where a wildfire in 1992 created an open view across the forest towards the Virunga Volcanoes. The **Rushara Hill Trail** is a three-hour trek to the top of the highest hill in the immediate area of Buhoma. The steep climb to 1915 m through fields and regenerating forest, can be strenuous, but you're rewarded with views across the Western Rift Valley to the Virungas to the south, and as far north as the Rwenzori Mountains on a very clear day. The 14-km **Ivi River Walk** is a six- to eight-hour return walk along a route cleared in 1970 for a never-completed road to Kisoro. The path, an important route for the local people, leads to the Ivi River at the southwestern boundary of the park. The 10-km **Buhoma–Nkuringo Trail** takes three to four hours, and crosses right through the park, connecting the two villages and offering impressive views as you ascend the hills towards Nkuringo. It may be possible to walk between the two and stay overnight at a place at either end and get your luggage taken by road – discuss this with your lodge.

Ruhija

Ruhija is in the east of the park and sits on top of a hill at 2345 m. This high-altitude section is the highest part of Bwindi, 1000 m higher than Buhoma, which means the climate is much cooler. It is especially favoured by keen birdwatchers and is one of only two areas (the other being Rushaga) where forest elephants reside (although they are seldom seen). Gorilla tracking, opened up here in 2009, is to the **Bitukura** and **Oruzoojo** groups, while the other habituated group, **Kyaguriro**, is visited for research purposes.

Getting there From Kabale it's 52 km to Ruhija and takes between 90 minutes and two hours. The signposted turn-off is 26 km on the Kabale–Kisoro road after passing the turn-off to Buhoma at Km 18. There's no public transport to Ruhija but you can get a special hire taxi from Kabale for around US$35-45. From Ruhija the road continues for another 50 km to Buhoma, but this is challenging, takes at least two hours in a 4WD and is usually only used by park staff.

Walks Guided walks (US$15-30 per person) of the forest can be started from the park gate and can be organized at the lodges. The winding six-hour **Bamboo Trail** leads to **Rwamunyoni Peak**; at 2607 m this is the highest point in the park. The climb is through the bamboo zone and montane forest and at the top on a clear day Lake Bunyonyi can be seen. Also of interest to birdwatchers is the four-hour **Mubwindi Swamp Trail**, which leads to a swamp of about 2 sq km, home to many birds. This is where Mubwindi Forest – meaning 'a muddy, swampy place of darkness' – is supposed to have got its name.

Nkuringo

Located on the southern boundary of the park, this became the second gorilla tracking point after Buhoma in 2004. There is one gorilla family here, the **Nkuringo group**, and the hike is fairly strenuous, as they are usually located some 600-700 m below the trailhead at Ntungamo village on Nteko Ridge. However, the walks along the top of the ridge are wonderful and provide superb views north towards Bwindi's forested hills and south to the Virunga Volcanoes. Lucky visitors may see as far as the glaciers on the Rwenzori peaks, some 160 km away.

Getting there From Kabale to Nkuringo is 105 km or three hours. The signposted turn-off is at Km 45 on the Kabale–Kisoro road (which also goes to Rushaga, see below), after passing the turn-off to Buhoma at Km 18 and the turn-off to Ruhija at Km 26. Follow the signposts and you'll reach a junction that goes right to Rushaga and left to the village of Rubugeri. Go through Rubugeri and then after 1 km you reach another junction which joins the road coming from Kisoro. Nkuringo is 11 km northwest of this junction near the village of Ntungamo.

The shortest route is from Kisoro (39 km and about 90 minutes), via Lake Mutanda (see page 159) and then Ntungamo. The turn-off to the lake and beyond is at the Agip petrol station in Kisoro on the Kabale–Kisoro road. From Kisoro you may be able to get sporadic

Mountain gorillas

The mountain gorilla is a subspecies of the genus *gorilla* and is the largest living primate. Mountain gorillas are the rarest of all the apes, and there are currently only 880 individuals in the mountainous and forested region that straddles Uganda, Rwanda and the DRC, which is the only environment in which they are able to survive. They have never been reared successfully in captivity and there are none in zoos.

They were first 'discovered' in 1902, when a German officer named Captain Oscar von Beringe shot two of them dead while on an expedition in the Virunga Volcanoes in Rwanda (then German East Africa). He managed to retrieve one of the bodies, a young male weighing 100 kg, which was larger than any apes the Germans had ever seen. The bones and skin were sent to the Berlin Zoological Museum for analysis and there it was acknowledged as a mountain gorilla – one of the two subspecies of the eastern gorilla (the other is the eastern lowland gorilla found in the area west of the Virunga Volcanoes). The captain's name, ironically, was attached to the new subspecies – *gorilla gorilla beringei*.

George Schaller was the first zoologist to study and live with the mountain gorillas of the Virungas in 1959. He was also the first to convey to the general public just how profoundly intelligent and gentle gorillas really are, and how very closely their behaviour parallels that of humans, contrary to then-common beliefs that they were aggressive and dangerous creatures as depicted in the famous 1933 *King Kong* movie.

Following Schaller, interest by archaeologist and naturalist Louis Leakey in the origins of mankind led to Dian Fossey founding the Karisoke Research Centre near Ruhengeri in Rwanda in 1967 (immortalized in the movie *Gorillas in the Mist*). In what would become an 18-year study of mountain gorillas, Fossey made new observations, completed the first accurate census, and established active conservation practices such as anti-poaching patrols. This culminated in humans making close and friendly contact with groups in their natural home – 'habituation' – and the subsequent development of gorilla tourism. Today, there are habituated groups in Uganda's Bwindi Impenetrable National Park and Mgahinga Gorilla National Park, Rwanda's Parc National des Volcans, and the DRC's Parc National des Virunga.

matatus to Ntungamo (particularly on Kisoro market days – Monday and Thursday), otherwise a special hire taxi will cost in the region of US$40.

Rushaga

Rushaga, in the southeast of the park, opened in 2009, and there are magnificent views south from here across to the Virungas. The region is dominated by high hills and because of this, the habituated gorilla groups have kept on separating and subdividing to take up different hills in the area. Mountain gorillas are non-territorial but will try as much as possible not to interfere with each other. At present three groups, **Shongi**, **Mishaya** and **Kahungye**, can be tracked from this point. As Rushaga is the closest trailhead to Kisoro (32 km) and Lake Mutanda (page 159), it's possible to stay at these places and still get to the gate by 0800 for gorilla tracking.

Getting there From Kabale and Kisoro the directions are the same as for Nkuringo (see above), except that you turn right to Rushaga at the junction 1 km before Rubugeri if coming from Kabale (65 km), and from Kisoro (32 km) you turn right at the Ntungamo turn-off and go through Rubugeri to Rushaga. Special hire taxis from Kisoro will cost around US$30-40.

As they are both on the southern side of the park, Rushaga and Nkuringo are becoming increasingly popular for visitors coming from Rwanda. Indeed Kigali **International Airport** is far closer to Bwindi than Kampala, and the route via the Uganda–Rwanda Cyanika border, 15 km south of Kisoro and Uganda's Mgahinga Gorilla National Park and 50 km from the Volcanoes National Park on the Rwandan side of the Virunga Volcanoes, has opened up many options for tour operators and independent travellers. (For more information about the border see box, page 163.)

Kisoro → *For listing, see pages 164-170. Phone code: 0486. Colour map 2, C1.*

Kisoro is in the extreme southwestern corner of Uganda, about 470 km from Kampala and 68 km from Kabale. It's a tiny town with a population of around 12,000, but it sees its fair share of visitors, given that it is the nearest town to the Mgahinga Gorilla National Park), 14 km away. The nearby Virunga Volcanoes, which straddle the border of Uganda, DRC and Rwanda, are made up of three extinct volcanoes: Mount Muhavura, meaning 'the guide' (4137 m); Mount Gahinga, meaning 'small pile of stones' (3474 m); and Mount Sabyinyo, sometimes spelt Sabinyo, meaning 'old man's teeth' (3674 m). There are endless views of these beautiful towering peaks throughout the region and they can be climbed from within Mgahinga Gorilla National Park. Kisoro also has a lively twice-weekly market (Monday and Thursday), incredible hill walking and clean, safe swimming lakes, such as Lake Mutanda and Lake Chahafi nearby.

Arriving in Kisoro

Getting there The construction of the new smooth tar road from Kabale to Kisoro and then on to Bunagana, the border with the DRC (12 km west of Kisoro) was completed in 2012. At Kisoro, a spur of the new tar now also connects it to the border with Rwanda at Cyanika, 15 km south of Kisoro (see Border crossing box, page 163). *Matatus* between

Kisoro

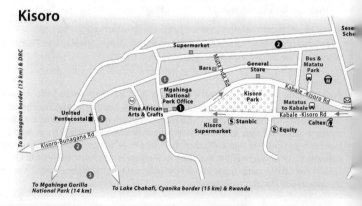

Kabale and Kisoro go throughout the day, and also link with the Cyanika border.
▶ See also Transport, page 170.

Tourist information Uganda Wildlife Authority (UWA) Mgahinga National Park office ① 13 Kisoro–Bunagana road, T0486-430098, www.ugandawildlife.org, daily 0800-1800, is a very helpful office that sells gorilla permits for both Mgahinga and Bwindi if you haven't already got one and if they are available. Also come here the day before to book for volcano climbs, golden monkey tracking and the Batwa Trail (all these activities are listed under Mgahinga, page 160). Payment is made either here or the park headquarters at Mgahinga and both accept US dollars, euro and GBP cash. The office also sells maps and a few souvenirs and you can pick up leaflets here for the other UWA parks.

Lake Mutanda

This pretty deep green lake north of Kisoro is nestled in the foothills of the Virungas at an altitude of 1800 m, from where there are outstanding views of the three volcanoes: Muhabura, Sabinyo and Gahinga. There are several tiny islands in the lake, and it is drained by the Rutshuru River that flows northwards to Lake Edward. It attracts a wide variety of birds, including pelicans, kites, sunbirds and weaverbirds, and is also home to otters, which are often spotted. The turn-off to the lake is at the Agip petrol station in town on the Kabale–Kisoro road. There are a few outstanding places to stay with gorgeous views at the northern side of the lake around 15-20 km from Kisoro (see Where to stay, page 166), which make a great alternative to the limited choice of accommodation in Kisoro itself. Beyond the lake this road eventually leads to the village of Rubugeri, which is close to the gorilla tracking trailhead at Nkuringo in Bwindi (page 156).

Another lovely trip is to hike to the **Mutanda Eco-Community Centre (MECC)** (see Where to stay, page 167), about 6 km or one to two hours' walk over the ridge above town and down to the water. Innumerable footpaths will take you there, but one of the best is over the hill at the end of Seseme School's playing field (then ask for directions). Beer and sodas are available on arrival at the **MECC**, and they can rustle up a local meal of, perhaps, grilled tilapia fish from the lake. The water is free of hippos, crocodiles and bilharzia and the centre has a swimming jetty and can organize canoes. It might be worth asking around for a taxi number to call from the lake to save you the return journey on foot, or someone from the MECC may be able to give you a lift.

Where to stay 🛏
Countryside
  Guest House **2**
Golden Monkey
  Guest House **1**
Kisoro Tourist **4**
Sawa Sawa Guesthouse **3**
Travellers Rest **5**

Restaurants 🍴
Coffee Pot Café **1**
Community Group **2**

Lake Chahafi

Another attractive walk with a stunning destination, about 9 km southeast from Kisoro close to the Rwandan border, is the route to **Lake Chahafi Resort** (see Where to stay, page 168). The first half is along the new tarred section of road to the Cyanika border, then branch off the road at Muganza opposite the church and the last 4 km or so is along beautiful country tracks, with breathtaking views and big skies. When you arrive you will find this charming, simple resort sitting right on the edge of the water, and the view from the deck is simply jaw-dropping. The beautiful, sleepy, papyrus-fringed lake (19.2 sq km) is scattered with lilypads and is home to some truly spectacular birds and it has a full-frontal view of the majestic Muhabura volcano. There's a good chance of seeing the African jacana, great blue heron, pelican, African fish eagle, pied kingfisher and bronze sunbird, amongst others.

Mgahinga Gorilla National Park → *For listing, see pages 164-170. Colour map 2, C1.*

This, the smallest national park in Uganda at just 34 sq km, was established in 1991 and sits high in the clouds at an altitude of between 2227 m and 4127 m. As its name suggests, it was created to protect the rare mountain gorillas that inhabit its dense forests, and it is also an important habitat for the endangered golden monkey. The park makes up the northeastern part of the Virunga Volcanoes and is contiguous with the Volcanoes National Park (Parc National des Volcans) in Rwanda and the Virunga National Park (Parc National des Virunga) in the DRC. The park takes its name from *gahinga*, a local word meaning 'piles of volcanic stones'. As well as being important for wildlife, the park has huge cultural significance, in particular for the indigenous Batwa pygmies, traditional hunter-gatherers who are considered to be the mountains' first human inhabitants.

Viewing the gorillas is the predominant reason for visiting Mgahinga, which is often less busy than Bwindi and is easier to access from cheaper accommodation in and around Kisoro than the limited choice of mainly high-end lodges in Bwindi. However, the excursion is far less reliable than Bwindi as the one group of habituated gorillas, the **Nyakagezi** group, frequently moves over into Rwanda or the DRC. Nevertheless, gorilla permits at Mgahinga are ONLY available 14 days in advance, which makes this is the better option to get last-minute permits (if the gorillas are *in situ*) compared to Bwindi where permits get booked out by the tour operators months, or even years, in advance. Mgahinga also offers the unique opportunity to go golden monkey tracking, attempt the challenging climbs of the volcanoes or visit the Batwa communities.▶ *For details of gorilla permits, see Essentials page 6.*

Arriving in Mgahinga Gorilla National Park

Getting there The **Ntebeko** entrance gate and visitor centre is 14 km from Kisoro along a dirt road that can be steep and rocky in places and can get slippery after heavy rain. Take the Kisoro–Bunagana road for 200 m after the **Travellers Rest Hotel** and turn left and then immediately right after about 100 m. It's clearly signposted. There are only walking paths within the park; vehicles can park at Ntebeko. A special hire taxi will cost around US$20 each way, and you can organize one at the UWA office in Kisoro (page 159) or the hotels. It's a good idea to get the taxi driver's phone number to arrange pickup after an excursion. You could get a *boda-boda* for a lot less but it's a very rough road. The new visitor centre at Ntebeko is the starting point for all activities: gorilla and golden monkey tracking, volcano climbs and the Batwa Trail (all listed below). You can book the day before at the office in Kisoro. It has a few displays about the Virunga environment, and about 800 m up the hill is a viewing platform that is great for birdwatching and has wonderful views of the volcanoes.

Virunga National Park

The DRC's Virunga National Park (Parc National des Virunga) just over the Bunagana border from Kisoro, is the other Virunga Mountain stronghold of the mountain gorillas along with the Ugandan and Rwandan side of the volcanoes. A UNESCO World Heritage Site since 1979, it's home to six habituated families of gorillas, and gorilla tourism has been an integral part of the park for more than 30 years. The trailheads for gorilla tracking can be accessed from Rwanda or Uganda, and Jomba, the nearest to Uganda, can be reached on foot from the Bunagana border. However, currently the park is closed to tourists, and has been since 2012 because of rebel activity in eastern DRC. But check locally as the situation could change at any time.

Sadly, this situation is nothing new and the park has routinely had to close since 1996 because of ongoing conflict and insecurity in the region. The park is administered by the Congolese Wildlife Authority (Institut Congolais pour la Conservation de la Nature: ICCN) who have made every effort to protect the park, even during the most intense periods of the DRC's conflicts. But it has not been without sacrifice as an estimated 140 ICCN employees have lost their lives in since 1996. The gorillas too have suffered considerably; not only have armed groups occupied their habitat, and poaching is rife, but in 2007 five members of one family, including the silverback, were massacred by rebels for no apparent reason.

The dedicated ICCN rangers continue to protect the park and its estimated 200 mountain gorillas, and they are supported by a number of international conservation groups and donors. These include the World Wildlife Fund (WWF) and the Frankfurt Zoological Society. Nevertheless, they constantly need funding, especially as the park is currently receiving no revenue from entry fees or gorilla permits.

For more information about the Virunga National Park, to read blogs from the rangers themselves about their tireless monitoring of the gorilla families, or to make a donation, visit www.gorillacd. org. This is the website of the ICCN and their employees and brings together all the people committed to protecting the Virunga National Park and its critically endangered mountain gorillas.

Background
The protection of gorillas on the Ugandan side of the Virunga Volcanoes began in the mid-1950s when game warden Walter Baumgartel took an interest in them. Baumgartel left Uganda in the late 1960s and in the years that followed there was much encroachment into the forest, particularly along the lower slopes of Muhavura, Gahinga and Sabinyo volcanoes. Poaching was also a threat and many of the gorillas retreated into better-protected areas in the neighbouring countries. It was not until 1989 that gorillas began to receive some protection under the **Gorilla Game Reserve Conservation Project**, which began to operate along the Virunga Volcanoes on the Uganda side. It became the **Mgahinga Gorilla National Park** in 1991.

Flora and fauna
The vegetation in the park includes montane, alpine and sub-alpine flora at each of the different levels up the volcano, varying with altitude. The lowest vegetation zone of the mountain is mainly bamboo and this is the area where the gorillas are more

likely to be found. The alpine zone is dominated by the impressive giant senecios and giant lobelias that are found at an altitude of between 3600 m and 4200 m. Apart from the mountain gorilla and golden monkey, the park is home to 76 species of mammal, although most are difficult to glimpse in the thick vegetation. These include giant forest hog, bush pig, buffalo, forest elephant, bushbuck, duiker and porcupine. Of the more than 180 species of bird are the Rwenzori turaco, crowned hornbill, black kite, crowned crane and paradise fly-catcher.

Gorilla tracking
① *Daily at 0800 sharp from Ntebeko. Permits US$600 including park entry. No under 15s. For details of getting gorilla permits, see Essentials, page 6).*
Mgahinga is home to the habituated **Nyakagezi group**, and the family includes the lead silverback **Bugingo** who is around 50 years old and father to most of the group. They are a fairly nomadic bunch and are known to cross the border frequently into Rwanda and the DRC. As a result, gorilla permits are ONLY available 14 days or less prior to the planned trek. If there any available after your arrival in Kisoro, they can be bought from the UWA office in Kisoro (page 159) or at the visitor centre at Ntebeko; otherwise you can ask at your hotel.

Golden monkey tracking
① *Daily at 0800 from Ntebeko. Permits US$50, plus park entry US$40. No under 15s.*
The highly endangered golden monkey (*Cercopithecus kandt*) is only found in the Virunga Mountains in highland forest, especially near bamboo stands, and two other forests in Central Africa. Similar to but separate from the blue monkey (*Cercopithecus mitis*), the golden monkey is no longer thought to be a subspecies of it. The monkey gets its name from the colour of its fur and, with its black limbs and a crown on its head, this monkey really is a lovely creature. Unfortunately, it is under great threat from poachers. There are an estimated 3000-4000 golden monkeys in the Virungas, of which a population of about 40-60 are habituated in Mgahinga for visitors to track, in the same way you track gorillas. Again permits can be bought from the UWA office in Kisoro (page 159) or at the visitor centre at Ntebeko. Treks usually last four hours, and again visitors spend a maximum of one hour with the group. This fairly new activity has also been developed over the border in Rwanda's Volcanoes National Park.

Climbing
① *Climbs are organized at the UWA office in Kisoro (page 159) or at the visitor centre at Ntebeko. They usually depart from Ntebeko at 0630-0700. US$60, plus park entry fee US$40.*
It's possible to climb to the peaks of Gahinga, Sabyinyo and Muhavura, although the pace set by the ranger and armed escort may be exhausting unless you are fit. The summit of **Mount Muhavura** ('The Guide') is the highest point of the park at 4137 m and is a typical cone-shaped volcano. It is a long steep climb over a distance of 12 km and elevation of 1700 m and takes four to five hours up and three to four hours down. Muhavura does not have the thick forest that Mgahinga and Sabinyo offer, and much of the climb is up a rocky surface covered by grasses and small shrubs. The low vegetation gives you excellent views of the area throughout the day. At the top is a small, beautiful crater lake, a great incentive to make it to the top. The view from the summit is frequently obscured by cloud, but if it's not, on a clear day you can see all the other Virunga Volcanoes, Lake Edward in Queen Elizabeth National Park and the peaks of the Rwenzori Mountains.

Border crossing: Uganda–Rwanda

Cyanika

The Cyanika border (0600-2100; 0500-2000 Rwandan time) is 15 km south of Kisoro and 50 km from the nearest large town on the Rwandan side, Musanze (formerly called and still widely known as Ruhengeri). This is a wonderful journey through the Virunga Mountains, which some say is the most beautiful part of Uganda and Rwanda. Ruhengeri lies near the twin lakes of Lake Burera and Lake Ruhondo and is the gateway to seeing the mountain gorillas in the Volcanoes National Park (Parc National des Volcans; PNV). Kigali is a further 93 km from Ruhengeri. *Matatus* link both sides of the border from Kisoro to Ruhengeri and the journey takes about three hours, but you'll have to swap vehicles at the border. The nearest banks and ATMs are in Kisoro and Ruhengeri, but there are money-changers at the border. Visas for both countries are available (but check with embassies), as is third-party insurance for drivers, and visas and vehicle costs are paid with US dollars cash. For more information on visas between the East African countries, see box on page 33. Remember, that traffic drives on the right in Rwanda so it's at the border that you swap over sides of the road. Also remember that Rwanda is one hour ahead of Uganda.

It is very feasible to go over the border for gorilla tracking in the PNV from Uganda (and many tour operators do so). There is also the option of flying into one country and flying out of the other. The park is home to 10 habituated gorilla families with eight visitors allowed per group; that's 80 permits per day. Like Uganda, the minimum age is 15 and the time allotted once the gorillas have been located is one hour. Gorilla permits in Rwanda are currently US$750 and are booked through the **Rwanda Development Board** (T+250 (0)252 580388; www.rdb.rw), although independent travellers can chance turning up at the park headquarters at Kinigi, 12 km northwest of Ruhengeri, to see if there are any available. However, like Bwindi, they are usually booked up months in advance by the tour operators so a better option is to go through a Rwandan tour operator. The gorilla excursion begins at 0700 each day from Kinigi, so you'll need at least one night near the park first if getting there from Uganda. There is plenty of accommodation in Ruhengeri. Rwanda Tourism is a good place to start for information about the country (www.rwandatourism.com).

Mount Sabyinyo ('Old Man's Teeth') offers a more varied, exciting and highly recommended climb, and the opportunity of straddling Uganda, Rwanda and the DRC simultaneously. It's an eight- to nine-hour return journey over 14 km and an elevation of 1300 m and there are three peaks to climb. Peak one is reached along a ridge on the eastern side. Reaching Peak two involves a traverse along the ridge with Rwanda on one side and Uganda on the other. Trekking to Peak three involves the use of a series of ladders, some angled, others horizontal, to help cover the terrain to the tri-border apex where, at 3669 m, you will be standing in Uganda, Rwanda and the DRC at the same time.

The **Mount Gahinga** ('Piles of Volcanic Stones') climb includes a pleasant walk through bamboo forest, known locally as *rugano*, before the gradient increases up to the summit. There was a small crater lake at the summit but it has turned into a swamp over time. It can be cloudy on top, but it does offer the opportunity to step into Rwanda. The round trip takes around six to eight hours, and covers a distance of 12 km.

The Batwa Trail

ⓘ www.thebatwatrail.com, US$80, including park entry for a full or half day. The trail is organized at the UWA office in Kisoro (page 159), at the visitor centre at Ntebeko or at Mount Gahinga Safari Lodge and Amajambere Iwacu Community Camp, both near the park gate (see Where to stay, page 168).

For generations, Mgahinga's dense forests were home to the indigenous Batwa pygmies – hunter-gatherers and fierce warriors who depended on the forest for shelter, food and medicine. When the national park was established in 1991, the Batwa were evicted from the forest and abandoned their low-impact, nomadic lifestyle. They now live in isolated villages around the base of the mountains and along the border with Rwanda near Lake Bunyonyi. The guided Batwa Trail was established as a result of a collaboration between the UWA and the United Organisation for Batwa Development. It runs across the lower slopes of the Muhavura and Gahinga volcanoes within the park boundaries. It's a highly enjoyable nature walk and learning experience about the Batwa's cultural heritage, but be aware it involves hiking at an altitude of around 2500 m for at least four to five hours. The Batwa guides demonstrate hunting techniques, gather honey, point out medicinal plants and demonstrate how to make cups and other implements out of bamboo. Some of the steep mountain slopes contain caves formed by lava tubes, one of them being the Batwa's sacred Garama Cave located 4 km from the Ntebeko visitor centre. It's over 340 m in length and 14 m deep, and used to be a refuge for the Batwa during their long-running conflicts with their neighbours over the centuries. The tour finishes here with a moving performance of Batwa song and dance, which is enhanced by the acoustics within the cave. Part of the tour fee goes directly to the guides and musicians, and the rest goes to the Batwa community to cover development initiatives such as paying for children's school fees and books, and for the purchase of new land near the park, which, in turn, deters illegal hunting within the park boundaries. Fun, interactive, informative and highly recommended; a far cry from other distasteful 'pygmy experiences'.

◉ The far southwest: gorilla land listings

For hotel and restaurant price codes and other relevant information, see pages 16-20.

● Where to stay

Bwindi Impenetrable National Park
p150, map p153

There is a large selection of accommodation available at Bwindi. Tour operators will secure gorilla permits and organize accommodation depending on budget. All places to stay can provide packed lunches for gorilla tracking and walks.

Buhoma *p152, map p153*
$$$$ Buhoma Lodge, reservations Kampala T0414-321470, www.uganda exclusivecamps.com. Well designed with

great use of natural materials, this has lovely forest views from 10 elevated timber and thatched cottages with verandas built up the hillside. The 1st-floor restaurant and bar overlook the Munyaga Valley. Nice touches include massages after gorilla tracking.
$$$$ Mahogany Springs, reservations Kampala T0414-3466667/8/9, lodge T0781-844354, www.mahoganysprings.com. This deservedly popular new luxury set up is a far cry from the usual safari-style. With ultra-modern decor and design, it offers 8 spacious rooms and a 2-room suite with forest-facing terraces, superb food and good wines and cocktails in the restaurant, and extras include afternoon tea on the deck.
$$$$ Sanctuary Gorilla Forest Camp, reservations through the website or the UK,

T044-(0)20-7190 7728, www.sanctuary
retreats.com. Positioned just inside the park
gate at Buhoma, and accessed up a very
steep hill, this upmarket camp has 8 large
tents equipped with bathtubs on wooden
decks looking straight into the forest. The
restaurant and bar is tastefully decorated
and serves excellent 5-course dinners and
a warming bonfire is lit at night.

\$\$\$\$ Volcanoes Bwindi Lodge,
reservations Kampala T0414-346464/5,
www.volcanoessafaris.com. From the
luxury Volcanoes Safari collection (also runs
Mount Gahinga Safari Lodge, page 168,
and **Kyambura Gorge Lodge**, page 186),
with 8 stone-and-tiled glass-fronted eco-
lodge *bandas*, pleasant communal areas with
large fireplace and veranda overlooking the
forest, very attentive staff and superb food,
extras include a complimentary massage.

\$\$\$ Engagi Lodge, reservations
Kampala T0414-321552, www.kimbla-
mantanauganda.com. The sister property
to **Lake Mburo Camp** (page 142), this is
a comfortable and friendly spot. 8 stone
cottages well camouflaged among the trees,
restaurant, lounge and library, and a bar built
out of rocks with a broad veranda for lovely
forest views.

\$\$\$ Silverback Lodge, reservations
Kampala T0312-259390, lodge T0772-
777855, www.silverbacklodge.com. A mid-
range place and still with only 12 rooms
in stone chalets, this is in fact the largest
lodge in the area. It's set high up on the hill
with wonderful views, a bar and restaurant,
and rents out mountain bikes.

**\$\$-\$ Buhoma Community Rest Camp
(BCRC)**, T077 2-384965), www.buhoma
community.com. A budget camp and
the backbone of the **Buhoma Mukono
Community Development Association**,
which has been involved in providing the
local Buhoma community with jobs and
funding since gorilla tracking began here
in 1993. 7 *bandas* and 6 safari tents, either
en suite or with communal bathrooms
(doubles from US\$60), a 6-bed dorm

(US\$20 per person) and a grassy campsite
(US\$10 per person). The small restaurant
serves hearty, basic meals; it's advisable to
pre-order. Within easy walking distance of
the park gates, with views similar to those
on offer nearby at 10 times the cost. It also
organizes walks in the park (see Walks,
page 155, and other activities, page 169).

**\$\$-\$ Bwindi View Bandas and Gorilla
Nest Rest Camp**, T0772-399224, www.
gorilladestination.com. This simple
backpacker-friendly place is just inside the
park gate, and is reasonably good value,
especially for groups as the 10 en suite
bandas have 3-5 beds, plus you can camp.
Neat gardens and restaurant and bar with
balcony. Doubles from US\$80, camping
US\$10 per person.

Ruhija *p156, map p153*

\$\$\$\$ Ruhija Gorilla Safari Lodge,
reservations Kampala T0414-503064, www.
gorillasafari.travel. The most upmarket option
in Ruhija with great views of the Virunga
Volcanoes. 14 timber and brick chalets with
balconies, well designed for warmth, given
that it is over 2300 m, restaurant and bar
with roaring fire and varied buffet meals.

\$\$\$-\$\$ Gorilla Mist Camp, T0772-563577,
www.gorillamistcamp.com. A sensibly
priced, locally owned place with 8 rooms
in either rustic cabins or large safari tents
under tin roofs, set on grassy terraces with
good forest views, handmade wooden
furnishings, elevated restaurant and bar
offering continental and local meals.

\$\$ Trekkers Tavern Cottages, T0772-
455423, www.trekkerstavern.com. On a
hilltop overlooking Bwindi about 2 km
south of the park gate at Ruhija but with
transfers for gorilla tracking. 5 simple en
suite cottages, friendly service and first-rate
food. Great for birdwatching, almost all of
the 34 species of Albertine endemics have
been seen around the lodge, and there's
easy access to walks to Mubwindi Swamp.

\$ Ruhija Community Rest Camp, T0771-
846635, ruhijac@gmail.com. Close to

the park gate in well-cared-for gardens, 4 double cottages with bathrooms (US$70), 2 twins without (US$50), which share ablutions with campers (US$10 per person). Bonfire in the evening and they provide hot water bottles. Good communal meals and all profits go directly into the Ruhija community, namely a nearby orphanage.

Nkuringo *p156, map p153*
$$$$ Clouds Mountain Gorilla Lodge, reservations Kampala T0414-251182, lodge T0772-489497, www.wildplacesafrica.com. This stunning luxury lodge has 8 double/twin and 2 family suites, each with a lounge, fireplace and sumptuous bathroom, a huge lounge and restaurant with massive wooden beams, and excellent food and wine. It was built in partnership with the **Nkuringo Community Development Fund (NCDF)**, which supports the local community.
$$$-$$ Nkuringo Gorilla Camp, T0774-805580, www.nkuringocampsite.com. Even though it's not in the luxury bracket, this is one of the most highly rated lodges in Bwindi and very popular with tour operators; book well in advance. On a 2161-m-high ridge, there are few better views in the whole of Uganda; you can see as far as the Rwenzoris and right across to the semi-active volcanoes in the DRC. There is a choice of 2 en suite cottages or 6 twin-bed rooms with communal bathrooms. Extra safari tents are put up during busy times. Great wholesome food using locally grown ingredients and fantastic staff.
$$-$ Bwindi Backpackers Lodge, 5 km before the park gate coming from Rubugeri, T0772-661854, www.bwindibackpackers lodge.com. One of the best options for independent travelers, simply because they provide a daily shuttle from Kabale (check the website for options and times) and can organize transfers from Kisoro and both the Rwanda borders. An attractive black-and-white timber-framed house with accommodation in en suite rooms (US$80 per double/twin), non-self-contained

rooms (US$25 per person), dorms (US$15 per person) and there's a campsite (US$10 per person). Good set meals, hot showers and Wi-Fi, and can organize all local hikes and village visits. 30% of profits go towards development initiatives.

Rushaga *p157, map p153*
As Bwindi's newest gorilla tracking trailhead, there's limited accommodation at Rushaga, but with an early start it's possible to reach the park gate for 0800 from Kisoro and around.
$$$$-$$$ Gorilla Safari Lodge, reservations Kampala T0414-345742, www.gorillasafarilodge.com. The best option at Rushaga and 1 km from the park gate, with 8 cosy cottages with fireplaces, 2 have 2 bedrooms for families or friends, verandas face the forest and pretty gardens, restaurant, bar and lounge; a nice touch is a boot-cleaning service after gorilla tracking.
$ Nshongi Camp, no phone, www. nshongicamp.altervista.org. Basic budget venture with 4 double *bandas* (US$25 per person) or you can camp (US$5 per person) in a pretty forest glade, shared bathrooms with hot bucket baths, good meals including a 3-course dinner and packed lunches, a 5-min walk to the park gate.

Kisoro *p158, map p158*
Remember that the southwest of the country has problems with running water. All the places to stay provide buckets/jerry cans of hot water for washing when there's none in the showers.
$$ Travellers Rest Hotel, Kisoro–Bunagana road, at the turn-off to Mgahinga, reservations Kampala T0414-200221, hotel T0772-533029, www.gorillatours. com. This old colonial hotel was known as the unofficial gorilla headquarters in the 1950-1960s as its owner, game warden Walter Baumgartel, was one of the first people to take an interest in gorillas and their protection. Dian Fossey stayed here often and it became a centre for primate

experts from around the world. Today it's set in mature gardens, a haven for birdlife, and has 12 comfortable rooms, a handsome rustic sitting room with an impressive collection of authentic Congolese masks for sale, the best restaurant in Kisoro (page 168) and activities include village walks, bike rides or visits to Lake Mutunda.

$$-$ Kisoro Tourist Hotel, Kisoro–Bunagana road, opposite the UWA office, turning down a small driveway, T0777-744410 www.kisorotouristhotel.net. Modern hotel, but a little concretey and characterless, with 14 rooms with DSTV, hot showers and sunny balconies. Restaurant food is mainly Western and the little bar has a warming fireplace.

$ Countryside Guest House, Kisoro–Bunagana road, near **Travellers Rest Hotel**, T0782-412741. Simple and spotlessly clean budget option with 14 en suite rooms around an inner courtyard. Doubles US$20 and you can camp in the grassy compound which has secure parking for US$3 per person. Bar and restaurant with DSTV and the staff are super helpful and will organize meals for early/late departures/arrivals and phone around for *boda-bodas* and taxis.

$ Golden Monkey Guest House, just behind the UWA office, T0772-43 5148, www.goldenmonkeyguesthouse.com. Centrally located and umissable thanks to its colourful murals of gorillas, this budget option is aimed at backpackers and has fantastically friendly staff. 12 rooms with en suite or shared bathrooms (from US$30, 4-bed rooms US$10 per person), the menu is varied and tasty and there's a bar. Also has its own vehicle for transfers to Mgahinga and the Rwanda border, among other destinations.

$ Sawa Sawa Guesthouse, directly opposite the **Travellers Rest Hotel** on the Kisoro–Bunagana road, T0774-472926. Best of the local cheapies and run by friendly female staff, 9 tiled rooms named after Mgahinga gorillas with or without bathrooms from US$12 per room in a compound behind a bar/dining room. *Sawa sawa* means 'all good' in Kiswahili.

Lake Mutanda p159

$$$ Chameleon Hill, 20 km from Kisoro, T0782-842707, www.chameleonhill.com. With unobstructed views of the lake, this new lodge has 10 lovely wooden chalets, each nicely decorated in bright colours and local crafts, the restaurant, bar and library lead out on to a wooden deck. Lots of activities including canoeing, and nature, village and birdwatching walks, plus Mgahinga activities can be arranged. Rates are full board.

$$$ Hotel Mucha, 6 km from Kisoro, not on Lake Mutanda but on the Mucha River on the way to the lake, T0784-478605, www.hotel-mucha.com. A new German venture opened in 2014 with a refreshing modern style in the event you've tired of all those thatched roofs, 10 rooms in long low buildings in the forest with verandas, minimalist modern decor, bistro-style menu, Wi-Fi, mountain bikes for hire and can organize pickups from town. Reports welcome.

$$$ Mutanda Lake Resort, 17 km from Kisoro, T0789-951943, www.mutandalakeresort.com. This is in a marvellous location on a wooded spit into the lake with 13 cottages raised on stilts, each with thatched verandas overlooking the lake and volcanoes, the Swiss chalet-style restaurant serves good buffet breakfasts, packed lunches and 3-course dinners. Can organize activities on and around the lake plus excursions to Mgahinga and Bwindi.

$ Mutanda Eco-Community Centre (MECC), 6 km from Kisoro, T0782-306973, www.lakemutandacamp.com. A local community venture in association with a Swedish NGO (volunteer placements can be arranged). Peaceful and rustc, activities include swimming, canoeing and village visits and, if you so desire, a guide will take you to look for the exceptionally large pythons that live around the lake. 4 simple *bandas* and a bunkhouse, hot water and filling local meals are provided. Doubles (US$50), dorm (US$10 per person), camping (US$6 per person).

Lake Chahafi *p159*
$ Lake Chahafi Resort, 9 km from Kisoro off the road to the Cyanika border, T0782-754496, www.lakechahafiresort.com. With volcano views, this rural retreat set in manicured gardens on the lakeshore has accommodation in furnished safari tents (US$50) dorms (US$20) and camping (US$8), all rates include breakfast and there's a restaurant and bar. Activities include canoeing, community walks and guided hiking in the hills on the Rwanda border, you can rent mountain bikes (US$10 per day) and there are also volunteer opportunities at the local school and clinic.

Mgahinga Gorilla National Park *p170*
You can easily get to the gate from Kisoro for gorilla tracking at 0800. Both of the following are located in the beautiful foothills of the Gahinga/Sabinyio volcanoes just outside the park entrance at Ntebeko.
$$$$ Mount Gahinga Safari Lodge, reservations Kampala T0414-346464/5, www.volcanoessafaris.com. With the volcanoes as a backdrop, this is the most luxurious option in the area with 9 very comfortable stone and tile *bandas* with fireplaces, set well apart from each other in the beautiful gardens. Full-board rates also include alcoholic drinks and a massage (a welcome touch after gorilla tracking). Offers accommodation and all the Mgahinga activities a s part of a 4-day/3-night safari with pickups at Kigali International Airport in Rwanda.
$ Amajambere Iwacu Community Camp, T0772-435148, www.amajamberecamp.org. This project is an income-generating community initiative run in association with the Mutanda Eco-Community Centre (see above). Friendly, clean with amazing

views, but a basic brick set up in gardens full of (oddly) hydrangeas, with single or twin *bandas* (from US$25), dorms (US$10 per person), a campsite (US$5 per person), bucket showers and a pit toilet. Basic meals can be prepared with notice and, thankfully given that it's over 2000 m, there are warming fires lit in the evening.

Restaurants

Kisoro *p158, map p158*
$$-$ Travellers Rest Hotel, see page 166. Daily 0700-2200, dinner at 1930. The best food in town with mouthwatering buffet dinners or 4-course set meals at less busy times (US$14), non-residents need to order by 1500. They use lots of salads and green vegetables, have a welcoming log fire, and lunches are served at outside tables in the mature gardens. Also provide packed lunches for those on activities.
$ Coffee Pot Café, next to the UWA office. Daily 0900-1800. This comfortable, well-furnished German-run café/craft shop is a welcome surprise in Kisoro, serving great sandwiches made from baguettes, burgers, salads, coffees, including café latte, and delicious home-made cakes.
$ Community Group Restaurant, on a back road between the main market and the top of Mutanda Rd. Daily 0700-2000. For the best local fare in town and popular with transport drivers, offers plates of sweet potato, *matoke*, yams, beans, meat stews and fat avocados, with large jugs of delicious fresh passion fruit juice.

Bars and clubs

Kisoro *p158, map p158*
The most lively place to be in the evenings is **Mutanda Rd**, which has a clutch of bars with cold beers and pool and table football tables, as well as delicious street food such as very tasty pork *muchomo* (roasted on a stick).

○ Shopping

Kisoro *p158, map p158*
Handicrafts
Fine African Arts and Crafts, at the **Coffee Pot Café** (see above) next to the UWA office. Daily 0900-1800. Has a great selection of locally made arts, crafts and jewellery, including some interesting carved masks and statues from the DRC. Also offers a decent choice of English, German and Dutch books to buy or exchange.

Markets
Kisoro market, held on Mon and Thu, is a fantastic and interesting spectacle and well worth a visit. It is very busy and colourful, attracting traders from Uganda, Rwanda and the DRC. It sells fresh fruit and vegetables, brightly colooured African fabrics, second-hand Western clothes, soap, kerosene lamps, and much more. The market used to take place on the Uganda–DRC border at Bunagana until the tense political situation prompted its move.

○ What to do

Buhoma *p152, map p153*
Buhoma Community Village Walk, run by the **Buhoma Mukono Community Development Association** at the **Buhoma Community Rest Camp** (page 165) just before the park gate, T0772-384965, www.buhomacommunity.com. This community initiative has been operating at Buhoma since gorilla tracking started in 1993. The popular 3-hr village walk includes a visit to a handicraft shop and a traditional healer, a singing and dancing performance, and a demonstration (and tasting) of how bananas are used to make juice, beer and gin. US$15 per person. They also run a 6- to 7-hr 13-km guided mountain bike trail that follows a well-maintained track from the park headquarters to the Ivi River. US$25 per person.

Nkuringo *p156, map p153*
Buniga Forest Walk, T0750-165738, www.bunigaforestwalk.org. Similar to the Batwa Trail in Mgahinga Gorilla National Park (see page 164), this is run by and visits the Batwa pygmy community who were largely displaced when both national parks were established. The 6-km walk departs from the **Nkuringo Community Conservation and Development Foundation (NCCDF)** office near the park gate and includes a walk through the Buniga Forest fragment of Bwindi, while a Batwa guide points out the medicinal and other traditional uses of plants and trees, followed by a visit to a Batwa settlement. US$25 per person.
Nkuringo Walking Safaris, T0774-805580, www.nkuringowalkingsafaris.com. Although listed here under Nkuringo, this outfit offers highly rated and incredibly scenic multi-day walking safaris between Kisoro and Buhoma or vice versa with overnights at a lodge at Lake Mutanda (page 167) and **Nkuringo Gorilla Camp** (page 166). The itinerary follows the western boundary of Bwindi and includes roughly 8 hrs of hiking each day and a 3-hr crossing of Lake Mutanda by canoe. Options can be tailor-made (largely depending on time, ability and gorilla permits) from 2 days between Lake Mutanda and Nkuringo to 4 days between Kisoro and Buhoma. Prices start from US$240 per person, excluding any park fees incurred.
Nkuringo Village Community Walk, book at **Nkuringo Gorilla Camp** (page 166) or **Clouds Mountain Gorilla Lodge** (page 166). Motivated by the success of the village walk at Buhoma, local guides at Nkuringo have now developed a 3- to 4-hr walk. It starts at **Nkuringo Gorilla Camp** and goes to the top of Nkuringo Hill to experience a 360° view of Bwindi, the Virungas and the DRC, and includes a visit to a primary school, blacksmith and sorghum beer producer, as well as a local youth group performance. US$10 per person.

⊖ Transport

The far southwest: gorilla land *p150*
A *boda-boda* to **Mgahinga Gorilla National Park** is a cheap option although you may have to walk over some of the roughest parts of the road. A special hire taxi will cost about US$20, more in the rainy season.

Matatus to **Kabale** go throughout the day, but although the 68 km is now tarred, it is steep and windy and takes the best part of 2 hrs, US$4.50.

To **Kampal**a buses depart around 0600 (10 hrs, US$14) and stop in Kabale (2 hrs, US$4.50), and **Mbarara** (5 hrs, US$7). There are *matatus* to the **Rwanda** border to cross to Ruhengeri, taking about 3 hrs, a scenic route through one of the most beautiful parts of Uganda (see Border crossing, page 163). Buses no longer go between Kisoro and Goma in the DRC, but they may resume as the Bunagana border was reopened in late 2013 after being closed for almost 2 years (but get up-to-the-minute advice before embarking on any travel to the DRC).

⊕ Directory

Buhoma *p152, map p153*
Medical services Bwindi Community Hospital, Buhoma, T0703-342891 (0800-1800), www.bwindihospital.com. Founded in 2003, this is wholly funded by UK and US charities and attends to more than 40,000 people a year in the communities around Bwindi. Visitors are welcome to make donations, whether or not they need to be attended to by the English-speaking doctors and nurses.

Kisoro *p158, map p158*
Banks Stanbic Bank, Kisoro. Currently has the only 2 ATMs in town, but do not rely on them having cash. The worst days to withdraw money are market days, Mon and Thu, and the first few days of the month, when civil servants are paid. Remember, gorilla permits and other Mgahinga Gorilla National Park fees are paid for in US dollars/euro/GBP cash, so bring enough with you.

Contents

Queen Elizabeth, Fort Portal & the west

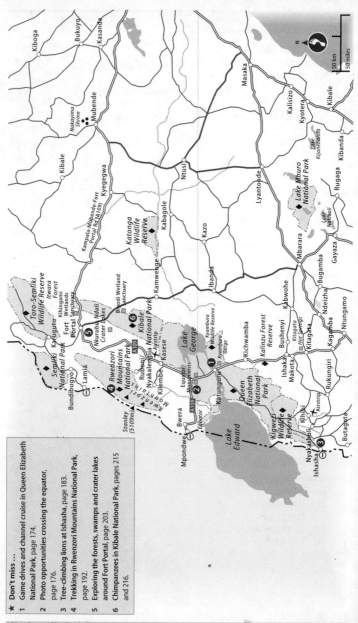

The Mbarara–Kasese road passes through the huge Queen Elizabeth National Park, and on its way it crosses the Kazinga Channel, the body of water that neatly connects Lake Edward in the west and Lake George in the east. The park is the best place in Uganda to see large species of plains game typical of East African savannah including lion and elephant. Many take a cruise along the famous Kazinga Channel to see the exceptionally large pods of hippos and some brilliant birdlife, or to visit the chimpanzees in the Kyambura Gorge.

Kasese is the gateway to the Rwenzori Mountains, the fabled 'Mountains of the Moon'. The border between Uganda and the DRC runs along the mountain peaks, demonstrating a huge change in vegetation as you climb to the icefields of Mount Stanley, the third highest peak in Africa at 5109 m.

Fort Portal, splendidly located in tea country in the west of Uganda, gives easy access to the Semliki Wildlife Reserve at the southern end of Lake Albert, Uganda's other royal lake. Hop over the northern spur of the Rwenzori Mountains and you can experience the huge central African rainforest which stretches for thousands of miles to the west in the Semliki National Park proper with its hot springs at Sempaya.

Other attractions around Fort Portal are chimp tracking in the Kibale National Park. This may not be anything like as exciting as gorilla tracking but it does give you a chance to experience chimpanzees in the wild and many more types of primates in the dense forest. Consider too cycling and hiking around the extraordinary Ndali-Kasenda crater lakes, an ideal place to stop and relax for a couple of days as there are lovely trails connecting the lakes.

Queen Elizabeth National Park (QENP)

The QENP lies across the equator in the southwest of Uganda. It is bordered to the southwest by Lake Edward and to the northeast by Lake George. The two lakes are joined together by the 33-km-long Kazinga Channel. The park covers an area of 1978 sq km, with mainly flat and gently undulating terrain that rises from the lakes to 1390 m above sea level at the crater area to the north of the Kazinga Channel. The park has a remarkable range of habitats: tropical forests, rivers, swamps, lakes and the volcanic craters. These provide a rich habitat for 95 mammal species and 606 bird species. To the northeast are the Rwenzori Mountains, often referred to as the 'Mountains of the Moon', which rise to over 5000 m. On a clear day it is possible to see the Rwenzoris from the park. As well as regular safaris by vehicle, other highlights of the park are launch trips on the Kazinga Channel, birdwatching, guided forest walks and tracking chimpanzees. ▸▸ *For listings, see pages 185-187.*

Arriving in Queen Elizabeth National Park → *Colour map 2, B1.*

Getting there

By air Aerolink ① *T0317-333000, www.aerolinkuganda.com*, see also Essentials, page 13, run return scheduled flights Monday-Friday between Entebbe International Airport and Kasese, for Mweya, and the airstrip at Kihihi, 22 km south of the Ishasha Gate (this flight also serves those going to Bwindi Impenetrable National Park). They operate the flight on demand, usually with a minimum of four passengers, and can also arrange charter flights. A special hire taxi from the airstrips to the lodges is then the option, or a tour operator will organize flights and transfers into a QENP fly-in package.

By road There are two bases for touring the park: **Mweya** in the north (see page 178) and its environs is the main one, and the more remote **Ishasha sector** (see page 183) in the southwest. As a result there are several approaches to the QENP, depending on which sector you're going to and which direction you're coming from. It takes about five or six hours to get to Mweya from Kampala either through Mbarara (420 km) or Fort Portal and Kasese (410 km); other routes lead to the Ishasha sector from Kampala, Kabale and Bwindi Impenetrable National Park.

There are several access points to the park from the **Ishaka–Kasese** road (97 km), which is in excellent condition (see below). Ishaka is 70 km northwest of Mbarara and 52 km north of Ntungamo, both on the Mbarara–Kabale road.

From Ishaka, the road goes up and down through forested hills dominated by tea estates. After 10 km it passes the turn-off on the left for Kalinzu Forest Reserve (see page 182), which is not part of QENP but is close enough to be included in this chapter. Then, when the road reaches Kichwamba on the top of the Rift Valley escarpment, 44 km north of Ishaka, the view of the plains of QENP suddenly opens up in front of you and to your left. A signpost on the left directs you to the Maramagambo Forest section of QENP (see page 181). From the cooler heights you descend into the hotter, dustier floor of the Rift Valley where the vegetation is mainly acacia bush and where the grass is sprinkled with occasional ant hills. Once on the floor of the valley, and about 3 km north of Kichwamba, the next turn-off is to the right to Kyambura Gorge in the Kyambura Wildlife Reserve, again part of QENP (see page 180). Another 8 km further on, and just before reaching the village of Katunguru, you'll come to another left turn that leads southwest

Queen Elizabeth National Park

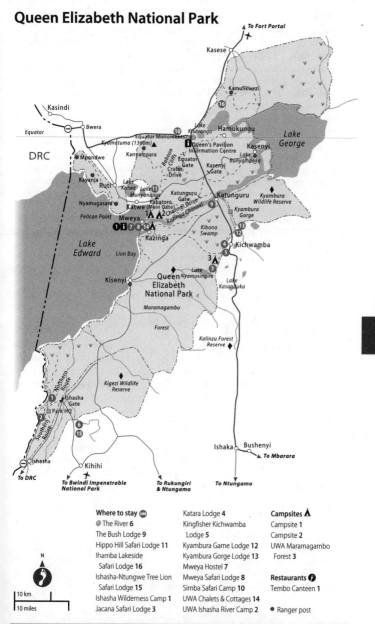

Where to stay 🏠
@ The River **6**
The Bush Lodge **9**
Hippo Hill Safari Lodge **11**
Ihamba Lakeside
  Safari Lodge **16**
Ishasha-Ntungwe Tree Lion
  Safari Lodge **15**
Ishasha Wilderness Camp **1**
Jacana Safari Lodge **3**

Katara Lodge **4**
Kingfisher Kichwamba
  Lodge **5**
Kyambura Game Lodge **12**
Kyambura Gorge Lodge **13**
Mweya Hostel **7**
Mweya Safari Lodge **8**
Simba Safari Camp **10**
UWA Chalets & Cottages **14**
UWA Ishasha River Camp **2**

Campsites ▲
Campsite **1**
Campsite **2**
UWA Maramagambo
  Forest **3**

Restaurants 🍴
Tembo Canteen **1**

● Ranger post

again. This is a public road that goes through the park to the Ishasha border with the DRC and is used by commercial traffic including heavy trucks bound for the DRC and Burundi. From Katunguru to the border it's 90 km and the road has benefited from recent, much-needed maintenance. Although this is not a game-driving road, and most of the animals shy away from it, it does go through the park and provides access to the southern Ishasha sector. You don't need to pay entry fees until you re-enter the park proper at Ishasha Gate, about 70 km (roughly two hours) after joining the road at Katunguru. For the other routes to the Ishasha sector, see page 183.

Back on the Ishaka–Kasese road at Katunguru, the road crosses an iron causeway over the Kazinga Channel, the natural channel that connects Lake George to Lake Edward. From here you can reach the main access points to Mweya (see page 178): turn left immediately after Katunguru to the Katunguru Gate from where it is 20 km to Mweya along a game-driving circuit known as Channel Drive (page 179). Alternatively, continue on the main road towards Kasese, turning left after 5 km on a public road to Katwe, a fishing village on the north shores of Lake Edward. After 15 km and 2 km before Katwe, you get to Kabatoro Gate, from where it is another 8 km to Mweya.

Back on the main road, opposite the Katwe turn-off, is the track going east to Lake George and the fishing village of Kasenyi (page 130), again part of QENP. Next and about 17 km north of Katunguru, on the left is the turn-off to the Equator Gate and Crater Drive (see page 179). This northernmost part of the park is the area of the crater lakes and it provides another 27-km route west to Mweya. Also here is the **Uganda Wildlife Authority (UWA) Queen's Pavilion Information Centre** ① *T0774-408124, www.ugandawildlife.org, daily 0730-1800*. The Queen's Pavilion was first built in 1959 to mark the visit of Queen Elizabeth II to Uganda and was renovated in 2007 for the visit of Prince Philip who reopened the centre. It has a kiosk for snacks and drinks, and a shop selling maps and books of the park.

Almost immediately after the centre, you cross from the southern to the northern hemisphere; on each side of the road there are large concrete circles marking the **equator** (like those on the Kampala–Masaka road, page 120), which make a fine photo opportunity. After the equator you are out of the park boundary and the main road splits: to the northeast it goes 26 km to Kasese, while the westwards branch goes 35 km to Bwera, after which it's another 5 km to the Mpondwe border with the DRC.

Park information
Uganda Wildlife Authority (UWA) ① *Mweya park headquarters T0483-44266, www.ugandawildlife.org; gate hours 0630-1930.* Park entry fees per 24 hours are US$40, children (5-15) US$20, foreign-registered vehicles: saloon car US$50, 4WD US$150, Uganda-registered vehicles: saloon car US$8, 4WD US$12.

Best time to visit
The park can be visited at any time and temperatures all year round average 18-25°C. June to September is the driest time when most animals remain near water, but be prepared for afternoon thunderstorms. Inside the park the tracks are fairly well maintained and in dry weather can be traversed in 2WD cars. The rainy seasons are from October to December and March to May, when a 4WD may be necessary as a lot of the park's tracks are on thick clay-type mud which can quickly get sticky.

Background

The depopulation of this region, once occupied by pastoralists, is largely a result of the ravages of rinderpest (a fatal disease that attacks cattle), as well as a smallpox epidemic in the 1890s, and then the arrival of tsetse fly in the early 20th century (another disease that kills livestock and gives humans sleeping sickness). In 1910, British officials decided to move the inhabitants away from the area around the lakes and in 1925 the Lake George Game Reserve and Lake Edward Game Reserve were established, in conjunction with the Parc National des Virungas across the border in the Belgium Congo (now DRC). These were later enlarged to include the crater areas and the area south of the Kazinga Channel. The Kibale Forest Corridor Game Reserve, to the north of Lake George, was also established, so elephants could pass to and from Kibale Forest. The reserves were combined and Kazinga National Park was gazetted in 1952. In 1954 it was renamed again following the visit by Queen Elizabeth II. The queen's first visit to Uganda was rather a sad and short one when, in 1952, she made a stopover at Entebbe Airport with the Duke of Edinburgh on their way to Britain for the burial of her father and her eventual accession as Queen. Her second visit was two years later on a Commonwealth tour, when she inaugurated the Owen Falls Dam on the Nile. The park headquarters were established in Mweya, and in 1960 the Nuffield Unit of Tropical Animal Ecology, later renamed the Institute of Ecology, was also developed there. During the Amin regime, the park was renamed Rwenzori National Park but it regained its original name in 1991 when Rwenzori Mountains National Park was gazetted.

Flora and fauna

The park is characterized by volcanic craters, grassy plains and tropical rainforests. It lies in the area of Africa where two types of vegetation meet: the rainforest which stretches out to the west for thousands of kilometres to the shores of the Atlantic, and the eastern and southern Africa grassland. The park, like much of Uganda, gets two rainy seasons each year, from March to May and from September to November. However, there is often rain during the rest of the year and prolonged droughts are unusual. The temperature varies from a minimum of 18°C to a maximum of 28°C.

Animals found in the park include hippo, lion (including the famous tree-climbers in the Ishasha sector), elephant, buffalo, Uganda kob, waterbuck, bushbuck and topi. Smaller animals that occur but not easily seen include warthog, hyenas, mongoose, red-tailed monkey, black-and-white colobus monkey, baboon, vervet monkey, and chimpanzees. Giant forest hogs live in the park, too, especially on the escarpment on the way up to Mweya, just outside the Maramagambo Forest. They look rather like large shaggy warthogs for which they can be easily mistaken.

Classified as an Important Bird Area by Birdlife International, the park is famous for its remarkably wide range of birdlife; an estimated 606 species have been recorded. It has the longest checklist of any park in East Africa due to the wide variety of habitats. The park's confluence of savannah and forest, linking to the expansive forests of the DRC, allow visitors to spot East as well as Central African species. In marshy and waterside areas larger species, such as the cormorant, goliath heron, egret, spoonbill, lesser and greater flamingo, pelican, fish eagle and sacred ibis can be seen. The 54 species of raptor, include African white-backed vulture, bateleur, martial eagle and Verreaux's eagle owl. The swamp areas in the Ishasha sector are a good place to look for the elusive shoebill stork. Migratory birds are present from November to April.

Mweya is the focal point and most frequently visited part of QENP, with better access and the widest choice of accommodation. The UWA's visitor centre is here, as is the launch site for the Kazinga Channel boat trip. From its elevated position, the peninsula commands gorgeous views of the channel, crammed with hippos and water birds, and its proximity to the surrounding savannah make it an ideal departure point for game drives.

Arriving in Mweya

Getting there By road Mweya is 420 km from Kampala via Mbarara, and 410 km via Fort Portal and Kasese. Both journeys take about five to six hours on good roads. From the Ishaka–Kasese road there are three different routes: via the Katunguru Gate along the Channel Track; via the Katwe road and the Kabatoro Gate; or via the Equator Gate and Crater Drive. See page 176 for details.

There is a Shell petrol station at **Mweya Safari Lodge** (page 185), which is pretty reliable for fuel, and you may well need to top up if you're doing a lot of game driving. Otherwise the nearest fuel is at Ishaka and Kasese.

Mweya is the only part of the park that can be reached relatively easily by public transport. From Kasese take a *matatu* going to Katwe; they leave daily in the morning. Ask to be dropped off at Kabatoro Gate, from where it is 8 km to Mweya; you can hitch, which is not difficult as there are plenty of private and UWA vehicles going from the gate. Alternatively, take any *matatu* going between Ishaka and Kasese and get off at Katunguru, and then take a special hire taxi, US$15-20. Taxis will take the Katwe road and drop you at Kabatoro Gate. UWA staff at the gate will probably let them take you the last 8 km to Mweya (and as they are only dropping you off, you will not be charged vehicle park entry fees). A special hire taxi from Kasese (55 km) will cost in the region of US$40-60 (depending on your bargaining skills); which is a reasonable price if there's a group of you. The journey should take little more than one hour.

Finally, if you find a taxi driver you feel confident with, make an offer to hire them for a day's game driving in the park. The fee for a Ugandan-registered vehicle s far less than for a foreign-registered vehicle. You will also have to pay park entry for the driver (US$6). If you're coming from Kasese, track a driver down the day before and get them to meet you at around 0500 at your hotel to maximize your day in the park. Once at Mweya, you can organize a UWA guide from the Mweya Visitor Information Centre (below) to come with you; not mandatory but recommended as they have extensive knowledge of the park, unlike the average Kasese taxi driver.

Park information **Mweya Visitor Information Centre** ① *100 m from Mweya Safari Lodge (page 185), Uganda Wildlife Authority (UWA), T0782-387805, www.ugandawildlife.org, daily 0800-1730*. The centre has information on game drive routes and accommodation and sells maps and postcards. There's a topographic model of the park and lots of informative exhibits describing the park within its Rift Valley setting. Visitors can enjoy the fantastic views of Katwe Bay, Lake Edward and the Rwenzori Mountains, 45 km away, from an outdoor decking area. The centre is the main booking office for activities such as the launch on the Kazinga Channel (see below), and for guides to go in your own vehicle (US$20 per vehicle per day). Taking an experienced guide in the early morning or at dusk is the most successful way to track down game, and guides are available from 0630 onwards; morning game drives should be booked the day before. You can also book guided walks here (US$30, children 5-15 US$15, per four hours), which include a walk around the Mweya Peninsula for birdwatching and lake views, or the trails in Maramagambo Forest (page 181). Park information is also available at the UWA's Queen's Pavilion on the Ishaka–Kasese road (page 176).

Launch trip on the Kazinga Channel

ⓘ UWA 2-hr launch trips run at 0900, 1100, 1500 and 1700. The UWA launch, a 40-seater pontoon-style boat, requires a minimum of 10 people, but they usually go at least twice a day. Book at the Mweya Visitor Information Centre, T0782-387805, US$30, children (5-15) US$15. The Mweya Safari Lodge (book at reception, page 185) has smaller boats (8-12 people) and run with a minimum of 4 and include snacks and drinks, from US$34 per person.

The Kazinga Channel is the wide, 33-km long natural channel that links Lake Edward and Lake George, and is a dominant feature of the QENP. Lake George, a small lake with an average depth of only 2.4 m, is fed by streams from the Rwenzori Mountains. Its outflow is through the channel which then drains into Lake Edward. It is almost impossible to tell which way the Kazinga Channel is flowing as the water level between the two lakes is just 40 cm and the channel moves extremely slowly. It does of course flow from east to west. The channel is famous as having one of the world's largest concentrations of hippos (approximately 2000), as well as many Nile crocodiles and monitor lizards. It's teaming with birds, and elephant and buffalo stride along the banks and are easily seen. The two-hour cruise is the most relaxing way to enjoy the QENP, in fact it's the highlight of any visit to the park, and the guides are very good at giving explanations about the animals. Birders can expect to tick off more than 60 species, some have boasted more than 100 in the two hours, and this could be the most surefire location in Africa to get that quintessential photo of a hippo yawning.

Channel Drive

The area along the north side of the Kazinga Channel between Mweya and Katunguru is perhaps the most popular for game drives and there is a network of roads to choose the length of drive that suits you. If you plan your route well there's no need to double back on yourself. By sticking to the main Channel Drive, it also provides access to Mweya from the Ishaka–Kasese road via the Katunguru Gate. Game in this area includes lion, elephant, hyena, buffalo, Uganda kob, waterbuck and warthog, and, while leopard favour the large trees along the channel, they are extremely difficult to spot. Hippo trails cross the road every so often; it has been observed that individual hippos tend to use the same route every night when they go inland to feed. If you do come across any hippos on land be sure to give them a wide berth and do not come between them and the water.

Crater Drive

Another access route to Mweya from the Ishaka–Kasese road, the hilly Crater Drive covers 27 km between Kabatoro Gate and the Equator Gate and Queen's Pavilion and takes two to three hours. Make sure you start this route by 1500 or 1600 to get to either gate by 1830. The road is generally good, but after rain there may be some muddy patches suitable only for 4WDs. Crater Drive takes in many of the park's 72 huge 'explosion craters'. These round basins scattered across the equator are evidence of the Albertine Rift's bubbling volcanic past. They are now filled with either patches of forest or woodland, water creating almost perfectly circular alkaline crater lakes or, quite by contrast, almost bare bowls of yellow grassland.

There is no permanent fresh water in this area so, apart from during the rainy season (March–June) when there are often herds of buffalo and elephant, you're unlikely to see many animals. However, there are always plenty of birds (particularly grassland varieties). It's a very scenic drive and, as well as the craters, there are superb views of the Kasinga Channel and the Rift Valley escarpment beyond. To the north are the Rwenzoris and on a clear day you can see the snow caps.

Lake George and Kasenyi

The track going east to Lake George and the fishing village of Kasenyi is on the Ishaka–Kasese road, opposite the turning to Katwe. The track goes through open grassland and is the Ugandan kob's main mating and breeding grounds and thus one of the best areas to spot lions. About 10 km from the main road look to your left and you should be able to see a Uganda kob *lek* (see box, page 182).

Just before you reach Kasenyi village you will see the small crater lake of **Bunyampaka**. You can take the track around the southern rim of the lake, which will also lead you to the Kazinga Channel, where there is good hippo-viewing, or continue east to Kasenyi village. The villagers here eke a living from salt panning and fishing and live in small semi-permanent huts on the sandy lakeside soil. On the way back, you can return along the main track and then turn right after 6 km. This leads you to the village of Hamukungu; turn left and you will go through a large swamp and then pass the crater lake of Kikorongo. This area is popular with elephant, and there's the possibility of sighting the shoebill in the swamp, while there are sometimes flamingoes on Lake Kikorongo. Just after the lake you are back to the Ishaka–Kasese road, opposite the Equator Gate and the Queen's Pavilion (page 176), and can return to Mweya along Crater Drive or turn left back to the Katwe road.

Lake Katwe and Pelican Point

To get to the village of Katwe, take the left turning just after Kabatoro Gate for about 2 km and on your right are the crater lakes of Katwe and Munyanyange. These provide Katwe inhabitants with their main sources of income: salt panning and fishing. The salt industry at Katwe dates back to the 16th century and still today provides the local inhabitants with an important source of income. The village and the crater lakes are in an enclave on Lake Edward outside the park boundaries so it is possible to leave your car. If you have come to Katwe straight from the Ishaka–Kasese road, then there are no park fees to pay. You can visit the salt works at Lake Katwe for a small fee; a guide will explain the methods by which salt is evaporated and purified. As **Lake Munyanyange** is an alkaline lake it is sometimes the home of lesser flamingos in varying numbers. It is possible to walk around the rim of the lake.

The road beyond Katwe is in very poor condition and it's advisable to avoid this route unless you have a 4WD. From the track you will be able to see the Nyamagasani Delta and the Kihabule Forest before you reach Pelican Point, where there are views across Lake Edward.

Kyambura Gorge

ⓘ *Chimpanzee tracking is organized by UWA; book in advance at UWA in Kampala (see page 42). It is possible to buy a permit at Kyambura Gorge, but there is no guarantee that there will be any available on the day. However, you can check with the Mweya Information Centre (page 178) or phone the office at the gorge, T0702-228292. Note: park entry fees apply* *but you do not have to pay fees again if you've already paid at another point of access into QENP within the last 24 hrs; you will need to show your receipt. Walks start at 0800 and 1400, 8 permits are available for each, and last 1-3 hrs, US$50, no under 15s. Mweya Safari Lodge (see page 185) and some of the other lodges can organize a trip to Kyambura Gorge for a group.*

The Kyambura Gorge (pronounced and sometimes spelt Chambura) and the Kyambura Wildlife Reserve that surrounds it, are part of the QENP. Take the road from Katunguru towards the Rift Valley escarpment for about 8 km. The well-signposted turn-off is to the left shortly before the road begins to climb to Kichwamba, and from here it is about 2.5 km to the edge of the gorge where there is a car park and pleasant picnic site. Without private transport, any bus or *matatu* can drop you at this junction, and you are permitted to walk along the 2.5-km track unguided.

The 10-km-long gorge is formed by the Kyambura River that flows off the Kichwamba escarpment and into the Kazinga Channel at Katunguru. On each side of the gorge is dry grassland savannah, and the river has created a wonderfully dense and tangled 'underground' forest 100 m below in the base of the gorge. The view from the edge is spectacular, and looking down on to the forest gives a fantastic view of the tops of the trees and any birds or animals that may be feeding off them. The gorge is best known for its resident chimpanzees, some of which are habituated and can be tracked through the forest with UWA guides. The chimpanzee tracking is not as reliable as in Kibale Forest (page 215), simply because there are fewer chimpanzees in a smaller area, and the UWA predicts an 80% success rate of seeing them. It's also more physically challenging as it's a bit of a scramble down the steep-sided gorge. Nevertheless, if you're unlucky, there's every chance of spotting other primates such as red-tailed, black-and-white colobus and vervet monkeys, and birds include various falcons, the blue-headed bee-eater and the rare African finfoot. In any event, there's also the possibility of hearing the chimps – the sound of their distinctive and high-pitched 'pant-hooting' rises from the gorge. If there are no permits available or you don't want to climb down the gorge, there's an alternative guided walk along the rim that takes around two hours (US$30 per person). The UWA are planning to put a campsite here; check with them.

Maramagambo Forest
① Guided walks are organized by UWA; book in advance at Myewa Visitor Information Centre (see page 176) or on arrival at the Maramagambo visitor centre; US$30 per guide per day. Note: park entry fees apply but you do not have to pay fees again if you've already paid at another point of access into QENP within 24 hrs; you will need to show your receipt.

Still part of the QENP, this is a medium-altitude, moist, semi-deciduous forest that spreads across the Rift Valley escarpment down to Lake Edward. The turn-off is at Kichwamba on the top of the escarpment, 12 km south of Katunguru (if you're visiting for the day it's 55 km from Mweya). The visitor centre at the start of the forest is 9 km along a steep track.

Maramagambo means 'the end of words' in a local language, and is based on a local legend. A group of people was lost in the forest for many days, and when they eventually found their way out, they were too exhausted to speak for a long time. Several species of primate live in the forest and you are likely to see olive baboons, and black-and-white colobus, vervet and red-tailed monkeys. There is a large population of chimpanzees, but as they are not habituated you are unlikely to see them. It's also a haven for birds, which include the rare forest flycatcher, white-naped pigeon and the striking Rwenzori turaco, as well as more common species such as shrikes, warblers and waxbills. You can also visit the 'cormorant house', a large tree that has been turned white by the birds that roost

Uganda kob

This is probably the most prevalent mammal in the Queen Elizabeth National Park with an estimated population of about 17,000. It prefers low-lying, open country without too much bush. Female kob and their young form loose herds of about 50. During the dry season they join up with males and with other groups to form herds of up to 1000 in areas where green grass is still available.

Male Uganda kobs mate with females in permanent grounds known as *leks*. Within a *lek* there is a cluster of small, usually roughly circular, breeding territories. For a few days the males will defend their territory by ritualized displays and by fighting when necessary, and there are frequent displays of them aggressively locking antlers. The females range freely within the *leks* and appear to favour males that hold territories in the centre of the *leks*. For this reason, most activity takes place within the central area, with these males constantly being challenged by other males.

The *leks* can be recognized by the flattened grass that is the result of being trampled on over many years. They are usually located in open grassland near water. During a prolonged dry season *leks* are usually abandoned and the herds join together in search of food and water.

here at night. Another curiosity of the forest is the long columns of soldier ants, some more than 100 m long. Avoid them though as the ants administer a nasty sting.

There are three walking tracks that go through the forest from the visitor centre, and you must be accompanied by a guide. One follows the forested shores of **Lake Kasanduka**, near the entrance, and takes no more than an hour. Another takes about three hours, and visits a bat cave that is home to thousands of fruit bats as well as a number of exceptionally large and well-fed pythons that feed on the bats. You're not allowed to go into the cave, but there's a viewing platform with glass windows. Interestingly, the platform built with funding from the Center of Disease Control and Prevention in the US following the death in 2008 of a tourist who contracted the Maburg virus (a highly contagious disease similar to Ebola) from the cave. There's no evidence of the disease now and you can see the bats and snakes from within the secure viewing facility. Maramagambo's third trail loops around the **Lake Nyamusingiri** and takes about half a day. The highlight of this pretty and vividly blue crater lake is the large population of greater and lesser flamingos and it is sometimes simply referred to as Flamingo Lake.

South of Maramagambo Forest is the **Kigezi Wildlife Reserve** which acts as a buffer zone between Maramagamba and the Ishasha sector of the QENP. It consists of forest to the north supporting the same animals as Maramagamba, while more open grasslands further south are shared by plains game from Ishasha. There are no visitor facilities at present.

Kalinzu Forest Reserve

ⓘ *T0772-568168, www.nfa.org.ug. US$15, guided walks US$15, chimpanzee tracking US$50 (no under 12s), camping US$9 per person. Chimpanzee tracking starts at about 0730 and takes up to 5 hrs (no under 12s).*

Located on the southern side of the Rift Valley escarpment, the 147 sq km Kalinzu Forest Reserve is adjacent to Maramagambo Forest but not within the boundary of the QENP. Instead it is under the management of the National Forest Authority (NFA). The turn-off is on the Ishaka–Kasese road 34 km south of Kichwamba and 10 km north of

Ishaka. The visitor centre is on the main road just north of the village of Butare, while the entrance gate is 4 km west. Without private transport, any bus or *matatu* can drop here, and you are permitted to walk along the track unguided or get a motorbike *boda-boda* from the village. There's a campsite within the forest with basic facilities, but you need to be self-sufficient.

Over 420 species of tree and shrub have been identified in the reserve including fig trees that provide bark-cloth, widely used in the local craft industry. Over 370 bird varieties have been identified in the forest, including the great blue turaco, black-and-white cascket, cuckoos and sunbirds. The forest is also rich in butterflies, moths and reptiles and gets occasional visitors from QENP including leopards, wild pigs and duikers. There are nine primate species here, including chimpanzees, black-and-white colobus and vervet monkeys. The chimpanzee population is put at about 270, of which two groups of about 70 each have been habituated, enabling them to be tracked by visitors (currently restricted to four permits per group per day). In theory this is a slightly cheaper option than other places for chimpanzee tracking and it can easily be reached using public transport. However, the reserve is little-visited and chimpanzee tracking here is not very well managed or organized; as a result, the chimpanzees are less used to human visitors and sightings are not as reliable as they are at Kyamburu Gorge (page 180) or Kibale Forest (page 215). Nevertheless, four forest trails have been developed that follow the contours of the scenic Rift Valley escarpment. The 2.5-km circular **River Trail** takes an hour and follows the course of the Kajojo (Elephant) River, named after a historically favoured bathing place. There is also the 5-km Palm Trail and the 3.5-km Valley Trail, both taking two hours, as well as the four- to five-hour Waterfall Trail through hilly terrain to the pretty Kilyantama Waterfall.

Southern sector (Ishasha) → *For listings, see pages 185-187. Colour map 2, C1.*

Made up of open partly wooded grasslands and riverine forests, heavily populated with animals, the southern and smaller part of the park is beautiful. It is less accessible than the northern part and so receives substantially fewer visitors. But those who venture this far may be rewarded with sightings of Ishasha's most famous residents – the tree-climbing lions – lounging in the branches while keeping a close eye on herds of Uganda kob. It is also home to the rare shoebill stork and is the only part of QENP where topi reside. Ishasha is a convenient place to pass through on the way to and from Bwindi Impenetrable National Park.

Arriving at Ishasha

Getting there From Mweya go back to the Ishaka–Kasese road and just south of Katunguru turn right on to the public road towards the town of Ishasha on the DRC border (page 176). Ishasha Gate is about 70 km (roughly two hours) after joining this road at Katunguru, and 20 km before the border.

To get there directly from Kampala and Mbarara, the shortest route is to go first to Ntungamo (page 138), 85 km southwest of Mbarara on the main road, and then on to a newly tarred road for the 45 km to Rukungiri. After that it's another 70 km on a dirt road to the Ishasha Gate via Kihihi. From the Bwindi Impenetrable National Park it's 65 km from Buhoma at Bwindi via Kihihi to the Ishasha Gate. From Kabale, follow the directions to Bwindi (page 150), but instead of taking the left turn at Kanyantorogo towards Buhoma at Bwindi, take the right turn to Kihihi and then on to the Ishasha Gate. The total distance on this route from Kabale to Ishasha Gate is 138 km. These are gravel roads and some sandy sections can be difficult when wet.

Although a tiny place, Kihihi, 22 km south of Ishasha Gate, is an important junction. It's a good idea to refuel at one of the petrol stations here, particularly if travelling between Bwindi and QENP and there's a branch of Stanbic Bank and a supermarket too. The airstrip serving Bwindi and the Ishasha sector of QENP is also at Kihihi.

Ishasha is tricky but not impossible to get to without your own transport. While there's every possibility of hitching on the public road from Katunguru to the gate on a truck bound for the DRC, this would be a fool-hardy option and the gate itself is in a remote spot in lion country. Another option is to get a bus or *matatu* to Kihihi (for details of Kampala–Butogota buses for Bwindi, which stop in Kihihi, see Getting there for Buhoma, page 154), and then hire a special hire taxi to the camps.

The UWA's Ishasha River Camp is on the east bank of the Ishasha River, 8 km southwest of Ishasha Gate in the far southwestern corner of the park close to the DRC border. It has campsites and simple *banda* accommodation (see Where to stay, page 187). The UWA Ishasha park headquarters is about 500 m before reaching the river and camp.

Southern and northern routes

Game viewing can begin at the Ishasha River Camp as close to Campsite Two is a large hippo wallow, which is also a watering point for various antelope and buffalo. The birdlife here is fairly extensive too, with herons, storks and ibises. Two game-viewing routes, each about 20 km long, run from here, called simply the southern and northern routes. As at Mweya, using a UWA guide will greatly improve your chance of spotting wildlife, not least because the game-viewing tracks are little-used and could be overgrown. Guides can be arranged at the park headquarters (US$20 per vehicle per day).

The tree-climbing lions live in the woodland along the southern route, but their sighting is far rarer than one is led to believe. If you do see lions in the giant fig and acacia trees count yourself very lucky. It is not known why they climb the trees to simply loll around in the branches, although it could be to escape the heat, enjoy the cool breeze and perhaps avoid biting tsetse flies at ground level. You may also see topi around here. These are splendid antelopes with beautiful coats, also found in Lake Mburo National Park (see page 133) and in a few national parks in Kenya and Tanzania.

The savannah along the northern route is favoured by elephant, but these migrate between Uganda and the heavily poached Virunga National Park in the DRC, and as a result they are easily scared by people and vehicles and are likely to run away. The northern route also touches on the Lake Edward floodplains which are the best place to spot the shoebill.

❹ Queen Elizabeth National Park (QENP) listings

For hotel and restaurant price codes and other relevant information, see pages 16-20.

⏱ Where to stay

Ishaka–Kasese road *p174, map p175*
For details of these locations, see Getting there, page 174.

$$$ Ihamba Lakeside Safari Lodge, 11 km north of the Queen's Pavilion and 16 km south of Kasese, reservations Kampala T0312-513675, www.ihambasafarilodge. com. Sensibly priced new lodge on the shores of Lake George in the northeast of the park. 6 spacious cottages, 1 for families, swimming pool, cosy lounge, restaurant, packed lunches available. Close to the water so hippos keep the lawns trimmed.

$$$ Katara Lodge, 2 km south of Kichwamba and then 2 km to the lodge, T0773-011648, www.kataralodge.com. The 7 thatched cottages are generous family sized with roll-away canvas walls and beds on wheels that can be rolled on to the balconies for glorious views from the escarpment. Swimming pool, and the food and service are excellent. The access road is very bumpy.

$$ Kingfisher Kichwamba Lodge, 500 m west of Kichwamba, T0774-15 9579, www. kingfisher-uganda.net. A mid-range option popular with families and conferences. The 18 rooms in white stone circular cottages are plain and the food mediocre, but there's a swimming pool and more of those sensational views across the Rift Valley, given that it's more than 250 m above the plains below.

$$-$ The Bush Lodge, Katunguru, 500 m from the bridge over the Kazinga Channel and 2 km west of the road, reservations Kampala, T0312-294894, www.naturelodges.biz. One of the least expensive options that overlooks the Kazinga Channel. At sunset the animals can be seen making their way to the channel

to drink, and you need a guard to take you to bed because of the many hippos. Simple accommodation is in 12 thatch and canvas elevated chalets (double US$120, extra bed US$22); safari tents with camp beds (double US$40); or camping (US$13 per person). All rates include breakfast, and there's a dining and bar tent serving delicious set meals.

$ Simba Safari Camp, just north of the equator, 2 km along the road to Bwera (for the DRC border), T0772-426368, www.safari-uganda.com. Set on a hill with great views over the park's northern boundary and Lake George and the closest accommodation for game drives in the Kasenyi area. 12 basic *bandas* (from US$70), dorms (US$12), and campsite (US$6 per person), plus a restaurant/bar. Used by many budget safari operators, including Great Lakes Safaris who run it and offer 3-day QENP trips from Kampala.

Mweya *p178, map p175*
$$$$-$$$ Mweya Safari Lodge, T0312-260260, www.mweyalodge.com. Located on the Mweya Peninsula on a bluff overlooking Katwe Bay and the Kazinga Channel, this is perhaps Uganda's best-known lodge. It was originally built in the mid-1950s and is still the main focal point of QENP. More reminiscent of a charming luxury country hotel than a safari lodge, accommodation is in 54 units in rooms, cottages, suites or safari tents. Facilities include a pool, gym, spa, gift shop, restaurant, and the **Tembo Bar** is superbly located. Rates start from US$295 for a standard double room, rising to US$970 if you want to stay in the presidential suite or Queen's Cottage. Non-residents can visit and eat here and they organize launches on the Kazinga Channel (page 179), bush dinners and breakfasts, and is the only lodge in the park that the UWA allow to operate spotlight night drives.

$$-$ UWA Chalets & Cottages, book through the Kampala office (page 42), or the Mweya Information Centre (page 178), T0782-387805, which is where you should go if you don't have a reservation and to check in, www.ugandawildlife.org. Opposite **Tembo Canteen** (page 187) and between the lodge and **Mweya Campsite**, these are renovated former park employees' houses: Jumbo sleeps 8, Cormorant and Pelican sleep 6. Each has 2 bathrooms and tea- and coffee-making facilities (from US$100 per chalet). The simpler cottages (US$8 per person) have 1 bare room and share bathrooms. **$ Mweya Hostel** (also called **Albertine Rift Hostel**), T0772-60-9969. Basic hostel in brick buildings close to **Mweya Safari Lodge** but with intermittent (or non-existent) water and power. However, it is clean and cheap (from US$20 per person). Accommodation is in 12 rooms with shared bathrooms or 2 houses each with 4-6 beds, a bathroom and a little kitchen. These can be used as dorms or family accommodation. There's also a small canteen-type restaurant serving local food and the likes of fish or chicken and chips.

Camping

$ UWA Campsites, book through the Kampala office (page 42), or the **Mweya Information Centre** (page 178), T0782-387805, which is where you should go to check in or if you don't have a reservation, www.ugandawildlife.org. There are 3 UWA campsites (US$6 per person) near Mweya Safari Lodge that have pit latrines, firewood, a thatched shelter and tap. Campsite 1, 4 km, and Campsite 2, 5 km, are both on Channel Drive next to the Kazinga Channel. The most convenient is **Mweya Campsite** on the south side of the peninsula overlooking the channel, 800 m from the lodge and about 500 m from **Tembo Canteen** (page 187). At all of them, you will encounter wild animals at night – at **Mweya Campsite** you can famously hear

hippos munching the grass around the tent-pegs from your tent at night. If you walk to the lodge or **Tembo Canteen** to eat, exercise extreme caution, stick closely together, use a powerful torch, and don't walk back after too many Nile Special beers.

Kyambura Gorge *p180, map p175*
$$$$ Kyambura Gorge Lodge, reservations Kampala T0414-346464/5, www.volcano essafaris.com. The latest offering from Volcanoes Safaris, with 8 luxury thatched *bandas*, lovely stone and wood decor with splashes of primary colours, so close to the gorge you can see the mist rising from the forest and may hear the chimps. The main building with restaurant, bar, patios, swimming pool and deck is a converted coffee-processing factory, and the decor throughout is wonderful with works of Ugandan art, historical black-and-white photos of the Rwenzoris and over-stuffed brightly upholstered furnishings. The cuisine and service is superb, and each guest gets a complimentary massage. Activities include a coffee tour, a visit to a bee-keeping project, and a cultural group performance.
$$$ Kyambura Game Lodge, reservations Entebbe T0414-322789, www.kyambura lodge.com. With great views across the QENP from its elevated position with 7 comfortable cottages well spaced out on the hillside. The restaurant serves excellent set meals using home-grown organic ingredients, there's a lovely pool with sundeck, evening campfire and traditional dancing.

Maramagambo Forest *p181, map p175*
$$$$-$$$ Jacana Safari Lodge, reservations Kampala T0414-258273, www.geolodges.com. Part of the quality **Geo Lodges** stable, on the edge of Maramagambo Forest with 10 cottages attractively arranged around Lake Nyamusingiri. It's a glorious location and the view is spectacular, especially after rain

at sunset. There's an elevated restaurant, pool, campfire and pontoon boat on the lake for sundowners.

Camping

$ UWA Maramagambo Forest Campsite, near the visitor centre at the entrance where you pay, www.ugandawildlife. org. Basic campsite in a forest glade with firewood, pit latrines and a cold shower, but plenty of birdlife and you can eat at **Jacana Safari Lodge** which is about a 1-km stroll (US$6 per person).

Ishasha *p186, map p175*
$$$$ Ishasha Wilderness Camp, just north of Ishasha Gate, reservations Kampala, T0414-321479, www.uganda exclusivecamps.com. Ishasha's most luxurious option, with 10 massive well-appointed tents situated in glades by the Ntungwe River, which has plenty of animal action to watch from the verandas. Excellent food including 5-course dinners, and bush breakfasts, guided birdwatching and river walks, and a campfire in the evening. Many guests arrive on fly-in packages to the airstrip at Kihihi.
$$$ Ishasha-Ntungwe Tree Lion Safari Lodge, outside QENP, 3 km from the Ishasha Gate towards Kihihi, T0772-60 02205, www.treelionsafarilodge.ug. 4 simple but comfortable safari tents, solar-heated hot water in the 'bush' showers, set in attractive forest, reasonable set meals and friendly staff. On the west bank of the Ntungwe River although it's a little swampy and narrow here.
$ @ The River, outside QENP, 4 km from the Ishasha Gate towards Kihihi, T0787-005888, www.attheriverishasha.com. Again on the Ntungwe River, a great budget option with

cottages (from US$60) and camping with your own tent or theirs (from US$10-30). Small splash pool, outdoor showers with a view, little beach area with good river views (elephant are regular visitors). The have their own vehicle for game drives, so independent travellers could get here from Kihihi (transfers can be arranged).
$ UWA Ishasha River Camp, 8 km southwest of the gate, near the park HQ where you pay, www.ugandawildlife. org. The campsite on the Southern route also has 2 twin-bed rooms and 2 *bandas*. Non-potable water only, cold shower, pit latrines, thatched shelter, fireplace and firewood available. Bring all food and cooking utensils.Beds US$12 per person, camping US$6 per person. There are 2 more campsites nearby, set among trees with their frontage on to the Ishasha River, the border with DRC, but they are sometimes closed if there's been any unrest near the border; check with the office. They're a wonderful place to view hippo and antelope coming to drink and they can still be visited for a picnic.

🍴 Restaurants

Mweya *p178, map p175*
$ Tembo Canteen, run by the UWA, between the lodge and **Mweya Campsite**, about 400 m to both. Daily 0600-2300. If you can't afford a meal on the veranda at **Mweya Safari Lodge**, then this is the next best thing, as it has views from the garden directly over Kazinga Channel. A surprisingly good choice; for example Spanish omelette for breakfast and peppered steak for dinner, plus there are cold beers and friendly staff.

Kasese and the Rwenzoris

The Rwenzoris (Ruwenzoris) are the fabled, glacier-topped 'Mountains of the Moon' that rise into almost permanent equatorial mists, their slopes covered with giant and strange vegetation. Sharing the border of Uganda and the DRC, they rise to a height of about 5109 m above sea level, and were formed from a block that was tilted and thrust up during the development of the Rift Valley. They were first described as the 'Mountains of the Moon' by Alexandrine geographer Ptolemy in AD 150 because they were believed to be the Lunae Montes predicted by the ancient Greeks to be the source of the Nile. The Rwenzori Mountains National Park, which was gazetted in 1991 and recognized as a UNESCO World Heritage Site in 1994, protects the highest peaks. These beautiful, often mist-shrouded mountains offer mountaineers and trekkers superb but challenging terrain and wonderful views. Huge tree-heathers and colorful mosses are draped across the mountainside with giant lobelias and 'everlasting flowers', creating an enchanting, fairytale scene. The approaches for trekkers are from Uganda's western town of Kasese, which is in the foothills, already at an altitude of 1000 m, and has good road and transport links from the rest of the country. ►► For listings, see pages 197-198.

Kasese

Where to stay
Margherita **2**
Rwenzori International **4**
Sandton **1**
White House **6**

Kasese is the main base for expeditions into the Rwenzori Mountains National Park as it is close to the trailheads into the park at Kilembe and Nyakalengija (see below). However, it is an unpleasant and extremely hot place, and the mosquitoes are most troublesome at night. It's best to pass through between the QENP and the far more attractive Fort Portal, 75 km to the north, or use it as an overnight for the trailheads of the Rwenzoris if you're trekking.

Kasese began life as an industrial town in the colonial 1950s, when copper was mined in the foothills of the Rwenzoris near Kilemba, and was once infamous for its dusty Wild West-style roads and rough mining-town atmosphere. While the copper was once an important source of foreign exchange for Uganda, and the mines employed more than 6000 people, they closed in the early 1980s, and the town suffered economically.

Nevertheless, today the Kasese Cobalt Company extracts high-grade cobalt from the residual sludge of the copper mines and employs much of the population. The plant is along the Kasese–QENP road, a few kilometres south of Kasese. Also, since the Kampala–Fort Portal road was completed in 2007, Kasese has established itself as a service centre for the A109 road, the busiest route for haulage trucks between Kampala (and ultimately Mombasa port on the coast) and Kisangani in the DRC, via the Mpondwe border, which is just over 60 km southwest of Kasese. However, while its economy may be recovering, its grimness is not.

Getting there
Kasese is 370 km west of Kampala via Fort Portal on a good tarred road. If you come via Mbarara on the southern route through Uganda, it's 420 km, so how you approach Kasese rather depends on where you've been first. From the northern reaches of the Queen Elizabeth National Park (at the equator) it's 27 km, and from Mweya it's 56 km, while Kasese is 75 km south of Fort Portal. There are direct buses from Kampala, and plenty of transport to and from the regional towns. There's an airstrip at Kasese, and Aerolink has scheduled and chartered flights. ▶▶ *See Transport, page 198.*

Visitor information
Rwenzori Tourism Information Centre ⓘ *Rwenzori Square, T0772-588161, www.rwenzori info.com, daily 0830-1700.* This office, set up and funded by a Belgium NGO involved in development issues in the region, cannot provide much information about Kasese (simply because there isn't really anything to see), but is helpful with information about the Rwenzori climbing operators (page 190), and can also organize community walks and advise on transport to the trailheads. If you want to get a special hire taxi to the QENP, they will be able to recommend a driver that has taken people before (see page 178).

Rwenzori Mountains National Park → *For listings, see pages 197-198.*
Colour map 2, B1.

The snow peaks of the Rwenzoris can be reached by hiking the Central Circuit and Kilembe Trail. However, it is demanding and tough going – the trails are variously steep, boulder-strewn, muddy and extremely boggy, and you will need to be fit with plenty of stamina – although many climbers consider the exceptional scenery and challenging achievement ample reward for their exertions. An eight- to 10-day trek will get skilled climbers to the summit of Margherita, though shorter, non-technical treks are possible to scale the surrounding peaks.

Arriving at Rwenzori Mountain National Park

Getting there There are two approaches for ascending the mountains: the Kilembe Trail starts at the Kyanjuki trailhead at the village of Kilembe, 14 km west of Kasese, and plenty of *matatus* ply the route or you can get a special hire taxi (about US$10) or a motorbike *boda-boda*; the Central Circuit starts from the Nyakalengija trailhead at the village of Ruboni. To get to Ruboni, travel 9 km along the main Kasese–Fort Portal road and take the turn-off to next to the Nkenda electricity sub-station. Continue on this fairly good gravel road for 12 km. Ruboni is also the starting point for hill walks, bird and nature treks and walks through the traditional homesteads of the local Bakonzo community (see box, page 196). From Kasese, there are *matatus* to Ruboni, or get a special hire taxi (about US$20). Coming from Fort Portal, get off at the Nkenda electricity sub-station and you should be able to get a motorbike *boda-boda*. **Note**: if you have heavy backpacks motorbike *boda-bodas* can be somewhat precarious and perhaps even a little dangerous, so consider the other options. Those with vehicles can arrange to park at a hotel in Kasese (try the **Hotel Margherita**), or at accommodation at the trailheads (see Where to stay, page 197).

Best time to visit The Rwenzoris have a justified reputation for being wet. As they are the main watershed for the River Nile, it rains throughout the year with exceptional heavy rains from March to June and September to December. Because of this, trekking here is possibly the muddiest in the world – when the mud stops, it's replaced by watery bog. It also means that the views are not so good with mist sometimes shrouding the mountains and peaks. The best times to visit are the driest months from late December to February and from mid-June to mid-August. Daytime temperatures average 10-15°C, with much colder nights; don't underestimate the equatorial chill at 4000 m.

Visitor information Entry fee per 24 hours, US$35; there is no vehicle access in the park. The first stop for trekkers should be the Rwenzori Tourism Information Centre in Kasese (see page 189). The **Uganda Wildlife Authority** (UWA) park headquarters ① *T0392-841133, www.ugandawildlife.org*, are close to Ruboni Community Camp (page 198) at Ruboni near the Nyakalengija trailhead, where they are in the process of building a new visitor centre. The offices of the two Rwenzori climbing operators are at the trailheads.

Rwenzori Trekking Services (RTS) ① *Kilembe, T0774-199022, Kampala, T0774-114499, www.rwenzoritrekking.com*, are the concessionaire to manage the Kilembe Trail for the UWA, the newer route that was opened by the UWA in 2008, see page 192. The office and starting point is at **Trekkers Hostel** at Kilembe (see Where to stay, page 197). Overall this foreign-owned company places a premium on safety and all guides to the main peaks have undertaken wilderness first-aid courses and carry satellite phones, there is a rescue stretcher in every hut, and they maintain a helipad at Bugata Camp (4062 m) in the event of serious emergencies.

Rwenzori Mountaineering Services (RMS) ① *Nyakalengija T0755-723581, Kampala T0784-308425, www.rwenzorimountaineeringservices.com*, is the concessionaire for the Central Circuit, see page 194, and their office and base is at the trailhead at Nyakalengija. They also maintain an office in Kasese on Rwenzori Road near the information office, but this appears to be mainly the accounts/admin office and they will most likely direct you to the Nyakalengija office. **Note**: Despite supporting local communities, RMS has received

The Mountains of the Moon

The Rwenzori range is 120 km long and 65 km wide and straddles the border between Uganda and the DRC. It is now generally accepted that Ptolemy (c AD 150), when writing of the 'Mountains of the Moon', the legendary source of the Nile, was referring to the Rwenzori massif. Unlike the other great mountains of Central Africa, they are not of volcanic origin but are the result of an upthrust associated with the formation of the Western Rift Valley, in which they stand. The highest reaches on the Ugandan side are protected in the 996-sq-km Rwenzori Mountains National Park, which is managed by the Uganda Wildlife Authority (UWA). About 70% of the park lies above 2500 m. On the DRC side, the highest peaks lie in the 7800-sq-km Virunga National Park. Both parks are UNESCO World Heritage Sites. At 5109 m, Margherita Peak on Mount Stanley is the highest peak in both Uganda and the DRC, and the third highest mountain in Africa. In fact, the Rwenzoris are statistically the highest mountain range in Africa. Mount Kilimanjaro (5968 m) and Mount Kenya (5225 m) are both higher, but are single volcanic peaks, Mount Stanley is a massif composed of six peaks.

negative feedback regarding the mountain huts, which are said to be in bad shape and poorly equipped compared to those of RTS. Nevertheless, established in 1987, they have taken countless people up the mountain and the local guides and porters have plenty of experience.

Equipment On the mountain, there is no opportunity to restock with equipment and supplies so be sure to bring everything you need. While meals are supplied on the treks, take plenty of snacks and sweets; supplies can be bought in Kasese or Fort Portal. It is wet for much of the year and cold at night, so come well prepared; sturdy hiking boots, waterproofs, plenty of warm clothing, a woollen hat, gloves and a decent four-season sleeping bag. Many people bring wellies (gum boots), which can be bought locally in the markets and are useful for the frequent boggy areas. Walking sticks are the most important piece of equipment for the trip, not only to steady yourself but also to probe the thickness of the mud and bog in your path; sunglasses or snow goggles, sunscreen, lip salve and a torch are also essential. Pack everything inside your backpack in plastic bags. Porters accompany all treks and are permitted to carry loads of up to 22 kg – 15 kg of your gear and 7 kg of their own.

Insurance Anyone climbing over 4000 m must have a comprehensive adventure and mountaineering insurance policy to cover all medical and rescue costs.

Flora and fauna
One of the most delightful aspects of the Rwenzoris is the diversity of plants and trees. Cultivation rarely extends above about 2000 m around the base of the mountain, and in many places it is considerably lower. In the foothills most of the vegetation is elephant grass, up to about 1800 m. Next comes the montane or true forest, a mixture of trees, bracken and tree ferns. In this zone, which extends to about 2500 m, it is possible to see orchids. Higher still is the bamboo zone, which continues up to about 3000 m. The vegetation here also includes tree heather and, in moister patches, giant lobelias. The

next fairly extensive zone is the heather forest, which extends from 3000 m up to 3800 m. The humid climate at this altitude causes vigorous development of mosses and lichens, which cover the ground and the trunks of living and fallen trees. At this level, on the better-drained slopes, tree groundsels and shrubby trees flourish, while the wetter parts are distinctly boggy. This zone also has brambles, orchids and ferns, all of which form a tangle that makes passage difficult. The highest vegetative zone, extending from about 3800 m to the snowline, is alpine. From here most of the common herbaceous plants disappear, leaving tree heaths, giant lobelias and senecios. Reeds grow in the marshes and shrubby bushes with everlasting flowers (*Belichrysums*) are abundant. The rocks are covered with a loosely adhering carpet of moss. Above 3000 m there is little sign of life except hyrax and other small rodents. Birds are also fairly sparse.

Although there is some wildlife in the park and it's home to more than 70 species of mammal, including elephant, leopard, chimpanzee and giant forest hog, these species are rare and very shy and there is little or no chance of seeing them in the dense vegetation. More commonly seen are the black-and-white colobus and blue monkeys, small antelope such as the bushbuck, and unusual reptiles including the three-horned chameleon. In the forest zone at around 1800 m there's a good chance of seeing some of the 217 recorded bird species. Of these there are 17 Albertine Rift endemics, including the Rwenzori turaco, long-eared owl, cinnamon-chested bee-eater, blue-headed and golden-winged sunbird, and several varieties of barbet.

Climbing the Rwenzoris

Margherita Peak can be reached on the Kilembe Trail with RTS, and on the Central Circuit with RMS, and can be attempted by trekkers with a peak level of fitness and stamina. Both also offer shorter hikes in the foothills through the montane and bamboo forests for those with less trekking experience and/or time. Some options go up to the lower huts or camps at about 3000 m to give travellers an opportunity to experience the mountain and its impressive vegetation. These start from US$180 for two days, US$330 for three days, US$450 for four days and so on, and include porters, food and accommodation but exclude park fees. Day walks start from US$40 plus US$35 park entry fee, and usually go up one of the closest river valleys where there are excellent opportunities to observe birds and the smaller primates. The northern spur of the Rwenzoris can also be trekked starting at Kazingo village near Fort Portal, see page 209, where the main focus is ascending the spectacular Karangora Peak, 3014 m.

The Kilembe Trail

The eight-day trek to **Margherita Peak** on the Kilembe Trail with **RTS** (page 190) for one or two people is currently US$1220 each; three or more pay US$1100, plus the UWA park entrance fee of US$35 per day (US$280), which is paid separately in cash. If an extra night on the mountain is needed (usually taken at Bugata Camp), because of bad weather or for acclimatization, it should cost in the region of US$150 plus US$35 park fees, so allow for this. Prices include all porters, food and accommodation whilst on the mountain, and equipment such as climbing ropes, harnesses with carabinas and crampons. Trekkers need to bring everything else but RTS do hire out warm sleeping bags. They also offer more specialist ascents to the glaciers on mounts Speke and Baker, although only those with experience in rock, snow and ice climbing should attempt these. Contact RTS for details and prices.

Exploration of the Rwenzori Mountains

In the 19th century, Samuel Baker observed the Rwenzoris (and called them the 'Blue Mountains') but failed to appreciate the importance of this natural feature. Sir Henry Stanley was the first to proclaim the existence of the Rwenzoris as snow mountains. In *Darkest Africa* he claims to have made the discovery himself, but in fact two members of his expedition, Surgeon Parke and Mountenoy-Jephson, had seen the snows a month before him, on 20 April 1888. The following year another member of the expedition, Lieutenant Stairs, ascended the mountains to a height of over 3050 m.

It is to Stanley that we owe the name Rwenzori (often spelt Ruwenzori). The word means 'the place from where the rain comes'. No name appears to have been given to the mountains by the local residents; their custom was to name the rivers running off the mountains rather than the actual peaks.

In the summer of 1891 Emin Pasha's companion Dr F Stuhlmann climbed up the Butagu Valley to a height of 4062 m and had the first close glimpse of the snow. A few years later naturalist GF Scott Elliott also made a number of expeditions, which were of significant botanical importance. In 1900 an expedition by CS Moore proved the presence of glaciers, and shortly afterwards Sir Harry Johnston reached the Mobuku glacier at a height of 4520 m. The first purely non-scientific climb, and the first by a woman, was in 1903 by the Reverend A B and Mrs Fisher.

The twin peaks of Mount Stanley, Alexandra and Margherita, were climbed for the first time in June 1906 by an expedition led by the Luigi Amedeo di Savoy, Duke of Abruzzi, a Spanish-born commanding officer in the Italian navy and acclaimed mountaineer and explorer. The expedition included six scientists, four alpine guides and the phenomenal Italian photographer and mountaineer, Vittorio Sella, who took photographs of mountains including the Alps and Karakorams, which are still today regarded as some of the finest ever taken. Today his photographs provide evidence of how rapidly the glaciers are receding on some of the world's highest peaks. With the help of over 300 porters, the Rwenzori expedition climbed to the tops of the six massifs in the range, and producing important scientific results and an excellent topographical survey of the mountains. It was this expedition that named most of the main peaks. Apart from Stanley (5109 m), there are Speke (4889 m), Emin (4791 m) and Baker (4843 m), and the duke chose to name the lowest peak on Stanley, Luigi di Savoia (4626 m), after himself.

Day 1 From Trekkers Hostel (1450 m), the first day involves a long steady climb through the montane forest and bamboo zone to (3156 m) in the heather zone.

Day 2 From Kalalama the route proceeds though the heather, passing several streams and waterfalls, all covered by green moss vegetation typical of this altitude. The arrival point of the day is Mutinda Camp (3688 m), named after the Mutinda Peaks. From this point, you can climb further to Mutinda Lookout (3925 m), about a 1½-hour walk plus one hour to descend back to the camp. It's worth the effort for the views down to Kasese town and Lake George.

Day 3 The trail from Mutinda Camp first crosses the Mutinda Valley and rises into the Alpine vegetation zone of tussock grass, everlasting flowers, giant groundsel and lobelia.

It then climbs a steep section up to Namusangi Valley (3840 m), from where there's a view up to the Mutinda Peaks. Along the valley it crosses various bogs as you steadily ascend to Bugata Camp (4062 m), from where you can see the peak of Mount Luigi di Savoia, often covered by snow.

Day 4 Although the start of the day's hike is up Bamwanjara Pass, and the trail climbs steadily with several long flat bogs, the route actually descends slightly in altitude on this day. On reaching the top of Banwamjara Pass (4450 m) there are excellent views of several glacial lakes far down in the valley, and all the main snow-capped peaks in front of you, and there's a small shelter to rest at and enjoy the scenery. The walk down to Kacholpe Lakes is steep and often very muddy, and then you climb to a ridge above the Butawu River to Butawu Camp (3974 m).

Day 5 The trail crosses several small rivers coming from Mount Baker, and then ascends the Scott Elliott Pass up the ridge of Mount Stanley to Margherita Camp (4485 m). This is sheltered with a ring of high rocks and is the original camp used by the Duke of the Abruzzi. From here you have great views back down Scott Elliot Pass, across to Mount Baker, and some of the high glaciers on Mount Stanley, above.

Day 6 This is the final ascent to Margherita Peak on Mount Stanley and the day usually begins at 0400-0500, so that you get to the glacier before sunrise. The glacier itself is steep, and can be a difficult scramble over the snow and ice, but there's a bolted static steel rope to assist climbers. Near the top is a climb around an exposed section of rock, which is again bolted and ropes are used, to get on to the ridge that runs up to the summit of Margherita Peak (5109 m). Once there, on a clear day, the views across the tops of the mountains are incredible. After reaching the summit you then descend directly to Butawu Camp, or in the case of bad weather, it may be necessary to stay again in Margherita Camp.

Day 7-8 The rest of the descent is via Bugata Camp (4062 m), and then either Kiharo Camp (3460 m) or Samalira Camp (3170 m), before arriving back in Kilembe.

Central Circuit
RMS (page 190) operates the seven-day Central Circuit to Margherita Peak which then returns on a different route. Current costs are US$990 for one or two people and US$150 per extra person, and an extra day on the mountain costs US$120. This includes UWA park entrance fees, guides, huts, porters and food for the guide and porters, but excludes equipment such as ropes, crampons, harnesses, etc, for which there is a one-off payment of US$25. There is an optional additional charge for food of US$120; a cook costs US$70. Again trekkers need to bring everything else but RMS hires out sleeping bags.

Day 1 Beginning at Nyakalengija (1600 m), the trail heads through a coffee plantation and then descends to the edge of the Mubuku River and into the forest. The day's final ascent is up a steep moraine ridge to Nyabitaba Hut (2651 m).

Day 2 This is the most difficult day of the Circuit, and will take at least seven hours from Nyabitaba to John Matte Hut. The trail follows the ridge through the forest and then forks down steeply to cross the Mubuku River. From here you climb up the other side –

the path gradually gets harder, becoming a slippery scramble – and continue on to the bamboo forest. It is here that you will start to go through heather and groundsel towards Nyamiliju Hut (3322 m); Nyamiliju actually means 'place of beards', a name that refers to the moss and lichen that hang from the trees. The hut is not used much any longer as most people prefer to push on to John Matte Hut. On a clear day you should be able to see Mount Stanley and Mount Speke as well as the glaciers, and Nyamiliju can make a good lunchtime stop. From here it is a further two hours to John Matte Hut (3505 m).

Rwenzori Mountains National Park treks

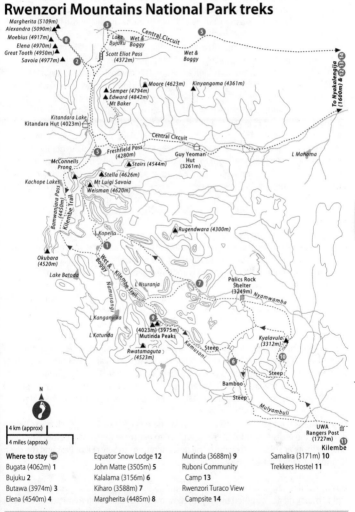

Where to stay 🛏
Bugata (4062m) **1**
Bujuku **2**
Butawa (3974m) **3**
Elena (4540m) **4**

Equator Snow Lodge **12**
John Matte (3505m) **5**
Kalalama (3156m) **6**
Kiharo (3588m) **7**
Margherita (4485m) **8**

Mutinda (3688m) **9**
Ruboni Community
 Camp **13**
Rwenzori Turaco View
 Campsite **14**

Samalira (3171m) **10**
Trekkers Hostel **11**

The Bakonzo people

Many of the people who inhabit the villages and farms in the Rwenzori foothills are the Bakonzo, commonly shortened to Konzo, and in the DRC they are known as the Banande. Most treks in the Rwenzoris hire the Bakonzo as guides and porters. Although slender and of medium height, they are astonishingly strong in the mountains and capable of covering enormous distances in a few hours of intense walking. Many traditional Bakonzo villages lie as high as 2300 m, and they consider the mountain peaks as the dwelling of their god Kitasamba, whose frozen sperm (the snow) melts into the rivers and lakes and fertilizes the land. The Bukonzo community around Ruboni (for the Nyakalengija trailhead) is thought to number about 2000. Community-run activities for visitors (US$15 per person) run by the Bukoma can be organized from the Ruboni Community Camp and Rwenzori Turaco View Campsite (see Where to stay, page 198). You can go on village walks as they demonstrate their daily activities, from tending to their animals and crops to preparing meals, and perhaps meet a blacksmith or traditional healer whose herb-based concoctions from the forests are believed to cure many ailments. You may also visit a village school, or see a crafts demonstration and a vibrant dance performance accompanied by lively drumming. There are also plenty of enjoyable nature walks going into the forests along the border with the national park. Trails go to waterfalls and the Mubuku River, and the guides can point out birds like the endemic Rwenzori turaco and cinnamon-chested bee-eater, as well as chameleons and black-and-white colobus and vervet monkeys.

Day 3 From John Matte Hut the trail crosses the particularly difficult Bigo bog and the Upper Bujuku Valley beneath the massive cliffs of Mount Stanley on your right (west) and Baker on your left (east). You will shortly reach the Kibatsi bog, which takes two to three hours to cross and from the bog there is another steep climb. The route then skirts Lake Bujuku to reach Bujuku Hut (3962m). You will find it almost impossible to avoid getting muddy on this section. Bujuku Hut has one of the loveliest settings of all the huts on the routes, with Mount Stanley and an incredible ice cave in the Peke Glacier on Mount Speke both clearly visible.

Day 4 The route climbs to Scott Elliot Pass (4372 m), and the track takes you through groundsel to a scree slope. There is a cleft in the rocks to the left and from here the descent continues with the vertical cliffs of Mount Baker on your side. There is an unforgettable view back down towards Mount Speke and Lake Bujuku down the U-shaped Bujuku Valley. The climb finishes at Elena Hut (4541 m) below the snowline of Mount Stanley.

Day 5 This is the big day for the ascent of Margerita Peak (5109 m), which starts before dawn for the chilly trek through snow and ice to get there for sunrise before the views and the route are obscured by mist. The descent returns to Scott Elliot Pass and the deep Kitandara Gorge back to the Kitandara Hut.

Day 6 The day begins with a steep climb to the Freshfield Pass (4282 m), a long flat of high alpine mossy glades carpeted by bright yellow mosses and offering tremendous views of mounts Stanley and Baker. It then descends through boggy areas to a rock overhang called Bujongolo. This is where the first expedition to explore the mountains in 1906 based itself. A muddy trail then leads down the Kabamba Valley to the Guy Yeoman Hut (3505 m).

Day 7 The remainder of the descent to Nyabitaba Hut (2652 m) follows the valley of the Mobuku and Kichuchu rivers, which is rich in plants and flowers of the heather zone before reaching the bamboo forest. Hikers can overnight at Nyabitaba or, if feeling fit, can continue to the trailhead at Nyakalengija (1600 m), which takes another two or three hours.

⊙ Kasese and the Rwenzoris listings

For hotel and restaurant price codes and other relevant information, see pages 16-20.

🛏 Where to stay

Kasese *p189 map p188*
\$\$ Hotel Margherita, 3 km west of town on the Kilembe road, T04834-44015, www.hotel-margherita.com. This former government hotel has a lovely setting but is a little characterless in a collection of plain concrete blocks. It is does, however, have 36 comfortable rooms with balconies and 1 self-catering apartment sleeping 5. The restaurant and bar is the place to head for a meal even if not staying and the spacious gardens have mountain views.
\$\$-\$ Sandton Hotel, Rwenzori St, opposite Stanbic Bank, T0483-445307, www.sandton hotelkasese.net. A fairly new neat option with rooms in the main building surrounding a large tiled courtyard and others in a nearby annex; a remarkable 66 rooms in total with a/c and DSTV. Good restaurant with a long menu of local and international dishes; again head here to eat even if not staying. Competing against the Margherita as the best in town.
\$ Rwenzori International Hotel, 1 Mbogo Rd, in the residential suburb of Kawaiba 3 km south of Kasese, T0483-444148, T078-228 2008, www.rwenzoriinternational hotel.com. This 35-room budget place offers excellent value. Doubles (US\$25-40) have DSTV and decent tiled bathrooms, plus there's a gym, tennis court (rackets

for hire), restaurant and bar. It's close to the Kasese–Ishaka road and the airstrip.
\$ White House Hotel, off Kilembe Rd, T04834-44706. The recommended shoestring option with 23 rooms, en suite or shared bathrooms and reliable hot water. Expect to pay around US\$10 per person. Restaurant, bar with DSTV, leafy beer garden, and internet café.

Rwenzori Mountains National Park
p189
Kilembe
\$ Trekkers Hostel (aka Rwenzori Backpackers), Kyanjuki Village, 12 km from Kasese and 2 km before Kilembe, T0776-114442 or T0774-199022, www.rwenzoritrekking.com. This is the base of RTS for the Kilembe Trail from the nearby Kyanjuki trailhead, but you don't need to be trekking to stay here. Situated 500 m above Kasese it is pleasantly cooler and can sleep about 30 in total in rooms (US\$15) and dorms (US\$8 per person) or there's a campsite (US\$3 per person). Good hot showers, restaurant, bar plus pleasant veranda next to the Nyamwamba River.

Nyakalengija
\$\$\$ Equator Snow Lodge, signposted from the village, 2 km on a bumpy road, reservations Kampala 0414-258273, www. geolodgesafrica.com. This new property from **GeoLodges** opened at the end of 2012 in a lovely spot next to the frothy Mubuku River. The 4 huge cottages have fireplaces

and are nicely designed from local timber and river stones. There's excellent food, some wine, a relaxing lounge with sofas and warm blankets, and the wooden deck looks straight into the forest.

$ Ruboni Community Camp, just opposite the RMS office, T0774-19 5859, www.rubonicamp.com. Near the park entrance and Nyakalengija trailhead, this camp offers a community experience in the Rwenzori foothills. En suite *bandas* and safari tents (US$20-25 per person) and camping (US$5 per person) with restaurant, bar and great veranda looking straight up into the mountains. Organizes guided village walks (see box, page 196).

$ Rwenzori Turaco View Campsite, 200 m from the Ruboni Community Camp, T0774-379564. Simple set up with grassy campsite (US$4 per person) and 7 cheap *bandas* with single beds, bedding and nets (from US$10 per person), compost toilets and bucket showers and a thatched communal hut. Can organize basic local meals with notice. Also arranges village walks, etc (see box, page 196).

O Shopping

Kasese *p189, map p188*
The main market in the centre of town has an excellent section of fruit and vegetables. **Hosanna Supermarket**, Margarita St, 0800-2200, has a good range of goods suitable for hiking such as dried soups and noodles, plus it sells frozen meat, fresh bread, alcoholic drinks and toiletries. **Titi's Supermarket**, Rwenzori Rd, close to the post office, is similar.

O What to do

Kasese *p189 map p188*
Rwefuma Safaris, T0772-573399, www.rwefumasafaris.com. Has a 4WD Landcruiser which can take 4 and a minibus for up to 8, from US$85 per day with driver excluding fuel, for local tours and transfers including QENP and Kibale Forest and will take you to/from Bwindi.

O Transport

Kasese *p189 map p188*
Air
Aerolink (T0317-333000, www.aerolinkuganda.com, see also Essentials, page 13) run 1 return scheduled flight Mon-Fri between Entebbe International Airport and the airstrip at Kasese. They operate the flight on demand, usually with a minimum of 4 passengers, and can also arrange charter flights. The flights also serve those going to the QENP and the northern sections of Bwindi.

Bus or matatu
Kasese is the terminus for the Kampala–Kasese via Fort Portal **Post Bus** route and it arrives and departs at the post office on Margherita St (see Essentials, page 14). Buses leave from the bus park, next to the taxi park at the southern end of town. To **Kampala**, 5-6 hrs, US$10-12, via **Fort Portal** or **Mbarara**. If travelling to the southwest, take a bus or *matatu* to Mbarara and change there. To Fort Portal, *matatus* leave frequently, 1-2 hrs, US$3.

Fort Portal and around

Located almost 300 km west of Kampala and 75 km north of Kasese at 1600 m above sea level, Fort Portal is situated in the foothills of the Rwenzoris and from the town is a beautiful view of the snow-capped mountains, although cloud often obscures the peaks. Heading to Fort Portal from Kampala, the journey, on a new tarred two-lane highway, passes through swampy areas with graceful papyrus beds and woodlands scattered with acacia trees. From Kasese it is another beautiful drive: the road climbs out of the dry plains and gradually enters the hilly greenness that surrounds Fort Portal. Some visitors base themselves at Fort Portal while organizing a trek up the mountains but, although not so pleasant, Kasese is more convenient. It is, nevertheless, the base for excursions to the northern spur of the Rwenzoris and the Kabale Forest National Park; several crater lakes and the Semliki Valley are also located near the town. ▸▸ *For listings, see pages 205-207.*

Kampala to Fort Portal → *For listings, see pages 205-207. Colour map 2, B5-B2.*

From Kampala, the direct route to Fort Portal is along what is known as the Kampala–Mubende–Fort Portal Road (A109), which is now tarred along its entire 294-km length. The journey time from Kampala to Fort Portal is about 4½ hours. **Mubende** is a small town, about midway between the two, and vehicles tend to stop here for snacks and drinks; the barbecued chicken on wooden skewers is particularly good. Mubende's best hotel is the good-value **Town View Hotel** ($; T0706-761407), with large rooms, hot showers, good views over the town and a restaurant, sited up the hill opposite Stanbic Bank.

If you have the time, you can climb the 213-m-high Mubende Hill about 4 km north of town, which has a flat tabletop that provides an excellent view over town and the surrounding area. At the top is the Nyakaima Shrine, an ancient 'witch tree', the base of which has large root buttresses forming nooks and fissures. It is visited by people paying homage to the matriarch Nakayima of the Bacwezi, a dynasty that is said to have flourished in the region in the 14th century. It was these people that are believed to have introduced coffee and Ankole cattle to what is now Uganda, from places further north along the Nile. Legend has it there was palace at the top of Mubende Hill, and Nakayima was a Bacwezi priestess who used to cure people of ailments from this hill. When she died, her spirit remained on the hill, from where she continues to treat and bless people who pay her homage. Many local people visit and make a wish at the tree by by placing a coffee bean into the nooks formed by the tree's roots.

Katonga Wildlife Reserve → *For listings, see pages 205-207. Colour map 2, B2.*

The 211-sq-km Katonga Wildlife Reserve was gazetted in 1998 and is named after the Katonga River, which flows from Lake Victoria to Lake George. The area is mixed savannah with acacia woodlands, and a few pockets of tropical and riverine forest. A large proportion of the reserve is wetlands, either permanent or seasonal, and most of the species of plant and animal in the reserve are specific to wetland habitats. However, the UWA is in the process of restocking the reserve with plains game since much of the wildlife was depleted during the unrest of the 1970 and 1980s. In 2013 two large herds of impala and zebra were relocated here from Lake Mburo National Park. The reserve for the moment can only be explored on foot with an armed ranger, and there are only camping facilities, although there are plans for more development.

Arriving at Katonga Wildlife Reserve

Getting there The most direct route is via the Kampala–Mubende–Fort Portal road. Some 48 km past Mubende, at the small town of Kyegegwa, take the left turn in a southerly direction. This unmade road takes you through the villages of Mpara and Karwenyi before reaching the reserve headquarters close to the Katonga River. Katonga is 42 km from Kyegegwa. A 4WD is needed during the rainy season. By public transport there are frequent *matatus* and buses to Kyegegwa. From here *matatus* run south, depending on road and weather conditions, as far as Karwenyi. From here walking is possible or hire a motorbike *boda-boda*.

The reserve can also be accessed from the Fort Portal–Mbarara road at a turning just south of Ibanda. From here, take the road east to Kazo and then the road north to Kabagole, which is just a short canoe trip across the Katonga River to the entrance gate to the reserve.

This is really only an option for the self sufficient as there are no facilities and you have to take everything with you, although water and firewood are provided. Accommodation is limited to camping, at US$8 per person (plus the reserve entry fee). The campsite is located on a hill overlooking the river valley. It has a thatched cooking shelter, or you can order meals through a local women's group. Another option is to cross the Katonga River by canoe and stay in basic board and lodgings in the small town of Kabagole.

Tourist information Uganda Wildlife Authority (UWA) ① *T0414-355000), www. ugandawildlife.org, US$10, children (5-15) US$5, guides for walks US$30.*

Flora and fauna

Katonga is one of the few places in Africa to have a large population of the extremely shy and reclusive sitatunga antelope, whose favoured habitat is papyrus swamps. Other mammals include elephant, hippo, black-and-white colobus monkeys, olive baboon, Uganda kob, waterbuck, duiker and reedbuck. The wetlands support a population of river otter, along with various reptiles and amphibians. In addition, there are over 150 species of bird recorded, including an abundance of kingfishers and storks.

Walks

The reserve has no roads at present, but three guided half-day walking trails have been developed to allow visitors the opportunity to see the various ecosystems within Katonga. These can be arranged by the park staff. The early morning walk along the **Sitatunga Trail** offers the best opportunity to spot the timid antelope. Other mammals are frequently seen as you walk through the savannah and later alongside the Katonga River. The **Kyeibale Trail** is a circular trek through the scrubland into the remnants of the forests, passing interesting rock formations and caves used for shelter by the animals. The **Kisharara Trail** traverses the savannah to the wetland canal, follows the Katonga River and continues up one of the tributaries through a variety of ecosystems, offering the visitor an opportunity to see the sitatunga antelope and various primates as well as other mammals and birds.

To Hoima and the north

About 55 km beyond Kyegegwa and the turn-off to Katonga Wildlife Reserve on the Kampala–Mubende–Fort Portal road, is the village of Kyenjojo, about 50 km before Fort Portal. There's a turn-off here to first the Kabwoya Wildlife Reserve (approximately 105 km), then Hoima (150 km) and Masindi (200 km) and then beyond to the Murchison Falls National Park (these are all covered in in the Murchison Falls and the north chapter, page 219). This road offers an alternative route from Fort Portal and the west of Uganda to the northern region. However, despite the road being considerably improved in recent years, it has a bad reputation of being very slippery in the wet. Nevertheless it is fantastically beautiful route; for the first part of the journey the landscape is one of low cultivated hills, but as you proceed north it becomes mountainous and partly forested. Every so often the road reaches a spot where you can see for miles. Those with a 4WD or a high-clearance vehicle may want to attempt it and it saves a long journey back via Kampala. For those that don't, or are using public transport, the good tarred roads from Kampala to Hoima and Masindi are the much better option.

Fort Portal → For listings, see pages 205-207. Phone code: 0483. Colour map 2, B2.

Small, quiet and refreshing, and with views of the Rwenzoris and a temperate climate, Fort Portal is one of Uganda's most agreeable towns. Thanks to the high altitude, good rainfall, and rich, dark volcanic soil, Fort Portal is the heartland of Uganda's tea-growing region. During the colonial period many **tea plantations** were run by Europeans on land leased from the government (and rarely owned). Now the land is mostly owned by a few large companies, but smallholdings are encouraged. Many of the original tea plantations fell into disrepair when the infrastructure of the country collapsed between 1972 and 1986. Since then a massive rehabilitation programme has been successful in restoring them to their former glory. The plantations that blanket the hillsides around the town are astonishingly green in the sun and glisten with silver when it rains. If you leave Fort Portal early to go chimp tracking in the Kibale Forest, you will notice lots of 'squads' getting ready to head out to work in the fields.

The town is a convenient base to explore the crater lakes, Kibale Forest, the Semliki Valley and the northern foothills of the Rwenzoris. You might also stop over here on the way to the Murchison Falls National Park (although it is a long day's travel to the north).

Arriving at Fort Portal

Getting there From Kampala, the direct route is via the Kampala–Mubende–Fort Portal road (A109), which is now tarred along its entire 294-km length. It takes 4½ hours and there are plenty of buses and the Post Bus stops here on its way to Kasese. There are frequent *matatus* to and from Kasese, which also has the nearest airstrip. ➤➤ *See also Transport, page 207.*

Background

Fort Portal was founded in 1893 under the name of Fort Gerry, and later renamed Fort Portal after the diplomat Sir Gerald Portal. Even though today his statue graces the main road, he never actually set foot in the town but contributed decisively to convincing the British government of the benefits of explorer Sir Frederick Lugard's plan that this area should become part of the British Empire, and was instrumental in the signing of agreements with the leaders of the kingdoms of Uganda that led to the formalizing of protectorate status for the country. The British-built fort itself is now part of the town's golf course and is little more than a pile of rocks.

Fort Portal is in the centre of the Toro Kingdom and the town was a base from which British colonial power protected the then Omukama (or King) of Toro. In 1876 Toro

Fort Portal centre

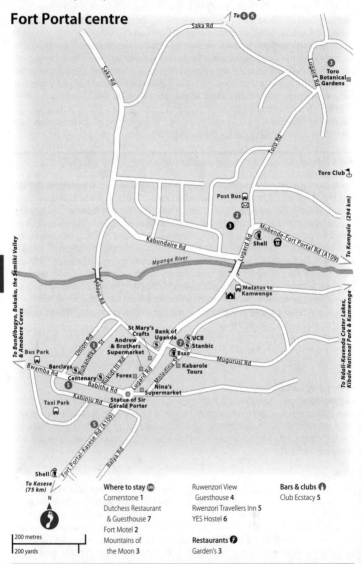

Where to stay 🛏
Cornerstone 1
Dutchess Restaurant
  & Guesthouse 7
Fort Motel 2
Mountains of
  the Moon 3

Ruwenzori View
  Guesthouse 4
Rwenzori Travellers Inn 5
YES Hostel 6

Restaurants 🍴
Garden's 3

Bars & clubs 🎵
Club Ecstacy 5

was captured by the Banyoro King Kabalega, but the British expelled him in 1891 and replaced him with a new Toro King, Kasagama. In later years Catholic and Protestant missionaries followed the colonial administration in order to establish churches, schools and hospitals. By 1900 the town was expanding rapidly, its development helped by the booming trade in cash crops. In the 1930s Europeans and Indians came to set up large tea estates, and shops and residential premises were built. The growth of the town was also helped by the establishment in 1952 of the railway line from Mombasa as far as Kasese, for the transportation of copper from the mines at Kilembe. However, the mines closed in the 1980s and subsequently the railway line was discontinued.

As with the other traditional kingdoms in Uganda, Toro was abolished in 1966 during Obote's first term of office. The previous king, Sir Tito Winyi IV, had been crowned in 1924, but was deposed when Obote abolished the monarchy. However, it was restored by Museveni in 1993, and the present Omukama, Rukirabasaija Oyo Nyimba Kabamba Iguru Rukidi IV, or simply King Oyo, was crowned in 1995 when he was only three years old (he is still today the world's youngest monarch). The Karambi Royal Tombs are located about 5 km out of Fort Portal on the Kasese road, on the right-hand side. These are the burial grounds for the Toro royal family, where Kasagama, Rukidi III and Kaboyo are buried among others. However, they are hopelessly overgrown and the land around them is used for grazing animals. There is some talk of restoring them.

Toro Botanical Gardens
① *Between the golf club and the Mountains of the Moon Hotel, 1.5 km out of town on the Kampala road, T0782-673188. Daily 0800-1700, guided walks US$2.*
Established in 2001 by retired Professor Rugumayo, the rationale for this 40-ha garden is to collect and conserve the local flora of the Albertine Rift region as well as raising local awareness; school children visit here. There are medicinal plants, herbs, spices and vegetables, as well as trees and flowers. Among them is sweet wormwood (*Artemisia annua*), an aromatic herb that produces artemisinin, containing anti-malarial properties. The workers' salaries are funded by sales of their produce that is packaged on site.

Around Fort Portal → *For listings, see pages 205-207.*

Amabere Caves → *Colour map 2, B2.*
Off the Bundibugyo Rd, after 6 km you branch off towards Nyakasura school, and follow the signs for 2 km to the caves. You can get here by motorbike *boda-boda*. Guides cost around US$5. You can negotiate to camp here.

A pleasant excursion from Fort Portal is to these caves, but don't expect anything too spectacular; the caves are small, just shallow overhangs of rock, and moss-covered pillars half conceal the entrance. There are stalagmites and stalactites (in the shape of a woman's breast, which is what the name Amabere means). The legends of the caves are more impressive than the caves themselves, and the guide will tell interesting stories about the traditional history of area. The caves are dark, so bring a torch. The first cave is dominated by a powerful waterfall that tips over the ridge of rock above and it's very refreshing to stand in the cave behind it and feel the spray.

Afterwards the guide can take you to the top of the Lake Saka crater rim, which has a beautiful view over the Fort Portal plateau and Rwenzori Mountains. Lake Saka is the largest of the three crater lakes in this area and is big enough for commercial fishing of tilapia, which is for sale in Fort Portal's market. From the viewpoint you can see the other two lakes: Nyabikere means 'place of frogs', and amphibians are plentiful in the lake; and Kigere which means 'footprint' in the local language. According to legend a footprint of a man was found in the stones of the caves after a volcanic eruption. The print has since disappeared but the lake and legend remain.

Around Fort Portal

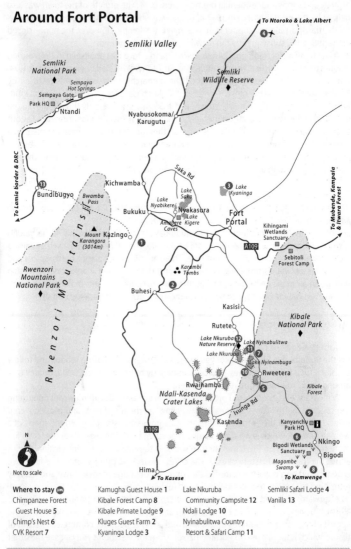

Where to stay 🏠
Chimpanzee Forest
Guest House **5**
Chimp's Nest **6**
CVK Resort **7**

Kamugha Guest House **1**
Kibale Forest Camp **8**
Kibale Primate Lodge **9**
Kluges Guest Farm **2**
Kyaninga Lodge **3**

Lake Nkuruba
Community Campsite **12**
Ndali Lodge **10**
Nyinabulitwa Country
Resort & Safari Camp **11**

Semliki Safari Lodge **4**
Vanilla **13**

Itwara Forest

Located 25 km northeast of Fort Portal and accessed off the Kampala road, this is the last sizeable patch of medium-altitude rainforest which is not within national park boundaries around Fort Portal. It officially covers 87 sq km, but is currently threatened by deforestation from firewood collection and from the surrounding tea estates. It is home to a large number of small mammals as well as a great range of birdlife. Primates include black-and-white colobus, red-tailed and red colobus monkeys, and there is also a small group of chimpanzees living in the forest but not much is known about them and they are rarely seen. Also found are the African palm civet, the giant forest squirrel and the scaly-tailed flying squirrel. Tourist facilities haven't been developed, but **Kabarole Tours** (page 207) in Fort Portal can organize a guided nature walk and transport and can perhaps combine the trip with a visit to a nearby tea factory. Since there are no established trails in the forest, it involves real bush walking and the guide carries a GPS.

◉ Fort Portal and around listings

For hotel and restaurant price codes and other relevant information, see pages 16-20.

◉ Where to stay

Fort Portal centre *p201, map p202*
Fort Portal has a way above average choice of accommodation both in town and the surrounding area.

$$$-$$ Mountains of the Moon Hotel
and Resort, 4 Nyaika Av, about 1.5 km from the town centre next to the Toro Botanical Gardens, T0483-423200, www.mountainsofthemoon.co.ug. Lovely renovated old colonial hotel, with 33 generous-sized rooms with verandas and Wi-Fi, set in 15 ha of beautiful grounds, which is an ideal place for an afternoon drink to look at the mountains. Facilities include pool, gym and sauna and the restaurant/bar areas feature massive fireplaces.

$$$-$$ RuwenZori View Guesthouse,
15 Lower Kakiiza Rd, T0772-722102, www.ruwenzoriview.com. Well signposted in Boma, a lush suburb about 500 m before the Mountains of the Moon Hotel. Excellent small hotel owned by a Dutch/English couple, 7 rooms with verandas in flowering gardens, way above usual standards, outstanding 4-course dinners, and the lounge has a display of locally made crafts for sale.

$$ Fort Motel, 2 Lugard Rd, T0772-501731, www.fortmotel.com. Stylishly restored old colonial house, with 10 comfortable rooms with DSTV and Wi-Fi, a small swimming pool, sauna, restaurant and neatly manicured gardens.

$ Rwenzori Travellers Inn, Fort Portal–Kasese Rd, T0775-299591, www.rwenzori travellersinn.com. Central, comfortable hotel on 3 storeys with 30 rooms and good value from US$40 for a double. Terrace restaurant, secure car park, and friendly staff. The popular bar on the 1st floor is fun and has great views over town but can get noisy so ask for a room away from it.

$ Dutchess Restaurant and Guesthouse, 11 Mugurusi Rd, just behind Stanbic Bank, T0704-879474, www.dutchessuganda.com. 4 double/triples and 1 single very comfortable guest rooms above the restaurant of the same name (see page 206). Large bathrooms, colourful decor, Wi-Fi, parking behind secure gate, run by friendly Dutch couple, can organize a guide for friendly walkabouts in town.

$ Hotel Cornerstone, T0483-422222, www.hotelcornerstone.com. A good budget choice in the centre near Barclays Bank in a neat white block with 24 spotless tiled rooms with DSTV, some with balconies, small bar and dining room. Newly built so everything is quite fresh. Doubles from US$30.

$ YES Hostel (Youth Encouragement Services), Kakiza Rd, Boma, T0722-780350, www.yesugandahostel.weebly.com. Located close to the **RuwenZori View Guest House**, this is a cheap hostel run by an NGO that supports orphans, with 6-8 bunks per dorm (US$7) and a campsite (US$3). Good hot showers, use of kitchen, or meals can be arranged. There are lovely views to the rear overlooking the pastures and the Rwenzoris.

Around Fort Portal *p203, map p204*
$$$$ Kyaninga Lodge, about 10 km from Fort Portal, take the Kampala road for 1.8 km, and turn left at the sign and follow this road for a further 6 km, T0772-999750, www.kyaningalodge.com. This Anglo-Ugandan project took over 6 years to build, and is an outstanding example of architecture and engineering perched on the rim of the Kyaninga crater lake with magnificent views of the landscape to the Rwenzoris. The 8 massive thatched log cabins are connected to the main lodge by elevated walkways, and top-notch facilities include a stunning pool, tennis and badminton courts, croquet, restaurant offering gourmet food and bar with a fine winelist. Easily one of Uganda's most attractive places to stay.
$$ Kluges Guest Farm, 15 km south of Fort Portal off the Kasese road; after 11 km branch off eastwards (signposted) at the **Kasusu Trading Centre** and continue for another 4 km, T0772-440099, www.klugesguestfarm.com. A German/Ugandan enterprise, this is a working farm, set in lovely countryside with the Rwenzoris as a backdrop. It offers 8 spacious cottages, a family guesthouse with 2 rooms and a kitchen, and camping (**$**), with your own tent or a hired one. Good food and there's a pool. Pick-ups from Fort Portal can be arranged.

🍴 Restaurants

Fort Portal *p201, map p202*
Again, Fort Portal has a surprisingly good choice of places to eat, and all the hotels have fine restaurants. The **Mountains of the Moon Hotel** has a good Sun lunch buffet in the garden, while the **Rwenzori Travellers Inn** offers tasty platters of Indian and Ugandan food.
$$-$ Dutchess Restaurant and Guesthouse, see Where to stay, page 205. Daily 0700-2130. Fort Portal's most popular hangout for expats and volunteer workers serving excellent espressos and cappuccinos, smoothies, burgers, salads, pizza and more elaborate meals for dinner. Pretty garden tables, internet café and Wi-Fi. Run by a lovely Dutch couple, also has a deli counter for home-made bread and cakes, cheese and yoghurt. Purified water is used to wash salads and to make ice cream.
$ Garden's Restaurant, opposite the market. Daily 1100-2100. Good-value Ugandan all-you-can-eat lunchtime buffet (starts around 1230) including chapattis, goat and beef stew, *matoke* and groundnut sauce. Other dishes such as pepper steak and chips available. Attractive outside bar, busy in the evenings, and bands play on Sun afternoons.

🍸 Bars and clubs

Fort Portal *p201, map p202*
The rooftop bar at the **Rwenzori Travellers Inn** is popular. **Ecstasy**, in a small alleyway opposite Barclays bank (open Wed, Sat and Sun) is a popular club.

🛍 Shopping

Fort Portal *p201, map p202*
The main market in the lower part of town between the Mpanga River and the junction of the Kampala road has a large choice of fruit, vegetables and bread.

Supermarkets
Andrew & Brothers Supermarket, Lugard Rd, T0483-22714. Daily 0800-1900. Well stocked with fresh bread, frozen meat, imported foodstuffs, toiletries, wines and alcoholic beverages. Also here is **Mary's Craft Shop**, with locally made crafts and cards.

⏱ What to do

Golf
Toro Club, a 20-min walk up Lugard Rd past the post office. Established in 1914, this pleasant 9-hole golf course is dotted with mature trees. It's on the site of the Old Fort (see page 202), and the remains of the moat can still be seen. Visitors are welcome and you can hire clubs.

Tour operators
Kabarole Tours, Moledina St, behind the Caltex station, T0483-4251156, T0774-057390, www.kabaroletours.com. Mon-Sat 0800-1800, Sun 0900-1500. A long-established company with friendly, helpful staff and excellent tour guides. Day trips to Lake Nkuruba, Rwenzori Mountains, Kihingmi Wetlands and Mpanga Waterfalls, among many other places, US$40-85. There are also local cycling tours visiting crater lakes, waterfalls and caves, and countrywide tours on short safaris. They are active in promoting ecotourism in this part of Uganda, and you can visit local communities and learn about their cultural traditions and farming practices. Just drop into the office and discuss what you would like to do and they will come up with some really interesting suggestions.

✈ Transport

Air
The nearest airport is Kasese (page 198).

Bus and matatu
The bus and taxi parks are in the centre of town around Bwamba Rd. The 2 alternative routes to and from **Kampala** are via **Mubende**, 294 km, 4½ hrs, or via **Mbarara**, and **Kasese**, 430 km, 4-5 hrs. Buses leave throughout the day on both routes, US$8-10, and stop at the major towns en route. The **Post Bus** stops in Fort Portal on the Kampala–Kasese route and it arrives and departs at the post office on Lugard Rd (see Essentials, page 14). Very few *matatus* now do the whole route between Kampala and Fort Portal. *Matatus* run to **Kasese** frequently, 2 hrs, US$2, and to **Masindi/Hoima** (changing in Kagadi), 7 hrs, US$10, but this is a long day on bad roads and the better option of getting to Hoima is on the tarred road from Kampala.

The Semliki Valley

The Semliki Valley (sometimes written Semuliki) lies at the base of the Albertine Rift, to the west of Fort Portal; the magnificent Rwenzori foothills are to the south and Lake Albert to the north. Four distinct ethnic groups live in the valley: Bwamba farmers live along the base of the Rwenzoris; the Bakonjo cultivate the mountain slopes; Batuku cattle-keepers inhabit the open plains; and Batwa pygmies, traditionally hunter-gathers, live on the edge of the forests. The Semliki River itself is 140 km long and starts in Lake Edward, flows west of the Rwenzori Mountains in the DRC and then forms part of the border between the DRC and Uganda in the Bundibugyo district, before emptying into Lake Albert on the Ugandan side. ▶▶ *For listings, see page 213.*

Fort Portal to the Semliki Valley → For listings, see page 213.

It is very easy to get confused over the Semliki Valley. There are two different parks: the Semliki Wildlife Reserve, which lies on the shore of Lake Albert and is home to the upmarket **Semliki Safari Lodge**, and the Semliki National Park, which is over the spur of the Rwenzori Mountains and lies along the Semliki River on the border with the DRC. Access to both is from the road that heads northwest from Fort Portal to Bundibugyo (a distance of 75 km). Once a rough rocky road that was treacherous if it rained, the journey has now been greatly simplified by a new super-smooth tarmac road that was completed in 2013. The road offers spectacular views as it skirts the northern spur of the mountains and in clear weather provides good views of the Kijura Escarpment and Lake Albert to the north.

At Karugutu, about 30 km from Fort Portal, a road branches off the Fort Portal–Bundibugyo road to the fishing village of Ntoroko on the southern shore of Lake Albert. This passes through the Semliki Wildlife Reserve and the distance is about 40 km to the lakeshore. Between Karagutu and Bundibugyo, the road loops around the northern spur of the mountains and as it descends into the Rift Valley, it drops from 1200 m to 720 m at the bottom of the escarpment. It is astonishing to find that the scarp is heavily cultivated; incredibly narrow terracing on a 60-degree slope contains a patchwork of fields – a green quilt, laced with black soil and dimpled by the cassava plants. It reaches the Semliki National Park's Sempaya Gate near the Sempaya Hot Springs, 59 km from Fort Portal. The park headquarters at Ntandi is 6 km further along the road. This 6-km section of public road runs through one of the loveliest tracts of forest in Uganda and provides views of birds and monkeys high up in the forest canopy. From Ntandi it's another 10 km to Bundibugyo.

Arriving in the Semliki Valley

There are *matatus* and at least one daily bus between Fort Portal and Bundibugyo (75 km). Now the road is finished, public transport is expected to become more frequent along this route. For Semliki Wildlife Reserve change at Karugutu; although there are few *matatus* along the Ntoroko route (40 km), there are trucks transporting fish from the lake to Fort Portal so it's possible to hitch and many local people do the same. For Semliki National Park, vehicles can drop you on the road as it goes past the Sempaya Gate and park headquarters at Ntandi en route to Bundibugyo.

Kazingo village

Kazingo village is in the foothills of the Rwenzoris, about 12.5 km west of Fort Portal, and is a base for treks into the northern sector of the mountains. Some people who are short of time or do not want to pay the high fees for the treks to the central mountains from Kasese, enjoy this shorter introduction to the Rwenzoris.

To get to Kazingo, take the Bundibugyo road and after 8 km branch off to the left at Bukuku. You can get a *matatu* up to Bukuku and walk the remaining 3.5 km to Kazingo. Alternatively, hire a special hire taxi or motorbike *boda-boda*. **Kabarole Tours**, see page 207, and the **AMA**, see below, can arrange trips through the northern Rwenzoris.

Visiting the northern spur of the Rwenzori Mountains

Abanya Rwenzori Mountaineering Association (AMA) ① *T0772-621397, www.rwenzori hiking.org*, based in Kazingo, is a community organization using local Bakonzo guides. From Kazingo there are several treks including the six- to eight-hour trek to the peak of **Mount Karangora** within the park (US$100, which includes the daily UWA Rwenzori Mountains National Park entry fee of US$35). This is physically tough going and begins in Kazingo at 1650 m and climbs through a dense forest and bamboo zone and along mossy ridges to Karangora's peak at 3014 m. But it's well worth it as, on a clear day, there are spectacular views of the Rift Valley some 600 m below, over the Semliki River and into the DRC.

Another AMA hike goes via the Bwamba Pass to Bundibugyo in the Semliki Valley. Long before a road was built in 1938 to link Fort Portal with the remote town of Bundibugyo local people followed the most direct route between these settlements over the steep north Rwenzori ridge, known as the Bwamba Pass. The distance between the two is perhaps no more than 20-25 km, even though by road around the spur of the Rwenzoris it's 75 km. The first day's seven- to nine-hour hike ascends through isolated mountain villages and bamboo forest from where there are superb Rift Valley views. From Kazingo, at 1650 m, it reaches a height of 2500 m before descending to 800 m on the floor of the valley. The trip includes an overnight stay in a Bundibugyo guesthouse, meals and return transport to Fort Portal (US$130 which includes the daily UWA Rwenzori Mountains National Park entry fee of US$35).

AMA also offer shorter hikes in the Rwenzori foothills to do some birdwatching, or follow a waterfall trail and identify medicinal plants. This area has some distinct ethnic groups: the Batoro of the lowlands, the Bakonzo of the mountains (see box, page 196) and the Batwa pygmies of the Semliki Valley. Visits to local communities to observe customs, culture and environment can be arranged. Short one- to four-hour tours that don't go into the national park cost US$15-25.

First established in 1929 and now covering 543 sq km, this is the oldest protected area in Uganda. Semliki Wildlife Reserve – previously known as the Toro Game Reserve and then the Toro-Semliki Wildlife Reserve – first entered European consciousness from 1864, when an expedition led by explorer Samuel Baker crested the rift escarpment bringing an immense body of water into view. Baker named it Lake Albert after Queen Victoria's husband. If any land was visible across the lake, it would have been a peninsula that juts northward into the lake, now the site of the fishing village of Ntoroko. The reserve was gazetted by the British after tsetse fly caused an outbreak of sleeping sickness in the region.

Arriving in the Semliki Wildlife Reserve
Uganda Wildlife Authority (UWA) ① *www.ugandawildlife.org, US$35, children (5-15) US$5, per 24 hrs.* There are no vehicle fees to use the public road to Ntoroko, 40 km from the junction at Karugutu, or to get to **Semliki Safari Lodge**, which is 25 km from the junction.

Visiting the Semliki Wildlife Reserve
Semliki is unique, gifted with geographic barriers that have formed a natural haven for wildlife and contains riverine forest, woodland and savannah. While most of the savannah game was decimated during the period of Amin and Obote's leadership (see box, opposite), lion, elephant and buffalo have returned and the number of Uganda kobs has multiplied and is now estimated to be over 8000. It is believed to be home to a substantial number of leopard and Semliki is one of the few places in Uganda where you can go on night drives with a good chance of seeing them. Many of the forest species survived the effects of the civil unrest and poaching, and monkeys, including black-and-white colobus, red-tailed and vervet are commonly seen, and troops of olive baboon are resident around the lodge. Although rarely seen, there are three, perhaps four, groups of chimpanzees in the reserve. They are often seen and heard along the Wasa River, and their pant-hoots are sometimes heard in forests flanking the Nyabaroga Valley. In the middle of the reserve is a study population along the Mugiri River and its tributaries, which has been partially habituated for research by the Semliki Chimpanzee Project, an NGO that is supported by Indiana University in the USA. The research is in its early stages, but guests at Semliki Safari Lodge are able to accompany the resident researchers into the forest. Birdlife is still plentiful, with over 420 species recorded. This is one of Uganda's most reliable places to see the rare shoebill stork, most easily viewed from a boat trip on Lake Albert. This is also an excellent opportunity to see other shore birds, hippo, and the Rift Valley escarpment plunging into the lake. The lodge can arrange this, or if only visiting the park for the day, at Ntoroko you can negotiate for a local motorized fishing boat to take you on the lake for a couple of hours. Note that you will be within the reserve on such a trip so ensure your park permit is valid should you be approached by rangers. **Semliki Safari Lodge** (the only place to stay – see page 213) offers numerous activities to explore this remote wilderness.

Semliki Valley history

At one time the Semliki Valley was famous for its very high density of wildlife including massive black-maned lions, buffalo, Jackson's hartebeest and forest elephants, known to the early hunting fraternity as 'Semliki rats'. Leopard, hippo, crocodile and giant forest hog were also common and the reserve had an estimated 10,000 Uganda kob (see box, page 182). Chimpanzees and black-and-white colobus monkeys were frequently seen and there was also prolific birdlife. Apparently, as game was so plentiful in the Semliki Valley in the late 1960s, and the habitat was similar to that in India, a proposal was mooted to breed tigers in the valley, in the hope that, in 10 years or so, the numbers would have multiplied sufficiently to allow tiger hunts to be offered in Africa. In the 1950s and 60s the Semliki Safari Lodge in what was the Toro Game Reserve was one of East Africa's most popular safari destinations, and the 40 rooms were said to run at an 80% occupancy. The drive across the grassland approaching the lodge was made amidst vast herds of Uganda kob, visitors recall watching from the veranda as lions stalked and killed them, and local people who worked there walked from the nearby villages with great trepidation.

Sadly most of the savannah game in the valley was decimated during the Amin and Obote years and the lodge was burned to the ground in the mid-1980s. There was frequent discussion of abandoning the Toro Game Reserve completely, de-gazetting it, and focusing on other conservation areas that held more promise. But in the early 1990s, Uganda National Parks (now the UWA) assessed the situation and made a commitment to save the Semliki Valley. It renamed the Toro Game Reserve and in 1993 gazetted the Semliki National

Park in the west of the valley. By 1998 a new **Semliki Safari Lodge** had opened in Semliki Wildlife Reserve. With ramped up anti-poaching activities and the presence of the new lodge and its staff, poaching declined and wildlife began a gradual recovery.

Despite these promising developments, political instability in western Uganda plagued the valley in the mid-1990s, slowing the recovery of wildlife and hampering conservation initiatives. On 16 June, 1997 a rebel group calling itself the Allied Democratic Front (ADF) engaged the Ugandan army (UPDF) in a bloody battle just outside the southern boundary of Semliki. For the next five years the ADF roamed the valley from Lake Albert in the north to the southern Rwenzoris, and east and west from the DRC border to Fort Portal. They took over the town of Bundibugyo and occupied the Semliki National Park headquarters, and by 2000 the Semliki Safari Lodge had all but been evacuated. Finally, in November 2001, UPDF forces fired mortars on to the Rift Valley escarpment in the largest and final UPDF-ADF battle. Although remnants of the ADF may still exist in the DRC, they were expelled from the valley by early 2002.

Today the valley is safe to visit and both the Semliki Wildlife Reserve and Semliki National Park are developing into viable tourist destinations. This has been further boosted by the new tarred road from Fort Portal to the border with the DRC that was completed in 2013. With persistent efforts from the UWA, the Semliki Safari Lodge, NGOs such as the Semliki Chimpanzee Project, and the surrounding communities, wildlife numbers and the rejuvenation of the valley's natural environment, is recovering significantly.

Semliki National Park → *For listings, see page 213. Colour map 2, A1.*

Semliki National Park lies 59 km northwest of Fort Portal, on the far side of the northern tail of the Rwenzoris. It was first declared a Forest Reserve in 1932 and it was gazetted as Semliki National Park in 1993. The park is dominated by the easternmost extension of the great Ituri Forest of the Congo Basin. This is one of Africa's most ancient and biodiverse forests; one of the few to survive the last ice age, 12,000-18,000 years ago. As such, it contains numerous features associated with central rather than eastern Africa, and is the only tract of true lowland tropical forest in East Africa. It is home to numerous central African animal and plant species (many of which reach the eastern limit of their range in Semliki) and the local population includes a Batwa pygmy community that originated from the Ituri.

Arriving in Semliki National Park

Uganda Wildlife Authority (UWA) ① *www.ugandawildlife.org. The park headquarters are beside the campsite at Ntandi, 6 km after Sempaya Gate, on the Fort Portal–Bundibugyo road. US$35, children (5-15) US$5, per 24 hrs. There is no vehicle access. Guided walks cost US$30.*

A short walking trail takes in the hot springs, and guided walks to other areas can be arranged through the park headquarters at Ntandi. There is no accommodation at the park, and only basic board and lodgings in nearby Bundibugyo, but now that the new road has been built, it's possible to visit on a long day trip from Fort Portal. Without your own transport you can negotiate a special hire taxi for the day, or book a car or minibus through **Kabarole Tours** (see page 207), who charge around U$60 for the two-way transfer. Bring a picnic from the great deli at the **Dutchess** in Fort Portal (see page 206). There is also the option of hiking from Kazingo to Bundibugyo (see page 209).

Visiting Semliki National Park

The vegetation is predominantly moist evergreen to semi-deciduous forest, but with some grassland, wetland and bamboo forest. The terrain is quite flat, with the Rwenzori range forming a backdrop to the east. It rains a lot, and visitors should bring waterproofs. The Semliki River defines the border with the DRC, and several tributaries run through the park, providing watering places and good spots to observe animals. It's home to about 50 mammal species including elephant, buffalo, leopard, civet, scaly-tailed flying squirrel and bush babies. Primates are well represented too, with eight species reported. Of these, De Brazza, Central African red colobus and Dent's monkeys are central African species, and this is the only place where they can be found in Uganda. More than 400 bird species and 300 butterfly species have also been observed. The **Sempaya Hot Springs** are Semliki's most famous attraction. Ringed by palm trees, they are boiling geysers that reach temperatures of a scalding 103°C and spurt bubbling water and steam up to 2 m high – the steam cloud can be seen from as far as 2 km away. The Batwa people used to cook their food in these boiling pools.

The Semliki Valley listings

For hotel and restaurant price codes and other relevant information, see pages 16-20.

Where to stay

Kazingo village *p209, map p204*
$ Kamugha Guest House, T0772-621397. Simple accommodation with beds and mattresses, but you'll need your own sleeping bag (US$4 per person) and a there's campsite (US$2 per person) in an enclosed compound. Warm showers, local food, soft drinks, coffee and tea available. Village walks and bike hire can be arranged and it's close to the AMA office for hikes (see page 209).

Semliki Wildlife Reserve *p210, map p204*
Plans are underway to establish a UWA camp (under the management of a concessionaire) near **Ntoroko**, at the northern tip of the Semliki Wildlife Reserve on the southern shore of Lake Albert.
$$$$ Semliki Safari Lodge, reservations Kampala T0414-251182, www.wildplaces africa.com. A luxury facility with 8 well-equipped tents under thatched roofs (1 is for families), a dining and relaxation area plus a pool. The food is simple but well prepared and very tasty. Activities include birding, guided walks, chimpanzee tracking (with researchers), boat rides and fishing for Nile perch and tilapia on Lake Albert. The night drive is a marvellous opportunity to see leopard, lion, spotted genet, white-tailed mongoose, eagle owl and nightjars. The guides are very knowledgeable. It takes about 1½ hrs to get here from Fort Portal and there's an airstrip for charter flights.

Semliki National Park *p212, map p204*
2 UWA camps are due to open:
1 near **Ntandi** and 1 at **Sempaya**.
$ Vanilla Hotel, Bundibugyo, about 300 m from the *matatu* stand. Very basic with intermittent power and (cold) water, but reasonably clean and currently the closest accommodation to the park, 10 km away. On the plus side it has a good view of the Rwenzoris from the terrace, cold beers and cheap plates of tasty chicken and beef stew with *matoke* or rice. If these don't sound appetizing, it may be a good idea to bring food from Fort Portal. It seems an odd name, but vanilla is grown in these parts.

Kibale National Park and around

Kibale National Park contains one of the loveliest and most varied tracts of tropical forest in Uganda. It harbours the greatest variety and concentration of primates found anywhere in East Africa and has superb birdwatching, easy access and a variety of interesting activities, making it a well worthwhile destination. Indeed it's on most tour operators' itineraries, simply because it offers the most reliable and successful chimpanzee-tracking option in Uganda; a primate encounter that is second only to meeting the gorillas. Kanyanchu, the primary centre for tourism activities, is 32 km southeast of Fort Portal. Sebitoli Forest Camp, the secondary tourism centre, is even easier to reach as it is 12 km east of Fort Portal on the Kampala road. Most people head straight for Kanyanchu, as this is the starting point for chimpanzee tracking, commonly known as the Primate Walk as other species are easily spotted too. A visit to Kabale National Park is almost always combined with visits to the nearby Ndali-Kasenda Crater Lakes, which lie to the west of Kanyanchu and are also accessed off the road from Fort Portal. This area is incredibly pretty, dotted with shimmering lakes and surrounded by views of the tea estates and Kibale Forest to the east, the Rwenzoris to the west and Lake George and the Rift Valley plains to the south. ▸▸ *For listings, see pages 217-218.*

Ndali-Kasenda Crater Lakes → For listings, see pages 217-218. Colour map 2, B2.

The **Bunyaruguru Volcanic Fields** cover an area which has numerous cones and craters, located about 30 km south of Fort Portal between the main Fort Portal–Kasese road and Kibale National Park. Crater lakes are formed when a violent eruption causes the top of a volcano to be blown off, leaving a crater. There are several lakes of varying size and character, and many have well-developed tourist facilities. In spite of their reputation, the crater lakes are not bilharzia-free, with the exception of Lake Nkuruba. They are therefore unsafe for swimming (and there are leeches too). However, they offer good fishing and the opportunity to do some serious birdwatching, with an estimated 300-400 species. The accommodation around the lakes is easily accessible to and from Kanyanchu for the chimpanzee tracking and other activities at Kabale.

Arriving at the Ndali-Kasenda Crater Lakes

Getting there Take the Kibale National Park road from Fort Portal for 17 km and then take the right fork at Kasisi, from where it is another 8 km to Lake Nkuruba. The left fork continues on to Kanyanchu, which is another 15 km. If you're coming from the Kanyanchu direction towards Fort Portal, there are signposted dirt roads that lead off to the camps and lodges around the lakes. There is little traffic on the roads to the crater lakes but *matatus* go from Fort Portal to the village of Rwaihamba, 40 minutes from Fort Portal, US$2. Lake Nkuruba is a 2-km walk from Rwaihamba, or you can take a *boda-boda* or special hire taxi from Fort Portal. **Kabarole Tours** (see page 207) in Fort Portal can arrange crater lake tours.

The lakes

Lake Nkuruba is a beautiful small crater lake and the only one to remain unspoilt by deforestation. It offers reputedly bilharzia-free, safe swimming, because it is the only lake clear of the freshwater snails that carry the fluke. **Lake Nkuruba Nature Reserve and Community Campsite** has accommodation (see Where to stay, page 218), but can also be visited for the day; the tranquil setting provides an ideal base to explore the other crater lakes with good walks to the 'Top of the World', neighbouring lakes, the Mahoma Falls and the explosion crater. Maps are available for different trips and walks. Around the lake live four species of primate, including a troop of red colobus monkeys, and banded mongoose are commonly seen running around the grassy lakeshore. **Lake Nyinambuga** is south of Lake Nkuruba, and this startlingly blue-green lake offers the only luxurious facilities in the crater lake area, **Ndali Lodge** (see Where to stay, page 217), while it is possible to walk from Lake Nkuruba to Lake Nyabikere in a leisurely two hours via Lake Nynabulita and Lake Nyamirima.

Kibale National Park → *For listings, see pages 217-218. Altitude: 1230 m. Colour map 2, B2.*

Kibale Forest National Park provides a rich and unique habitat for more than 70 species of mammal and over 375 species of bird. Kibale adjoins Queen Elizabeth National Park to the south in the northern section near Lake George, thus creating a 180-km-long corridor for wildlife between Sebitoli in the north of Kibale National Park to Ishasha, in the remote southern sector of Queen Elizabeth. The animal species famously include 13 primates; the highest concentration in Africa, and the viewing of chimpanzees in their natural environment is the main attraction. The national park's emblem is a black-and-white colobus monkey. The park covers 795 sq km and is divided into seven zones for management purposes: research, natural reserve, civic-cultural, recreation, harvest, community and protection. There is an emphasis on conservation, sustainable utilization and non-consumptive use of the forest. Nature trails into the forest have been created and, quite apart from the chimps, the walks are wonderful.

Arriving at Kibale National Park

Getting there Kanyanchu, in the central part of Kibale, is the main trailhead for the park's famous forest walks and is 32 km southeast of Fort Portal on the Fort Portal–Kamwenge–Mbarara road. It is well signposted. Frequent *matatus* leave Fort Portal from the Kamwenge stage, just near the bridge over Mpanga River and opposite the market on Kibale Road, passing Kanyanchu on the way. There is also the option of getting a special hire taxi or *boda-boda* to Kanyanchu. The good gravel road should be fully tarred by the time you read this and it shouldn't take more than 45 minutes, but check locally what time you should leave Fort Portal for Kanyanchu if you're doing the Primate Walk that starts at 0800. Alternatively, you could stay the night in or near Kibale (see Where to stay, page 218). The Sebitoli section of the park is 15 km from Fort Portal along the Kampala road and any public transport will drop off/pick up there.

Tourist information Uganda Wildlife Authority (UWA) ① *information office at Kanyanchu, T0486-424121, www.ugandawildlife.org*. Park entry fees are US$40, children (5-15) US$20, per 24 hours. There is no vehicle access, and there's a car park at Kanyanchu. No fees are charged for driving through the park on the Fort Portal–Kamwenge road or for visiting the Bigodi Wetland Sanctuary (see page 216). Guided walks cost US$30, guided night walks US$40, two-hour children's walks (5-12) US$5, Primate Walk daily 0800 and 1400 which lasts approximately three hours (no under 12s) costs US$150 (including park entry fee).

Flora and fauna

Kibale's varied altitude supports different types of habitat, ranging from wet tropical forest (moist evergreen forest) on the Fort Portal Plateau, through dry tropical forest (moist semi-deciduous), to woodland and savannah on the Rift Valley floor. Some 351 tree species have been identified in the park, and many have broad buttress roots and rise to over 55 m high and are over 200 years old.

Kibale's 1450 chimpanzees represent Uganda's largest population of this endangered primate. The forest is also home to East Africa's largest population of the threatened red colobus and the rare I'Hoest's monkey. Other primates include the black-and-white colobus, red colobus, blue- and red-tailed monkeys, the grey-cheeked mangabey, olive baboon, bushbaby and potto. At least 70 mammal species are present in the park though ground-dwelling animals are difficult to see in the dense forest. An estimated 500 elephant are present, along with buffalo, leopard, warthog, bush pig, golden cat and duiker. However, many of these are reclusive and you will be lucky to see them. A keen observer may spot reptiles and amphibians as well as a 250 colourful and varied species of butterfly.

Chimpanzee tracking and other walks

Tracking the habituated chimp troops is conducted by well-trained guides who will also be able to tell you about the forest generally. The group of chimps in the Kanyanchu community is probably the largest in Kibale Forest, numbering about 45, and the chances of locating them are excellent. However, this activity in never 100% guaranteed as, unlike gorillas, chimps are often high up in the trees or moving quickly away. The Primate Walk (chimpanzee tracking but so called as there's every chance of seeing other primates too) leaves twice daily from Kanyanchu at 0800 and 1400 and lasts about three hours. A maximum of three groups of six people can go in a morning or afternoon. The morning walk is reported to offer a better opportunity of seeing the chimps, usually to be found feeding in the fig trees.

Two-hour birdwatching tours start at 0700 at Kanyanchu Rare species include the papyrus gonolek, white-winged warbler, white-collared oliveback and papyrus canary. When chimpanzees and other forest residents rest up at dusk, a nighttime shift of rarely seen creatures becomes active. Night walks though the darkened forest use powerful torches to seek nocturnal creatures such as the potto, bushbaby, nightjar, cricket and tree hyrax, with its chilling shriek, as well as the occasional civet or serval cat. Night walks leave Kanyanchu at 1930 and last between 1½ and two hours. Short and interesting one- to two-hour children's walks can be arranged in the forest immediately around Kanyanchu to learn about the ecosystem (children of 12 years and under are not allowed to go on the Primate Walk).

Bigodi Wetland Sanctuary and Magombe Swamp

ⓘ *Just north of the village of Bigodi on the Fort Portal–Kamwenge–Mbarara road , 40 km from Fort Portal, and 6 km beyond Kanyanchu, T0772-468113, www.bigodi-tourism.org. 3-hr guided walks depart at 0800 and 1500, US$20.*

Managed by the Kibale Association for Rural Development (KAFRED), the sanctuary is a community-based organization that supports ecotourism initiatives and funds local projects, including a school, health centre and library. In the morning and late afternoon you can take a guided swamp walk along a trail with occasionally muddy boardwalks. The Magombe Swamp is rich with a variety of vegetation. The most common tree species are wild palms, polita figs and wild rubber trees. In addition there are ferns, water lilies, flowers such as those of the Ipomea species, fire lilies, wetland grasses, sedges and reeds. The dominant vegetation is the papyrus. Primates such as the red colobus, black-and-white colobus and red-tailed monkey live in the swamp, along with over 138 bird species, including the great blue turaco, and a large number of butterflies. The guides are excellent at identifying the birds, more visible during the morning excursions. Make sure you take precautions against red ants ascending your legs by wearing closed shoes or boots, avoiding open-toed sandals and tucking trousers into socks.

Beside the visitor centre for the swamp walk is the **Tinka-Homestay ($)**, where you can be a guest in a Ugandan home and enjoy home-grown, freshly harvested traditional food. Cultural activities like storytelling and dance take place.

Sebitoli and Kihingami Wetlands Sanctuary
A northern entrance to Kibale National Park called Sebitoli is on the main road from Fort Portal to Kampala, 15 km from Fort Portal. It's easy to get to by public transport or you could hire a bike from **Kabarole Tours** (page 207). Designed to take pressure off the Kanyanchu section, this site offers guided forest walks and a chance to encounter primates such as red colobus, black-and-white colobus and blue monkeys, among other primates and visitors may also spot a variety of aquatic, forest and savannah birds and enjoy views of the Mpanga River. However, there's no chimpanzee tracking available here as none have been habituated in this part of the forest. Adjoining and just outside the Park boundary, is the Kihingami Wetlands Sanctuary, which is part of the Kihingami Community Enviromental and Development Association (KICEDA), a community-based project that was founded in 2002 to protect the wetlands from encroaching tea-growers and firewood collection. They also offer guided walks that take up to two hours, starting from the Kihingami Vocational Institute for Tourism (just off the main road) and cost US$15 per person; the revenue pays for the guide and maintenance of the trails in the wetlands.

◉ Kibale National Park and around listings

For hotel and restaurant price codes and other relevant information, see pages 16-20.

● Where to stay

Ndali-Kasenda Crater Lakes *p214, map p204*
$$$$ Ndali Lodge, Lake Nyinambuga, T0772-221309, www.ndalilodge.com. Colonial farm homestead on a narrow ridge overlooking the lake 100 m below, stunning 360° views of the crater lakes to the east and north. 8 cottages set on the hillside in a well-kept garden and baths with a view. Service is impeccable and beautifully presented 5-course dinners are served, and

there's Wi-Fi, a library, pool, sauna and yoga platform. Activities include boat trips and you can walk around Lake Nyinambuga which takes around 1½ hrs.
$$ Chimpanzee Forest Guest House, 23 km south of Fort Portal on the Kamwenge road, T0772-486415. With Lake Nyabikere views, this offers 2 rooms in the house, 4 cottages or camping (US$8 per person) in 4 ha of wonderful grounds, including gardens, indigenous forest and tea plantations. Built in the 1950s, it was previously the home of the British District Commissioner. Good country-style food including home-made bread and pancakes for breakfast.

$$-$ Nyinabulitwa Country Resort & Safari Camp, 19 km south of Fort Portal on the Kamwenge road, T0712-984929, www.nyinabulitwaresort.com. One of the newest options in the area with a row of spacious cottages and a campsite sitting on the rim of Lake Nyinabulitwa. There's a bar, a craft shop and a good restaurant using home-grown ingredients. A pleasant excursion is to cross the lake by rowing boat and climb a treehouse in the forest for bird- and monkey-watching.

$ CVK (Crater Valley Kibale) Resort, 20 km south of Fort Portal on the Kamwenge road, T0772-906549, www.cvklakeside. com. Perched on the rim of Lake Nyabikere, this has been popular with backpackers and overlanders for many years and is well placed for the Primate Walk at Kabale. Accommodation is in a neat row of en suite rooms (double US$28), or cheaper *bandas* (US$10 per person) and a campsite (US$8 per person). Restaurant, bar, guided walks and canoe hire.

$ Lake Nkuruba Community Campsite, T0773-266067, www.nkuruba.com. A relaxing spot where accommodation ranges from campsites (US$4 per person) and *bandas* (US$8 per person) to the romantic lakeside house (US$15 per person). Cold beers and sodas, delicious evening meals made with locally grown vegetables and chapattis are baked fresh to order or you can use the kitchen to self-cater.

Kibale National Park *p215, map p204*
$$$ Kibale Primate Lodge, Kanyanchu, reservations Kampala T0414-267153, www.ugandalodges.com. Run by Uganda Lodges, which also has properties in QENP and Murchison Falls, with 8 safari tents, 7 cottages. The bamboo and natural stone decor is attractive, and there's a restaurant and bar with deck looking straight into the forest. There's also a campsite (**$**). Located only a couple of mins' walk from the trailhead for tracking chimpanzees.

$$-$ Chimp's Nest, T0774-669107, www.chimpsnest.com. Dutch enterprise near Nkingo village, about 15 mins' drive from the start point for chimpanzee tracking and close to the Bigodi Wetland Sanctuary; it overlooks a swampy area with giant overhanging trees that are alive with birds, and is occasionally visited by forest elephants. 7 cottages, a 6-m-high treehouse, backpacker rooms or camping available, and there's an attractive thatched hilltop restaurant and bar.

$$-$ Kibale Forest Camp, 2 km south of Bigodi, T0779-820695, www.naturelodges. biz. Set in a pretty forest glade close to Bigodi Wetland Sanctuary. 10 comfortable en suite safari tents, or 'lazy camping' in pre-erected dome tents under thatch with camp beds and bedding, or a regular campsite. Friendly staff and tasty food, especially the Indian dishes.

Contents

Footprint features

Murchison Falls & the north

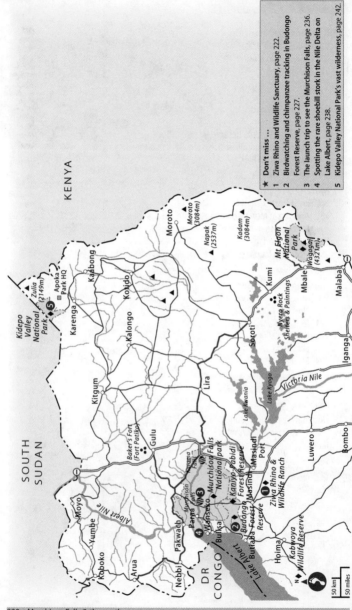

★ Don't miss...
1 Ziwa Rhino and Wildlife Sanctuary, page 222.
2 Birdwatching and chimpanzee tracking in Budongo Forest Reserve, page 227.
3 The launch trip to see the Murchison Falls, page 236.
4 Spotting the rare shoebill stork in the Nile Delta on Lake Albert, page 238.
5 Kidepo Valley National Park's vast wilderness, page 242.

Northern Uganda contains two of Uganda's jewels: Murchison Falls National Park in the northwest and Kidepo Valley National Park in the northeast. The vast Murchison Falls is the main attraction for most travellers and, thanks to good tarred highways, is easily accessible from Kampala. The game viewing is good although it is mainly restricted to north of the river around Paraa. Many consider the boat trip up to the mighty falls, where the Victoria Nile squeezes through a tiny gap creating a furious explosion of whitewater, as the highlight because many animals, including elephants, come down to the river. The Nile crocodiles and pods of hippos are also very impressive, as are the birds; best seen from a cruise in the river's delta with Lake Albert.

In the far northeast abutting the borders with South Sudan and Kenya is Kidepo Valley National Park, an area of beautiful wilderness nestling between two mountain ranges. The scenery is dominated by vast arid savannah plains, in marked contrast to the forested south of the country. It has one of the greatest diversities of wildlife in Uganda, with 82 species of mammal recorded, but receives the fewest visitors as a result of its remoteness. However, there is the option to fly there and avoid a long dusty journey by road, and all visitors will be well rewarded by having the park almost entirely to themselves.

The north includes the towns of Lira, Gulu and Kitgum. These areas suffered from civil unrest during the period of activity by the Lord's Resistance Army, when many local people were displaced and travel was fraught with insecurity. But peace has prevailed since 2006 and development in northern Uganda is now booming. Nevertheless, many of these towns are still home to aid workers from various NGOs dealing with the post-conflict problems.

Kampala to Murchison Falls National Park

The fast road from Kampala to Masindi means that Murchison Falls National Park is a popular weekend destination for inhabitants of the capital. The park is bisected by the Victoria Nile, and the falls – where the river is squeezed through a gap only 7 m wide – are truly spectacular. Murchison has some of Uganda's best game-viewing and it is one of the few places in the country where giraffes can be seen. South, and within the park boundary, is the Kaniyo-Pabidi section of the Bundongo Forest Reserve, which is another of Uganda's places to go on an exciting chimpanzee-tracking excursion. An alternative route to the park is a pleasant drive up the east bank of Lake Albert and there are some great views across the lake to the Blue Mountains, which are in the DRC, on the far shore. On the way to the park from Kampala, the Ziwa Rhino and Wildlife Ranch is worth a stop to see the only free-ranging rhino in Uganda; sadly the last of the wild population was shot out in Murchison Falls in the 1980s.
▶▶ *For listings, see pages 229-231.*

Kampala to Masindi → *For listings, see pages 229-231.*

The road to Masindi leaves Kampala heading north starting at the Wandegeya roundabout near Makerere University passing through Bombo and Luwero, before swinging westwards. The journey from Kampala to Masindi is 215 km on a good road (which is part of the Kampala–Gulu Highway) and takes about three hours. About 30 km out of Kampala you cross into the Luwero district and reach the army town of **Bombo** with row upon row of barracks. In the early 20th century the Sudanese Volunteers in the King's African Rifles, known as the Nubians, were based here. Known as the **Luwero Triangle**, the area was severely affected during the Obote II regime when army atrocities resulted in the killing of many thousands of people, their houses looted and burnt and destruction of the surrounding *shambas*. Little evidence remains apart from a couple of burnt-out tanks left to rust on the roadside.

Although it is not visible from the road, there is a big lake system just to the north of Luwero as the Victoria Nile flows through Lake Kyoga and then Lake Kwania before reaching first the Karuma Falls and then the Murchison Falls and eventually flowing into Lake Albert. The countryside for miles around is low-lying and rather swampy.

The tarmac Kampala–Gulu Highway reaches an important junction 176 km from Kampala at Kafu Bridge. Left goes on to Masindi, another 45 km, and this is the best route to Paraa at Murchison Falls National Park (page 232). The Kampala–Gulu Highway veers northwards, and after 115 km reaches Karuma where it crosses the Nile on the Karuma Falls Bridge. Just north of the bridge is the turn-off to the Chobe Gate of the Murchison Falls National Park and then this road continues to Pakwach, past the Wankwar and Tangi gates to the park. In Pakwach it again crosses the river, and goes on to Arua and, eventually, the DRC. From the Karuma Falls Bridge it's another 75 km north to Gulu, and yet another turn-off takes you east to Lira, 80 km from the bridge.

Ziwa Rhino and Wildlife Ranch → *For listings, see pages 229-231.*

Arriving at Ziwa Rhino and Wildlife Ranch
Getting there The ranch is 178 km northwest of Kampala, and 42 km before Masindi. All buses from Kampala going to Masindi can drop off at Nakitoma, from where it is a short *boda-boda* ride to the ranch's main gate.

Tourist information ① *T0775-521035, www.ziwarhino.com, rhino tracking US$35, children (5-12) US$18.* There are also canoe rides and swamp and bird walks US$15, per guide, per group.

Visiting the ranch

This private, non-profit sanctuary is a joint enterprise between **UWA**, the **Uganda Rhino Fund** and **Ziwa Ranchers Ltd** who reintroduced rhinos to Uganda in 2005, and this is still the only place in Uganda where they can be seen. Once found in all the parks, rhinos became extinct in Uganda in 1982 after years of poaching and the internal armed conflict. Initially there were six reintroduced white rhino (*Ceratotherium simum*), four of which were translocated from a reserve in Kenya and two came from Disney's Animal Kingdom in Florida in the US. Thanks to a carefully monitored breeding programme, they now number 14.

The 7000-ha sanctuary is enclosed by a 60-km-long by 2-m-high solar-powered electrified fence, designed to keep out human predators and protect the rhino, and built by local people, giving much-needed employment. The rhinos have transmitters in their horns and are closely guarded by armed rangers 24 hours a day. Guides can take visitors very close to the animals, given that they are partially habituated, and tracking is partly by vehicle and partly on foot. The tracking excursion lasts on average between one and two hours, and other animals found on the ranch include monkeys, oribi, bushbuck, leopard, hippo, crocodile and around 350 species of bird. You can enjoy a sundowner around the fire pit at the **Amuka Lodge**, although insect repellent is needed as the mosquitoes are prolific, and there is also a campsite and backpacker accommodation (see Where to stay, page 229).

Masindi → *For listings, see pages 229-231. Phone code: 0465. Colour map 1, C2.*

Masindi is 215 km from Kampala en route to the Murchison Falls National Park. It is a pleasant town with lots of flowers and greenery, although the main street, Masindi Port Road, is typical of the area, being rather dry and dusty. Masindi has a lively market, located just behind the main street. It's a good place to refuel and buy supplies before visiting the park. The **Masindi Hotel** (see Where to stay, page 229) is well worth a stop even if it's just for a coffee on the terrace to soak up the wonderful colonial atmosphere. Built in 1923 by the East African Railways and Harbours Company, this is Uganda's oldest colonial hotel, and it has preserved its charming, stylish exterior. Many famous people have stayed here, including Humphrey Bogart and Katherine Hepburn whilst filming *The African Queen* at Masindi Port in 1951 (see box, page 101), and Ernest Hemingway, who recuperated here after surviving two plane crashes in a week in 1954 at Murchison Falls and at Butiaba airstrip (see box, page 235).

Arriving in Masindi

Getting there *Matatus* and buses run between Kampala and Masindi throughout the day and the **Post Bus** stops in Masindi on its Kampala–Hoima route. Frequent *matatus* travel to Hoima. Transport to Paraa at Murchison Falls is non-existent, but there is always the option of organizing a special hire taxi from Masindi for the 88-km journey, or alternatively go on a tour (see Tour operators, page 230). ▶▶ *See also Transport, page 231.*

Tourist office UWA's **Murchison Falls Conservation Area Tourist Office** ① *T0465-420428, www.ugandawildlife.org, daily 0800-1800,* is signposted north from the main road, opposite the town council buildings, 50 m west of the post office. The staff are extremely helpful and can also give you information about Budongo Forest.

Around Masindi → *For listings, see pages 229-231.*

Two kilometres from town on Kihande Hill is **Kihande Palace**, the palace of the King or Omukama of Bunyoro, Solomon Gafabusa Iguru. The Bunyoro Kingdom and kingship were abolished in 1967 during the Obote I regime. President Museveni restored the kingdoms returning their ceremonial powers in 1993. In the interim, people settled and built houses and gardens on royal sites such as the Kihande Palace, so unfortunately there's nothing to see anymore. Although Omukama Solomon normally resides in his palace in Hoima, there are plans to renovate this old palace.

Excursions to **Lake Albert** can be made from Masindi. Head for the town of Butiaba on Lake Albert, a distance of 57 km; *matatus* make the journey and take about one hour. The drive over the escarpment of the Rift Valley is an experience in itself and the air on top is fresh and invigorating. Once you get to Butiaba ask the local fishermen and you should be able to hire a boat for the day.

Masindi Port

Easily confused with Masindi, Masindi Port lies about 40 km to the east, on the Victoria Nile at the western end of Lake Kyoga, which extends across much of central Uganda. In the early 20th century the town of Masindi was a transit point for many goods and produce from the northern Congo and southern Sudan destined for export to European markets. Cargo was shipped across Lake Albert, trucked from Butiaba on the lakeshore up to Masindi's customs sheds, and then trucked on to Masindi Port, where they were shipped down to Soroti and then by railway to Mombasa on the coast. When steamers on the Nile were an important mode of transport, both Karuma Falls and Murchison Falls were major obstacles to travelling upriver. Coming from Lake Victoria, the steamers travelled the Victoria Nile and into Lake Kyoga. Passengers and goods then disembarked at Masindi Port and travelled overland to Butiaba on Lake Albert. From here they continued their boat journey north. Masindi Port has since declined in importance and is now mainly a market town with a population of around 8000. It is possible to negotiate with a fisherman for a canoe ride on the lake, which is good for birdwatching. To get there simply follow Masindi Port Road (the main street in Masindi) east out of town; it crosses the Kampala–Gulu Highway again and then goes to the lakeshore. *Matatus* link the two. Alternatively you can make a detour off the Kampala–Gulu Highway.

Hoima → *For listings, see pages 229-231. Phone code: 0465. Colour map 2, A3.*

Before or after going to Murchison Falls from Masindi, you can take an excursion to Hoima, 56 km to the southwest and linked by *matatus*, which provides access to Kabwoya Wildlife Reserve (see page 225). There are, however, other approaches to Hoima, and ultimately Masindi, so this is an alternative way to get to Murchison Falls. The most direct route to Hoima from Kampala (200 km) is on a sealed road via Kiboga, which is an interesting journey first through hilly landscape with a scattering of huge boulders amongst the farmland.

Soon after leaving Kiboga the road begins a gradual descent into the plain beyond which Hoima, the capital of Bunyoro, is located. The plain is punctuated by the occasional bare hill, and Hoima itself is spread across two such hills. Hoima can be seen from quite a distance, surrounded by eucalyptus trees that were planted as an anti-malarial measure during the colonial era.

The final route is from the southwest and the turn-off is 50 km east of Fort Portal on the Kampala–Mubende–Fort Portal road. This rough road goes first past the Kabwoya Wildlife Reserve (approximately 105 km), and then Hoima (150 km). However, despite the road being considerably improved in recent years, it has a reputation for being very slippery in the wet. Nevertheless, it is a fantastically beautiful route: for the first part of the journey the landscape is one of low cultivated hills, but as you proceed north it becomes mountainous and partly forested; every so often the road reaches a spot where you can see for miles.

On entering Hoima you pass through the instantly recognizable old colonial part of town: fading government offices and bungalows with wide verandas set in large gardens. The town centre overlooks a deep valley with a number of buildings, including one of the town's churches, on the opposite side. Hoima itself has presently got a population of about 42,000, and was until recently a sleepy backwater town where the economy depended on small-scale agriculture. However, thanks to the recent discovery of oil deposits in the Lake Albert area, it is now going through a mini oil boom, and a US$2 billion refinery is being built on the outskirts by the Uganda government in collaboration with the Chinese. As a result, the Kampala–Hoima road has been tarred and you'll notice lots of construction work, including hotels, going on around town.

Around Hoima

Katasiha Fort is located 3 km along the Butiaba road, which leads north out of town towards Lake Albert. The fort was established in 1894 by Colonel Colville when he was trying to subdue Cwa II Kabalega, the Omukama (king) of Bunyoro. All that survives of the fort are a rampart and a ditch.

The **Mparo Tombs**, 3.5 km from Hoima on the road to Masindi, are the burial places of the two most influential Bunyoro kings: Kabalega who died in 1923, and Sir Tito Winyi who died in 1971. Both tombs have a thatched roof supported by a circular stone wall, and inside, the tombs are covered with stretched cow hides and surrounded by a collection of the kings' traditional personal belongings. As well as the two monarchs, several other members of the royal family are buried at Mparo. The site is surrounded by bark-cloth trees and a reed fence. Once you're there, ask around for a guide (they live close by) who will show you around for a tip. Along with Uganda's other traditional kingdoms, the Bunyoro Kingdom was abolished during the Obote period, but was restored in 1993 by the Museveni government. The current Omukama is Solomon Iguru I. His modern palace is just out of town on the road to Butiaba.

Kabwoya Wildlife Reserve → *For listings, see pages 229-231. Colour map 2, A3.*

Arriving at Kabwoya Wildlife Reserve

Getting there The reserve is 70 km southwest from Hoima; it's a 90-minute journey. Drive 5 km along the Hoima–Butiaba road and take the second turning left at the signpost for Karongo. The road passes through Biseruka village then heads south to Kabaale. Continuing south for another 8 km you reach Kaseeta, then turn right (west) and the escarpment is a further 8 km. The lodge and lake are another 15 km west.

Visitor information Entry fee US$10, children (5-15) US$5, per 24 hours. Fees are paid at the lodge.

Visiting Kabwoya Wildlife Reserve

Kabwoya Wildlife Reserve was gazetted in 2002, and then formerly opened in 2006, making it Uganda's newest reserve. Located between Lake Albert and the escarpment of the Albertine Rift Valley, it is mostly savannah and riverine forest in an area that was decimated of wildlife during Uganda's troubles or used by pastoralists for grazing domestic livestock. However, numbers and varieties of wildlife are now rapidly rising, and include hippo, buffalo, Uganda kob, bushbuck, oribi, duiker, warthog, black-and-white colobus monkey and olive baboon, along with the occasional leopard. Birdlife is prolific with over 450 varieties. Re-introduced species include Jackson's hartebeest and waterbuck, which were transferred from Murchison Falls when the reserve opened. However, the reserve is rarely visited and there's only one place to stay; the **Lake Albert Safari Lodge** (see Where to stay, page 230), which also has a campsite. On a clifftop overlooking Lake Albert, guests will simply have the whole reserve to themselves and the lodge organizes all safari activities.

Masindi to Murchison Falls National Park → *For listings, see pages 229-231.*

There are two routes between Masindi and Murchison Falls, and both provide access to the Budongo Forest Reserve (page 227) located on the southern boundary of the park. Budongo Forest is the biggest mahogany forest found in the whole of East Africa, as well as habitat to the largest number of chimpanzees in Uganda. The major tourist sites within this forest are Kaniyo-Pabidi and Busingiro.

Of the two routes from Masindi, the first is the direct and most commonly used route to Paraa, 88 km, which takes about two hours and enters the park through the Kichumbanyobo Gate. The Paraa route goes past Kaniyo-Pabidi.

The second and more beautiful route is via Bulisa. From Masindi you take the Butiaba road and then, before reaching Butiaba, on the shores of Lake Albert, you head north. (If you're coming from Hoima there is a direct road for the 50 km or so to Butiaba to save going to Masindi at all). Then the northwards drive is a very attractive route looking across the Rift Valley towards Lake Albert and across to the DRC on the other side. When you reach the village of **Bulisa** it is 18 km to the **Bugungu Gate** and 23 km to Paraa. In total this route is 135 km from Masindi to Paraa; it takes three to four hours and goes past the Busingiro section of Budongo Forest.

Both routes are dirt but are well maintained except after heavy rains when they become a little slippery and a 4WD may be necessary. Both sections of Budongo offer something different: visitors to **Kaniyo-Pabidi** can enjoy chimpanzee tracking, birding and wonderful accommodation in a beautiful natural setting, while **Busingiro** offers even better birding along what is referred to as the Royal Mile, but only has a simple campsite. So if you intend to stop on the way to the park, it's in Masindi that you have to make a decision about which way to go. Alternatively, neither is that far from Masindi so they can be visited independently of the park, and by public transport, given that vehicles are not allowed into the forest, which can only be explored on foot.

When planning your approach, the final issue to note is that Kaniyo-Pabidi is an extension of, and is within the Murchison Falls National Park boundary and UWA fees apply. To get there, you would have already passed through the park's Kichumbanyobo Gate and paid entry fees; remember UWA fees are per 24 hours so it's not unfeasible to continue on to Paraa after visiting Kaniyo-Pabidi is you want to overnight there. Busingiro isn't within the park and you only need to pay for a guide for walks. It is perhaps the option of seeing the chimpanzees that will ultimately sway the decision.

Budongo Forest Reserve → *Colour map 1, C2.*

The 825-sq-km reserve of grassland and forest near Lake Albert – with 482 sq km of the reserve semi-deciduous, tropical forest – is the largest area of unexploited mahogany forest in East Africa, and the huge trees grow up to 60 m high. The habitat consists of primary forest with medium understory vegetation density allowing for good visibility of the canopy (and thus of the chimpanzees). The presence of savannah and grassland areas neighbouring the primary forest present an interesting opportunity for viewing different ecosystems. The reserve has exceptional biodiversity with 24 species of small mammal, nine being primates; 465 species of tree and shrub; 359 species of bird; 289 species of butterfly; and 130 species of moth. As in all rainforests, conditions are often very wet, so suitable clothing is needed.

Background Budongo Forest Reserve was gazetted in 1932. However, commercial extraction of timber was ongoing from 1915 until the mid-1990s and there are estimates that about 75% of this forest has been cut down at least once. Researcher Vernon Reynolds first studied chimpanzees in this forest in 1962, writing a book about the forest and its chimpanzees in 1965. He is considered one of a trio of pioneer field researchers into chimpanzees in East Africa at the time (the others being Jane Goodall and Adriaan Kortlandt). During the bleak 1970s and 1980s of unrest and civil war, and the accompanying breakdown of law and order, chimpanzee mothers were shot and the infants taken from the forest and smuggled to collectors in Asia, Europe and America. Reynolds returned to Uganda in 1990 to determine whether a viable population of chimpanzees still existed in Budongo. The research team renovated and occupied buildings that had been constructed for the Budongo Sawmills Ltd, and had been abandoned during the regime of Amin. In 1991, the **Budongo Forest Project** became a Ugandan NGO and today is known as the **Budongo Conservation Field Station** (www.budongo.org). By 1995 some 50 chimpanzees had been identified, and this figure remained constant until 2000 when the numbers started rising; fantastically, the number of chimpanzees today is put at around 800.

In 2006, the **Jane Goodall Institute** (JGI) entered into an agreement with the **National Forestry Authority** (NFA), to take over the management and infrastructure of the actual forest. The objective of this was that the JGI could establish appropriate development of chimpanzee tracking and tourism, while ensuring that the chimpanzee communities were not put at risk as a result of these activities. At the same time, all profits made from the venture were to be returned back into the protection of Budongo through monitoring, conservation education and community collaborative projects. Since then the JGI has improved the NFA's **Kaniyo-Pabidi Eco-Tourism Site** (now known as the **Budongo Eco Lodge**) – the visitor centre, accommodation, campsite and walking trails.

Kaniyo-Pabidii

① *UWA entry US$40, children (5-15) US$20 per 24 hrs. Activities commence from Budongo Eco Lodge which is managed by Great Lakes Safaris (see Where to stay, page 230, for contacts) and pre-booking for activities is advised. Chimpanzee tracking 0730 and 1330, US$60; low-season rates (1 Mar-15 Jun, 1 Oct-15 Dec) US$50, no under 12s. Forest and bird walks, 1½/4 hrs, US$15/20, full-day bird walks US$30. Kaniyo-Pabidi is 29 km north of Masindi on the road to Paraa. There's no public transport, but you can hire a special hire taxi or boda boda in Masindi.*

Budongo Eco Lodge, also known by its old name of Kaniyo-Pabidi Eco-Tourism Site, is the centre of activities in this section of the Budongo Forest Reserve. There's accommodation (page 230), a visitor centre with a small museum exhibiting a display of fossils, animal skeletons and snares that have been removed from the forest, a craft shop with a small selection of locally made crafts and a restaurant. More than 100 km of walking trails radiate from the lodge. The twice-daily chimpanzee excursions usually last two to four hours, and six people are permitted on each walk. Once they are found (never 100% guaranteed), one hour is permitted to watch them. On the walk, the guides will point out other wildlife in the forest that may be seen, including black-and-white colobus and blue monkey and olive baboon, as well as some of the giant mahogany trees.

In addition to the chimpanzee tracking, chimpanzee habituation sessions lasting five to 10 hours accompanying the field researchers are available for up to two adults per day (not July-September); US$150 per person. Habituation of chimpanzees is a slow process. Researchers follow the chimps every day and stay at a distance of 10 m, getting them used to the presence of humans. It's a good opportunity to study their behaviour over more than the hour permitted on the tracking excursion.

Other forest and bird walks are available from 1½ to four hours. The four-hour Pabidi Hill walk is best done mid-morning, taking a packed lunch to eat on top of the hill, which has great views over Murchison Falls National Park, Lake Albert and the mountains in the DRC. It's also a unique opportunity to go through tropical rainforests and savannah in the same walk, and as there are lions in the area, an armed guide goes with you.

Busingiro → *Colour map 1, C2.*

ⓘ *42 km from Masindi on the road west to Butiaba. Matatus to Butiaba will drop off, 1 hr, US$3, or take a private hire taxi or boda-boda from Masindi. US$15 for a 3-hr guided forest and bird walk.*

This is the other NFA ecotourism site within the Budongo Forest Reserve, with a visitor centre that offers information and organizes guides, and an education centre for schools. It's outside the Murchison Falls Protected Area so is cheaper to visit than Kaniyo-Pabidi and you only have to pay for a guide. They are very knowledgeable, particularly with regards to bird calls, and they carry binoculars and a field guide. Chimpanzee tracking in Busingiro was discontinued a few years ago because after habituation the chimps lost their fear of humans and started raiding nearby crops. They remain in the forest but are rarely spotted. Other primates are black-and-white colobus, vervet, red-tailed and blue monkey, potto, and olive baboon, along with giant forest squirrels and the bizarre chequered elephant shrew. Birdlife is excellent with 366 species recorded, and the paths are clouded by butterflies. The Royal Mile, so called because it was a favourite location of Bunyoro King Kabalega, is a wide avenue of trees between the Nyabyere Forestry College and the Research Station, with abundant birds. This is Uganda's best forest birding site and contains a number of endemic species, including the sought-after African dwarf, blue-breasted and chocolate-backed kingfishers. It's 15 km away from the Busingiro centre and is only accessible with private transport and you need to pick up a guide first. Currently, there is no accommodation in Busingiro but you are permitted to camp if self-sufficient. An upgrade of the former *banda* camp is expected.

⦿ Kampala to Murchison Falls National Park listings

For hotel and restaurant price codes and other relevant information, see pages 16-20.

⦿ Where to stay

Ziwa Rhino and Wildlife Ranch *p222*
$$$$ Amuka Lodge, T0771-600812, www.amukalodgeuganda.com. A fairly new luxury lodge that is nicely built using mahogany columns, beams and flooring recovered from a now-redundant sawmill. 12 chalets, 2 for families, set well apart and linked by pathways through the bush, sun deck and swimming pool, restaurant with open barbecue kitchen. Nocturnal animals that have been known to visit the lodge include genet cat and porcupine. 10% of profits go to **Rhino Fund Uganda**.
$$-$ Ziwa Guesthouse, T0775-521035, www.ziwarhino.com. Accommodation offered by the ranch is set in a grassy clearing where bushbuck and crowned cranes can often be seen walking around. The guesthouse has pleasant 1- and 2-bed en suite rooms (US$40 per person), or basic backpacker rooms with shared hot showers (US$15 per person), camping with their tents (US$15 per person), or camping your your own tent (US$10 per person), plus a restaurant that can organize packed lunches.

Masindi *p223*
$$-$ Masindi Hotel, 22-34 Butiaba Rd, 1 km out of town past the police post on the road to Hoima, T0772-420130 www.masindihotel.com. After Independence, the hotel was part of the **Uganda Hotels** chain for nearly 30 years. But it was privatized in 2000 and has been well refurbished since then, retaining its colonial charm. 28 pleasant, spacious rooms leading off broad verandas, plus there's 1 self-catering cottage, a dorm room and a campsite in the grounds. Quiet library, the **Kabalega Restaurant** serves good food, including Indian dishes, and the

Hemingway Bar has a lovely courtyard to sit in as the formidable man himself once did.
$ Kopling Guesthouse, 500 m north of the Caltex petrol station on the main road, T0782-394992, www.kolpingguesthouses-africa.com. Quiet, clean church-run guesthouse with 4 en suite rooms and 2 rooms sharing a bathroom, with a small restaurant and bar (serving beer) and large spacious lawned grounds where you can negotiate to camp. Doubles/twins from US18.
$ New Court View Hotel, 200 m from Masindi post office, T0465-420461, Nyanga Rd, www.newcourtviewhotel.com. Set in the garden are 15 small, round, comfortable and very clean cottages, the restaurant serves excellent food, including some surprisingly leafy salads, and can provide packed lunches if you're on the way to the park. The gift shop sells a range of locally produced crafts. You can negotiate to camp here.

Hoima *p224*
$ Crown Hotel Hoima, 54-58 Mandela Rd, T0465-442741, www.crownhotelhoima.com. Predominantly a local conference venue with 22 tiled rooms with DSTV and reliable hot water, and worth mentioning because of its large swimming pool set in neat gardens with thatched bar and restaurant alongside. Day visitors are welcome for a meal and a swim.
$ Kon Tiki Hotel, 2 km out of town on the Kampala road, T0772-775005, www.hoimakontiki.com. A great-value and surprising find for backwater Hoima with 25 rooms set in thatched cottages among palm trees, each with veranda, doubles/twins from US$50, extra bed US$10, camping US$10 per person. Good food, including pizza and Indian, bar, also has stables for horseriding, can organize village walks and trips to Mparo Tombs, and provides a birdlist for a walk around the hotel's garden; 50 species have been recorded.

$ Kopling Guesthouse, Butiaba Rd, T0782-394992, www.koplingguesthouses-africa.com. This is an almost identical church-run guesthouse to the one in Masindi. Again clean, pleasant, in nice gardens and a restaurant serving local and international dishes. The **Kopling Society** (named after a 19th-century German Catholic priest) also has guesthouses in Kenya, Tanzania and Nigeria.

Kabwoya Wildlife Reserve *p225*
$$$ Lake Albert Safari Lodge, T0772-221003, www.lakealbert.com. Set on cliffs that overlook Lake Albert with wonderful views westwards of the mountains in the DRC. 12 thatched cottages, good food and a well-stocked bar, the small pool is shared by guests and the occasional wildlife. You can also camp here for US$20-60 per person depending on how many meals you want provided. Horseriding, day and night game drives, fishing, village visits and nature walks cost US$10-30 per activity.

Kaniyo-Pabidii *p227*
$$-$ Budongo Eco Lodge, at Kaniyo-Pabidi in the Budongo Forest Reserve, reservations through **Great Lakes Safaris**, T0414-267153, www.safari-uganda.com. Hidden in the forest are 5 attractive en suite solar-powered cabins sleeping 1-3, plus 4 spacious 4-bed dorms with shared bathrooms. Rates include either breakfast or half board and the restaurant has a lovely terrace facing the forest. Pre-booking is also advised for chimpanzee tracking as numbers are limited; there's a US$5 surcharge if you pay on site.

🍴 Restaurants

Kampala to Masindi *p222*
$$-$ Kabalega Diner, Kafu Bridge, on the Kampala–Gulu Highway, T0414-691910, www.kabalegadiner.com. Daily 0700-1900. Probably the nearest thing to a motorway service station to be found in Uganda,

this lies 165 km from Kampala, 165 km to Gulu, and about 4 km before the turn-off to Masindi. It's the brainchild of 2 friends; formerly a safari guide and a camping safari chef. There's a long menu from French toast and Spanish omelette for breakfast, or light meals like soups, sandwiches and salads, to tilapia fish and chips, chicken curry and spaghetti bolognaise. Drinks include great coffee, beer and wine.

Masindi *p223*
It's another 2-hr drive (88 km) to Paraa in Murchison Falls National Park, so Masindi is a popular spot for refreshments on the journey from Kampala. In addition to the hotels, which all offer food, consider:
$ Traveller's Corner, on the main road next to the post office, T0772-799969. Daily 0900-2100. Popular with expats and tour groups on their way to the park, and owned by the **New Court View Hotel**. Attractive wooden veranda, bar with pool table and cosy restaurant decorated with murals painted by local school children. Good food, including sandwiches, burgers, fish or chicken and chips/rice; most meals won't take more than 20 mins to prepare, and the friendly, helpful staff can advise about the park.

🛍 Shopping

Masindi *p223*
There are 2 small supermarkets, **Lucky 7** and **Wat General Agencies**, on Commercial St, which offer a few basics. Fresh fruit and vegetables are available in Masindi market.

⏰ What to do

Masindi *p223*
Tour operators
Local agents who can arrange excursions into Murchison Falls National Park are:
Yebo Tours, office next to Barclays Bank on Masindi Port Rd in the middle of town, T0772-637493, yebotours2002@yahoo.

com; **Masindi Hotel** and **New Court View Hotel** (see Where to stay, page 229); and **Traveller's Corner** (see Restaurants, page 230). Each can organize a driver and 4WD vehicle for about US$80 and a minibus for around US$100 (excluding fuel) for a day trip to Murchison Falls, expect to depart from Masindi at about 0500; make all arrangements the day before. You'll have to pay UWA park fees for the vehicle and driver but these are considerably less than foreign visitor fees – US$6 for the driver/ guide, and US$12 for the vehicle. **Yebo Tours** has tents, so it's possible to organize a 24-hr trip with a night in a campsite just outside of the park.

⊖ Transport

Masindi *p223*
The bus and taxi park is in the middle of town on Masindi Port Rd on the opposite side to Barclays Bank. There are frequent buses and *matatus* to and from **Kampala** (4 hrs, US$5-7). The **Post Bus** stops in Masindi on the Kampala–Hoima route (see Essentials, page 14). Frequent *matatus* travel to **Hoima** along a murram road (1 hr, US$2).

Hoima *p224*
The bus and taxi parks are to the southwest of the market. There are frequent buses and *matatus* to and from Kampala (3 hrs, US$4-6), or you can come and go via Masindi using the Kampala–Gulu Highway, which adds another hour on to the journey and you'll have to swap vehicles in Masindi. Hoima is the end of the Kampala–Hoima **Post Bus** route via Masindi; it departs again for Kampala from the post office at 0630 (5 hrs, US$7). Regular *matatus* go to Masindi US$2. You could get to Fort Portal by *matatu*, but it would probably take all day as, while there are *matatus*, they link the villages along the way and it's a rough road.

Murchison Falls National Park

The Murchison Falls National Park is the largest national park in Uganda, covering an area of nearly 4000 sq km. The even larger Murchison Falls Protected Area (MFPA), which includes the adjoining Karuma and Bugungu wildlife reserves, is 5072 sq km. With spectacular scenery covering hills, rainforest and savannah in the northwest of the country, it offers game viewing safaris by vehicle and river and fishing. The park is cut in half by the River Nile where it has to squeeze itself through the famous Murchison Falls, an impossibly narrow 7-m gap in a cleft of rock creating a powerful explosion of whitewater into the deservedly named 'Devil's Cauldron' 50 m below. The mighty cascade drains the last of the river's energy, transforming it into a broad, placid stream that flows quietly across the Rift Valley floor into Lake Albert.

The best way to see the falls is from the river – a three-hour boat trip departs from park headquarters at Paraa going upstream to the foot of the falls. Some of Africa's largest crocodiles are found at the base – up to 4.5 m in length – thanks to an ever-available menu of Nile perch. The game viewing from the river is superb and the boat is steered from shore to shore through hippo pods and past sandbanks where these huge and contented crocodiles bask in the sun. Nile perch and tigerfish provide an exciting challenge to anglers, and fishing is available above and below the falls.

There is much more to the park than a frothing river, although game numbers are much lower than in other East African parks, and wildlife numbers suffered terribly in this region during Uganda's conflict years. But animal numbers have recovered significantly, and the park's palm-dotted hills to the north of the river offer rewarding game drives in search of Uganda kob, oribi, hartebeest, giraffe, lion, elephant and buffalo. ➤➤ For listings, see pages 237-238.

Arriving in Murchison Falls National Park

Getting there

By air Pakuba airstrip is 19 km from the north side of the Nile at Paraa, and there's another airstrip at Bugungu just to the south of Paraa on the south side of the Nile. **Aerolink** ① *T0317-333000, www.aerolinkuganda.com, see also Essentials, page 13*, run return scheduled flights Monday-Friday between Entebbe International Airport and Murchison Falls. They operate the flight on demand, usually with a minimum of four passengers, and can also arrange charter flights. The lodges in the park will pick up from the airstrips, or a tour operator will organize flights and transfers into a Murchison Falls fly-in package.

By road From Kampala it is 300 km and takes about four to five hours (two to three hours on tarmac and two hours on murram road) to Paraa in the park, via Masindi. There are two approaches from Masindi; one is 88 km through Kichumbanyobo Gate (passing Kaniyo-Pabidi on the way), and the other is 137 km via Bugungu Gate; see page 226 for detailed descriptions of both. **Paraa**, meaning 'home of the hippo' in the local Luo language, is the park's tourism hub. All the park's access roads converge here as the northern and southern banks of the river are linked by a passenger and vehicle ferry, which runs at roughly hourly intervals throughout the day (0700-1900). Several of the accommodation options are located nearby. Additionally, a UWA visitor centre with a small museum and gift shop can be found on the north bank, and most game drives, launch trips and nature walks commence from here. **Note**: you need to be at Paraa before 1900 as driving in the park is not permitted after dark, so plan your route accordingly.

There is no direct public transport into Murchison, although you can travel by public transport to Masindi and from there arrange a trip with one of the tour operators (see page 230).

The park can also be entered via the Chobe, Wankwar and Tangi gates north of the Nile. These are reached from the Kampala–Gulu Highway which crosses the Nile at Karuma Falls Bridge in the northeastern corner of the park. If coming from Kampala, instead of going to Masindi you stay on the Kampala–Gulu Highway for another 115 km after the junction at Kafu Bridge. The highway travels parallel with the eastern boundary of the park, to the Karuma Falls Bridge, 260 km from Kampala. Just north of the bridge is the turn-off to the Chobe Gate of the Murchison Falls National Park and then this road continues to Pakwach, past the Wankwar and Tangi gates to the park. In Pakwach it again

Murchison Falls National Park

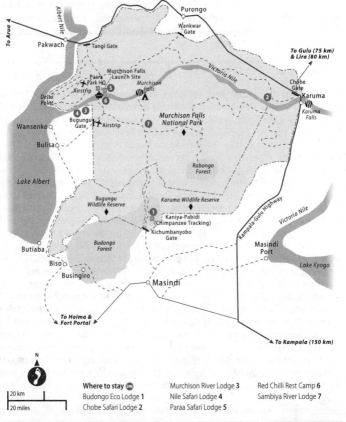

Where to stay 🛏
Budongo Eco Lodge 1
Chobe Safari Lodge 2
Murchison River Lodge 3
Nile Safari Lodge 4
Paraa Safari Lodge 5
Red Chilli Rest Camp 6
Sambiya River Lodge 7

crosses the river, and goes on to Arua and, eventually, the DRC. Back on the Kampala–Gulu Highway, beyond the Karuma Falls Bridge, it's another 75 km to Gulu, and yet another turn-off takes you to Lira, 80 km from the bridge.

Park information

Uganda Wildlife Authority (UWA) ① *Park headquarters T0392-881348, www. ugandawildlife.org. Gate hours 0630-1930. Entry fees per 24 hours, US$40, children (5-15) US$20, foreign-registered vehicles: saloon car US$50, 4WD US$150, Uganda-registered vehicles: saloon car US$8, 4WD US$12.*

Best time to visit

The park can be visited at any time and temperatures all year round average 25-32°C, which makes this one of the hotter regions of Uganda. Nights are a little cooler and drop to 18°C. December to late February and from June to September are the driest times when most animals remain near water. The best time for birdwatching is January to March, which tends to have plenty of bird activity with fewer tourists, but be prepared for afternoon thunderstorms. Inside the park the tracks are fairly well maintained, but in the rainy seasons from October to December and March to May a 4WD may be necessary as a lot of the park's tracks can be muddy.

Background

In 1907 during the colonial years, Winston Churchill strolled the 88 km from Masindi just to see the Paraa area. Already it was famed as having spectacular numbers of wild animals around the impressive Murchison Falls. Explorer Samuel Baker had named the falls after Sir Roderick Murchison, president of the **Royal Geographical Society**, after he 'discovered' them in 1863. On reaching the falls at Paraa, so captivated was he by their beauty, he wrote: "The fall of water was snow-white, which had a superb effect and contrasted with the dark cliffs that walled the river, while the graceful palms of the tropics and the wild plantains perfected the view. This was the greatest waterfall of the Nile, and in honor of the President of the Royal Geographical Society, I named it the Murchison Falls, as the most important object throughout the entire course of the river."

The park was first gazetted as a game reserve in 1926, and then designated as a national park in 1952, at a time when wildlife was plentiful. For a while in the 1960s Murchison Falls was considered to be the most visited park in Africa, and some 60,000 safari-goers went every year. The big attraction was its exceptionally large herds of elephant, some 500-stong, and the park's population was put at over 14,000. Unfortunately the wildlife was dramatically reduced by the decades of civil unrest in Uganda. The park was temporarily renamed Kabalega Falls National Park by Amin's regime in 1973, in honor of the king of Bunyoro who fought Samuel Baker in 1870s. It is during the late 1970s and early 1980s when the conflicts were particularly devastating in the northwest of the country, that the elephant population was reduced to fewer than 200 individuals and the rhino became extinct. It was said that wayward soldiers used animals as target practice. Things changed in the early 1990s as the region became secure again and wildlife populations have steadily increased since then. Numbers of some species such as buffalo and lion have at least doubled in the last two decades, and elephants today are thought to number about 1200.

Apart from Churchill, other notable visitors include Theodore Roosevelt, Ernest Hemingway (see box, above) and several British royals, and much of the 1951 movie *The*

Hemingway at Murchison

Ernest Hemingway made a couple of visits to Africa. The first was in 1933, when Hemingway, then 34, and his second wife Pauline spent a couple of months hunting and fishing in Tanzania. It was another 20 years before Hemingway would visit Africa again, and this was to be an altogether more eventful trip. By now he was with his fourth wife, Mary. In 1953 they stayed on the Percival farm in Kenya (Percival was one of the foremost white hunters), and went on safari, where Ernest shot a big, black-maned lion, zebra and gerenuk.

Ernest began getting into the spirit of Africa with some gusto. He shaved his head, dyed his suede jacket and two shirts with Masai red ochre and went leopard hunting with a spear. He took a liking to an Akamba girl, Debba, and brought her and some friends back to the camp where the celebrations became so enthusiastic that they broke one of the beds. Some months later Ernest observed that he should now be a father in Africa.

In 1954 Ernest and Mary flew from Nairobi, piloted by Roy Marsh. They stopped at Fig Tree camp then headed for Mwanza in Tanzania where they refuelled, before staying over at Costermanville (now Bukavu) in the DRC. As they circled the glassy waters, dotted with islands and hemmed in by green hills, Mary thought Kivu was the most beautiful lake she had ever seen. They then put down in Uganda at Entebbe. The following day, circling Murchison Falls, the plane hit a telegraph wire and plunged onto the crocodile-infested shores of the Nile not far from the Murchison Falls. The three lit a fire and slept under coats. Next day a boat visiting the falls gave them a lift to Butiaba. They engaged a plane and a pilot to fly them from Butiaba airstrip to Entebbe, but taking off from the bumpy runway, the plane suddenly stopped, and burst into flames. Roy Marsh kicked out a window and managed to drag Mary through. Ernest butted the jammed door open and struggled out. Though alive, he was in poor shape with concussion, ruptured liver, spleen and kidney, a crushed vertebra and burns. A policeman drove them to Masindi, and they stayed at the Masindi Hotel before reaching Entebbe and Lake Victoria Hotel. A few days later they flew to Nairobi.

In the meantime, a civilian airliner had reported the plane wreck; the world thought Hemingway had died and newspapers published obituaries. When Hemingway finally arrived in Entebbe by car, the *New York Times* was part of the media scrum who were there to meet him, and filed this report: "He was carrying a bunch of bananas and a bottle of gin... He joshed his wife, saying her snoring had attracted elephants as they camped overnight near the wreckage of the first plane that crash-landed Saturday near Murchison Falls on the upper Nile near Lake Albert. 'We held our breath about two hours while an elephant twelve paces away was silhouetted in the moonlight, listening to my wife's snores,'" Mr Hemingway roared...". In 1956 there were plans to make a third trip to Africa, but poor health meant that it never materialized. Hemingway's experiences on safari provided the material for many short stories, a fine collection of which are in *The Green Hills of Africa*.

African Queen starring Humphrey Bogart and Katherine Hepburn was filmed on Lake Albert and the Nile in Murchison Falls National Park (see box, page 101).

Flora and fauna

The park is worth visiting as much for the variation in its scenery as for its wildlife, although mammal numbers have greatly increased over the past two decades. The south of the park borders the Budongo Forest and is green and lush, while the further north you travel, the drier, hotter and more savannah-like it becomes. Some parts are quite extraordinary, with long, wide alleys of date palm trees and other exotics stretching from left to right to the horizon. These were planted centuries ago by Arab slave traders to mark their route in and out of inland black Africa.

The park is home to 76 species of mammal, including Ugandan kob and numerous other species of antelope, buffalo, hippo, baboon, crocodile, lion, leopard and elephant. It is also one of the few places in Uganda where you can see giraffe, and the savannah-dwelling patas monkey is only found here and in Kidepo Valley National Park. Of the 451 species of bird, the stars of Murchison's show are the shoebill stork (see box, page 72), the goliath heron – the largest heron in the world – and pairs of elegant grey-crowned cranes, Uganda's national bird.

Game viewing

For the best game viewing you have to go to the north of the park; there are very few animals on the south bank apart from small herds of Ugandan kob. If you are south of the river, getting to the north bank necessitates crossing the river by **ferry** ① *0700, 0900, 1100, 1200, 1400, 1600 and 1800; vehicles US$8.50, drivers and passengers US$2.* Early mornings are unquestionably the best time to see and photograph animals. The Nile valley is one of the hottest places in Uganda and animals tend to look for shade and rest towards 1100. It is always advisable to take food and water with you on a game drive. There is the option of taking a UWA guide with you in your own vehicle, US$20, which can be arranged at park headquarters north of the ferry.

The best route for viewing animals is the **Buligi Circuit**, which includes the Buligi, Victoria Nile, Queens and Albert Nile tracks. Depending on the time available, there are numerous ways to explore this area. It is recommended that at least four to five hours are set aside for a thorough safari; expect to cover 120-170 km.

Launch trip

① *UWA 3-hr launch trips run from Paraa at 0900 and 1400, US$30, children (5-15) US$15. The double-decker boat takes 40 and at least 10 people are needed, but this is never really an issue. The Paraa Safari Lodge (book at reception, page 237) and Wild Frontiers (see page 238) also have boats for the trip.*

This trip is thoroughly recommended and you are guaranteed to see hippos, with reportedly 4000 in this stretch of the river, and some huge Nile crocodiles. There is a good chance of viewing elephant, red-tailed and black-and-white colobus monkey, as well as some magnificent birdlife at close quarters. Other game found along the river bank includes buffalo, giraffe and a range of antelope, all of which you will notice keep a wary eye out for crocs as they come down to drink.

You will hear the falls before you see them, as the thunderous roar begins well before the boat rounds the bend and the falls come into view. The waters violently compress through the narrow gorge, spraying mist and creating a permanent rainbow. It is a breathtaking natural spectacle, the most powerful rush of water anywhere in the world.

It is possible to stop at the base of the falls from one of the boats to walk up the steep footpath to the top. Alternatively, the drive from Paraa to the Baker Point viewpoint on the southern side takes about 45 minutes and is roughly 30 km. A visit here should form an integral part of any trip to the park. There is a small campsite and ranger post at the falls, the starting point for a short walk downhill to the water's edge. Here it is possible to get within a few metres of the fenced-off falls, but care is required as the surrounding area can be slippery underfoot. The narrow gap and the volume of water that rages through it, vibrating the ancient rocks, can only truly be appreciated from this vantage point. You can also view the Nile splitting into the smaller Uhuru Falls, created in 1962 when the river burst its banks. Try to be here at sunset, when hundreds of bats fly over the falls chased by birds of prey. You can also stop off at the north bank during a game drive, and walk down a set of steps to stand within meters of the rapids above the falls, but you can't see the actual falls from here.

◉ Murchison Falls National Park listings

For hotel and restaurant price codes and other relevant information, see pages 16-20.

◉ Where to stay

$$$$-$$$ Chobe Safari Lodge, on the north bank of the Nile 14 km west of Chobe Gate in the east of the park, reached via the Karuma Falls Bridge route (page 233), reservations Kampala T0312-259390, www.chobelodgeuganda.com. The original lodge was destroyed during the 1970s conflict when it was a rebel base. It reopened in 2010 and is now part of the **Marasa** stable along with **Paraa Safari Lodge** (below) and **Mweya Safari Lodge** in the QENP (page 185). Accommodation is in 36 luxury rooms, 9 with a/c and Nile-facing balconies or terraces, 21 safari tents, 4 suites, and a presidential cottage. The unique 3-tiered swimming pool sits right on the Nile, and there's superb restaurant, bars, gym and spa.

$$$$-$$$ Paraa Safari Lodge, at Paraa on the north river bank, facing the launch jetty, reservations Kampala T0312-259390, www. paraalodge.com. This was built in 1953 and Queen Elizabeth, the Queen Mother, stayed here in 1959 in the **Queen's Cottage**. It was then gutted by rebels during the armed conflicts but reopened in 1997 and is now run by **Marasa**. There is a colonial theme

with lots of pictures of the early explorers and other memorabilia, and 54 rooms, 2 with disabled facilities, 2 suites, each with a balcony and a splendid view over the Nile. Top-notch facilities include a large pool with bar, restaurant, and gift shop, and has its own boat for excursions. Wildlife is frequently seen around the lodge.

$$$ Nile Safari Lodge, on the south bank of the Nile outside the park boundary near the Bugungu Gate, reservations Kampala, T0414-258273, www.geolodgesafrica.com. Not ideal for early morning game drives on the north bank of the river but is in one of the best locations for birdwatching and seeing elephant coming to drink. 10 rooms in safari tents or chalets with balconies on wooden stilt frames, the restaurant offers a varied menu, and the swimming pool also has Nile views. If you approach via the Bulisa route from Masindi (page 226) you don't need to pay park fees.

$$$-$ Murchison River Lodge, on the south bank of the Nile outside the park boundary near the Bugungu Gate, reservations Kampala T0714-000085, www. murchisonriverlodge.com. Opened in 2010, and an informal family-run option, this is near **Nile Safari Lodge** and again if you approach via the Bulisa route from Masindi (page 226) you don't need to pay park fees. Accommodation is in 4 comfortable en suite thatched double-storey cottages each sleeping up to 4, or cheaper safari tents with chemical toilets and bush showers. There's also 'lazy camping' in dome tents with proper beds, and a campsite for own tents, both sharing an ablution block. There's an open-sided thatched restaurant and bar with river views, pool and craft shop.

$$$-$ Sambiya River Lodge, on the south bank, only 20 mins' drive from the top of the falls, about 40 km north of Kichumbanyobo Gate, reservations Kampala T0414-233596, www.sambiya riverlodge.com. This open-fronted lodge with a pool has 20 thatched cottages with veranda, some have 2 bedrooms for families or friends making it quite economical, and there are also 10 small budget *bandas* with shared bathrooms. Quiet and relaxing atmosphere with an attractive bar and good homely cooking. The surrounding savannah plain and riverine forest is ideal for birdwatching and fishing in the Sambiya River, which is a tributary of the Nile.

$ Red Chilli Rest Camp, Paraa, south of the river and 500 m from the ferry, reservations Kampala T0312-202903, T0772-509150, www.redchillihideaway.com. Run by Red Chilli Hideaway in Kampala (page 56), with twin/double/family *bandas* with or without bathrooms (US$25-70), plus 12 large twin safari tents (US$20), and a campsite (US$5 per person). Good shared showers with solar power for hot water, though rarely needed in Murchison as its hot most of the time, pleasant thatched restaurant and bar, good set dinners with 3 choices, packed lunches organized, plenty of game around including hippo coming up from the river at night. Pre-book

at **Red Chilli** in Kampala, or go on one of their bargain 3-day safaris from Kampala; from US$320, US$380 with a visit to Ziwa, including park entry fees.

Camping

There is a basic **UWA** campsite at the top of Murchison Falls, about 30 km or 45 mins from Paraa; a 4WD is needed for the hill. It's a pretty spot but apart from pit latrines and a simple thatched shelter there are no facilities so bring everything with you and book and pay at park HQ in Paraa. US$8 per person. You can also camp at **Red Chilli**.

☉ What to do

Wild Frontiers (aka G&C Tours), T0773-897275, www.wildfrontiers.co.ug, offers the launch trip from Paraa to see the falls daily at 0830 and 1430 for US$32 on their 35- or 14-seater boats. Also runs a 20 km, 4-hr cruise downstream into the Lake Albert Delta in the opposite direction of the falls, Tue/Thu/Sat/Sun at 0700, US$55 including breakfast on board. This is excellent for birdwatching and the shoebill and other papyrus species may be spotted. Can also organize sport fishing for the mighty Nile perch; catfish and tigerfish are also found in the river. Fishing can be done from the shore or from boats, and rates start at US$110 for half a day, depending on arrangements and numbers, excluding UWA fishing licenses which are US$50 for one day and US$150 for 4 days. **Marasa**, operators of the **Paraa Safari Lodge** (page 237) and **Chobe Safari Lodge** (page 237) can also organize similar fishing excursions from their lodges.

Kidepo Valley National Park and the northwest

For decades, the populations in northern Uganda suffered terrible loss of life and livelihoods through armed conflict and widespread insecurity. From the mid-1980s to when peace was brokered with the Lord's Resistance Army (LRA) in 2006, some 1.8 million people were displaced. But since peace has returned to the north, many towns like Lira, Gulu and Kitgum are burgeoning, and throughout the region much progress has been made in reconstructing schools, health centres, roads, and water and sanitation facilities. For visitors, the options of exploring the north have opened up; road travel is safe, public transport is plentiful, and the towns have decent amenities. Most importantly, the population of northern Uganda is energetic; the people are friendly and welcoming even though they struggle in conditions of extreme poverty to put the past behind them. Away from the towns, Kidepo Valley National Park is a particular draw for tourists; a beautiful wilderness that was all but abandoned during the crisis and now holds potential as one of the country's highlights for wildlife-watching. ▸▸ *For listings, see pages 244-246.*

North to Gulu → *For listings, see pages 244-246.*

The obvious access to the northern towns is along the tarmac Kampala–Gulu Highway. From Kafu Bridge, 176 km northwest of Kampala where there is the turn-off to Masindi, the highway veers northwards to Karuma (115 km) where it crosses the Nile on the Karuma Falls Bridge.

The small town of Karuma is dominated by truck stops and is currently going through a little insurgency thanks to construction workers on the Karuma Power Station, which is currently being built a few kilometres upstream. From the bridge over the river you can see the foamy Nile lined with steep tree-covered banks – the northern side lies within the Murchison Falls National Park boundary. The Karuma Falls themselves are a series of rapids below the bridge and it is from here that the Nile gathers momentum as it approaches its impossibly tight squeeze through the Murchison Falls.

Just north of the bridge is the turn-off to the Chobe Gate of the Murchison Falls National Park and then this road continues to Pakwach, past the Wankwar and Tangi gates to the park. In Pakwach it again crosses the river, and goes on to Arua and, eventually, the DRC. From the Karuma bridge it's another 75 km to Gulu, and yet another turn-off takes you to Lira, 80 km from the bridge.

This is also the recommended route from Kampala to the Kidepo Valley National Park in the extreme northeast of the country, simply because the roads are better and hence it's quicker. There is another route north from Mbale near Mount Elgon and the Kenya border that goes up the northeast side of the country via Soroti and Moroto (see page 111), and also cuts across to Lira and Gulu.

Lira → *Phone code: 0473. Colour map 1, B4.*

With a population of around 110,000, and situated in the middle of the northern region, Lira is 342 km from Kampala via the Kampala–Gulu Highway, and roughly 450 km from Kampala via Jinja, Mbale and Soroti, so how you get to Lira rather depends on where you're coming from. However, despite it being a pleasant enough place with tree-lined streets, there's little reason to go at all as it's a nondescript administrative centre. There is, in fact, no need to veer off the highway for the 80 km from Karuma if you are heading

The Lord's Resistance Army (LRA)

The LRA was initially formed to resist government suppression and Museveni's National Resistance Army (NRA), when it took over power in Uganda through military means in 1986. The LRA is a militant movement and perhaps one of the least understood rebel movements in the world, with an ideology, as far as it has one, which is difficult to define or understand. Described by some as a Fundamentalist Christian movement or a cult, the LRA claimed to want to establish a theocratic state based on the Ten Commandments and supposedly 'purify' the Acholi people (the predominant ethnic group in northern Uganda). Its leader, Joseph Kony, himself an Acholi from Gulu, proclaims to be a spokesman of God and a spirit medium. But in contrast to any wholesome Christian beliefs, over a period of 20 years the LRA led a series of attacks on civilians and committed widespread human rights violations, including murder, abduction, mutilation, child-sex slavery, and forcing children to participate as child soldiers.

From the mid-1990s, the LRA was strengthened by military support from the government of Sudan, which was retaliating against the Ugandan government for supporting rebels there in what would become South Sudan. With increased military arsenal, the LRA fought with vigour against the NRA army, which led to mass atrocities such as the killing or abduction of several hundred villagers in the north. In response, the Ugandan government created the so-called 'protected camps' from 1996. Hundreds of thousands of Acholi people were moved from the Gulu district into camps, ostensibly for their protection. This policy expanded to encompass the entire rural Acholi population of four districts, and over the next decade the LRA attacks and the government's counter-insurgency measures resulted in the displacement of nearly 95% of the Acholi population all over northern Uganda. By 2006, 1.8 million people lived in more than 200 internally displaced person (IDP) camps. These camps had some of the highest mortality rates in the world, and in 2005 an estimated 1000 people were dying weekly, chiefly from malaria and AIDS.

Finally, peace talks held in Juba in Sudan promised some relief to these people, and the Ugandan government and the LRA signed a truce on 26 August 2006. Under the terms of the agreement, the LRA forces had to leave Uganda. Since then, they have reportedly been active in South Sudan, the DRC, and (most recently in 2012) in the Central African Republic (CAR). Kony himself has remained elusive, despite being wanted for war crimes and crimes against humanity by the International Criminal Court in The Hague. In late 2013, he was reported to be in the CAR and in poor health.

In Uganda, the last of the camps were finally closed in 2009 and people gravitated back to their villages all over northern Uganda. Some of the camps were converted into makeshift villages; the huts that were once protected by military now form new farming communities. But the long civil war in northern Uganda has had devastating effects on the Acholi people and their traditional ways of life have largely been changed forever. There is still quite a prominent NGO presence in the region, especially as the aftermath of the conflict left many orphans and widows, and still today a substantial number of impoverished people rely on charities, as well as government handouts, for survival.

further north, though Lira serves as a useful stop if you are travelling between the northwest and northeast of Uganda.

Gulu and around → *For listings, see pages 244-246. Phone code: 0471. Colour map 1, B3.*

Gulu is 337 km north of Kampala and is the largest town in northern Uganda. Historically it is the heartland of the Acholi (also Acoli), a northern Uganda Luo Nilotic ethnic group, and the region is often commonly referred to as Acholiland. Originally from southern Sudan, the Acholi have lived in northern Uganda since the 13th century. The north was denied much development under the British colonial administration who viewed it as a marginal, agriculturalist and primitive region. Under the British, the Baganda people of the south were favored as colonial administrators and thus gained political power, while the Acholi people of the north were often employed as manual labour on cotton or sugar plantations, or recruited into the Ugandan military or to serve as police and prison guards. After Independence, the region continued to be marginalized economically and has suffered higher rates of poverty than other areas of the country. The livestock-raising Acholi from the north were also resented for dominating the army and police. The Acholi are known to the outside world mainly because of the long insurgency of the Lord's Resistance Army (LRA) led by Joseph Kony, an Acholi from Gulu (see box, opposite).

After peace returned, Gulu with its potholed streets and worn out colonial buildings got a new buzz; Indian traders who had fled came back to open businesses. More than a dozen banks have opened, hotels have flourished and, thanks to the new Kampala–Gulu Highway, which continues to the border with South Sudan, traffic has increased along with the services associated with a busy transport route for trucks.

Arriving in Gulu
Getting there Gulu is 337 km from Kampala and is accessible via Lira from the east and Masindi from the west. The road from Kampala via Karuma is sealed and in good condition and the journey can be done in four hours and there is plenty of public transport. The South Sudan border at Nimule is 120 km north of Gulu and 190 km southeast of Juba, the capital of South Sudan. However, travel there is currently ill advised because of renewed violence between factions since the country gained its Independence in 2011. ▶ *See Transport, page 246.*

Places in Gulu
Baker's Fort is located at Patiko, 32 km north of Gulu and is sometimes referred to as **Fort Patiko**. It was formerly used as a base by slave traders but was taken over by Sir Samuel Baker in 1872 when, as Governor of Equatoria Province, he drove the traders out and used it as a base from which to crush the slave trade. It was later occupied by Emin Pasha. The fort centres on a large *koppie* consisting of several separate rock outcrops and a number of massive boulders. Three mortared stone structures still stand on the central plateau and there are the remains of a defensive ditch below. You can get here by special hire taxi from Gulu, and although it's rarely visited, if you ask around the village a guide may materialize.

Kitgum → *Colour map 1, A4.*
Located 110 km northeast of Gulu and 435 km from Kampala, Kitgum is generally flat, savannah woodland, with the Lamwo and Agoro mountain ranges to the northeast.

There are gentle hills by the Aswa river valley. Kitgum gets few tourists, apart from those en route to Kidepo Valley National Park 140 km further northeast. It is little more than one street, with several small shops and basic restaurants, but has everything a traveller is likely to need.

Kidepo Valley National Park → *For listings, see pages 244-246. Colour map 1, A5.*

Gazetted as a national park in 1962, and covering an area of 1334 sq km, Kidepo is one of the most spectacular national parks in Uganda but, being the most isolated, it is also one of the hardest to visit. It lies in rugged, semi-arid valleys in the far northeast of the country on the South Sudan border and close to the Kenyan border. But the few who make the long journey north through the wild frontier region of Uganda would agree that it ranks among Africa's finest wildernesses. From Apoka, in the heart of the park, a savannah landscape extends far beyond the gazetted area, towards horizons outlined by distant mountain ranges. During the dry season, the only permanent water in the park is found in wetlands and remnant pools in the broad Narus Valley near Apoka. But these scarce and fragile water sources still manage to sustain 77 mammal species as well as around 475 birds, including large birds such as the ostrich and kori bustard.

Arriving in Kidepo Valley National Park

Getting there By air: Aerolink ① *T0317-333000, www.aerolinkuganda.com, also see Essentials, page 13,* run return scheduled flights Monday to Friday between Entebbe International Airport and the Apoka airstrip in Kidepo. They operate the flight on demand, usually with a minimum of four passengers, and can also arrange charter flights. The lodges will pick up from the airstrip, or you can arrange for the UWA to pick you up; contact them in advance.

By road: Driving here from Kampala is between 571 km (Kampala–Karuma–Gulu–Kitgum–Kidepo) and 792 km (Kampala–Mbale–Soroti–Moroto–Kotido–Kabong–Kidepo), depending on the route chosen. The Gulu route is the more obvious option and the drive to Kidepo from Kampala will take around 10 hours: Kampala–Gulu five hours (sealed road), Gulu–Kitgum two hours (reasonable murram road) and Kitgum–Kidepo three hours (poor murram road). The route to Kidepo from Soroti is along a rough murram road, particularly hair-raising during the rainy season (see page 111 for details of this route). Whichever direction you take, Kidepo itself is a vast and unspoiled wilderness and road conditions are poor and a 4WD is essential. Before embarking on the trip get up-to-date information from the **UWA in Kampala** ① *T0414-35 5000, www.ugandawildlife.org,* or the **Apoka Safari Lodge** (see page 244).

Park information

Uganda Wildlife Authority (UWA) ① *park HQ T0392-899500, www.ugandawildlife.org.* Gate hours 0630-1930. Entry fees per 24 hours, US$35, children (5-15) US$5, foreign-registered vehicles: saloon car US$50, 4WD US$150; Uganda-registered vehicles: saloon car US$8, 4WD US$12.

The **Apoka Tourism Centre**, overlooking the game-rich Narus Valley, is where **Apoka Safari Lodge** and the **UWA** camp are located and is the park's hub and UWA headquarters (see above). You can organize guides to go in your own vehicle (US$20) and game walks (US$30), and for those without their own transport (if you've flown in), park trucks can be hired (from US$30) if there are any available. There is a craft shop with books and souvenirs; bottled water, sodas and beers can also be purchased here. The park also has a small museum displaying pieces of skeletons as well as some insect specimens, plus photographs of some rangers involved in earlier efforts at conservation.

Visiting the park

Kidepo's altitude ranges from 1350 m to 2750 m. The **Napore Nangeya mountain range** is located to the west and the **Natera hills** to the east. In the distance to the north you will be able to see the peak of Mount Lotukei (2797 m) in South Sudan. The vegetation is typical savannah with some acacia woodland, home to many tsetse flies, with occasional stands of borassus palms. Sand rivers necessitate the use of 4WDs, especially in the east.

One problem that Kidepo suffers from more than the other national parks in Uganda is that of water shortages although the plants and animals of the area have adapted. Low rainfall and a long and severe dry season of almost six months are characteristic of this region as a whole. The effects of this are best appreciated between October and March when the national park is progressively baked, bleached and burnt by sun and often by fire. Every scrap of moisture, except that which manages to survive in a few waterholes and dams, turns to dust under the scorching breath of the tireless northeast wind. Unattractive as this may sound, it is in fact the best time to visit as it creates conditions that are good for game viewing. Animals are more tied to the available water sources, and there tends to be a concentration of animals around **Apoka** in the **Kidepo Valley** at the height of the dry season. The **Narus dam** and the water hole near the tourism centre are perfect observation points for game during this time. The animals leave Kidepo Valley, which dries out very rapidly once the rains have ceased, and head for the comparatively lush savannahs and woodlands of **Narus Valley,** where there is enough water to see them through until the rain falls again in March or April. Once the rains begin the animals drift back to the Kidepo Valley, and from April to October, when the grass is shorter, this is probably the best viewing area.

Game in Kidepo suffered badly during the period of turmoil and lawlessness, but recovery is well underway. The animals include lion, buffalo, elephant, zebra, leopard, giraffe, bushbaby, spotted hyena and black-backed and side-striped jackal, as well as a wide range of antelope including oribi, waterbuck and dik-dik. The greater and lesser kudu, eland and cheetah that inhabit Kidepo are found nowhere else in Uganda. Kidepo also has an extensive bird list of around 475 species, making it second only in Uganda to Queen Elizabeth National Park. Kidepo is notable for its birds of prey. Of the 56 species recorded, 14 – including Verreaux's eagle, Egyptian vulture and pygmy falcon – are believed to be endemic to the Kidepo and Karamoja region.

The **Kanangarok Hot Springs** that cross the Kidepo River are worth a visit. The Kidepo River is a 50-m wide sand river, which only flows visibly for a few days of the year. However, below the sand, at depths that vary from a few centimetres to a few metres, there is water; the depth depends on how far into the dry season it is. The animals of the park dig holes to reach the water. This also explains why on the banks of an apparently dry river the vegetation is oftengreener and lusher than elsewhere in the park. The name Kidepo in fact means 'to pick from below' in a local language.

Idi Amin had a lodge, the now-derelict **Grand Katurum Lodge**, built on the edge of a precipitous cliff in Kidepo Valley. Abandoned 30 years ago these ruins with magnificent views south into the valleys of Acholi have been designated by UWA as a potential site for redevelopment.

For hotel and restaurant price codes and other relevant information, see pages 16-20.

◉ Where to stay

Lira *p239*

$ Gracious Palace Hotel, 5A Akalo Rd, T0392-941392, www.graciouspalacehotel.com. Newish hotel with 31 neat tiled rooms with balconies and DSTV, good service and garden with secure car park. Free Wi-Fi in public areas and restaurant serves generous portions.

$ Lillian Towers Hotel, 14-18 Inomo Rd, T0774-19 2310. A fairly modern block with 25 basic rooms and tired decor, though some have a/c and there's a decent restaurant with pleasant outside dining area serving good breakfasts, local dishes, steak, pastas and pizzas. The small 10-m pool doesn't always have water in it.

$ Lira Hotel, 8-10 Erute Rd, T0473-420024, www.lirahotel.com. Surrounded by a grassy open space that once was the golf course (government officials stay here when visiting Lira), with 42 comfortable rooms and DSTV. Well-stocked bar though the choice in the restaurant is limited to local meals and the likes of chicken and chips. Recently refurbished so everything is quite fresh.

Gulu *p241*

$$ Bomah Hotel Gulu, 8 Eden Rd, next to the Gulu Referral Hospital, T0779-945063, bomahhotelltd@yahoo.com. Sited on the northern side of town where NGOs have their offices. Easily the best hotel in town with 60 a/c rooms in a 5-storey modern block (there's an elevator), with DSTV and mini-fridge. The hotel is set in pleasant gardens and has a comfortable bar and dining area. The menu is varied and reasonable but service can be slow. Sauna, massage, steam room and lovely pool that's popular with expats at the weekend for the poolside barbecues. A website might soon be up and running; in the meantime, book through **Gulu Tours** (page 246).

$ Acholi Ber Country Hotel, Market St, just below the market, T0372-280387, acholibercountryhotel@gmail.com. The best value in town for clean, basic B&B accommodation from US$20 a double. All rooms are self-contained and beds have nets. Restaurant has Italian and Indian food and it is centrally located and next to **Café Larem ($)**, which offers the best coffee in Gulu including cappuccino, as well as ice cream, and it sells some handicrafts.

$ Acholi Inn, 4-6 Elizabeth Rd, T0471-432880, acholiinn@yahoo.com. A reasonable option on the northern side of town with 60 rooms with a/c, DSTV and mini-fridge. Pleasant gardens, pool (US$3 for non-residents), sauna and gym. The decor is a little faded but service is good and there's free Wi-Fi in the lobby. The original parts date to 1936.

$ Hotel Pearl Afrique, Paul Odongo Rd, T0471-432055, www.hotelpearlafrique.com. Off Acholi Rd which leaves Kampala Rd between Caltex petrol station and Stanbic Bank. Modern brick block with 36 rooms with balconies and DSTV, reliable hot water, pleasant terrace restaurant/bar with Wi-Fi. Good management and popular with business travellers, currently expanding with another 60 rooms. About 5 mins' walk from the bus park.

Kitgum *p241*

$ Fugly's Hotel, T0754-500555. A basic hotel in well-maintained grounds with a small pool. Has 4 en suite rooms with hot water or a dorm house with 5 rooms (all with nets) and communal bathrooms. The restaurant and bar is open to non-residents too, serving good food in generous quantities. Note that Kitgum has problems with electricity. Also operates the Nga'Moru Wilderness Camp at Kidepo Valley National Park (below).

Kidepo Valley National Park *p242*

$$$$ Apoka Safari Lodge, reservations Kampala T0414-251182, www.wildplaces africa.com. Overlooking the Narus River valley this luxurious lodge has 10 large rooms built of wood, canvas and thatch, solar-heated power showers, verandas and outdoor bathtubs carved into the rockface. The thatched main lodge houses the restaurant and bar, and the swimming pool is set in a rocky outcrop. Apart from the manager and partner and the chef, all the staff are local Karimojong. The price is all inclusive of game drives and walks; breakfasts and dinners can be arranged in the bush.

$$$ Nga'Moru Wilderness Camp, T0785-551991, www.ngamoru.com. Just outside the park boundary and 4 km from the Katarum Gate (hence park entry fees do not apply for overnight stays). Located on a hill, there are amazing views across the Narus Valley and savannah plains with 3 double/twin safari thatched tents and 2 cabanas sleeping 4 with hot bush showers. The dining and bar area is a large mess tent and there are plans to build a permanent structure on the rocks. Wildlife frequently wanders through camp.

$ UWA Apoka Rest Camp, T0392-899500, 500 m from the lodge, park HQ T0392-899500, reservations Kampala T0414-355000, www.ugandawildlife.org. This modest UWA camp has 21 double *bandas*, en suite or with shared bathrooms (US$30/20) in what used to be UWA employees' accommodation. Self-catering and a gas cooker and utensils can be hired or pre-arranged meals can be ordered at reasonable prices. Aside from the friendly, though elusive staff, other camp residents include elephant who often cruise around the *bandas* checking out the new intake.

Camping
There's a UWA campsite at the **Apoka Rest Camp**, and another 2 at **Kakine** and **Nagusokopire**; both about 2 km from Apoka to the west and south respectively and in marvellous scenic locations in the Narus Valley. You need to pick up an armed ranger at the park HQ. Each site has a thatched shelter, pit latrine, firewood and tap; US$8 per person.

🍴 Restaurants

Lira *p239*
$ Sankofas, opposite mayor's garden on the top floor of a tall yellow building, T0772-712198. Daily 0900-2300. The hotels have adequate restaurants and there are plenty of cheap places to eat local food around town, but this place has a few treats and is worth seeking out. Restaurant and internet café serving burgers, pizza, cakes and biscuits, and delicious milkshakes and passion juice plus beers. Great relaxed environment with comfy chairs, good views from the balcony and a lovely breeze as it's on the top floor. DSTV and Wi-Fi and popular with NGOs and volunteers.

Gulu *p241*
Again the hotels are the best bet, or for lunch try the **TAKS Art Centre** (see Shopping, below).
$ Butterflies Bar and Restaurant, 1 Jinnah Rd, about 100 m east of Stanbic Bank on the Lira–Gulu road, T0784-227692. Daily 1100-2400. A lively modern spot with friendly Belgium owner, a small gravel garden and outside thatched bar and barbecue, Wi-Fi (though never guaranteed in this part of the world), serves coffees, stews and curries, fish and chips, and lighter meals like sandwiches and grilled meat and chicken kebabs.
$ Sankofas, 1 Samuel Doe Rd, T0776-712198. Daily 0800-2200. The sister branch to the one in Lira offering hamburgers, local dishes, cakes, breakfasts and snacks, such as samosas. Although they take a while, the pizzas are excellent, made with hard-to-find ingredients like anchovies and chorizo sausage. Wi-Fi and fat sofas to relax in. Down a side street to the east of the Gulu–Lira road, most *boda-boda* drivers know it.

Kidepo Valley National Park *p242*
The **UWA Rest Camp** can provide dishes of local food but you need to book in advance. Otherwise bring food and drink. **Apoka Safari Lodge** only serves its guests.

○ Shopping

Gulu *p241*

There are plenty of supermarkets around town to stock up on supplies. The best is the double-storey branch of **Uchumi**, Lima–Guru road near Centenary Bank, daily 0800-1800, which has a good selection of fresh fruit and vegetables, frozen meat, booze and a bakery. There are small supermarkets and a market in Kitgum, but with a limited choice.

TAKS Art Centre, 3-5 Upper Churchill Dr, behind **Acholi Inn**, www.takscentre. blogspot.com. 1000-1500. Sells a variety of handicrafts made by local groups, and doubles up as a lunchtime restaurant for cheap local dishes including some tasty stews and cold sodas and beers and an internet café. Outside tables are set under a giant mango tree. Produces weaving, tie and dye, embroidery, beads and ceramics and there are some unusual designs.

○ What to do

Gulu *p241*

Gulu Tours, 2-4 Lagara Rd, T0758-660020, www.gulutours.com. Day trips around Gulu including to Fort Baker and 3-day tours to Kidepo staying at **Apoka Safari Lodge** or the **UWA** accommodation, depending on budget. Expect to pay in the region of US$130 per day for a 4WD with driver depending on numbers and arrangements.

Kidepo Valley National Park *p242*

Buffalo Safari Camps, T0782-085639, www.buffalosafaricamps.com. Can arrange safaris to Kidepo either overland from Gulu, or will pick up from **Aerolink** flights at Kidepo. They use their own camping equipment for accommodation and vehicles for game drives. A 3-day/2-night road safari from Gulu starts from around US$250 per person, and a fly-in safari from US$850 per person depending on numbers. Meals and park entry is included. Can be combined with fly/drive safaris

to Murchison Falls, and can also arrange departures from Kampala or Jinja. Discuss with them what you would like to do.

○ Transport

Lira *p239*

Lira's main bus and taxi park is to the south of Oyum Rd near the Bank of Baroda in the centre of town. The roads to and from **Gulu** and **Soroti** are sealed and in good condition, and both are linked by frequent buses and *matatus* which take about 2 hrs to both (US$4). There are direct buses to **Kampala** which go via **Karuma** (5-6 hrs, US$12). To get to **Masindi** (for Murchison Falls National Park) see Gulu, below. To get across from Lira to southeastern Uganda, there are daily buses (if there is the demand) to **Mbale** via **Soroti**; they will depart very early in the morning so enquire at the bus park the day before.

Gulu *p241*

The **Post Bus** leaves Kampala at 0800 and Gulu for **Kampala** at 0700, US$7. The post office is on the Gulu–Lira road opposite Gulu Hospital and the police station. There are also plenty of faster direct buses (4 hrs, US$10), and the bus and taxi park is north of Acholi Rd opposite Stanbic Bank. To **Masindi** (for Murchison Falls National Park) take the Kampala bus and change at **Kigumba**, a small town on the Kampala–Gulu Highway about 60 km south of Karuma, and then get another vehicle from there the 42 km to Masindi. There are frequent *matatus* to/from Gulu and **Lira** (2 hrs, US$4), and infrequent ones to **Kitgum** (2-3 hrs, US$5.50).

Kitgum *p241*

The bus and taxi park is next to the market. There are infrequent *matatus* to/from Gulu (2-3 hrs, US$5.50) covering the bumpy 108 km on a murram road. Although there is the occasional direct bus from Kitgum to **Kampala** (roughly 8 hrs), the better option is to get one from **Gulu**.

Contents

Background

History of Uganda

Before the arrival of the British there were as many as 30 different ethnic groups in the area that now forms modern Uganda, each with its own language, culture and social organization.

The political organization of these different states ranged from those with a highly developed centralized rule, through small chiefdoms, to areas with no obvious system of government. Buganda, Toro, Bunyoro and Nkore (Ankole in the colonial period) were all of the first type, all had a highly developed centralized system with a monarch in place, and are still today referred to as traditional kingdoms. Until 1830 Toro was part of Bunyoro, but broke away when Prince Kaboyo rebelled against his father. For some time Bunyoro was the strongest and most powerful of the four, but from the second half of the 18th century it was overtaken by Buganda. In Nkore the system was rather different as the minority pastoral Bahima ruled over the majority agriculturalist Bairu.

Other areas had no obvious system of government and interpersonal relations were controlled by fear of spirits and the supernatural.

The first foreigners to arrive in the area were Arab traders in the 1840s. From about 1850 the first Europeans began to arrive. John Speke reached Buganda in 1860 and was the first European to identify the source of the Nile (see box, page 86).

The late 19th century was a period of instability in much of Uganda, and there were wars on a surprisingly large scale. In 1888 the British East Africa Company was given a Royal Charter and their control over the area was consolidated by a treaty with the Kabaka (ruler or king) of Buganda (the central and most prominent kingdom) in 1891. However, the Company found the administration of the territory too much to manage, and in 1894 the British government took over responsibility and Buganda was declared a protectorate. Similar status was given to Bunyoro, Toro and Ankole in 1896. During the following years the boundaries of the country were finalized, with a section of Uganda being transferred to Kenya as late as 1912.

Buganda Agreement of 1900

The so-called 'Buganda Question' goes back to the signing in 1900 of the Uganda Agreement (at this time, and until about 1906, the British referred to the District of Buganda as Uganda). It proved to be a watershed in the history of Buganda and, indeed, the whole of Uganda. It formalized the association between the British and the Buganda that had been developing since Speke's arrival in 1862.

One of the most important aspects of the agreement was that it secured a remarkably privileged position for Buganda in comparison with its neighbours. The constitutional relationship between the protectorate government and the government of the Kingdom of Buganda was set out at some length, and it emphasized Buganda's political identity while assuring it a greater measure of internal autonomy than the other districts enjoyed. Some of the other districts had their own agreements, but none were as comprehensive or as favourable as that accorded to the Buganda.

The agreement led to important changes in land tenure. It won over the majority of the chiefs by giving them land grants known as *mailo*, and in doing so it recognized that land was a marketable commodity. The land not given to the Kabaka and chiefs became Crown land to be used for the benefit of the kingdom. The agreement thus created a landed class. It also gave, for the first time, recognition to the notion of indirect rule through the chiefs. The colonialists needed local allies to help them administer with the minimum expenditure, and to produce an economic surplus that could pay for the administration. In time the interests of the chiefs and the government became more closely interwoven. The chiefs collected regular salaries and promoted government policies, and in the public's mind they began to be associated with the administration of the protectorate.

The benefit of the agreement added to the natural advantages that Buganda already had, with its fertile soils, regular rainfall, and a location on the shore of Lake Victoria that ensured good transport links. Missionary activity in the area, stimulated by competition between the Protestants and Catholics, led to a greater concentration of hospitals, schools and other educational facilities. Britain encouraged the production of cotton, the major cash crop in the south, while parts of the remaining areas were discouraged from growing cash crops and were instead developed as labour reserves. This served to accentuate further the differences between Buganda and the rest of the Protectorate, with the south producing cash crops and the north providing migrant labour. In keeping with this division, the north also provided soldiers to the army throughout the colonial period. Buganda's farmers benefited greatly from high coffee prices after the war, and in the early 1950s industrial and commercial development were concentrated in the south generally and in particular in Buganda with its locational and educational advantages.

The period of British rule in Uganda saw dramatic changes in the politics and economy of the country. Most of the wars and disputes were brought under control and the peace that grew up became known as Pax Britannica. The country was divided into districts, each headed by a District Commissioner, and the districts into counties (*saza*), sub-counties (*gombolola*), parishes (*miruka*) and sub-parishes (*bukungu* or *batongole*). A system of indirect rule was developed, with local people used at all these levels. In cases where a system of government was already in place the incumbents were used, but where this was absent other Ugandans – usually Baganda – were brought in. This meant that in many parts of Uganda in the early years of British administration, the British controlled large areas of Uganda through appointed Baganda chiefs.

While the south of the country developed into an agriculturally productive area producing mainly cotton and coffee, the north and southwest became labour pools. Migration into the southern and central region became crucial to maintaining the high production in these areas. There was also a great deal of migration from outside Uganda to the central region. This was mainly from what was then known as Ruanda Urundi (later to be Rwanda and Burundi) but was also from Tanganyikya and the Congo. Migration was not just for large-scale government employment, such as the building of the railway and the army, but also to work for individual cotton and coffee farmers in Buganda. There were some big European-owned farms and plantations in Uganda, but they were never as extensive as in Kenya and it was always planned that Uganda should be developed primarily for Africans. During the Depression of the late 1920s and early 1930s, the Uganda colonial government was not prepared to give the Europeans financial support to get them through the difficult times. Many went bust and left the country. A number of the plantations were later bought up by Asians and were developed into the sugar plantations that can be seen on the road from the Kenya border to Kampala.

The Christian missions arrived in Uganda early and their impact was enormous. Islam was also introduced into Uganda but never made the same impact. The first schools and hospitals were all mission run; the Catholics and Protestants tried desperately to win the most converts, and the key was to provide superior education. The two Christian faiths

The history of East Africa

Archaeological sites at Olduvai Gorge in Tanzania and at Lower Awash River in Ethiopia suggest that man began to evolve in the Rift Valley more than 3 million years ago, and hunter-gatherer communities were established. The area then experienced an influx of people from West Africa (the Bantu Expansion), beginning around 500 BC. In the Horn it is thought that Cushitic immigrants came from Mesopotamia (now Iraq) around 300 BC. The newcomers were cultivators and pastoralists, and they began to change the pattern of subsistence away from hunting and gathering.

Contact with other areas began as seagoing traders arrived from the north, sailing down the east coast of Africa and coming from as far as India and China. A sprinkling of settlements by Islamic people from Shiraz in Persia were established along the coast from about AD 1000.

European contact began with the arrival of the Portuguese who sailed round the southern tip of Africa and passed up the east coast from 1500 onwards. They set up fortified settlements to consolidate their trading presence, several of which remain, most notably Fort Jesus in Mombasa.

A struggle for dominance of these coastal strips began between Arab groups drawing support from the Persian Gulf and vying with the Portuguese for the trade in gold, ivory and slaves. By the end of the 17th century the Portuguese found themselves stretched to retain their hold in East Africa, and Fort Jesus fell to the Arabs in 1698. For most of the next two centuries Arab rule prevailed at the coast, and they began to penetrate the interior with caravans to capture slaves and ivory. These set out from Bagamoyo and Kilwa on the coast of present-day Tanzania, following routes that stretched over 1000 km to the Great Lakes, Uganda and beyond.

In the interior, meanwhile, pockets of centralized rule and formalized social structures emerged, particularly to the west of Lake Victoria.

European exploration began in the 18th century. A Scot, James Bruce, in 1768-1773 travelled from Suskin on the Red Sea up the Abara River to join the Nile.

The origins of the White Nile (which joins the Blue Nile at Khartoum) began to exercise the imagination in Europe, and the source was eventually traced to Lake Victoria by John Hanning Speke in 1860. The two great journeys by David Livingstone in 1858-1864 and 1866-1873

divided the country up between themselves so that, for example, the White Fathers went to Southern Uganda, the Mill Hill Fathers to Eastern Uganda and the Verona Fathers to the north. The Church Mission Society (CMS) is to be found across most of the country and its influence was significant.

Countries under colonial rule have usually achieved independence when a growing nationalist movement has been successful, both in mobilizing a large section of the population and in extracting concessions from the colonial power. In Uganda however, it has been said that it was not nationalism that produced independence but rather the imminence of independence that produced nationalist parties. It was assumed that independence would be granted at some stage, and the focus was turned to the position and role that Buganda would take in an independent country. The Baganda did not wish for their role to be diminished after Independence. By the same token, the rest of the country had no wish to be dominated by the Baganda.

reached Lake Tanganyika and beyond, and were followed by Stanley's expedition in 1874-1877 which crossed the continent from east to west.

The activities of the explorers were followed by missionary activity and a campaign to end the slave trade. Although slavery was made illegal in 1873, it was some time before it was finally eliminated.

The European nations formalized their presence with the British occupying Kenya, Uganda and Zanzibar, and the Germans establishing themselves in what is now mainland Tanzania, Rwanda and Burundi. The Belgians held the eastern Congo.

Economic progress had taken place in the interior as iron implements replaced more primitive stone and wooden tools, and cultivators accumulated farming knowledge. However, droughts, locusts, rinderpest and local conflicts contrived to keep populations fairly stable. Progress accelerated with the advent of European occupation. Diseases were controlled, new crops introduced, roads and railways were built. Death rates fell, birth rates remained high and the population began a steady expansion. Living standards improved and significant sections of the population received basic education.

After the First World War the British took over the part of German East Africa that became Tanganyika, and Belgium absorbed Rwanda and Burundi. Settler presence increased, particularly in Kenya, and the Asian communities consolidated their positions in commerce.

Nationalist movements began to emerge as significant political factors after the Second World War. In Kenya, where there was by now a substantial settler population, there was an armed conflict in the 1950s (the Mau Mau uprising) over land grievances and generally in support of self-determination. All three British territories obtained Independence in the early 1960s. The immediate post-Independence period typically saw the establishment of single-party regimes. In Uganda, Rwanda and Burundi, there have been disastrous collapses of peace and security. Economic development was pursued by the adoption of socialist development strategies with heavy reliance on the public sector. A slowdown of economic progress followed. In the 1980s most countries began to reverse their economic policies. Multiparty political systems were introduced in the 1990s, although Uganda has retained a form of non-party rule.

Uganda's territory was not affected by the hostilities in the First and Second World Wars. However, Ugandan troops served in the Kings African Rifles in both conflicts, and experience abroad, hearing of former colonies that had become independent, was a factor in the movement for self-determination.

Kabaka Crisis of 1953-1955 and Independence

The issue of Baganda separatism came to a head when Sir Andrew Cohen was appointed governor in 1952, and indicated that he was determined to push Uganda as quickly as possible along the road to self-government. A vital principle underlying his policies was that Uganda must develop as a unitary state in which no one part of the country should dominate any other. Thus a strong central government was required, in which all districts, including Buganda, would be represented on an equal footing. This challenged the privileged position that the Buganda had enjoyed since 1900.

The crisis of 1953-1955 was sparked off by a chance remark in London by Sir Oliver Lyttleton, the colonial secretary, about the possibility of introducing a federal system in East Africa embracing the three British territories of Kenya, Uganda and Tanganyika. This was very unpopular with all Ugandans as it was feared that the federation would be dominated by the Europeans in Kenya. The Baganda were even more fearful that they would be unable to safeguard their privileged position in a wider union. Cohen responded to Lyttleton's remarks by giving public reassurances in the Legislative Council that there would be no imposition of a federation against public wishes. The Kabaka, Mutesa II, accepted these reassurances but took the opportunity to ask for the affairs of Buganda to be transferred from the Colonial Office to the Foreign Office. This would be a clear indication that Baganda was not just another colony, but had a more privileged position as a protected state whose monarch had invited British protection. Finally, Mutesa asked for a timetable for Independence to be drawn up.

The Kabaka then went a step further and rejected the policy of a unitary state and asked for the separation of Buganda from the rest of the country. Cohen demanded assurances in line with the 1900 agreement that the Kabaka would not publicly oppose the government's policies for Uganda's development. However the Kabaka refused, pleading that he first needed to consult the *Lukiko*, the Buganda council of elders. On 30 November 1953 Cohen signed a declaration withdrawing Britain's recognition of Mutesa as Native Ruler in Buganda, deported the Kabaka by air to Britain and declared a State of Emergency. Troops were deployed around Kampala but there was no outbreak of violence.

Following the Kabaka Crisis discussions to attempt to resolve the situation led to the Namirembe Conference of July-September 1954. In October 1955 the Kabaka returned to Uganda and signed the Buganda Agreement that was the outcome of the conference. The agreement declared that Buganda should continue to be an integral part of the Protectorate of Uganda, and recommended that the *Lukiko* should agree to elected Baganda participation in the Legislative Council, a step which, fearful of being submerged, it had consistently rejected. The Kabaka in theory returned as a constitutional monarch stripped of political power, but in reality the crisis had served to unite the various clans of the Baganda firmly behind the Kabaka, and thereby increase his political influence.

The crisis had a number of major effects. First, the question of federation with the rest of East Africa was ruled out. Second, the Buganda continued to have a special position and virtual internal self-government. Third, the Kabaka's personal power and popularity increased. Fourth, a statement was made in the British House of Commons that Uganda would be developed primarily as an African country, with proper safeguards for minorities. Fifth, non-Baganda members of the Legislative Council adopted an increasingly nationalist attitude and began to question the special treatment accorded to the Buganda, sowing the seeds of confrontation. And finally, now that Independence in Uganda was clearly just a matter of time, the major question was related to who would hold the power after Independence, and to a definition of the future role of the Buganda and the Kabaka.

From the mid-1950s the first political parties were formed. The Democratic Party (DP), led by Benedicto Kiwanuka, had particular support among Catholics. They wanted a unitary state after Independence and wanted to limit the powers of the Baganda –

so initially they did not find much support in Buganda. The Uganda National Congress (UNC) was more nationally based and wanted greater African control of the economy in a federal independent state. In 1958 a splinter group broke off from the UNC and formed the Uganda People's Congress (UPC), led by Milton Obote. A political party called Kabaka Yekka (KY) – 'The King Alone' – also formed, representing the interests of the Baganda.

In the immediate run-up to Independence the Baganda did not co-operate, fearing the loss of their political identity as part of a unitary state and becoming increasingly hostile towards the protectorate government. They refused to proceed with elections for Buganda's legislative councillors until Buganda's role in a future central government and the role of the Kabaka had been determined. On 31 December 1960 the Baganda declared themselves independent but this was a meaningless gesture as they did not have the power to make Independence a reality.

In 1961 an inquiry was set up to look into the question of the relationship of the various parts of Uganda with the centre. It recognized that Buganda enjoyed what was virtually a federal relationship with the rest of the protectorate, and recommended that this should continue. Uganda should therefore become a single democratic state with a strong central government, with which Buganda would have a federal relationship.

The first elections were held in 1961 – the two main parties being UPC and DP. The Baganda boycotted the election so that only 3% of the Buganda electorate voted, allowing the DP to make a clean sweep in Buganda. Overall UPC won a majority of votes but DP's success in Buganda gave them the majority of the seats. Obote, as leader of the UPC opposition, and the Kabaka were both anxious to eject the DP from power in the 1962 elections, and so Obote agreed to support Buganda's demands – particularly for indirect elections to the National Assembly – in return for Buganda's return to the centre and acceptance of a single central government. Thus Buganda participated in the Constitutional Conference in London in September 1961.

Obote I

At the 1961 conference the structure of the future government was agreed and the date of full Independence was set for 9 October 1962. Buganda obtained virtually everything that it had demanded. There would be a federal relationship with the centre, and the constitution would define all matters concerning the Kingdom of the Kabaka and traditional institutions (three other Kingdoms were recognised: Bunyoro, Ankole and Toro). This opened the way for the Baganda to participate once again in central government, which they did through the Kabaka Yekka party, formed in 1961. They made an alliance with the UPC and the February 1962 elections in Buganda were really a fight between KY and DP; KY won 65 of the 68 seats. The KY victory determined the composition of the new government formed after the national, pre-Independence elections, in April 1962. Obote's UPC won a comfortable victory over DP outside Buganda, within it the KY-UPC alliance ensured a majority of seats for the alliance. In May 1962 Obote was sworn in as prime minister of the UPC-KY government and the Kabaka's role was that of constitutional monarch. On 9 October 1962, the day Uganda became an independent nation, Obote spoke of the joy felt by all in Uganda at the achievement of Uganda's Independence, particularly as this had been reached in an atmosphere of peace and goodwill. He went on to speak of the need for a unity of purpose, mutual understanding and respect, and a resolve to place country above tribe, party and self.

However, the coalition between UPC and KY was fragile and by 1964 enough KY and DP members had crossed the floor to join the UPC so that the alliance was no longer necessary. Obote dismissed KY from the government.

In February 1966 Obote suspended the constitution, deposed the president and transferred all executive powers to himself. Shortly afterwards an interim constitution was imposed, which the parliament had neither read nor debated, withdrawing regional autonomy, and introducing an executive presidency – assumed by Obote who thus became head of state with absolute power. This became known as the 'pigeon-hole constitution' because MPs were told to vote on it before they were allowed to read it – it was simply placed in their pigeon-holes for them to read afterwards. When the Baganda demanded the restoration of their autonomy, troops led by the second-in-command of the army, Colonel Idi Amin, seized the Kabaka's palace. The Kabaka fled to Britain, where he died of alcohol poisoning in exile in a Bermondsey council flat – an ignominious end for a man who had been a captain in the Grenadier Guards, and once spent much of his time at Cambridge travelling to the engineering works in Derby to supervise the carving of ivory from elephants he had shot to make the switches for the dashboard of his Rolls Royce.

Colonel Idi Amin

The late 1960s saw the beginning of the years of trouble for which Uganda was later to became notorious. Detentions and repression became increasingly common. A 'Move to the Left' was introduced, which redistributed resources by way of nationalization and increased central power. Obote, who had used the army to prop up his own regime, was to be ousted by that same army under the command of Amin. The takeover occurred in January 1971 while Obote was out of the country at a Commonwealth Conference. Amin declared himself the new head of state and promised that there would be a return to civilian government within five years. This, however, was not to be.

It is worth remembering that Amin was initially greeted with widespread support among the Ugandan population, particularly the Baganda, as well as in the Western world. Not long into his regime, however, Amin suspended all political activity and most civil rights. The National Assembly was dissolved and Amin began to rule the country by capricious decree. In August 1972 he announced the expulsion of all non-citizen Asians. The directive was later expanded to all Asians, although under pressure he did backtrack on this. However, in the event the atmosphere that had been established drove all but a handful of the 75,000 Asians to leave the country. Most went to Britain, while many others went to Canada and the United States. Britain cut off diplomatic relations and imposed a trade embargo. By the end of the year most other Western countries had followed suit. The businesses that had been owned by Asians were Africanized, that is, given to various cronies of Amin. The expulsion of Asians and policy of Africanization was popular with the majority of the Ugandan population, many of whom had resented the success of the Asian businesses. However, many businesses collapsed and the sudden and dramatic loss of technical skills brought other enterprises to a standstill. Amin also attempted to gain the popularity of the Baganda by returning the body of the Kabaka for burial in the Kisubi Tombs outside Kampala.

Amin's administration was propped up by military aid from the Soviet Union and Libya, but the infrastructure – water supply, schools, hospitals, roads – collapsed. Many former cash crop producers returned to subsistence production in an effort to survive.

Unexplained disappearances increased, particularly among the Acholi and Langi people. There was conflict within the army.

In 1976 a group from the Popular Front for the Liberation of Palestine hijacked an Air France flight that was bound for Israel and forced it to land at Entebbe. The terrorists were welcomed by Amin. The passengers were transferred to the terminal and released except for the Israelis and Jews. The Air France crew elected to stay with the hostages. The terrorists demanded the release of 53 Palestinians held in Israeli jails and around the world, threatening to kill the hostages. A raid by Israeli commandos, landing under cover of darkness at Entebbe in four transport planes, succeeded in freeing the hostages and destroying 11 Ugandan Mig-17 fighters on the ground. Four hostages lost their lives, as well as the leader of commandos, 46 Ugandan soldiers, and the six terrorists. The episode was a major humiliation for Amin.

In 1978, in an attempt to detract attention from the internal turmoil, Amin launched an attack on Tanzania. The Kagera Salient in southwest Uganda has, since the drawing of international boundaries, been rather a problematic area. Just to the west of Lake Victoria the international boundary is a straight line following the 10° latitude. However, the Kagera River forms a loop to the south of this. There is, therefore, an area of land that is part of Tanzania but, because of the river, has more contact with Uganda. One of the most important agreements that the Organization of African Unity (OAU) reached soon after its formation was that, however unfair or illogical the international boundaries drawn by the colonial powers, they should not be disputed. Amin's claim to the Kagera Salient was clearly in breach of this. Amin's undisciplined troops were no match for the Tanzanian army and the 1979 war led to massive destruction, as the army fled north pillaging and destroying as it went. Amin fled and went into exile, first in Libya, and later in Saudi Arabia.

His Excellency, self-styled Field Marshal and Life President of Uganda, Amin awaited the call to return once the 'misunderstanding' that led to his overthrow was cleared up. At his villa in Jeddah, he remained convinced that his people still loved him. The money he took with him from Uganda was soon gone, but the Saudi government granted him an allowance. He died in Jeddah in 2003.

Following the war, the Tanzanian army remained in Uganda to maintain the peace. Meanwhile, on the political front, the Tanzanians arranged the Moshi Conference in March 1979. At this conference Dr Lule (who had formerly been vice-chancellor of Makerere) was chosen to be the leader of the National Consultative Committee of the Uganda National Liberation Front, which, together with a military commission, undertook the interim rule of Uganda. In April Lule was sworn in as president. However, in June he was voted out of office by the 30-strong National Consultative Committee, and former Attorney General Binaisa was put in his place. His length of office was to be only a year and in May 1980 the UNLF's military commission took over. This was headed by Paul Mwanga and was supported by Museveni as vice-chairman. Elections were set for December 1980 and were contested by four political parties: UPC (headed by Obote) and DP (headed by Paul Ssemogerere), as well as a newer party, the Uganda Patriotic Movement (UPM), headed by Yoweri Museveni, and the Conservative Party, largely a Buganda-based party derived from Kabaka Yekka.

Obote II

This election for which Uganda had such high hopes is widely believed to have been fixed; crowds had gathered in the streets of Kampala as the first results came out and word was that the DP had won. However, Mwanga announced that no further results of the election could be released before they had been approved by him. Needless to say, when the results were finally published – announcing a UPC victory – there was widespread belief that they had been falsified. The truth of the election result will probably never be known but in the end the UPC had a majority of 20 seats, and Obote was proclaimed president with Mwanga as vice-president. The election of the new government did not, however, bring peace and stability to the country. The policies that the UPC put forward were aimed at attracting World Bank and IMF-sponsored economic reconstruction, but rebuilding the country was not to be easy. On the security side the situation in many parts of the country deteriorated still further.

The dissatisfaction that resulted from the doubts over the elections led to a number of groups going into the bush from where they carried on a guerrilla war. These included the National Resistance Army (NRA), led by Yowari Museveni, a political science graduate from the University of Dar es Salaam. The NRA was based largely in the southern part of the country. It was well organized and grew from a small collection of fighters into a powerful army. The atrocities perpetrated by the government in what became known as the Luwero Triangle, an area to the north of Kampala, were an attempt to rid the NRA of civilian supporters. Large numbers of people displaced by these atrocities joined up with the NRA, including children orphaned by the civil war.

Meanwhile there was also trouble within the Uganda National Liberation Army (UNLA), an ethnic division within the army largely made up of Acholi and Langi, which was to lead to another change in leadership in July 1985. This was led by the two Okellos (Tito and Basilio, not related). Obote fled to Kenya and from there to Zambia, to die of kidney failure in a Johannesberg hospital in 2005.

Tito Okello took over as president. The NRA did not join Okello but remained fighting and within a few months had taken over Fort Portal and Kasese in the west of the country. By the end of the year the NRA was within a few miles of Kampala. There were efforts at negotiation at a conference in Nairobi, and in late December a peace treaty was signed. However, just three weeks after the signing, Museveni's troops advanced on Kampala.

Museveni

Okello's troops fled north, Museveni was sworn in as president and formed a broad-based government with ministries being filled by members of all the main political factions. However, fighting continued in the north. By the late 1980s, under an amnesty offered to the rebels, almost 30,000 of them had surrendered.

Museveni, however, has not been without his critics. An Amnesty International report published in late 1991 accused the NRA of torturing and summarily executing prisoners during the operations against the rebels in the north. The criticism most commonly aimed at Museveni, particularly by the Western donors, is his apparent avoidance of democratic elections. When he first came to power political parties were suspended and it was announced that there would be no elections for three years. In October 1989 the NRM extended the government's term of office to a further five years from January 1990, when their mandate was due to run out. Museveni argued that the time was not ready for political parties and that a new constitution had to be drawn up before elections could take place. In March 1990 the ban on political party activities was extended for five years. A new constitution was adopted in 1995, which provided for an assembly with 305 members, 214 elected, the remainder nominated or ex officio.

The Coronation of the Kabaka

This event eventually took place at the end of July 1993. There had been a number of delays since it was first announced that the son of Edward Muteesa II could return to Uganda and be crowned. An amendment had to be made to the constitution and it was made clear that the new Kabaka would not have any political powers but would be a cultural leader. The occasion also gave rise to much discussion as to the future of the other four kingdoms in Uganda; the people of at least one of these kingdoms (the Ankole) did not want their king to return.

Finally it was declared that the coronation could go ahead and suddenly the Baganda found they had a huge amount to organize before the great day. There were invitations to be sent out, a hill-top to clear, large grass-thatched constructions to be built, a road to be surfaced, not to mention all the traditional rituals that the Sabataka (the one who was to be King) had to perform before he could be pronounced the Kabaka. These included the tuning of the drums and a series of visits to culturally important sites around Buganda.

In the weeks before the coronation day hordes of volunteers gathered at the site at Namugongo near the famous Kings College, Budo, and set about clearing the hill top. Groups of women sat around cleaning and preparing the reeds used for the construction of walls of the buildings. They were dressed in the Ugandan basuti, many made from bark cloth. The atmosphere was one of great anticipation, and they frequently broke into song.

Eventually the great day arrived. Events began at daybreak with a mock cane fight in which the Sabataka had to prove his worthiness to become the Kabaka. Thousands of people began to arrive in traditional dress and gathered on the hill top. It was a wonderful sight, with fine views of Buganda all around and, as the sun rose, the mist gradually cleared.

Foreign dignitaries took their places in the shade of a pavilion. President Museveni and his wife were the last of the guests to arrive and the president was greeted extremely warmly as the Baganda thanked him for returning their king to them. The ceremony was split into two parts: the first being the traditional one under a tree, and the second, in view of many more people, was the religious ceremony when prayers were said. The Sabataka was carried into the enclosure where the coronation was to take place and took his seat on a covered with bark-cloth throne underneath the traditional tree. As part of the ritual he prodded a cow (in the past he would have killed it) and as the ceremony progressed he was dressed in layers of bark-cloth covered by animal skins.

Just after the actual crowning, dark clouds started to gather and the wind suddenly rose. There had been no rain in the area for a few weeks and now it looked as if there was to be a thunderstorm, which would forebode ill. But after just a few spots of rain the clouds cleared and the sun came out – and the Bagandans said: God is being kind to us.

Museveni was elected president in 1996, and re-elected in 2001. In 2005 a constitutional amendment sanctioned a multi-party system and abolished the limit on the number of terms a president could serve. Museveni was duly re-elected in 2006 and in the February 2011 elections Museveni was returned to power for another five-year term. Opponents accused his party of using state resources to bribe voters, and EU observers expressed concern at ruling party candidates' widespread distribution of money and gifts to voters during their electoral campaign. Nevertheless he achieved a 68% majority with 59% of registered voters having voted.

The Kabaka of Baganda was allowed to return to the country and to be crowned in a highly publicized ceremony in 1993 (see box, page 257). This was obviously immensely popular with the Baganda, although his role is purely ceremonial without any political function. The kingdoms of Bunyoro Busoga and Toro have also been restored. The Ankole, however, declined the restoration. This was attributed to the fact that the former Ankole Kingdom had been a rigid, almost caste-like social structure and many Banyankole (Ankole people) did not want its return.

The Asian community have been encouraged to return, and the property they relinquished on their departure has been restored. The Asians have been cautious, but they are once again filling positions in all sectors of the economy.

In 1990 the security situation in outlying parts began to be a matter of concern for the government. There were four areas where there were regular outbreaks of fighting. In the north, the Lord's Resistance Army (LRA), led by Joseph Kony, mounted attacks on communities around Gulu and Kitgum, abducting prisoners, including many children (see box, page 240). Although the LRA initially had the aim of setting up a Christian state in Uganda, it quickly descended into kidnapping and banditry which became a way of life for its members. It received support from Sudan, and Uganda has retaliated by giving support in southern Sudan to the Sudan People's Liberation Army (SPLA), which was fighting for secession from the Islamic government in the north. In December 1999 Uganda and Sudan reached an agreement whereby each country would not offer refuge or support to the other country's rebels. Uganda followed this up with an offer of an amnesty to the LRA, held open for six months. There was a disappointing response to these initiatives. In March 2002 the LRA attacked a Sudanese garrison meaning that the attitude of the Sudanese government hardened towards their former allies and they allowed the Ugandan army to pursue the LRA inside Sudan. Attacks by the LRA on Sudanese citizens caused the SPLA to contemplate targeting the LRA. This move has embarrassed Uganda as it could hardly co-operate with the SPLA having agreed earlier not to support it. As all parties were by now opposed to the LRA, there was more optimism that they could be hunted down and their ghastly activities terminated.

In the northeast of Uganda there was fighting between clans of the pastoralist Karamajong. During the Amin and Obote II periods firearms were acquired, and they were used to try to settle disputes over cattle thefts. Several hundred people were reported killed, and the government became involved in trying to maintain law and order by implementing a programme to disarm the Karamajong.

There was also rebel activity in the west of the country, around Kasese. A series of bomb attacks on buses and two serious assaults on Kasese displaced some 70,000 people. It is thought that the groups forming the Allied Democratic Forces (ADF) were opportunistic rather than idealistic, and numbered only around 200 activists. Material support was said to come from Libya, Iran and the United Arab Emirates, and the ADF is believed to have a strong Islamic element. Finally, in November 2001, UPDF forces fired mortars on to the Rift Valley escarpment in the largest and final UPDF-ADF battle. Although remnants of the ADF may still exist in the DRC, they were expelled from Uganda by early 2002.

In addition to the internal worries, Uganda has also become involved in the conflict in the Democratic Republic of Congo (DRC). Uganda was concerned to prevent incursions by armed groups formed mostly from Hutu displaced by the troubles in Rwanda and Burundi. In March 1999, eight tourists and four rangers were killed by Rwandan Hutu rebels in the Bwindi Impenetrable National Park. Museveni responded by improving security for visitors in the area.

Uganda supported Laurent Kabila in overthrowing the rule of President Mobutu, in the hope that an ally in the DRC would help in achieving secure borders. However, Uganda rapidly became disenchanted with Kabila, and, with Rwanda, began supporting the Rassemblement Congolais pour la Democratie (RCD) against the DRC government. RCD split into factions based on Goma (supported by Rwanda) and Kisingani (backed by Uganda). As a result there was fighting between Rwandan and Ugandan troops who were at one time allies. In 1999 there was a peace agreement signed in Lusaka, with the UN committing 500 observers and promising 5000 peace keepers after a ceasefire was established.

The assassination of Kabila in January 2001 saw the leadership of DRC pass to Joseph Kabila, the former president's son. There were hopes that the new regime would show a more sympathetic approach to an effective peace deal. However, the ongoing conflict in the DRC has continued unabated resulting in the borders with Uganda and the DRC being routinely closed and refugee camps being established in Uganda as people have fled insecurity in the eastern regions of the DRC. In July 2012, the UN accused Uganda of sending troops into DRC to fight alongside the M23 rebel movement. It was a charge Uganda denied and in response to UN accusations, in November 2012, Uganda announced its intention to withdraw from UN-backed international peacekeeping missions. By February 2013, 11 countries, including Uganda, signed a UN-mediated agreement pledging not to interfere in the DRC.

Today the LRA is fragmented and the 'army' is not now believed to number more than 1000 individuals. After a peace agreement with the Ugandan government in 2006, the LRA left Uganda and first became established in northeast DRC, and is now thought to have a presence in the Central African Republic (CAR). In 2010, the Ugandan army claimed it killed Bok Abudema, a senior commander of the LRA in the CAR, but Kony has not yet been captured. Since 2006 when the LRA rebels were driven out of northern Uganda much reconstruction progress has been made.

Economy of Uganda

Given the state of the economy following the Amin period and its aftermath, Uganda has made an excellent recovery. In May 1987 Museveni ended the period of indecision over Uganda's economic strategy when agreement was reached on a programme with the IMF on a return to a market-based economy. The Kampala Stock Exchange opened for business in January 1988.

Uganda has substantial natural resources, including fertile soils, regular rainfall, small deposits of copper, gold and other minerals, and recently discovered oil. GDP in 2014 was US$50.77 billion, and in terms of economic size it is a medium-sized economy among the East African countries. But the average annual income is estimated to be US$1400 per head, placing Uganda firmly in the low-income category.

Agriculture provides 24% of GDP. It is even more important in that it provides the livelihood of around 82% of the population. Industry generates 28% of GDP, but incomes are high in this sector, as it comprises only 5% of total employment. Similarly services contribute 49% of GDP, but make up only 13% of employment.

Exports make a contribution at 22% of GDP, although this probably underestimates export activity as the main crop, coffee, is easy to smuggle out through neighbouring states, where prices are often higher. Exports are 70% coffee, with gold at 8% and fish at 6%. Other exports include horticultural products such as tea, cotton and flowers. Imports are 36% of GDP; mostly petroleum, machinery and transport equipment. Tourism is the fastest-growing sector of the Ugandan economy and is a major driver of employment, investment and foreign exchange. From just 160,000 visitors in 1995, numbers have been rising rapidly: there were 470,000 arrivals in 2005, 845,000 in 2008, and 1.2 million in 2012. Numbers are predicted to rise by at least 10% per year and the revenue generated by tourism is currently put at about US$850 million per annum.

Social conditions

The population in mid-2014 was estimated at 34.75 million. The uplands in the east and west form the most densely populated areas, whereas the west has low population densities. The average population density is 168 people per sq km, which is about four times the African average. Urban population, at 16% of the total, however, is low. Turmoil in the past has led many to flee the towns to survive by subsistence agriculture in the countryside. As urban employment opportunities have expanded only slowly, many people have been reluctant to return.

The population growth rate at 3.3% a year is high. Regionally, Uganda's population growth rate is about the same as that of Tanzania; considerably greater than Kenya at 2.75% and Rwanda at 2.9%. The high rate results from one of the world's highest birth rates, with 6.6 children born, on average, to each woman. The average age of a mother's first birth is 18.9 years. Uganda has one of the youngest populations in the world and, in 2012, 78% of Ugandans were below the age of 30 and 52% below 15. Life expectancy was 58 years in 2013, which has improved dramatically from just 46 years in 2000.

Adult literacy, at about 73%, has recovered significantly from the disruption of the Amin years and the aftermath. In 1997, Uganda introduced free primary education for four children per family and within two years the numbers of children enrolled had doubled to six million. The enrolment rate is now around 97%. Secondary and tertiary provision is less good with enrolments at 22% and 4% respectively. Despite the encouragement of enrolment, there is the compounding problem of lack of school places, poor infrastructure (more than one quarter of primary schools in northern Uganda are still outside under trees) and lack of teachers. Although 60-70,000 students in Uganda leave secondary school each year qualified to go on to higher education, only some 35% of them (at most 25,000) are able to find places at the limited number of institutions. Makerere University in Kampala (MUK) has about 95% of the total student population in Uganda's universities. The remainder is distributed among the more than 20 private universities and a smaller number of non-university institutions.

Culture of Uganda

People
The largest ethnic group in Uganda are the Baganda (Bantu) with 16% of the total. Other main groups are the Soga (Bantu) with 8%; the Nkole (Bantu) with 8%; the Teso (Nilotic) with 8%; the Kiga (Bantu) with 7%; the Lango (Nilotic) with 6%; the Gisu (Bantu) with 5%; the Acholi (Nilotic) with 4% and the Alur (Nilotic) with 4%. In all, there are 14 groups with more than 1% of the population, while 29% of the total population is made up of groups with less than 1% including Asians and Europeans. Prior to their expulsion by Amin in 1972 the Asians comprised about 2% of the total, and their community numbered 70,000. Many Asian families returned, and today are thought to number about 15,000. The country's smallest ethnic groups include the Batwa and Bambuti Pygmies, relics of the hunter-gatherer cultures that once occupied much of East Africa and in Uganda are now confined to the hilly southwest. Another small group, the Ik, are remote mountain people who inhabit a chain of volcanic mountains in the northeast of the country between the Timu Forest bordering Kenya and Kidepo Valley National Park.

Religion
Religion plays an important part of daily life in Uganda. Over four-fifths of Ugandans are Christian, either Protestant or Catholic; faiths that were introduced by missionaries in the 19th century. Around 10% are Muslim, a legacy of the Arab traders who arrived in the 18th century. Ugandans are strong in their faith and see no conflict in holding on to some traditional beliefs and may also consult a local oracle or healer. Many Ugandans believe that sacrifices to ancestors or spirits can protect them from harm and shrines are still in active use.

Uganda land and environment

Geography
Uganda covers 236,040 sq km and is a medium-sized landlocked African country bordered by South Sudan, Kenya, Tanzania, Rwanda and the Democratic Republic of Congo (DRC). Uganda lies astride the equator between latitude 4° North to 1° South and longitude 30° West to 33° East. It has semi-desert areas in the northeast, swampland along the Albert Nile in the northwest and savannah across the central regions. It is in the heart of the Great Lakes region, and with eight major rivers and five huge lakes, water covers nearly one-fifth of the country. Uganda has a 43% share of Lake Victoria, which with a surface area of 68,800 sq km, is Africa's largest lake and the world's second largest freshwater lake by surface area. The White Nile has its source in Lake Victoria; as the Victoria Nile, it runs northward through Lake Kyoga and then westward to Lake Albert, from which it emerges as the Albert Nile to resume its northward course to South Sudan.

About 8% of land is covered by forest, including the tropical montane forests of the west and southwest, some of which border the central African Congo forests. The country has a rim of mountains along most of its borders. Along the western border with the DRC, in the Ruwenzori Mountains, Margherita Peak on Mount Stanley reaches a height of 5109 m; in the south are the northernmost of the Virunga Volcanoes which share the border with Rwanda and the DRC; while on the eastern border with Kenya,

Ugandan peoples

Situated at the geographical heart of Africa, Uganda has long been a cultural melting pot, with over 30 ethnic groups. The peoples of Bantu origin occupy southern Uganda, and in total comprise about half of the population. They are not an ethnic group, but are identified by unique linguistic similarities. They are thought to have migrated from West Africa in several waves over the period AD 1000 to AD 1300.

Of these the Baganda, the largest ethnic group estimated at 16% of the total population, live in central and southern Uganda. In western Uganda several ethnic groups are found including the Bakiga from the far southwest, the Banyankore who live in the Kingdom of Ankole, centred around Mbarara, the Batoro from the Kingdom of Toro in the foothills of the northern Rwenzori mountains around Fort Portal, the Bamba bordering the DRC in Bundibugyo district and the Bakojo from the Kasese district. Further north the Banyoro peopled the ancient Bunyoro-Kitara Kingdom, and their descendants are found around Kibale and Mubende districts and part of Luwero district. In eastern Uganda, the Basoga occupy the area around Jinja, and to the north the Bagisu inhabit Mbale and the foothills of Mount Elgon.

Nilotic groups migrated from north of present-day Uganda somewhat later than the Bantu, around the 15th to 18th centuries. The Teso, of Nilo-Hamitic origin (sometimes referred to as the Iteso), are a major group in eastern Uganda mainly living in and around Soroti district. Northeast Uganda is where the hunter/pastoralist Karamajong people are found. Classified as Nilo-Hamitic they are believed to have common origins with the Teso and the Lango, one of the largest ethnic groups, from northwest Uganda. The Acholi, also classified as being of Nilo-Hamitic origin, occupy the area north of the Langi up to the border with Sudan. Two major groups of Sudanic peoples are found in the far northwest Uganda: the Lugbara and the Madi.

Mount Elgon rises to 4321 m. By contrast, the Western Rift Valley, which runs from north to south through the western half of the country, is below 910 m on the surface of Lake Edward and Lake George and 621 m on the surface of Lake Albert. Generally speaking, the south of the country is agricultural and the north is pastoral.

Climate

Temperatures vary little in an equatorial climate but are made cooler and wetter by altitude. Rainfall, greatest in the mountains and the Lake Victoria region, reaches an annual average of up to 200 cm. Elsewhere it averages 125 cm but the dry northeast and parts of the south receive less than 75 cm. The dry season lasts only one month in the centre and west, but three months (June, July and August) in the south. There are two dry seasons in the north and northeast, in October and from December to March, making two harvests possible.

Books on Uganda

Fiction and memoirs

Burton, RF *The Lake Regions of Central Africa*. The original 1860 account of the charismatic explorer's travels around Lake Victoria. Burton's journal entries document the Arab slave trade, safari life in the days of human porters and mules, and the flora and fauna he encountered.

Churchill, W *My African Journey*. Engaging account by the young politician, which displays an infectious enthusiasm for Uganda and which coined the phrase 'Pearl of Africa'.

Foden, G *The Last King of Scotland*. Fictionalized account of a medic serving in Uganda, engaged as Idi Amin's personal doctor. Captures well the mood of Uganda in the 1970s. Made into a film of the same name in 2006.

Gee, M *My Driver*. A clever and laugh-out-loud novel about the adventures of a plucky but accident-prone white writer who goes to Uganda for an African writers' conference and to visit her former cleaner who is now the successful executive housekeeper of Kampala's Sheraton Hotel. It follows on from *My Cleaner* about her family's relationship with the Ugandan cleaner in London.

Murphy, D *Ukimwi Road*. A trip by bicycle from Kenya to Zambia, taking in Uganda by an intrepid sexagenarian Irish traveller.

Theroux, P *Fong and the Indians*. One of Theroux's earliest novels and a comic-moral tale about an innocent Chinese grocer living in Kampala in the 1960s.

Theroux, P *Sir Vidia's Shadow: A Friendship Across Five Continents*. The story of the travel writer's friendship with Nobel Prizewinner for Literature VS Naipaul, which began when they met as lecturers at Makerere University in Kampala in 1966 and ended in 1997 in London.

History

Allen, T *The Lord's Resistance Army: Myth and Reality*. Provides the most comprehensive analysis of the group available, from the roots of the violence to the oppressive responses of the Ugandan government and the failures of the international community to intervene. It includes a remarkable first-hand interview with Joseph Kony himself.

Bierman, J *Dark Safari*. The life of Henry Morton Stanley, who found David Livingstone at Ujiji in Tanganyika and who later made 2 great journeys across Africa from coast to coast, from the east in 1874-1877 and from the west in 1887-1889, passing through Uganda on both occasions.

Coster, G *Corsairville: The Lost Domain of the Flying Boat*. Splendid account of the flying boat service from Southampton to Durban, touching down on Lake Victoria. Written around a flying boat that turned left by mistake on leaving Port Bell, Kampala, crash landed on the River Dunga in the then Belgian Congo, and was (eventually) successfully repaired and flown out.

Jagielski, W *The Night Wanderers: Uganda's Children and the Lord's Resistance Army*. A gritty account of the civil war with the LRA in northern Uganda by a Polish journalist and former BBC correspondent. Succeeds in capturing the haunted atmosphere of Acholiland through the tales of the thousands of children who were caught up in the conflict, many of whom were captured by the LRA to become child soldiers.

Jeal, T *Explorers of the Nile: The Triumph and Tragedy of a Great Victorian Adventure*. Entertaining account of the 5 British explorers on the seemingly impossible task of discovering the source of the White Nile from 1856 and 1876; they were Richard

Burton, John Hanning Speke, Samuel Baker, David Livingstone and Henry Morton Stanley. The book was adapted for BBC Radio 4 in 2011.

Low, A *Fabrication of Empire: The British and the Uganda Kingdoms, 1890-1902.* During the 1890s and the Scramble for Africa, the interior carved out by the British first encompassed some 20–30 African kingdoms. This book examines how and why the British were able to dominate these rulerships and establish a colonial government.

Miller, C *Lunatic Express.* Weaves the history of East Africa round the story of the building of the Uganda Railway, from Mombasa to Kampala, well researched, engagingly written, and with a fine eye for the bizarre and amusing.

Rice, A *The Teeth May Smile But the Heart Does Not Forget: Murder and Memory in Uganda.* An enthralling account of the murder of an administrative chief in rural southwestern Uganda because of his political opposition to the Amin regime, and the victim's son's efforts, 30 years later, to get a measure of justice with a murder investigation and trial.

Speke, J H and Grant, J *Journal of the Discovery of the Source of the Nile.* First published in 1863, the tale of Speke's epic journey, which finally established that the source of the Nile is at Jinja in Uganda.

Twigger, R *Red Nile: The Unexpurgated Biography of the World's Greatest River.* Impressively researched and the most up-to-date assessment of the Nile and the countries it travels through from ancient times to the Arab Spring.

Natural history

Briggs, P *East African Wildlife.* Bradt's comprehensive field guide on the animals you are likely to see on safari and illustrated by photographs or watercolour drawings.

Hosking, D and **Withers, M** *Wildlife of Kenya, Tanzania and Uganda (Traveller's Guide).* This popular Collins guide describes 475 species of bird, mammal, snake, lizard, insect and tree and is well illustrated with colour photographs. Also includes tips on wildlife photography.

Schaller, G *The Year of the Gorilla.* Very readable account of George Schaller's 2 years of observation of mountain gorillas in the late 1950s in the Virunga Volcanoes. He also recounts the adventures he experienced as a solitary researcher living in the forests.

Van Perlo, B *Birds of Eastern Africa (Collins Field Guide).* An easy-to-use Collins guide featuring over 450 species found in Kenya, Tanzania, Uganda, Ethiopia and Somalia, including full-colour illustrations and distribution maps.

Contents

Footnotes

Index → *Entries in bold refer to maps.*

Notes

Acknowledgements

Lizzie would like to thank, as always, friends, expats and ex-overlanders who have settled in Uganda for constantly keeping me in the loop on what's going on in the tourist industry in East Africa and, of course, for the odd bed for the night. Thanks to the Uganda Wildlife Authority (UWA), of which I met many enthusiastic staff and guides at the park gates and offices around the country. Many thanks go to John Dahl, Leslie Carvell, Markie-Mark Vine, Nash Karanja and all other staff from Nile River Explorers (NRE) in Jinja and Bujagali for the wheels (the NRE 'yellow beast'), and exceptionally helpful information. Also in Jinja, thanks to PK from All Terrain Adventures, Emily Wall from Kayak the Nile, Cam Mcleay and Yasin Kabunga from Adrift, Kaz Mikkelsen from Safari Wildz, and a special mention must go to Colin Cheetham for fixing my 1000-miler Havaiana flip-flops which stayed on my feet for my 1600-km journey around Uganda. For their exceptional hospitality thanks to Debbie and Emmanuel at Red Chilli in Kampala, Merryde and Helen at Gately's Inn and Diana and Hendrick at 2 Friends, both in Jinja and Entebbe, Hennie at Mweya Safari Lodge and Rukia Mwai at Marasa head office, Phiona, Francis and Robert at Kyambura Gorge Lodge and Ros Boycott from Volcanoes Safaris, Glen and Ingrid at Wildwaters Lodge on the Nile where UK guests Tom and Lyn Fryatt also gave me essential birding information, Gitta at Birdnest@Bunyonyi, Jennifer and Molly at the Traveller's Rest in Kisoro, Chris and Katie at Rwakobo Rock at Lake Mburo, and in Fort Portal thanks to Heleen and Michael at the Dutchess Guesthouse & Restaurant, and Aubrey and Bo at Ndali Lodge. Grateful thanks must go to Michael Hodd and Angela Roche for their work in compiling the earlier editions of this book. Finally thanks to Patrick Dawson, Felicity Laughton and the rest of the dedicated team at Footprint for making it all make sense.

Credits

Footprint credits
Editor: Felicity Laughton
Production and layout: Emma Bryers
Maps: Kevin Feeney
Colour sections: Angus Dawson

Publisher: Patrick Dawson
Managing Editor: Felicity Laughton
Advertising: Elizabeth Taylor
Sales and marketing: Kirsty Holmes

Photography credits
Front cover: Olivier Goujon/SuperStock
Back cover: Dmitryp/Dreamstime.com

Colour section
Page i: Superstock: Rolf Schulten/imagebr/imagebroker.
net. Page ii: Superstock: Marka. Page v: Dreamstime:
Agap13. Page vi: Superstock: Tom Cockrem/age fotostock.
Page vii: Superstock: Herbert Hopfensperger/age fotostock;
Minden Pictures. Page viii: Superstock: Minden Pictures;
Luis Domingo/age fotostock. Page ix: Dreamstime:
Dmitry Pichugin. Page x: Superstock: Martin Zwick/age
fotostock; Gilles Barbier/imageb/imagebroker.net

Wildlife section
Page i: Superstock: Hugo Alonso/age fotostock.
Page ii: Superstock: Kaehler, Wolfgang. Page iii:
Superstock: Rolf Schulten/imagebr/imagebroker.net;
age fotostock; Philip Crosby/age fotostock. Page iv:
Superstock: Philip Crosby/age fotostock; Oberholzer
David/Prisma. Page v: Superstock: Biosphoto; Caren
Brinkema; Robert Harding Picture Library. Page vi:
Superstock: Minden Pictures; age fotostock; Biosphoto;
Gilles Barbier/imageb/imagebroker.net. Page viii:
Superstock: Philip Crosby/age fotostock; Kaehler,
Wolfgang. Page ix: Superstock: Robert Harding
Picture Library; age fotostock. Page x: Superstock:
age fotostock; Minden Pictures; Ivan Vdovin/age
fotostock. Page xi: Superstock: Christian Hütter/imag/
imagebroker.net. Page xii: Superstock: Lilly/imagebroker/
imagebroker.net; age fotostock. Page xiii: Superstock:
Biosphoto; Luis Domingo/age fotostock. Page xiv:
Superstock: Water Rights; Oberholzer David/Prisma.
Page xv: Superstock: age fotostock. Page xvi: Superstock:
Oberholzer David/Prisma.

Printed in India by Thomson Press Ltd,
Faridabad, Haryana

Publishing information
Footprint Uganda
3rd edition
© Footprint Handbooks Ltd
August 2014

ISBN: 978 1 910120 00 2
CIP DATA: A catalogue record for this book
is available from the British Library

® Footprint Handbooks and the Footprint
mark are a registered trademark of
Footprint Handbooks Ltd

Published by Footprint
6 Riverside Court
Lower Bristol Road
Bath BA2 3DZ, UK
T +44 (0)1225 469141
F +44 (0)1225 469461
footprinttravelguides.com

Distributed in the USA by Globe Pequot
Press, Guilford, Connecticut

Every effort has been made to ensure that
the facts in this guidebook are accurate.
However, travellers should still obtain
advice from consulates, airlines, etc about
travel and visa requirements before
travelling. The authors and publishers
cannot accept responsibility for any loss,
injury or inconvenience however caused.

Map symbols

□ Capital city
○ Other city, town
≈ International border
≈ Regional border
⊖ Customs
◯ Contours (approx)
▲ Mountain, volcano
⇆ Mountain pass
⊔⊔ Escarpment
▱ Glacier
▦ Salt flat
▨ Rocks
▾▾▾ Seasonal marshland
▨ Beach, sandbank
⑆ Waterfall
⌁ Reef
═══ Motorway
─── Main road
─── Minor road
┄┄┄ Track
⋯⋯⋯ Footpath
─── Railway
┅■ Railway with station
✈ Airport
🚌 Bus station
Ⓜ Metro station
- - - Cable car
++++ Funicular
⛴ Ferry
═══ Pedestrianized street
)(Tunnel
→ One way-street
⫿⫿⫿ Steps
⇌ Bridge
▪▪▪ Fortified wall
▦ Park, garden, stadium
● Sleeping
❷ Eating
♫ Bars & clubs

▨ Building
▣ Sight
✝ ✝ Cathedral, church
☗ Chinese temple
🛕 Hindu temple
⚑ Meru
☪ Mosque
⌂ Stupa
✡ Synagogue
🅸 Tourist office
🏛 Museum
✉ Post office
ⓟ Police
Ⓢ Bank
@ Internet
♩ Telephone
♙ Market
✚ Medical services
🅿 Parking
🅟 Petrol
⛳ Golf
∴ Archaeological site
◆ National park,
     wildlife reserve
✻ Viewing point
▲ Campsite
⌂ Refuge, lodge
🏯 Castle, fort
✇ Diving
♈♙♐ Deciduous, coniferous,
     palm trees
❀ Mangrove
⌂ Hide
🍷 Vineyard, winery
⏶ Distillery
⌐ Shipwreck
✕ Historic battlefield
▱ Related map

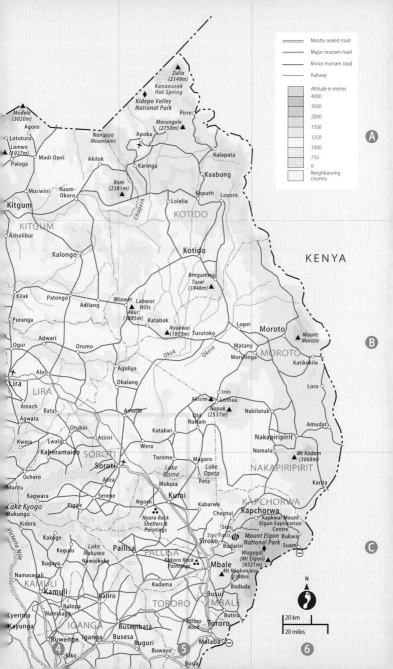

A

B

C

KENYA

Zulia
(2149m) ▲
Kananorok
Hot Spring
Kidepo Valley
National Park
Pirre

▲ Modole
(3020m)
Agoro
Lotuturu
▲ Lamwo
(1927m)
Paloga
Madi Opei
Akilok
Nangeya
Mountains
Morungole
(2750m) ▲
Apoka
Karinga
Kalapata
Kaabong
Koputh
Loyoro

Mucwini
Naam-
Okoro
Rom
(2381m) ▲
Lolelia
KOTIDO

Kitgum
Chapeth
KOTIDO

Acholibur

Kalongo
Kotido

Kilak
Patongo
Adilang
Wiawer
Labwor
Hills
Akur
(1885m) ▲
Katabok
Nyakwai
(1803m) ▲
Turutoko
Lopei
Amgamwa
Toror
(1948m) ▲
Moroto
▲ Mount
Moroto

Puranga

Ogur
Adwari
Orumo
Aguliya
Obalang
Okok
Okere
Matany
Morulinga
MOROTO
Katikekile

Lira
LIRA
Aloi
Amuria
Akisim
Iriri
Lothaa
Napak ▲
(2537m)
Old
Nanam
Nabilatuk
Loro

Amach
Bata
Agwata
Otuboi
Atiriri
Katakwi
Wera
Amudat

Kwera
Lwala
Kaberamaido
SOROTI
Torome
Magoro
Namalu
Nakapiripirit
Mt Kadam
(3068m) ▲

Ochero
Soroti
Atira
Lake
Bisina
Lake
Opeta
Peta
NAKAPIRIPIRIT
Karita

Muntu
Kagwara
Pigire
Serene
Mukura
Ngoro
Kumi
Kabarwa
KAPCHORWA

Lake Kyogo
Bukungu
Kidera
Kakoge
Lake
Nakuwa
Nawaikoke
Nyero Rock
Shelters &
Paintings
Cheptui
Sipi
Sipi Falls
Siroko
Budariri
Kapchorwa
Kapkwai Mount
Elgon Exploration
Centre
Bukwa
Suam

Victoria Nile
Bugoya
Kagulu
Pallisa
PALLISA
Kakoro Rock
Paintings
Mbale
Wagagai
(Mt Elgon)
(4321m) ▲
Mount Elgon
National Park
Bukwa

Namasagali
KAMULI
Bulopa
Kaliro
Kadama
Mt Nkokonjeru
(2348m) ▲
Bududa

Kyerima
Naminage
Kamuli
IGANGA
Busembata
TORORO
Busui
MBALE
Butiru

Kayunga
Buwenge
Iganga
Busesa
Buguri
Tororo
Rock
Tororo
Malaba

Kiko
Buwayo
Busia

N

20 km
20 miles

4
5
6

Map 2

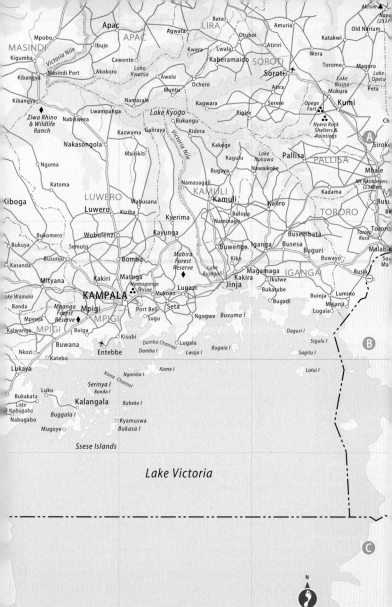

Footprint story

It was 1921

Ireland had just been partitioned, the British miners were striking for more pay and the federation of British industry had an idea. Exports were booming in South America – how about a handbook for businessmen trading in that far away continent? The Anglo-South American Handbook was born that year, written by W Koebel, the most prolific writer on Latin America of his day.

1924

Two editions later the book was 'privatized' and in 1924, in the hands of Royal Mail, the steamship company for South America, it became The South American Handbook, subtitled 'South America in a nutshell'. This annual publication became the 'bible' for generations of travellers to South America and remains so to this day. In the early days travel was by sea and the Handbook gave all the details needed for the long voyage from Europe. What to wear for dinner; how to arrange a cricket match with the Cable & Wireless staff on the Cape Verde Islands and a full account of the journey from Liverpool up the Amazon to Manaus: 5898 miles without changing cabin!

1939

As the continent opened up, the South American Handbook reported the new Pan Am flying boat services, and the fortnightly airship service from Rio to Europe on the Graf Zeppelin. For reasons still unclear but with extraordinary determination, the annual editions continued through the Second World War.

1970s

Many more people discovered South America and the backpacking trail started to develop. All the while the Handbook was gathering fans, including literary vagabonds such as Paul Theroux and Graham Greene (who once sent some updates addressed to "The publishers of the best travel guide in the world, Bath, England").

1990s

During the 1990s the company set about developing a new travel guide series using this legendary title as the flagship. By 1997 there were over a dozen guides in the series and the Footprint imprint was launched.

2000s

The series grew quickly and there were soon Footprint travel guides covering more than 150 countries. In 2004, Footprint launched its first thematic guide: Surfing Europe, packed with colour photographs, maps and charts. This was followed by further thematic guides such as Diving the World, Snowboarding the World, Body and Soul escapes, Travel with Kids and European City Breaks.

2014

Today we continue the traditions of the last 91 years that have served legions of travellers so well. We believe that these help to make Footprint guides different. Our policy is to use authors who are genuine experts who write for independent travellers; people possessing a spirit of adventure, looking to get off the beaten track.

Join us online...

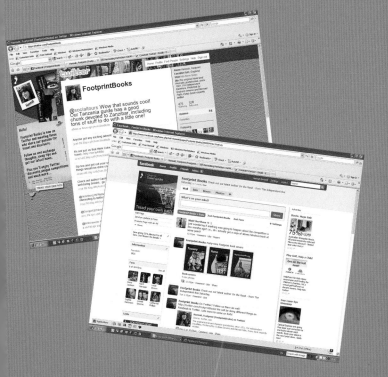

Follow us on **Twitter** and **Facebook** – ask us questions, speak to our authors, swap your stories, and be kept up to date with travel news and exclusive discounts and competitions.

Upload your travel pics to our **Flickr** site – inspire others on where to go next, and have your photos considered for inclusion in Footprint guides.

And don't forget to visit us at footprinttravelguides.com